Lecture Notes in Business Information Processing   **523**

LNBIP reports state-of-the-art results in areas related to business information systems and industrial application software development – timely, at a high level, and in both printed and electronic form.

The type of material published includes

- Proceedings (published in time for the respective event)
- Postproceedings (consisting of thoroughly revised and/or extended final papers)
- Other edited monographs (such as, for example, project reports or invited volumes)
- Tutorials (coherently integrated collections of lectures given at advanced courses, seminars, schools, etc.)
- Award-winning or exceptional theses

LNBIP is abstracted/indexed in DBLP, EI and Scopus. LNBIP volumes are also submitted for the inclusion in ISI Proceedings.

Boris Shishkov

Editor

Business Modeling and Software Design

14th International Symposium, BMSD 2024
Luxembourg City, Luxembourg, July 1–3, 2024
Proceedings

 Springer

Editor
Boris Shishkov
Bulgarian Academy of Sciences
Institute of Mathematics and Informatics
Sofia, Bulgaria

Faculty of Information Sciences
University of Library Studies and Information
Technologies
Sofia, Bulgaria

Interdisciplinary Institute for Collaboration
and Research on Enterprise Systems and Technology
Sofia, Bulgaria

ISSN 1865-1348   ISSN 1865-1356 (electronic)
Lecture Notes in Business Information Processing
ISBN 978-3-031-64072-8   ISBN 978-3-031-64073-5 (eBook)
https://doi.org/10.1007/978-3-031-64073-5

This Springer imprint is published by the registered company Springer Nature Switzerland AG
The registered company address is: Gewerbestrasse 11, 6330 Cham, Switzerland

If disposing of this product, please recycle the paper.

Preface

In most current information systems, we observe "too much of everything" – too much sensing, too much processing, too much tracking, too much reasoning, too much machine learning, and so on, compared to what we had at the beginning of the millennium. At the same time, developed information systems are not bringing higher levels of user satisfaction and software failure rates remain high. In our view, an issue then and an issue now is that developed software remains insufficiently aligned to its enterprise environment; in tune with this, technology-driven (as opposed to user-centric) software artefacts are often offered to customers. Here one problem is the suboptimal system behavior from the perspective of satisfying user needs, while another issue is the limited software fit as it concerns a broader social context. Therefore business (enterprise) modeling and software design need to be adequately aligned in a way that allows sensitivity to the actual user needs and also to the broader social context. Considering these challenges brings us together in the BMSD Community – Business Modeling and Software Design.

This book contains the *proceedings* of BMSD 2024 (the 14th International Symposium on *Business Modeling and Software Design*), held in *Luxembourg, Grand Duchy of Luxembourg*, on *1–3 July 2024* (https://www.is-bmsd.org). *BMSD* is an annual event that brings together researchers and practitioners interested in enterprise modeling and its relation to software specification.

Since 2011, we have enjoyed **thirteen successful BMSD editions**. The first BMSD edition (**2011**) took place in **Sofia, Bulgaria**, and the theme of BMSD 2011 was: "Business Models and Advanced Software Systems." The second BMSD edition (**2012**) took place in **Geneva, Switzerland**, with the theme: "From Business Modeling to Service-Oriented Solutions." The third BMSD edition (**2013**) took place in **Noordwijkerhout, The Netherlands**, and the theme was: "Enterprise Engineering and Software Generation." The fourth BMSD edition (**2014**) took place in **Luxembourg, Grand Duchy of Luxembourg**, and the theme was: "Generic Business Modeling Patterns and Software Re-Use." The fifth BMSD edition (**2015**) took place in **Milan, Italy**, with the theme: "Toward Adaptable Information Systems." The sixth BMSD edition (**2016**) took place in **Rhodes, Greece**, and had as theme: "Integrating Data Analytics in Enterprise Modeling and Software Development." The seventh BMSD edition (**2017**) took place in **Barcelona, Spain**, and the theme was: "Modeling Viewpoints and Overall Consistency." The eighth BMSD edition (**2018**) took place in **Vienna, Austria**, with the theme: "Enterprise Engineering and Software Engineering - Processes and Systems for the Future." The ninth BMSD edition (*2019*) took place in **Lisbon, Portugal**, and the theme of BMSD 2019 was: "Reflecting Human Authority and Responsibility in Enterprise Models and Software Specifications". The tenth BMSD edition (**2020**) took place in **Berlin, Germany**, and the theme of BMSD 2020 was: "Towards Knowledge-Driven Enterprise Information Systems". The eleventh BMSD edition (**2021**) took place in **Sofia, Bulgaria** (*We got back to where we once started!*), and the theme of BMSD 2021 was: "Towards Enterprises and Software that are Resilient Against Disruptive Events." The twelfth BMSD edition (**2022**) took place in **Fribourg, Switzerland**, with the theme: "Information Systems Engineering and Trust", and the thirteenth edition (**2023**) took place in **Utrecht, The Netherlands**, with the theme: "Incorporating Context Awareness in the Design of Information Systems." The current edition brings BMSD back to Luxembourg (ten years after BMSD-Luxembourg-2014). BMSD-Luxembourg-2024 marks the **14th EVENT**, with the theme: "*TOWARDS SOCIALLY RESPONSIBLE INFORMATION SYSTEMS*."

We are proud to have attracted distinguished guests as keynote lecturers, who are renowned experts in their fields: **Willem-Jan van den Heuvel**, *Tilburg University*, The Netherlands (2023), **Hans-Georg Fill**, *University of Fribourg*, Switzerland (2022), **Manfred Reichert**, *Ulm University*, Germany (2020), **Mathias Weske**, *HPI -University of Potsdam*, Germany (2020), **Jose Tribolet**, *IST - University of Lisbon*, Portugal (2019), **Jan Mendling**, *WU Vienna*, Austria (2018), **Roy Oberhauser**, *Aalen University*, Germany (2018), **Norbert Gronau**, *University of Potsdam*, Germany (2017 **and 2021**), **Oscar Pastor**, *Polytechnic University of Valencia*, Spain (2017), **Alexander Verbraeck**, *Delft University of Technology*, The Netherlands (2017 **and 2021**), **Paris Avgeriou**, *University of Groningen*, The Netherlands (2016), **Jan Juerjens**, *University of Koblenz-Landau*, Germany (2016), **Mathias Kirchmer**, *BPM-D*, USA (2016), **Marijn Janssen**, *Delft University of Technology*, The Netherlands (2015), **Barbara Pernici**, *Politecnico di Milano*, Italy (2015), **Hend**erik **Proper**, *Public Research Centre Henri Tudor*, Grand Duchy of Luxembourg (2014), **Roel Wieringa**, *University of Twente*, The Netherlands (2014 **and 2023**), **Kecheng Liu**, *University of Reading*, UK (2013), **Marco Aiello**, *University of Groningen*, The Netherlands (2013), **Leszek Maciaszek**, *Wroclaw University of Economics*, Poland (2013), **Jan L. G. Dietz**, *Delft University of Technology*, The Netherlands (2012), **Ivan Ivanov**, *SUNY Empire State College*, USA (2012), **Dimitri Konstantas**, *University of Geneva*, Switzerland (2012), **Marten van Sinderen**, *University of Twente*, The Netherlands (2012), **Mehmet Aksit**, *University of Twente*, The Netherlands (2011), **Dimitar Christozov**, *American University in Bulgaria – Blagoevgrad*, Bulgaria (2011), **Bart Nieuwenhuis**, *University of Twente*, The Netherlands (2011), and **Hermann Maurer**, *Graz University of Technology*, Austria (2011).

The high quality of the BMSD 2024 technical program is enhanced by a keynote lecture delivered by an outstanding Dutch scientist: **Bert de Brock**, *University of Groningen* (the title of his lecture is: "Developing Information Systems Accurately"). Next to that, the presence (physically or distantly) of former BMSD keynote lecturers is much appreciated: *Alexander Verbraeck* (2017, 2021), *Roy Oberhauser* (2018), and *Mathias Kirchmer* (2016). The technical program is further enriched by a panel discussion (featured by the participation of some of the abovementioned outstanding scientists) and also by other discussions stimulating *community building* and facilitating possible *R&D project acquisition initiatives*. Those special activities are definitely contributing to maintaining the event's high quality and inspiring our steady and motivated Community.

The BMSD'24 Technical Program Committee consists of a Chair and more than one hundred members from more than thirty countries – all of them competent and enthusiastic representatives of prestigious organizations.

In organizing BMSD 2024, we have observed **highest ethical standards**: We guarantee *at least two reviews per submitted paper* (this assuming reviews of adequate quality), under the condition that the paper fulfills the BMSD'24 requirements. In assigning a paper for reviewing, it is our responsibility to *provide reviewers that have relevant expertise.* Sticking to a **double-blind review process**, we guarantee that a reviewer would not know who the authors of the reviewed paper are (we send anonymized versions of the papers to the reviewers) and an author would not know who has reviewed his/her paper. We require that a reviewer *respects the reviewed paper* and would not disclose (parts of) its content to third parties before the symposium (and also after the symposium in case the manuscript gets rejected). We *guarantee against conflict of interest* by not assigning papers for reviewing by reviewers who are immediate colleagues of any of the co-authors. In our decisions to accept/reject papers, we **guarantee against any discrimination based on age, gender, race, or religion**. As it concerns the EU data protection standards, **we stick to the GDPR requirements**.

We have demonstrated for a 14th consecutive year a high quality of papers. We are proud to have succeeded in establishing and maintaining (for many years already) a high scientific quality (as it concerns the symposium itself) and a stimulating collaborative atmosphere; also, our Community is inspired to share ideas and experiences.

As mentioned already, BMSD is essentially leaning toward **ENTERPRISE INFORMATION SYSTEMS (EIS)**, by considering the **MODELING OF ENTERPRISES AND BUSINESS PROCESSES** as a basis for **SPECIFYING SOFTWARE**. Further, in a broader context, BMSD 2024 addresses a large number of EIS-relevant areas and topics.

BMSD 2024 received 54 paper submissions from which 20 papers were selected for publication in the symposium proceedings. Of these papers, 13 were selected for a 30-minute oral presentation (full papers), leading to a **full-paper acceptance ratio of 24%** - an indication for our intention to preserve a high-quality forum for the next editions of the symposium. The BMSD 2024 authors come from: Belgium, Brazil, Bulgaria, Czechia, Finland, Germany, Luxembourg, Portugal, Spain, The Netherlands, and USA (listed alphabetically); that makes a total of 11 countries to justify a strong international presence. Three countries have been represented at all fourteen BMSD editions so far – **Bulgaria**, **Germany**, and **The Netherlands** – indicating a strong European influence.

Clustering the BMSD'24 papers has been inspiring, opening different perspectives with regard to the broad challenge of adequately specifying software based on enterprise modeling. (a) As it concerns the BMSD'24 Full Papers: some of them are directed towards BUSINESS PROCESS MANAGEMENT (AND PROCESS MINING) AND DIGITAL TRANSFORMATION, while others are touching upon BUSINESS CAPABILITY MAPS AND ENTERPRISE DATA MODELS, DECLARATIVE SEMANTICS, the relation between BUSINESS PROCESS MODELS and CONCEPTUAL MODELS of the software-to-be, as well as the gap between the SOCIAL WORLD of the business organization and the FORMAL WORLD of software development; a paper addresses the VR-DRIVEN VISUALIZATION OF SOFTWARE DEVELOPMENT, while other papers consider SMART CONTRACTS, BLOCKCHAIN TECHNOLOGY, and DIGITAL IDENTITY WALLETS; a paper explores PRIVACY and MONETARIZATION -related issues concerning the so called "BRAIN-COMPUTER INTERFACE", another paper considers DATA ASPECTS IN CYBER-PHYSICAL SYSTEMS (particularly stressing upon NEURAL NETWORKS), while yet another paper is touching upon IoT-BASED SOFTWARE with a stress upon FIRMWARE ANALYSIS. (b) As it concerns the BMSD'24 Short Papers: a paper is touching upon CONTEXT AWARENESS while other papers are directed towards REQUIREMENTS ENGINEERING and FUNCTIONAL SOFTWARE SPECIFICATIONS; a paper addresses DATA ANALYTICS, while other papers consider the VISUAL-CHARACTERISTICS-BASED DETECTION OF OBJECTS and GEOLOCATION concerning LOGISTICS; yet another paper is touching upon DevSecOps (DEVELOPMENT, SECURITY, and OPERATIONS).

BMSD 2024 was organized and sponsored by the *Interdisciplinary Institute for Collaboration and Research on Enterprise Systems and Technology (IICREST)*, co-organized by the *University of Luxembourg*, and technically co-sponsored by *Cesuur B.V.* and *Scheer Americas Inc.* Cooperating organizations were *Aristotle University of Thessaloniki (AUTH)*, *Delft University of Technology (TU Delft)*, the *Dutch Research School for Information and Knowledge Systems (SIKS)*, and *AMAKOTA Ltd.*

Organizing this interesting and successful symposium required the dedicated efforts of many people. First, we thank the *authors*, whose research and development achievements are recorded here. Next, the *Program Committee members* each deserve credit for the diligent and rigorous peer reviewing. Further, appreciating the hospitality of the *University of Luxembourg (UL)*, we would like to mention the excellent organization provided by the *IICREST team* (supported by its *logistics partner, AMAKOTA Ltd.*) – the team (words of gratitude to *Aglika Bogomilova*!) did all the necessary work for delivering a stimulating and productive event, supported by the *UL team*. We are grateful to *Coen Suurmond* and *Alexander Verbraeck* for their inspiring support with regard to the organization of BMSD 2024. We are also grateful to *Springer* for their willingness to publish the current proceedings and we would like to especially mention *Ralf Gerstner* and *Christine Reiss*, appreciating their professionalism and patience (regarding the preparation of the symposium proceedings). We are certainly grateful to our *keynote lecturer, Prof. Bert de Brock*, for his inspiring contribution and for his taking the time to synthesize and deliver his talk.

We wish you inspiring reading! We look forward to meeting you next year in *Milan, Italy*, for the *15th International Symposium on Business Modeling and Software Design (BMSD 2025)*, details of which will be made available on: https://www.is-bmsd.org.

June 2024   Boris Shishkov

The original version of the Bookfrontmatter was previously published without an Abstract before TOC. A correction to the Bookfrontmatter is available at https://doi.org/10.1007/978-3-031-64073-5_21

Organization

Chair

Boris Shishkov   Institute of Mathematics and Informatics - BAS, Bulgaria
University of Library Studies and Information Technology, Bulgaria
IICREST, Bulgaria

Program Committee

Marco Aiello	University of Stuttgart, Germany
Mehmet Aksit	University of Twente, The Netherlands
Amr Ali-Eldin	Mansoura University, Egypt
Apostolos Ampatzoglou	University of Macedonia, Greece
Paulo Anita	Delft University of Technology, The Netherlands
Juan Carlos Augusto	Middlesex University, UK
Paris Avgeriou	University of Groningen, The Netherlands
Saimir Bala	Humboldt University of Berlin, Germany
Boyan Bontchev	Sofia University St. Kliment Ohridski, Bulgaria
Jose Borbinha	University of Lisbon, Portugal
Frances Brazier	Delft University of Technology, The Netherlands
Bert de Brock	University of Groningen, The Netherlands
Barrett Bryant	University of North Texas, USA
Cinzia Cappiello	Politecnico di Milano, Italy
Kuo-Ming Chao	Coventry University, UK
Michel Chaudron	Chalmers University of Technology, Sweden
Samuel Chong	Fullerton Systems, Singapore
Dimitar Christozov	American University in Bulgaria - Blagoevgrad, Bulgaria
Jose Cordeiro	Polytechnic Institute of Setubal, Portugal
Robertas Damasevicius	Kaunas University of Technology, Lithuania
Ralph Deters	University of Saskatchewan, Canada
Claudio Di Ciccio	Sapienza University, Italy
Jan L. G. Dietz	Delft University of Technology, The Netherlands
Aleksandar Dimov	Sofia University St. Kliment Ohridski, Bulgaria
Teduh Dirgahayu	Universitas Islam Indonesia, Indonesia

Olga Ormandjieva	Concordia University, Canada
Paul Oude Luttighuis	Le Blanc Advies, The Netherlands
Mike Papazoglou	Tilburg University, The Netherlands
Marcin Paprzycki	Polish Academy of Sciences, Poland
Jeffrey Parsons	Memorial University of Newfoundland, Canada
Oscar Pastor	Universidad Politecnica de Valencia, Spain
Krassie Petrova	Auckland University of Technology, New Zealand
Prantosh K. Paul	Raiganj University, India
Barbara Pernici	Politecnico di Milano, Italy
Doncho Petkov	Eastern Connecticut State University, USA
Gregor Polancic	University of Maribor, Slovenia
Henderik Proper	Vienna University of Technology, Austria
Mirja Pulkkinen	University of Jyvaskyla, Finland
Ricardo Queiros	Polytechnic of Porto, Portugal
Jolita Ralyte	University of Geneva, Switzerland
Julia Rauscher	University of Augsburg, Germany
Stefanie Rinderle-Ma	University of Vienna, Austria
Werner Retschitzegger	Johannes Kepler University Linz, Austria
Jose-Angel Rodriguez	Tecnologico de Monterrey, Mexico
Wenge Rong	Beihang University, China
Tamara Roth	University of Arkansas, USA
Ella Roubtsova	Open University, The Netherlands
Irina Rychkova	University Paris 1 Pantheon Sorbonne, France
Shazia Sadiq	University of Queensland, Australia
Ronny Seiger	University of St. Gallen, Switzerland
Denis Silva da Silveira	Federal University of Pernambuco, Brazil
Andreas Sinnhofer	Graz University of Technology, Austria
Valery Sokolov	Yaroslavl State University, Russia
Richard Starmans	Utrecht University, The Netherlands
Hans-Peter Steinbacher	FH Kufstein Tirol University of Applied Sciences, Austria
Janis Stirna	Stockholm University, Sweden
Coen Suurmond	Cesuur B.V., The Netherlands
Adel Taweel	Birzeit University, Palestine
Bedir Tekinerdogan	Wageningen University, The Netherlands
Ramayah Thurasamy	Universiti Sains Malaysia, Malaysia
Jose Tribolet	IST - University of Lisbon, Portugal
Roumiana Tsankova	Technical University - Sofia, Bulgaria
Martin van den Berg	Utrecht University of Applied Sciences, The Netherlands
Willem-Jan van den Heuvel	Tilburg University, The Netherlands
Han van der Aa	University of Mannheim, Germany

Marten van Sinderen	University of Twente, The Netherlands
Damjan Vavpotic	University of Ljubljana, Slovenia
Alexander Verbraeck	Delft University of Technology, The Netherlands
Hans Weigand	Tilburg University, The Netherlands
Roel Wieringa	University of Twente, The Netherlands
Dietmar Winkler	Vienna University of Technology, Austria
Shin-Jer Yang	Soochow University, Taiwan
Benjamin Yen	University of Hong Kong, China
Fani Zlatarova	Elizabethtown College, USA

Invited Speaker

| Bert de Brock | University of Groningen, The Netherlands |

Developing Information Systems Accurately
(Abstract of Keynote Lecture)

Bert de Brock

University of Groningen, The Netherlands
e.o.de.brock@rug.nl

Abstract. How to develop functional requirements for an information system in a straightforward way, given some problem space? Both data (the statics) and processes (the dynamics) must be developed, in an integrated way. The statics and dynamics of a system are closely related: They are the two sides of the same coin. We will sketch a concrete and complete development path for functional requirements, from initial (vague) user wishes until software specifications. The development steps are mutually aligned. Our aligned development pipeline supports traceability. The development pipeline includes concrete validation and explanation steps. An intermediate Conceptual Model (CM) has a central role in the development. The CM is a kind of functional 'blue print' and is implementation-independent. From the CM we can deduce the software specifications for the target platform in a straightforward way. The original question now reduces to the question how to specify the functional requirements for a given problem space. Actually, this splits Developing into Specifying and Realizing. The Conceptual Model of a system should model the statics as well as the dynamics of the system. The statics can be specified by a Conceptual Data Model (CDM) and the dynamics by a Conceptual Process Model (CPM). In short: CM = CDM $\oplus$ CPM. A CDM consists of one data model, while a CPM typically consists of several (usually many) 'interaction descriptions', in the form of System Sequence Descriptions (SSDs). The constructions in our SSD-language have a formal semantics.

Contents

Short Paper

Full Papers

Analysis of the Strengths of Process Mining Techniques in the Optimization of Logistics Processes

Radim Dolak[1]([⊠]) [iD], Michal Halaska[1] [iD], and Jakub Chmelicek[2]

[1] School of Business Administration in Karvina, Silesian University in Opava, 733 40 Karvina, Czechia
{dolak,halaska}@opf.slu.cz

[2] Company TP+, 709 00 Ostrava, Czechia

Abstract. The paper analyzes the adequacy and strengths of Process Mining techniques for logistics process optimization. The theoretical part of the paper will mention the main benefits of utilizing Process Mining techniques for logistics processes. In this, we refer to related work and analyze theoretical aspects concerning Process Mining techniques in general and their utilization for logistics processes. The practical part will be in the form of a case study. It will describe all necessary steps of Process Mining, such as the acquisition of data, preparing dataset, importing and analyzing data from a logistics software tool. The primary goal is to use Process Mining software based on the Disco tool to identify flaws and potentially improper operations in the chosen logistics process.

Keywords: Process Mining · Logistics · BPM

1 Introduction

The paper deals with analyzing and optimizing logistics processes using Process mining techniques.

The theoretical part of the paper will aim to define the main benefits of utilizing Process Mining techniques for logistics processes. There will be also a brief overview of related already published works on the use of process mining in logistics.

The main objective of the case study, with the help of the process mining software Disco, is to detect errors and possibly incorrect procedures in the selected logistics process. This disclosure will allow further possibilities to perform the individual steps within the process correctly. To do all this, it is necessary to first describe the whole logistics process and process mining issue. The next step will be optimizing the selected process obtained from event logs within the IT company TP+ and one logistics international company. The case study is based on a master's thesis called "Logistics process analysis and optimization design using process mining methods" [8]. The application of academic knowledge obtained at Silesian University in Opava was paired with the hands-on experience of a student working as a programmer as part of the thesis writing process.

© The Author(s), under exclusive license to Springer Nature Switzerland AG 2024
B. Shishkov (Ed.): BMSD 2024, LNBIP 523, pp. 3–15, 2024.
https://doi.org/10.1007/978-3-031-64073-5_1

2 Logistics and Process Mining

Process mining is defined as a relatively young research discipline that sits between computational intelligence and data mining on the one hand, and process modeling and analysis on the other hand [1]. The process mining spectrum is a quite broad and extends far beyond process discovery and conformance checking. Process Mining can help fight complexity, provide new insights, and support digital transformation. Process mining aids in discovering process, control, data, organizational, and social structures from event logs, providing a comprehensive view of underlying processes [6].

Process mining techniques have been increasingly applied in logistics case studies to analyze and optimize various processes. These techniques offer a data-driven approach to understanding and improving business processes [4]. Process Mining applies in logistics both for the sourcing transport from supplier to manufacturer as well as for the delivering transport from manufacturer to customer. Throughput times and on-time deliveries are of critical importance for customer satisfaction and cost efficiency [16].

Furthermore, process mining can be instrumental in analyzing inter-connected processes, such as procurement processes, by providing valuable insights for optimization [5]. By utilizing process mining bottleneck analysis techniques, logistics practitioners can identify and address bottlenecks in processes, leading to enhanced operational efficiency [4].

Moreover, the application of process mining in logistics case studies has shown the potential to streamline operations, reduce inefficiencies, and enhance overall performance [17]. By leveraging process mining techniques, logistics organizations can gain valuable insights from event data to drive process improvements and ensure better decision-making [2]. Overall, process mining plays a crucial role in logistics case studies by providing a systematic approach to analyzing and optimizing processes for increased efficiency and effectiveness.

Process mining has also been acknowledged as a useful method for material movement analysis in warehouse business processes, indicating its relevance in logistics operation optimization. The integration of process mining with warehouse business processes allows for the identification of improvement opportunities and the enhancement of overall efficiency [9]. Process mining techniques have been recognized also for their potential in process management, highlighting further opportunities for their application in optimizing processes [7]. Real-life processes often exhibit more variability than expected, a fact that process mining techniques bring to light, emphasizing the importance of understanding and adapting to this variability in logistics processes [13]. In the logistics context, the optimization of processes using genetic algorithms and ant colony optimization has been explored, demonstrating the potential for advanced optimization techniques to enhance logistics operations [18]. Additionally, the application of data mining technologies in logistics management has been shown to improve customer satisfaction, enhance the scientific nature of logistics management, and provide strong support for logistics operations [22]. The integration of process mining techniques with optimization algorithms and data mining technologies presents a promising avenue for improving the efficiency and effectiveness of logistics processes in various industries.

Logistics and transportation examples often focus on the efficiency but also fluidity of their processes. We can find a list of examples of using process mining in logistics and transportation published by Fluxicon [10]. There is a collection of process mining examples case studies such for example:

- Boris Nikolov from Vanderlande applied process mining in logistic process automation. He validated and optimized test scenarios during some of the most critical phases of a project - acceptance testing and operational trials [14].
- Marc Gittler and Patrick Greifzu from DHL analyzed the parcel delivery process based on hundreds of millions of events. They also reduced their audit time by 25% in comparison to classical data analytics by using process mining to analyze the quality of their audit process [12].
- Bram Vanschoenwinkel from AE worked with a package delivery company in Belgium, which processes around 300,000 packages daily [20].

If companies want to optimize logistics processes it is necessary to know the real process and for this purpose is very beneficial process mining technology. We can find out many advantages that we can get from using process mining analysis of logistics activities in companies. There are many software tools for process mining analysis such as ARIS Process Mining 10, Appian Process Mining, Apromore, Celonis, Disco, IBM Process Mining, ProM, QPR, UiPath Business Automation Platform or SAP Signavio Process Intelligence [11].

Using process mining analysis for logistics processes gives essential insights to cut costs and speed up deliveries. Process mining combines logistics data into one place and visualizes real logistics processes, increasing the overall transparency of logistics. Advanced analytics allow companies to focus on the most critical areas of improvement [15]. Visualization is key to process analysis, allowing companies to easily see where things go wrong. With process mining, companies will be able to identify inefficiencies that slow their business down, using up valuable time and resources. It is possible to streamline shipments, warehousing, and packaging processes [21].

What are the benefits of applying process mining to logistics? With process mining, logistics teams can: [3].

- Understand logistics processes
- Improve on-time delivery
- Save costs: 40% in warehousing costs
- Discover key regions where payment is on time
- Benchmark and observe the amount of returned goods
- Identify root causes for order changes
- Monitor lead times

3 Case Study: Logistics Process Analysis and Optimization Using Process Mining Methods

The following case study uses Process Mining to map individual processes, identify areas that take the longest, and then enhance the current process. We will start with a brief overview of the IT company TP+ s.r.o., and then we will introduce the selected logistics process. The main part of the case study deals with importing event logs into Disco and creating a Process mining map. The most important process mining analysis is presented with possible optimization of the selected logistics processes such as optimizing the frequency of activities, time-consuming optimization, or overview of longest-lasting processes.

3.1 Case Briefing

IT company TP+ s.r.o. has specialized in the delivery of software solutions for forwarding, logistics, and transport since its foundation in 1993 [19]. Among the most frequent clients are small and large freight forwarding, logistics, and transport companies. This company has been implementing projects focused on IT systems in the field of supplier-customer relations, especially in the field of logistics. TP+ develops a system for the distributed organization of consignments with intermediate storage, for the transport of pallet goods. It also develops a universal freight forwarding system, allowing to organization of all kinds of road consignments, from data acquisition to invoicing. The best applications developed by the company include the shipping applications xSped, xRays and its successor xxRays, xApollo, xLink. Of course, the company also provides a service tied to this software. There is also a special tool for the organization of consignments using a mobile scan, where it develops an application allowing the loading and unloading of individual entities, pieces, and consignments for transport and the recording of various events for consignments.

3.2 Introducing the Logistics Process

The logistics process is the total life cycle of the shipment, which is recorded from its creation to its end. The whole life cycle is the process by which the shipment is made at the manufacturer and delivered to the final destination to the customer. A case in point is the production of discs for a car, where a product is made at the point of origin, which in our case is a disc for a car. Once this product is made, the company can order it. At this point comes the start-up process, when the specific company is approached, for transport from production site A to the chosen destination B. At the moment this happens, the first LC status of the shipment is created in the ENT state, which tells us that the activity has started. This is located at point A, the continuation of which is to get the shipment to point B. The total process of LC states, which are recorded throughout in the form of an event from the life-cycle process, is detailed in the following Table 1, which contains all possible event states that may occur.

The actual implementation of the process is based on the movement of the shipment from its very creation from loading to unloading. The default information system processing these shipments is the xxRays software, which is a desktop application WPF (Windows Presentation Foundation), which is written in C# and XAML using the.NET Framework libraries. The xxRays application is a successor to the xRays application, which was created in the already unsupported and obsolete Microsoft Silverlight platform. In the application, based on the available data in the database, is possible to monitor the life cycle of the shipment, which is intertwined with many processes and associated applications, mainly intertwined with the myTruck application, which is available in the scanner of every person involved who physically manipulates the shipment from the storekeeper to the driver. Within this process, there are certain hierarchies in the role

Table 1. List of life cycle activities.

ID	ItemCode	ItemValue	ID	ItemCode	ItemValue
1	ENT	Entered	26	XIR	Xdock IN error
2	SUB	Submitted	27	XOR	Xdock OUT error
3	VAL	Valid	28	DED	Delayed departure
4	INV	Invalid	29	XMI	XDock IN myTRUCK
5	ACC	Accepted	30	XMO	XDock OUT myTRUCK
6	REJ	Rejected	31	AC1	AcceptedToCDC
7	CNC	Cancelled	32	AC2	AcceptedToFTL
8	PLG	Planning	33	AC3	AcceptedPostoponed
9	PLD	Planned	34	TTX	Sent to CarO
10	EXE	Executed	35	POH	Sent to Pohorelice
11	PUL	Pickup location	36	ACP	Reservoir Pohorelice
12	PUO	Pickup OK	37	TTM	Sent OST T1 do CarO
13	NPU	Not picked up	38	TTR	Sent FBR do CarO
14	PUE	Picked up – exception	39	ACM	Reservoir Mošnov
15	INT	In transit	40	LFS	Disabling delivery date to LFS
16	XDI	XDock IN	41	CON	Confirmed
17	XDO	XDock OUT	42	TTS	Send AVI to CarO
18	DLL	Delivery location	43	TTF	Send FBR to CarO
19	DLD	Delivered	44	TTO	Send OST T1 to CarO
20	EDL	eDelivered	45	FBO	WGP Booked
21	DLE	Delivered with exception	46	CNL	CDC Unloaded
22	NDL	Not Delivered	47	OHD	On Hold
23	POD	Proof of delivery	48	RFO	Ready to Invoice
24	UPD	Order Update	49	VDF	VDA4987 Error
25	POC	Proof of collection			

Source: TP+ internal documentation.

of individual LC statuses, which have their own clearly defined procedure. This allows a company to move from one state to another only in clearly defined conditions. This means that it is not possible to jump from one LC state to any other LC state, but only to the set of states that are possible within the previous state. It is not possible to have a state of unloading the shipment if there is no state of loading the shipment etc.

3.3 Importing Event Logs into Disco

We have used shipment data in the data range of planned loading from 01-11-2021 00:00:00 to 01-12-2021 23:59:56. However, these data are not the input set itself, which is used in Disco. The above-mentioned data are used for narrowing the set, to which we had to download the respective events in the next step, which are the input data for Disco. In the data range from which we have received the shipments, there were 2778 shipments. These shipments are linked to events about their life-cycle. To the number of 2778 shipments, 58143 logs were available at the time of data acquisition. After successful activation and creation of an academic license, we can jump into importing data. Data into Disco can be exported from different types of files. For this use, it is best to import data from an XLS file, which we prepared based on the data collected from the database. At the moment we upload the file to Disco, we will see a desktop where we will set what data we want to use and assign them their roles.

In this case, it will be set as CaseID my ObjectID field, which contains the shipment ID, as an activity it will set the ToLCStatus column, which contains the current activity. Next, we need to set TimeStamp, where we want to use the EventTime column. Still, since the data was only 91% usable due to bad syntax, so we decided to use the data from the InsertionDT column, which contains the date and time of the record in the database and is the same as EventTime, but with better higher accuracy.

To describe the events, there will be just one shipment from the mentioned 2778, over which it was selected only its events linked to life-event. Each event log contains the following.

- EventID – unique event code
- EventType – type of event, executed in a process or system
- ObjectID – connection to a unique object 1: N (shipment)
- EventTime – time of events acquisition
- UserID – user ID
- InsertionDT – record creation date
- FromLCStatus – previous state
- ToLCStatus – current state

We can see the structure of the dataset for the import into the Disco tool in the following Fig. 1.

3.4 Process Mining Map

Disco allows us to perform process mining in a nice design environment, which is very intuitive and well-processed. After the first import, the processes of all events are displayed as they follow each other from the start. In the application, this means that we have activities set to 100% and paths to 0% in the right part of the window, therefore we see even the least involved activities. This view of the process can be found in Fig. 2, where we can see all activities, their numbers, and even time-consuming.

Additional options for event exploration are available in other tabs available. These tabs are the statistical view tab, where the data is displayed within the table. It is also possible to display in the last tab using the cases. This tab allows the user to view events from an event perspective, where we can see the percentage of event variants from a similarity perspective. Based on this view, we can get an interesting overview of the data being examined.

EventID	EventType	ObjectID	EventTime	UserID	InsertionDT	FromLCStatus	ToLCStatus
45841340	ENT	1853781	13.01.2021 4:01	1552	2021-01-13 04:01:45.82 40038	ENT	ENT
45841341	ENT	1853781	13.01.2021 4:01	1552	2021-01-13 04:01:58.24 59138	ENT	INV
45841343	PRC	1853781	13.01.2021 4:02	1552	2021-01-13 04:02:50.68 35370	INV	PLD
45841349	SYS	1853781	13.01.2021 4:02	1552	2021-01-13 04:02:53.77 73033	INV	CON
45841765	PRC	1853781	13.01.2021 4:24	1526	2021-01-13 04:24:02.48 30354	PLG	CON
45841766	PRC	1853781	13.01.2021 4:24	1526	2021-01-13 04:24:06.57 68000	CON	PLD
45841776	PRC	1853781	13.01.2021 4:24	1526	2021-01-13 04:24:11.46 74023	PLG	XDI

Fig. 1. Dataset for the import into the Disco tool

Disco also allows the user to set any filtering over events that can change the offered view of the data. This filter offers several options that can be combined. This allows you to work with the displayed data more efficiently.

Previous representations of the process map of all processes may not always be clear enough, so it is advisable to display only those activities that occur most frequently. This is achieved by downloading the percentage of activities to 0 percent in the right part of Disco and getting a graphical representation of the most used processes, mapped in order as the shipment proceeds within the process. This representation can be seen in Fig. 3.

Figure 3 shows that there are two different processes PLG - Planning and CON - Confirmed within the whole process, which are repeated within the lifetime of the shipment. We will address this fact during optimization and exploration and try to find out why these processes are repeated and try to find some other cycling that could be optimized.

Disco also includes a real-time display option, which allows you to view the progress of individual shipments in real-time. This allows me to see in real-time how individual shipments pass between states within time. This display can be manually controlled within the time axis in the Disco environment. This display allows us to usefully explore the flow of shipments. By displaying it, we can see which parts of the process are the most time-consuming and which parts of the process occur most frequently. The graphical display is also very useful for presentation to lay surroundings, who can get an idea of the progress and flow of the shipment process.

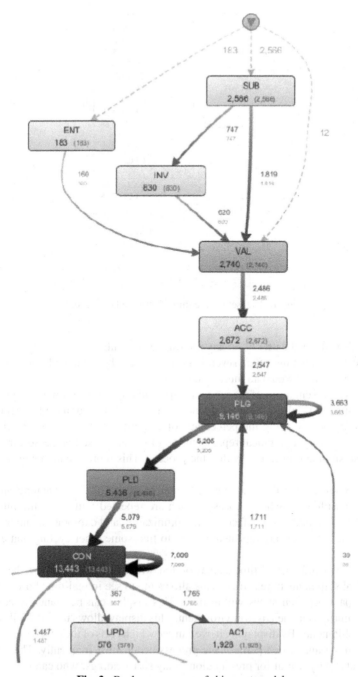

Fig. 2. Real process map of shipment model

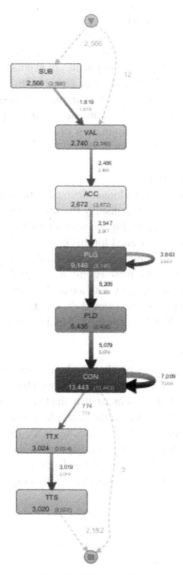

Fig. 3. Main activities

3.5   Results and Discussion

The most important process mining analysis is presented with possible optimization of the selected logistics processes such as optimizing the frequency of activities, time-consuming optimization, or overview of longest-lasting processes.

Optimizing the Frequency of Activities

As the above problem has already been declared, we would perform an appropriate optimization over a portion of the activities that are cycling according to the mapping. In terms of bitrate, this is the creation of duplicates of events that are shown again. This phenomenon is caused by a bad procedure or an error in the application. Therefore, it would be advisable to optimize the aforementioned processes PLG – Planning and CON – Confirmed so that these events are unique within the process. This finding will help in the further monitoring and elimination of problems that may arise from this cycling.

Time-Consuming Optimization

The second part of the research was no longer devoted to the actual amount of processes, but the Disco application was used to display the time-consuming events. Within this display it was found that when changing the state of XDO – XDock OUT to the state of TTX – Send to CarO, the time needed for this process is 5.1 days. This time interval interested us the most, because compared to other large time delays, where in combination with the frequency of events there is only a negligible amount of shipments. In selected intervals with this time delay, over a thousand shipments are paused. Therefore, as an additional possible optimization, it would choose the option of decreasing the time interval between the state of XDO – XDock OUT and the state of TTX – Send to CarO.

Longest-Lasting Processes

The next analysis that was done was within the long duration of some shipments. For this discovery, based on the selected filter in Disco, we chose a different set of records. These are shipments for which the processes were the longest. After setting up the filters, it was found that these were 15 percent of the cases. As a result of the research itself and the logistics process of the shipment's lifecycle, we made the following findings: there are cycling activities in the logistics process that need to be removed due to improper procedure, cycling, and writing duplicates to the database.

We can see the Process time-consuming in the following Fig. 4.

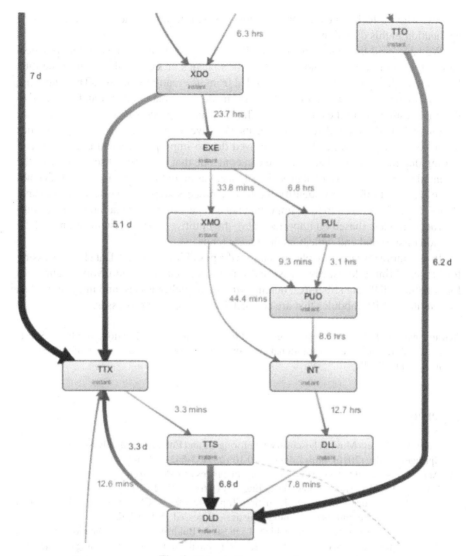

Fig. 4. Process time-consuming

4   Conclusion

The primary goal of the paper's theoretical section was to outline the advantages that the utilization of Process Mining approaches offers many benefits for logistics processes. We can conclude the adequacy and strengths of Process Mining techniques concerning logistics process optimization based on the related works and case studies that were published. Process mining techniques have been increasingly applied in logistics case studies to analyze and optimize various processes so we can generally considered using

Process Mining techniques in logistics analysis as relevant because of the increasing application in this direction.

We have used the Disco software tool for Process Mining analysis in the practical part in the form of a case study based on the logistics process in the form of the total life cycle of the shipment, which is recorded from its creation to its end. The whole life cycle is the process by which the shipment is made at the manufacturer and delivered to the final destination to the customer. We have managed process analysis that was done within the long duration of some shipments. We have found that some cycling activities in the logistics process need to be removed due to improper procedure, cycling, and writing duplicates to the database. We can conclude that using the Disco tool gives the potential to produce a variety of process perspectives including maps and other previews. There we could effectively identify ineffective process steps that need to be adjusted. Hence, Disco is claimed to have important advantages, such as the automatic discovery of process models (based on imported data), the intuitive process visualization, and the creation of start and end indicators in process maps.

In our future research, we plan to analyze the possibilities of ERP Data Preprocessing for Process Mining logistics process analysis. This research would involve techniques for handling ERP data structures, dealing with data quality issues, and integrating data from multiple ERP modules that are connected with logistics processes.

Acknowledgment. "This paper was supported by the Ministry of Education, Youth and Sports Czech Republic within the Institutional Support for Long-term Development of a Research Organization in 2024".

References

1. Aalst, W.: Process Mining: Discovery, Conformance and Enhancement of Business Processes. Springer, Berlin (2016). https://doi.org/10.1007/978-3-642-19345-3
2. Augusto, A., et al.: Automated discovery of process models from event logs: review and benchmark. IEEE Trans. Knowl. Data Eng. **31**(4), 686–705 (2019)
3. AI Multiple. Process Mining in Logistics: Top 3 Benefits & Challenges in '23. https://research.aimultiple.com/process-mining-logistics/. Accessed 18 Mar 2023
4. Bemthuis, R., Slooten, N., Arachchige, J., Piest, J., Bukhsh, F.: A classification of process mining bottleneck analysis techniques for operational support. In: Proceedings of the 18th International Conference on e-Business, pp. 127–135. SciTePress, Location (2021)
5. Berti, A., Jessen, U., Park, G., Rafiei, M., Aalst, W.: Analyzing inter-connected processes: using object-centric process mining to analyze procurement processes. Int. J. Data Sci. Anal. (2023)
6. Jagadeesh Chandra Bose, R.P., van der Aalst, W.: Trace alignment in process mining: opportunities for process diagnostics. In: Hull, R., Mendling, J., Tai, S. (eds.) BPM 2010. LNCS, vol. 6336, pp. 227–242. Springer, Heidelberg (2010). https://doi.org/10.1007/978-3-642-15618-2_17
7. Brzychczy, E., Napieraj, A., Sukiennik, M.: Modeling of processes with use of process mining techniques. Sci. Pap. Silesian Univ. Technol. Organ. Manag. Ser. **2018**(116), 23–36 (2018)
8. Chmelicek, J.: Logistics process analysis and optimization design using process mining methods [Master's thesis]. Silesian University in Opava. Master's thesis supervisor: Dolak, R. (2021)

 9. Er, M., Astuti, H.M., Wardhani, I.R.K.: Material movement analysis for warehouse business process improvement with process mining: a case study. In: Bae, J., Suriadi, S., Wen, L. (eds.) AP-BPM 2015. LNBIP, vol. 219, pp. 115–127. Springer, Cham (2015). https://doi.org/10.1007/978-3-319-19509-4_9
10. Fluxicon. https://fluxicon.com/blog/2022/04/process-mining-logistics/. Accessed 18 Mar 2023
11. Gartner. https://www.gartner.com/reviews/market/process-mining. Accessed 18 Mar 2023
12. Gittler, M., Greifzu, P.: Increasing the Audit Process Efficiency at DHL. https://fluxicon.com/camp/2016/5. Accessed 18 Mar 2023
13. Maggi, F.M., Bose, R.P.J.C., van der Aalst, W.M.P.: Efficient discovery of understandable declarative process models from event logs. In: Ralyté, J., Franch, X., Brinkkemper, S., Wrycza, S. (eds.) CAiSE 2012. LNCS, vol. 7328, pp. 270–285. Springer, Heidelberg (2012). https://doi.org/10.1007/978-3-642-31095-9_18
14. Nikolov, B.: Process Mining in Logistics. https://fluxicon.com/camp/2019/7. Accessed 18 Mar 2023
15. QPR. https://www.qpr.com/process-mining/logistics. Accessed 18 Mar 2023
16. Reinkemeyer, L.: Process Mining in Action: Principles, Use Cases and Outlook. Springer, Cham (2020). https://doi.org/10.1007/978-3-030-40172-6
17. Rubin, V., Mitsyuk, A., Lomazova, I., Aalst, W.: Process mining can be applied to software too! In: Proceedings of the 8th ACM/IEEE International Symposium on Empirical Software Engineering and Measurement (2014)
18. Silva, C., Sousa, J., Runkler, T.: Rescheduling and optimization of logistic processes using ga and aco. Eng. Appl. Artif. Intell. 21(3), 343–352 (2008)
19. TP+ s.r.o. https://www.tpplus.cz/. Accessed 18 Mar 2023
20. Vanschoenwinkel, B.: Process Mining at AE. https://fluxicon.com/camp/2012/6. Accessed 18 Mar 2023
21. Wang, G.: Process Mining and Automation in Logistics. UiPath. https://www.uipath.com/blog/industry-solutions/process-mining-and-automation-in-logistics. Accessed 18 Mar 2023
22. Xu, L.: Construction mode of efficient logistics system under the big data environment. In: Conference: Information Science and Industrial Applications (2016)

Process-Led Digital Transformation: Mastering the Journey Towards the Composable Enterprise

Mathias Kirchmer[1,2,3](✉)

[1] Scheer Americas, Inc., Saarbrücken, Germany
mathias.kirchmer@outlook.com
[2] University of Pennsylvania, Philadelphia, USA
[3] Widener University, Philadelphia, PA, USA

Abstract. Digital transformation is a key topic for most organizations, leading to the development of a "composable enterprise" that adopts seamlessly to changing business conditions. However, how can this transformation happen without overwhelming the organization? Process-led digital transformation provides an answer to this question. It helps to prioritize processes to achieve best value, touch the process during the transformation the right way and sustains the achieved results. Process-led transformation helps to standardize, optimize and innovate processes, as required by the overarching strategy and the related business model.

Keywords: AI · Business Process Management · Composable Enterprise · Digital Transformation · Innovation · Optimization · Process Design · Process Governance · Reference Models · Standardization

1 Process-Led Digital Transformation to Realize the Composable Enterprise in a Specific Company Context

Most organizations have started their digital transformation journey [1]. The desired result is more and more often described as a "composable enterprise" that can adjust seamlessly to changing business conditions [2]. However, how can this transformation happen without overwhelming the organization? Process-led digital transformation provides an answer to this question.

In the first section of this article key characteristics of the composable enterprise are described followed by a short discussion of key challenges in realizing this concept. Then it is explained how process-led digitalization addresses this situation. The following sections walk through the phases of the process-led transformation approach, from setting the appropriate priorities through design, realization of the digital processes to the sustainment of the achieved results.

1.1 The Composable Enterprise as Transformation Target

The composable enterprise is a company that is agile, flexible, innovative and efficient through a combination of appropriate information systems and a decentralized

B. Shishkov (Ed.): BMSD 2024, LNBIP 523, pp. 16–31, 2024.
https://doi.org/10.1007/978-3-031-64073-5_2

process-oriented organizational structure [2]. This concept was initially introduced by the industry-analyst Gartner Group with a focus on the digital technologies involved [3]. Scheer added the organizational component and expanded the overall integrated vision. A composable enterprise componentizes its business process and technology capabilities. This allows to quickly assemble components to new processes with appropriate information technology (IT) support as response to a changing business environment.

Core of the technology architecture is the move from large mega software systems to smaller software components, referred to as Packaged Business Capabilities, and an Application Composition Platform supporting a no or low code developed of the business capabilities as well as the required integration and workflow capabilities [2]. This allows a fast adjustment to changing market conditions and related technology requirements. The organizational structure is process-oriented to achieve the desired agile and flexibility as well as the focus towards the market. A Shared Services organization supports the decentralized product units to enable the desired resource efficiency. The product units are organized in end-to-end processes so they can adjust quickly and deliver best value to clients [2].

The described key components of the Composable Enterprise are visualized in Fig. 1 [2]. In the next section we briefly discuss key challenges to realize this vision.

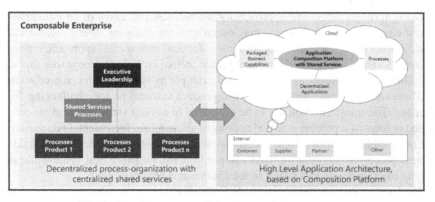

Fig. 1. Key Components of the Composable Enterprise [2]

1.2 The Challenge Realizing the Composable Enterprise

Moving toward the Composable Enterprise means a company-wide transformation. According to Scheer, this is realized through an approach structured in 8 phases [2]:

1. Enterprise Analysis
2. Innovation and Business Model
3. Composable Process and Enterprise Architecture
4. Application Composition Platform
5. Development and Implementation
6. Execution

7. Insights through Mining
8. Improvement Actions

In the Enterprise Analysis stage, the fundamental needs for the transformation are determined based on client, partner, supplier and other market requirements. On this basis, the strategic innovation requirements are defined, and an appropriate business model is defined. The process and enterprise architecture define how the business model is realized, aligning business process flows and related technology components. Entrance point into the process hierarchy is the operating model, identifying the processes necessary to realize the business model. Key for the realization of the processes is the Composition Platform. It allows the low or no-code development and implementation of the re-usable business capabilities; hence, the required software components as well as their integration and use in the process flow are based on appropriate data models. After the implementation of a process type, specific process instances are executed based on the process design and the underlying technology infrastructure. The ongoing process execution is controlled using the insights from process mining systems providing the necessary performance and conformance information. This allows the definition of necessary improvement actions. These can be either executed though the different end-users or in focused improvement projects if larger changes are required. Steps 3 to 8 form the ongoing business process lifecycle.

Going through this entire approach for all business processes of an enterprise is in most cases not practical since it may overwhelm the company. Many organizations avoid "boiling the ocean" and look for a more focused incremental approach, realizing the overall vision and strategy in manageable steps [4]. Scheer recognizes this and gives hints how to address this situation, for example by starting with one product unit [2]. However, even transforming an entire product unit can be too challenging for a Company. The transformation has to be organized in smaller steps. These steps can be defined in form of a process-oriented approach, allowing the incremental realization of the Composable Enterprise. Process-led digital transformation specifies how individual business processes can be prioritized and put in place, targeting best value while still working towards the overall vision of the composable enterprise [5, 6].

The journey towards the Composable Enterprise on a process-by-process basis can be further simplified by providing guidance for the process design. This makes it easier to "touch" processes the required way. It helps to minimize resource and related budget needs for the transformation initiative. Companies can avoid "re-inventing the wheel" since they benefit from existing experiences and good practices. Therefore Process-led Digital Transformation defines how to apply different design paradigms within the overall approach to realize the Composable Enterprise.

Process-led digital Transformation builds on the vision developed in phases 1 and 2 of the overall approach defined by Scheer [2] to ensure that all process transformation and improvement initiatives are aligned and realize the overall strategy. It guides through key steps of the transformation journey and specifics of the phases 3 to 8 of the overall approach further from a business point of view.

1.3 Process-Led Digital Transformation to Organize the Journey

Process-led Digital Transformation structures the overall enterprise-transformation into smaller initiatives, aligned with the specific company context. It starts with a prioritization of processes identified through the operating model and the underlying process hierarchy. Hence, it uses the results of phases 1 and 2 of Scheer's approach as a starting point to set realization priorities for the following phases. It delivers a roadmap to guide the transformation considering available resources. The process design approach distinguishes standardization, optimization and innovation. Hence, it defines how to touch the processes to make them a component of the future Composable Enterprise while delivering immediate value. The process design lays then the foundation for technology and people-based implementation of the processes and the definition of a governance structure to realize the expected value and initiate further change initiatives when required. Design and Realize address phases 3 through 5 of the Scheer's approach. Phases 6 and 7 are specified in the Sustain step.

The approach of Process-led Digital Transformation is shown in Fig. 2. The following sections discuss key components of this approach.

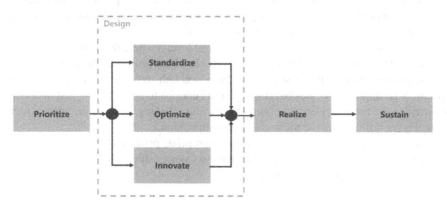

Fig. 2. Process-led Digital Transformation Approach

The approach for Process-led Digital Transformation combines the general phases to realize the Composable Enterprise with the appropriate elements of Value-driven Business Process Management to operationalize the approach further [4, 7]. It focuses transformation activities on business outcomes to deliver short-term value while realizing the long-term vision of the composable enterprise. It uses the business process management capabilities to derive value systematically [8].

2 Prioritize

The incremental transformation requires a systematic prioritization approach to identify the processes that deliver best value to the organizations through the digitalization initiatives. The prioritization and selection of business processes for the digitalization is based on the Targeting Value approach of Value-driven Process Management [9]. It uses the overall enterprise analysis, business model and operating model as starting point. This provides the understanding of the company context and the end-to-end processes. These processes are then evaluated based on their impact on the company strategy and their maturity level. High impact low maturity processes are best candidates for the immediate transformation initiatives They help most realizing the strategic goals of the company. The short, mid and long-term transformation initiatives are then defined in the transformation roadmap, outlining the journey towards the Composable Enterprise.

2.1 Understand the Context

The operating model of a company identifies the top level then end-to-end business processes. It normally consists of 8 to 12 processes [4]. This is the first level of the process hierarchy, either delivered through pre-work to prepare for the Composable Enterprise or defined as starting point for the prioritization exercise. Depending on the size of the organization and the differences between products, the operating model may have to be defined in two steps: Level 0 identifies the end-to-end processes per product unit as well as the support service processes, level 1 ten details the product unit processes. Figure 3 shows an example for the definition of an operating model for a technology manufacturing company with one main product line.

The operating model is then decomposed until level 3 where the whole organization is described through 150–200 processes [4]. This level has proven the best level of detail for the prioritization of processes. It is detailed enough to allow the identification of specific high impact processes but still high level enough to avoid getting lost in details. It provides the necessary end-to-end context while allowing to focus on what matters most. Figure 4 illustrates the hierarchical decomposition.

The level 3 processes are evaluated to set appropriate priorities based on the strategy of the organization and the overall goals for the Composable Enterprise. This is done through a process impact assessment.

2.2 Target Value

The business strategy is operationalized through a value-driver tree. It identifies the overall company priorities, decomposes those into goals that are then further specified through measurable value-drivers. Value-drivers describe the 8–12 operational objectives an organization has to get right to deliver on its strategy. These value-drivers are used to evaluate the impact of the difference level 3 processes. Figure 5 shows an excerpt of a sample value-driver tree.

In a next step, the impact of each level 3 process on each value-driver is defined. This can be done through a detailed formal analysis or through stakeholder interviews. In practice, stakeholder interviews have proven to be efficient and sufficiently accurate. The total of the individual impacts of a process on each value-driver represents the overall process impact. This allows to identify the 15–20% of the high impact processes of an organization. These processes are most important for the strategy execution of the company and are therefore prime transformation targets. The process impact assessment is visualized in Fig. 6.

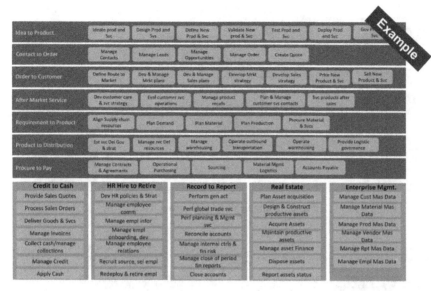

Fig. 3. Example of an Operating Model for Technology Manufacturing Company

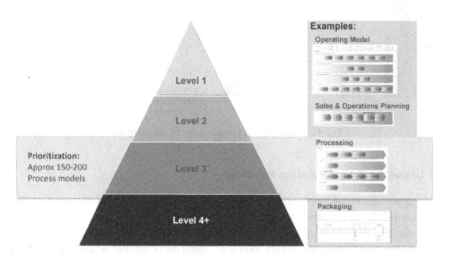

Fig. 4. Hierarchical Decomposition of Operating Model to prepare for Prioritization Activities

Then a process maturity assessment determines how well a process is currently executed. High impact low maturity processes are the first transformation targets since the initiatives will deliver best value for the overall strategy.

Some of the 80%+ commodity processes may be included in a first transformation steps, for example when they are on a very low maturity level. This maturity assessment can be also conducted through stakeholder interviews or the use of process management tools, especially analytics tools.

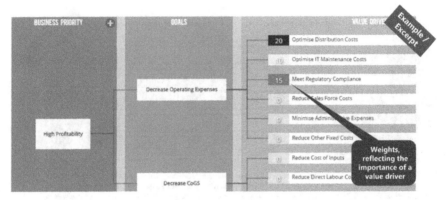

Fig. 5. Example of a Value-driver Tree

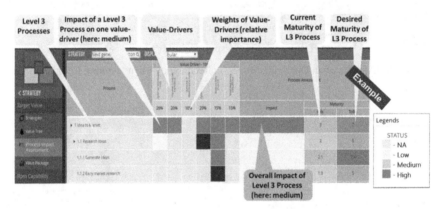

Fig. 6. Example of a Process Impact Assessment

2.3   Define the Transformation Roadmap

Once impact and maturity of the level 3 business processes is identified, specific transformation projects or "work packages" can be defined, reflecting those process priorities. Therefore, the transformation effort of potential process transformation options is roughly estimated. The processes are then segmented into transformation waves, reflecting the company's capabilities to address digital transformation projects from a resource and budget point of view. Figure 7 shows an example of such a transformation roadmap.

The transformation initiatives in wave 1 are directly started, wave 2 are planned initiatives. Future, less specifically defined initiatives, are part of wave 3 that serves as "parking lot" for the digitalization activities that will be evaluated further at a later point of time. This leads to a rolling adjustment of the transformation roadmap.

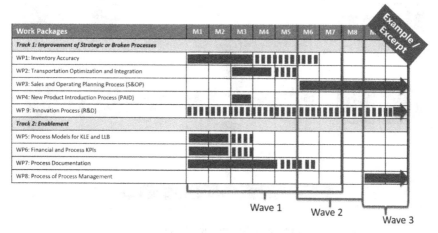

Fig. 7. Example of a Transformation Roadmap

3 Design

The to-be design of the processes in scope lays the foundation for the realizing the expected value from the digitalization. The design reflects the business impact of the digital technologies defined in the enterprise architecture or helps to identify additional technology support. In most cases, the capturing of as-is processes and their analysis is required as input for the design and to develop or validate the business case as well as prepare the people change management.

The process design documented in process models becomes a key asset for an organization. Since many digital technologies are delivered through the cloud [10], the assets that stay in the company are the resulting business processes [11]. These process assets are produced as side-effect of a process-led digital transformation and housed in process repositories enabling the simple and effective re-use.

Depending on the transformation goals and the company specific context, the process design is used to standardize, optimize or innovate processes. An organization defines which design paradigm to choose to achieve the defined objectives. The following discussion helps to understand the key options as basis for the decision. This helps to streamline the journey towards the Composable Enterprise.

The process design leverages the ARIS framework developed by Scheer to ensure a systematic approach [12] and address all aspects of a process. It outlines key components of a business process and their relations, as shown in Fig. 8 [11].

Each component of the business process can be described on the business level and the information technology level, addressing the digital realization of the process components.

Main modelling method is the industry standard BPMN [13]. This allows a process description of business level by using a small subset of the method as well as a further specification on IT level to drive the configuration of the composition platform and the development of the business capabilities as well as their integration.

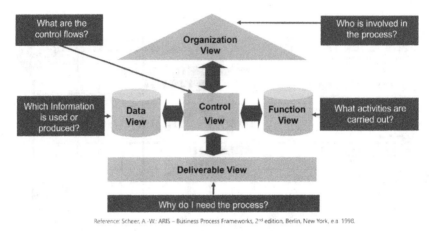

Reference: Scheer, A.-W.: ARIS – Business Process Frameworks, 2nd edition, Berlin, New York, e.a. 1998.

Fig. 8. ARIS Framework [12]

The core process models in BMN are complemented though information models addressing individual ARIS views, such as data models. This allows addressing aspects that cannot sufficiently described in BPMN.

3.1 Identify the Design Approach

The decision if the initial transformation is about standardization, optimization, innovation or a combination of approaches depends on the specific objectives of the organization. The overall approach how to "touch" the process must be defined before moving into the process design.

In many cases, starting with a standardization initiative is beneficial since it simplifies the digital transformation while delivering initial benefits, such as agility or the reduction of IT maintenance cost [14]. Typical examples that trigger a standardization are the following:

- Consistent customer experience across business units
- Compliance requirements
- Reduction of IT maintenance cost through system consolidation
- Simplify company-wide future adjustments of processes

Basis for the standard could be good existing practices or processes based on existing business capabilities provided through the composition platform. The standardization initiative is often followed by a further optimization project to realize the full potential of the digitalization.

High impact processes with a low maturity level may justify starting with optimization activities before standardizing across locations or even different business units. Typical triggers for a start with optimization are the following:

- Efficiency improvements, especially cost and cycle time reductions
- Quality improvements, e.g. increase of service level or reduction of rework
- Increased scalability

The optimized process can be used as a reference model for a potentially following standardization.

Disruptive changes through new business models and corresponding operating models may require new or significantly changed processes, delivered through appropriate process innovation [15]. Business process innovation is often triggered through the following topics:

- Business model changes that require new high impact processes, e.g. to support new products, markets, channels or address new competition.
- Market changes that require new or significantly enhanced processes.

If this innovation is relevant for different areas in the organization, a standardization initiative can be used to drive the roll-out of the new processes.

3.2 Standardize

Process standardization [14] can be used to support the creation of central services through a shared service organization, create consistent practices across different locations of a product unit or even to leverage synergies between product units. Hence, the standard processes may occur only once on corporate level or multiple time in different business areas.

Process standardization focuses on identifying a standard that addresses the defined goals while minimizing performance reductions through its roll-out. Process simulation can be used to clarify the standardization impact.

Many standardized processes still require variations to reflect specific needs, for example due to different legal regulations in locations of international companies or product specifics. The level of detail of the definition of the standard determines the degree of freedom in applying the standard. In some processes this freedom may be minimal to enforce compliance requirements, in others larger, for example to manage customer relationships in a specific cultural context. The level of abstraction defines how a standard process is executed, which specific digital technologies are used. It could, for example, request the re-use of defined business capabilities, hence existing software modules, and a specific composition platform or the leverage of a defined ERP systems. The process standardization approach [15] is illustrated in Fig. 9.

Standardization is accelerated through the use of process reference modes. They reflect, for example, the impact of digital technologies or industry best and common practices. Those models can be company specific or procured externally, for example, from consulting companies or industry organizations [11, 16].

A major technology manufacturer, for example, was able to standardize the processes of five locations managing technical aspects of customer orders based on existing good practices and related application software. This resulted in reduced cycle by over 30%, a consistent customer experience and higher agility for process adjustments.

Process standardization can be considered a specific form of optimization. Improvements are mainly achieved through the consistent execution of a group of processes instead of best performance of one single process.

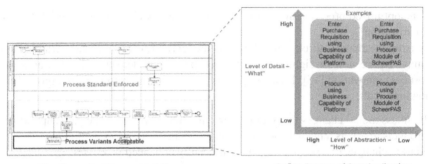

Identify required Process Variations   Define Degree of Standardization

Fig. 9. Process Standardization Considerations

3.3 Optimize

The term "optimization" is commonly used, however, slightly misleading since it is in a process improvement context difficult to define what an optimum is. In the context of process-led digitalization the term is used to refer to an improvement of an existing process that is consistent with the defined goals. The optimization starts with capturing existing processes, goes through a thorough analysis to identify the improvement opportunities and defines the to-be state realizing those improvements. The ARIS framework can be used to identify possible improvements systematically by identifying opportunities regarding all views on a business process [11]. The to-be processes leverage the identified digital technologies, such as the composition platform or existing and planned software business capabilities. The to-be design can be accelerated leveraging process reference models as starting point [16]. Those models are then modified to address the improvement opportunities.

The effects of improvements are validated through thorough process simulation, in general of different alternative process scenarios. An insurance company, for example, found, that the automation of their underwriter process using a no-code platform and developing appropriate business capabilities would reduce cost by over 40% and increase scalability by a factor 9.

Another insurance company discovered through simulation of different scenarios that the cost related to placement and policy servicing can be reduced by over 50%. It was also determined through the simulation that over 60% of the required business capabilities for the automation are already available through their composition platform and that most of the additional capabilities were already in the plan for upcoming development projects. Hence, the process-led digitalization delivers significant value – and moves the company towards the Composable Enterprise. The simulation results are illustrated in Fig. 10.

3.4 Innovate

Process innovation can be achieved by leveraging a design thinking approach. Using process management techniques this approach is operationalized [15]. Stakeholder journey maps provide an outside in view on processes, reference models are used to transfer

Placement and Policy Servicing Benefit Summary					
Placement		Policy Servicing		Overall	
As-is Costs	To-be Costs	As-is Costs	To-be Costs	As-is	To-be
$819,700	$445,990	$293,191	$97,608	$1,112,891	$543,597
46%		67%		51%	
$373,711		$195,583		$569,294	

Placement and Policy Servicing - Capabilities Required			
Capabilities Identified	Existing Business Capabilities	Business Capabilities in Backlog	Gaps Identified**
42	21	14	7
Cost Realization^	$370,962	$119,544	$78,789

Fig. 10. Simulation for Placement / Policy Servicing – leveraging existing Business Capabilities

practice from one sector into another, and the evaluation of different process scenarios enables an agile realization approach. The operating model and related process hierarchy provides the context for supporting story telling about the impact of the innovation. These components of an innovation initiative are shown in Fig. 11.

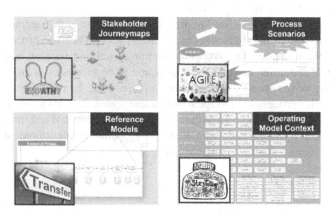

Fig. 11. Applying Design Thinking for Process Innovation

The process scenarios provide the opportunity to check the business impact of new technologies. Artificial Intelligence (AI), for example, can be brought in the context of a business process. This enables the validation of the business impact of AI [17].

A biologics company used elements of this approach to reduce their document related compliance issues by over 90% through the roll-out of new simple digital checking tools. This process innovation is in most cases applied in product specific high impact processes that are important for the competitive positioning of an organization.

4 Realize and Sustain

The design of the process types is the foundation for their implementation, execution and control of specific process instances. We discuss this implementation briefly from a business point of view since the technology side is outlined in the overall approach [2]. Details are technology specific or covered through existing project management approaches. Appropriate process governance is required to sustain achieved results and leverage the agility and flexibility achieved through the digital technologies, especially the Composable Enterprise.

4.1 Implement

The to-be design is used as guideline for the configuration, development and integration of the required software components, leveraging the technology and software information of the enterprise architecture [2]. This addresses specifically the use of the composition platform, available business capabilities and, if applicable, integration of external systems, such as ERP packages. It provides the top-level requirements for the development of new business capabilities which can be delivered either through business departments in case of simpler adjustments or a specialized IT department. The outlined process control flow helps to identify the integration requirements. The required integration of various software components is in many cases a key challenge requiring sophisticated capabilities of the platform.

The same process design is used to drive the people change management, ensuring the alignment of people and technology capabilities [4, 11]. The to-be processes provide the basis for the necessary information, communication and training activities. The identification of the differences between as-is and to be processes is an indicator for the significance of the change, hence, helps to prepare for the right degree of change management. This process-led change management approach helps to create culture of cross-departmental collaboration and the focus on value to external and internal clients.

This approach for integrated technology configuration and development as well as people change management is visualized in Fig. 12.

4.2 Govern

Process governance organizes the ongoing management of the business process to realize the expected value and trigger new improvement or transformation initiatives in case of changes in the business environment [4, 18]. Hence, appropriate governance helps to benefit from the agility and flexibility that the Composable Enterprise provides.

At the core of the governance approach is the definition of the process ownership and related accountabilities. To make this work, the process related goals and how they are measured is defined. Appropriate knowledge about the process and the necessary insights enables fast well-informed decisions and related actions. The process governance is guided through the process definition in the operating model and the strategic priorities, reflected in the enterprise-wide value-drivers.

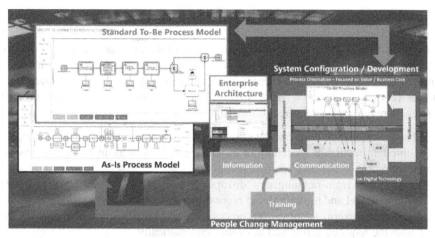

Fig. 12. Integrated Technology Implementation and People Change Management

The governance approach is realized through and overall governance model and the related detailed governance processes. Figure 13 shows an example of a governance model for a mid-sized biologics company.

The dynamic of today's business environment and the related agility of the Composable Enterprise require a digitalization of the governance processes themselves [18]. Process modelling and repository tools as well as mining applications for performance and conformance management play a key role. These tools are used to support the governance processes that are defined as component of the overall process of process management.

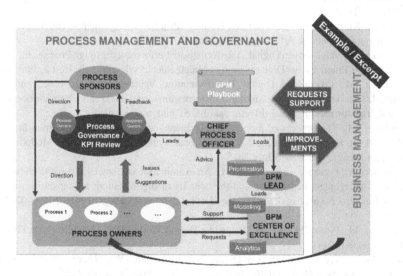

Fig. 13. Example of an overall Process Governance Model

5 Continue to Enhance the Journey

Process-led Digital Transformation or components of the approach have been applied in numerous successful initiatives in practice. The approach allows a controlled way to transform the enterprise without overwhelming the organization. The process-orientation enables a consequent focus on business value. To continue to enhance the transformation journey more research is required, for example in the following areas:

- Value-driven use of Artificial Intelligence (AI) for the approach itself, for example through intelligent modelling or mining tools, as well as an enabler of process innovation for operational business processes.
- The transition from defining new disruptive business model into am appropriate operating model and the underlying process hierarchy.
- Aligning the governance of various processes to an overall governance approach the realizes the required agility and flexibility systematically.

Process-led digitalization enables ambitious but pragmatic company transformation. It paves the way to the Composable Enterprise.

References

1. Kirchmer, M., Franz, P., Lotterer, A., Antonucci, Y., Laengle, S.: The Value-Switch for Digitalisation Initiatives: Business Process Management. BPM-D Whitepaper, Philadelphia, London (2016)
2. Scheer, A.-W.: Composable Enterprise: Agile, Flexible, Innovative – Gamechanger fuer Organisation, Digitalisierung und Unternehmenssoftware, 4th edn. Springer, Berlin (2023). https://doi.org/10.1007/978-3-658-43089-4
3. The Gartner Group (ed.): Future of Applications: Delivering the Composable Enterprise. ID: G00465932 (2021)
4. Franz, P., Kirchmer, M.: Value-Driven Business Process Management – The Value-Switch for Lasting Competitive Advantage, New York (2012)
5. Kirchmer, M.: Value-driven Digital Transformation: Performance through Process. In: IM+io, Best & Next Practices aus Digitalisierung I Management I Wissenschaft, Heft 2, Juni 2019
6. Kirchmer, M.: Process-led Digital Transformation: Value-driven, Data-based and Tool-enabled, October 2022. https://digital-transformation.cioreview.com/vp/bpmd/process-led_digital_transformation:_value-driven,_data-based_and_tool-enabled/
7. Kirchmer, M.: The process of process management – mastering the new normal in a digital world. In: Proceedings of the 5th International Symposium on Business Modelling and Software Design, Milan, 6–8 July 2015
8. Antonucci, Y., Fortune, A., Kirchmer, M.: An examination of associations between business process management capabilities and the benefits of digitalization: all capabilities are not equal. Bus. Process Manag. J. (2021). ahead-of print. https://doi.org/10.1108/BPMJ-02-2020-0079
9. Kirchmer, M., Franz, P.: Targeting Value in a Digital World. BPM-D Publications, Philadelphia, London (2014)
10. Abolhassan, F. (ed.): The Drivers of Digital Transformation – Why There is No Way Around the Cloud. Springer, Berlin (2016). https://doi.org/10.1007/978-3-319-31824-0

11. Kirchmer, M.: High Performance Through Business Process Management – Strategy Execution in a Digital World, 3rd edn. Springer, Berlin (2017). https://doi.org/10.1007/978-3-319-51259-4

12. Scheer, A-W.: ARIS – Business Process Frameworks, 2nd edn. Springer, Berlin (1998). https://doi.org/10.1007/978-3-642-58529-6

13. Fisher, L: BPMN 2.0 Handbook – Methods, Concepts, Case Studies and Standards in Business Process Modelling Notation (BPMN), 2nd edn., Lighthouse Point (2012)

14. Kirchmer, M.: Realizing appropriate process standardization – basis for effective digital transformation. In: Shishkov, B. (eds.) BMSD 2023. LNBIP, vol. 483, pp. 18–31. Springer, Cham (2023). https://doi.org/10.1007/978-3-031-36757-1_2. ISBN: 978-3-031-36756-4

15. Kirchmer, M.: Agile innovation through business process management: realizing the potential of digital transformation. In: Shishkov, B. (ed.) BMSD 2022. LNBIP, vol. 453, pp. 21–34. Springer, Cham (2022). https://doi.org/10.1007/978-3-031-11510-3_2. ISBN: 978-3-031-11509-7

16. Kirchmer, M., Franz, P.: Process reference models: accelerator for digital transformation. In: Shishkov, B. (ed.) BMSD 2020. LNBIP, vol. 391, pp. 20–37. Springer, Cham (2020). https://doi.org/10.1007/978-3-030-52306-0_2. ISBN: 978-3-030-52305-3

17. Hang, H., Chen, Z.: How to realize the full potential of artificial intelligence in the digital economy? – A literature review. J. Digit. Econ. 1, 180–191 (2022)

18. Kirchmer, M.: Digital transformation of business process governance. In: Shishkov, B. (ed.) BMSD 2021. LNBIP, vol. 422, pp. 243–261. Springer, Cham (2021). https://doi.org/10.1007/978-3-030-79976-2_14. ISBN: 978-3-030-79975-5

From Value Streams and Capability Maps to Protocol Models and Back

Ella Roubtsova(✉) 🆔

Open University of the Netherlands, Valkenburgerweg 177, 6419 AT Heerlen,
The Netherlands
ella.roubtsova@ou.nl

Abstract. Value Streams with supporting Capability Maps are a popular trend in modern enterprise architecture design. However, the existing definition of a capability as a collection of selected functionality is imprecise and often results in unmanageable capabilities and capability maps. Conceptual and process models, which are traditionally used to select functionality for system modules are considered too detailed at the strategic level, where capabilities are represented. This paper defines requirements and constraints for manageable capabilities and capability maps. The paper also proposes a method for the design of manageable capabilities and capability maps. This method employs the definition of requirements and constraints, as well as protocol modeling, to achieve this goal. Protocol models of capabilities are defined at the level of business objects and functionality chunks. The composition technique inherent to protocol modeling allows for the seamless movement of business objects and functional chunks between capabilities, thus facilitating the design of a manageable capability map. Furthermore, all protocol models of capabilities and capability maps can be simulated. The simulation process enables the identification of unmanageable and missing capabilities within a capability map. The proposed method can be employed as a reference for the design of manageable capability maps.

Keywords: Enterprise Modeling · Value Streams · Design a Manageable Capability Map · Protocol Models · Simulation as Mental Management

1 Introduction

Modeling techniques and design trends reflect the needs of the changing world.

When enterprises were relatively small, focused on production, and seen as machines [1], the design methods for values and enterprise architectures reflected the internal values of efficient production processes [29].

As enterprises started to collect finances from different shareholders, got management teams and started to be seen as organisms [1], the design methods for values and enterprise architectures were focused on efficient communication processes of subsystems of organismic enterprises [3] and on economic values [6].

© The Author(s), under exclusive license to Springer Nature Switzerland AG 2024
B. Shishkov (Ed.): BMSD 2024, LNBIP 523, pp. 32–47, 2024.
https://doi.org/10.1007/978-3-031-64073-5_3

Modern enterprises are globally dispersed groups and institutions often called social systems [17], and they are global not only in terms of global market, but also in covering different domains. Enterprises as social systems provide many economic and non-economic values to different categories of customers. For example, the Starbucks not only sells coffee, but also selects producers and monitors their production process to ensure that the production is nature and worker friendly. Information about the monitoring of the coffee bean production is displayed in all Starbucks stores and on every cup of coffee, with the goal of building reputation among different groups of customers. Another example is Warby Parker, which not only produces eyeglasses, but also contacts medical institutions to find out the needs of patients, produces extra glasses and "donates a pair of eyeglasses to someone in need for every pair sold" [21]. So the new pair of glasses is one value, and the donation is another value to the customers.

Enterprise modeling techniques for social enterprises should be able to assess the ability of an enterprise to cover different domains and deliver the value associated with each domain covered. Therefore, the trend in enterprise architecture modeling is to build enterprise architectures based on value streams and on the business capabilities that support them.

Although the idea of such enterprise architectures has been proposed, and capabilities have been drawn as modules of such architectures, the requirements for the selection of functionality for the capability modules and the constraints for the communication of capability modules have not been defined. Without these definitions, a capability can be designed in many different ways.

This paper proposes

- The requirements for designing of capabilities and the constraints for the communicating of capabilities in a capability map to achieve manageable capabilities and the capability map;
- A modeling method that uses these requirements and constraints and the protocol modeling approach [12] for designing capabilities in a capability-based enterprise architecture.

The requirements and constraints are derived from the needs of enterprise architects of modern social enterprises.

The protocol modeling approach was chosen because it has a unique built-in composition operator that allows the free movement of business functions, business objects, and behaviors when composing and decomposing them into modules. This is in contrast to the conceptual and process models, which have a well-known problem called the tyranny of the dominant decomposition [4] that restricts the composition and decomposition of business functions, business objects, and behaviors.

Section 2 reviews the existing definitions and frameworks for designing value streams and capability maps for modern social enterprises.

Section 3 derives the requirements for a capability and the constraints on the communication of capabilities for an enterprise. The combination of requirements and constraints results in the definition of a manageable capability. Then, the semantic advantages of protocol modeling are presented and a method for designing value streams and manageable capabilities is proposed.

Section 4 illustrates the proposed method with a case study.

Section 5 concludes the paper with a reference to the classification of value streams and capabilities in an enterprise and the future application of the proposed method for their modeling.

2 Status of Value Stream and Capability Map Design

The terms "value" and "capability" are used differently in many approaches. We focus on the definition proposed in standards for modern social enterprises.

2.1 Definitions

The TOGAF standard emphasizes that "within the context of business architecture, it is important to think of **value** in the most general sense of usefulness, advantage, benefit, or desirability, rather than the relatively narrow accounting or financial perspective that defines value as being the material or monetary worth of something" [20].

Value streams "are represented by value stream stages, each of which creates and adds incremental stakeholder value from one stage to the next.... A key principle of value streams is that value is always defined from the perspective of the stakeholder, the customer, end-user, or recipient of the product, service, or deliverable produced by the work" [20].

"**Capability** is an ability and capacity of an enterprise to deliver value, either to customers or to shareholders, right beneath the business strategy" [20].

The TOGAF® Series Guide Value Streams [19] presents an example of a value stream and the mapping of value stages to capabilities. It states: "Creating value streams and mapping them to business capabilities should not require going down to operational levels of detail. That is normally the domain of business process design. The operational level of detail can be derived from the value streams but that detail does not usually provide the overall, end-to-end perspective that is needed for strategy-level discussions and analysis" [19].

Although the need for an end-to-end perspective is accepted [10,27,28], the statement that "creating value streams and mapping them to business capabilities should not require going down to operational levels of detail" is not shared by practitioners. Without some level of detail, the mapping of value streams to capabilities often splits the functional chunks that should be performed in the same capability. The separation of some functional chunks into different capabilities can result in an architecture that is difficult to change and plan resources for. In addition, the mapping of value streams to capabilities, designed from a purely strategic perspective, is often incomplete, i.e. some capabilities required by value stages are missing. Incomplete mapping leads to planning errors. This means that the mapping of value streams to capabilities should be modeled at a level of detail that reveals when functional chunks are incorrectly separated and shows why one separation is manageable and another is not.

The need for a certain level of detail in the design of capabilities is supported by the research of Wißotzki and SandKuhl [28]. They conducted "an analysis and discussion of the literature on capabilities in EAM (Enterprise Architecture Modeling)" and proposed "a conceptualization of EAM capability". The authors have found that "the notion of capability is related to the notions of resource, business, goal, enterprise context, process(activity), knowledge, actor(role)" [28]. The authors identified the subtypes of external and internal capabilities. External capabilities are dynamic and innovative. They include the development and delivery of both new products and services. Internal capabilities are divided into core business ("enabling and supplemental") and IT capabilities. The authors refer to their subtypes as "combinable", but they do not present a methodology for combining (or separating) capabilities.

The Object Management Group (OMG) proposed the Value Delivery Modeling Language (VDML) to standardize business object names used to model value streams. VDML proposes value stream diagrams as activity diagrams that label the arrows between activities with a deliverable object that flows. Representing value stream stages through activities and processes contradicts the TOGAF definition of value streams. This is because value streams are meant to be measured, and measurement is only possible in states.

2.2 Frameworks

Some enterprise modeling frameworks attempt to incorporate the concepts of value, value stream, and capability.

The 4EM framework [5,11,24] proposed a meta-model that relates capabilities to goal, process, and concept models. Such a set of models is traditionally used in enterprise modeling. "Process is a series of actions that are performed in order to achieve particular result. A process supports Goals and has input and produces output in terms of information and/or material. When initiated, a process consumes resources. A process describes the actions that need to be performed to deliver a capability" [5]. However, concept diagrams represent all states of modeled business objects, not the states of objects before and after a process in a process diagram. In addition, the well-known modeling phenomenon, called the tyranny of the dominant decomposition, indicates that there are always scattered and tangled functional chunks (also called aspects) that cannot be separated in process diagrams and objects [4]. The 4EM does not provide a method to guide the selection of functional chunks for each capability.

The need to model values and relate them to other enterprise views has led to a formal transformation of the e3value approach [9] into ArchiMate [25] via the DEMO framework [8]. The use of transaction rules makes it possible to separate the functional chunks and to sort them into capabilities. Nevertheless, further work is required to provide guidance on the selection of transaction rules for each capability and each value stage.

Our review shows that the useful semantics for capability design are still being sought, and that the methods of capability design are still evolving. This paper is a contribution to that search.

3   Method for Designing Value Streams and Capability Maps Using Protocol Modeling

3.1   Manageable Capability Map

To design an enterprise architecture consisting of value streams and capability maps, it is necessary to define the requirements for the capabilities as modules of this architecture and to define constraints on their communication. The requirements are derived from the needs of modern social enterprises to cover many domains, to plan the resources and the responsible roles for each capability, and to ensure that any problem in delivering a value in the designed value stream can be localized in a capability module.

Given that, each value in a value stream and the corresponding capability module covers a different domain, it is essential that the capability modules have as few dependencies as possible.

From the design point of view, the functionality chunks formulated for capabilities can be seen as functions of a life cycle of a business object (from the set: create, read, update, delete) or other functional aspects like different checks and derivations. So, we formulate the requirements and constraints in terms of functions of life cycles of business objects and other functional aspects.

Requirements for capability design: All life cycle functions of a business object used in a capability map should be placed in one single capability. A capability module can contain several closely related business objects and their life cycle functions. A capability module can include repeated functional aspects into business modules.

Constraint on communication of capabilities in a capability map: The business objects placed in one capability module of the capability map can only read the state and attribute values of business objects in another capability module, but cannot change them.

A capability map is considered manageable if it meets the requirements for capability design and the constraint on communication of capabilities in the capability map.

A capability map that meets the formulated requirements and the constraint is manageable because it allows for the assignment of roles and resources to a capability. The roles and resources will control the business objects included in the capability and will not depend on business objects of other capabilities and the roles and resources assigned to them. The requirements and the constraint enable the localization of business problems and changes to capabilities in an enterprise that implements such a capability map.

3.2 Protocol Modeling

Protocol model [14] contains all the necessary modeling elements for capability modeling: actions (event structures that model transferred data), objects, and object states. Protocol modeling combines concept and action diagrams in one notation and enriches them with object states.

In addition, protocol models have the semantics of derived states, which are used to separate chunks of functionality called mixins [16]. A mixin is not necessarily a complete behavior of an object, but it is a functional chunk recognized at the business level.

Functional chunks modeled as objects or mixins are called protocol machines. Protocol machines are protocol models and they can be combined in submodels with in the protocol model.

The protocol machines and combined submodels are uniformly composed by the rules of CSP-parallel composition, which are part of the protocol modeling semantics. The rules of CSP-parallel composition state that (1) an event can be recognized by several objects; (2) only if all objects that recognize an event are ready to accept the event, the event can proceed. Otherwise, the event is refused [12].

Protocol models are executable for testing the reachability of the states. There is a tool ModelScope that supports the execution of a protocol [13].

Protocol modeling has been used for modeling in various domains [15] and the models remains at the business level. For example, a protocol model for a crisis management system [2], a reference model for a service level agreement in the domain of information sharing services [7], a protocol model for health insurance business [26], a reference model for measurement and analysis with KPIs [23], and a reference model for privacy control capabilities [22].

This paper demonstrates the use of protocol modeling in the design of value streams and supporting capabilities.

3.3 Method Description

Given the semantic benefits of protocol modeling for separation and composition of business objects life cycle functions and other functional aspects, we propose a method for designing value streams and capability maps.

1. The first version of a value stream map and a capability map is proposed.
2. The capabilities of the capability map are modeled as protocols. The set of protocol models of capabilities is already a protocol model of the capability map (because of the CSP-parallel composition of protocol models of capabilities).
3. The protocol models are simulated. Since the protocol models are composed (semantics of the CSP-parallel composition), both each protocol model of a capability and the composition of selected capabilities can be simulated for resource planning, manageability checking, correction, and completion.

(a) If the life cycle events of a business object are handled by different capabilities, the chunks of functionality for that business object are moved into one capability. Go to (2)

(b) If there are chunks of functionality that belong to undefined business objects, the missing capability is added and new business objects and all their behaviors are placed into this added capability. Go to (2)

(c) If the new business objects add a value stage to a value stream, the value stream sequence is redrawn to include the new value stage. Go to (2)

(d) If the simulation of the protocol model of the capability map allows each assigned actor (role) to perform the necessary life cycle events (from the set: create, retrieve, modify and delete) for each business object placed in the capability, and if business objects of one capability only read the state and do not change the objects of other capabilities, the capability model is manageable.

4. The new, manageable version of the capability map is redrawn from the protocol model. The corrected capabilities are abstracted one-to-one from the corrected protocol model, resulting in a new capability map.

The next section presents a method application case study. It demonstrates how to identify unmanageable capabilities using protocol models, how to identify missing capabilities, and how to make capabilities and capability maps manageable.

4   Value Stream and Capability Model from Unmanageable to Manageable

4.1   The First Version of a Value Stream and Capability Map Is Proposed

Figure 1 shows a value stream of a health insurance business. The value stream and the capabilities are proposed based on the information provided by the business developers in a previous project, as referenced in [26]. The value stream provided to customers by the health insurance business contains three value stages: V1: Insurance Product, V2: Insurance Policy, and V3: Claim Handling (Fig. 1).

The value stream is mapped to capabilities.

– The capability "C1:To define an Insurance Product" is mapped to the value stage "V1: Insurance Product". C1 is refined to smaller capabilities. Namely, "To create a medical procedure", "To create a group of medical procedures", "To create a coverage of a group of medical procedures", and "To create an Insurance product from coverages". An insurance product is a collection of coverages. It is then ready for sale.

- The capability "C2: To sell a Policy of an Insurance Product" is mapped to the value stage "V2: Insurance Policy" and it is refined into smaller capabilities: "To create and delete a policy corresponding an insurance product for a registered person", "To activate coverage-counters for the policy". The coverage counters with initial values of parameters are created for each customer.
- The capability "C3: To handle a claim" is mapped to the value stage "V3: Claim Compensation". The capability C3 aggregates the capabilities "To submit a claim", "To sort a claim for a coverage", "To transfer the amount of a sorted claim to the account", and "To modify a counter for a coverage".

The capabilities and the smaller capabilities refining them, seem logical at the first glans.

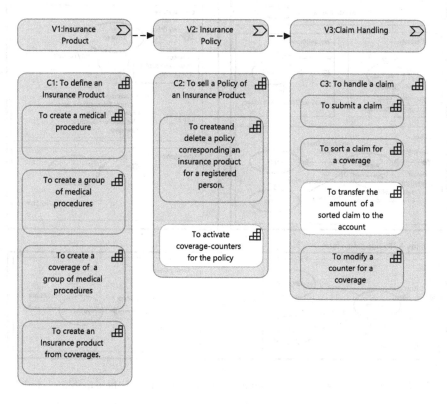

Fig. 1. Value Stream and Capability Map of an Insurance Business. Difficult to manage.

Capability 1:
To define an Insurance product

Capability 2:
To sell a Policy of an Insurance Product

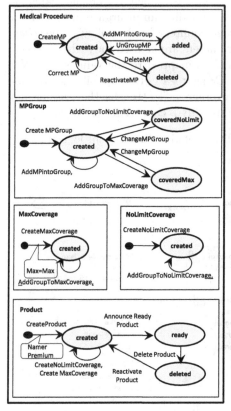

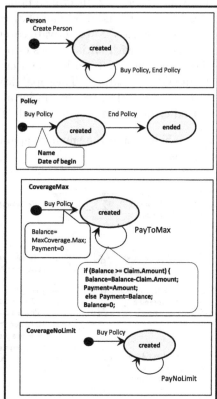

Capability 3: To handle a claim

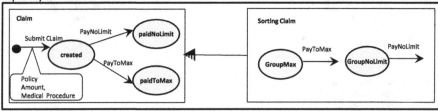

Fig. 2. Protocol models corresponding to the first version of the capability model

4.2 The Capabilities from the Capability Map Are Modeled as Protocols

The capabilities suggested by strategic designers have been used to be presented as protocol models. Figure 2 presents the graphical view on three capabilities C1, C2, C3 as protocol machines.

The protocol model of capability C1 shows that each business object Medical Procedure has to be defined. After that, the groups MPGroups are created and each Medical Procedure is added to an MPGroup (event AddMPintoGroup). Events synchronize the behaviors of objects. For example, the AddMPIntoGroup event is used for synchronization of a Medical Procedure and a MPGroup. There are different types of coverage for compensation of groups of medical procedures. For simplicity, we model only two types of coverage. The business object called Max Coverage, which has an attribute called Maximum and states that the medical procedures are compensated until the Maximum is reached. We model the business object NoLimit Coverage, which means that medical procedures are always compensated. We also model the business project Product. There are events CreateMaxCoverages and Create NoLimitCoverage for each Product.

The capability C2 protocol model indicates that a Person purchases a Policy, which involves agreeing to product coverages and paying the premium to the insurance company. Coverage counters for each policy are then created. The CoverageMax Counter object starts in the initial state with attributes $Balance = Max$, taken from the MaxCoverage of the Insurance Product, and

$$if\ (Balance >= Claim.Amount)$$

$$then\ Balance = Balance - Claim.Amount;\ Payment = Claim.Amount;$$

$$else\ Payment = Balance;\ Balance = 0;$$

The CoverageNoLimit Counter object ensures that any claim filed under this coverage will always be compensated. The reachability of the state "created" for a Policy object of a Person object and for the objects displayed operational coverages for the Person object indicates that value stage V2 achieved in capability C2. Note, that a Policy object is created from an object of type Product in the state "ready", but does not change it.

The capability C3 protocol model shows the life cycle events of the business object Claim. The Sorting Claim is a mixin, presenting a decision-making behavior. It is included in the object Claim. The derived state GroupMax is reached when the medical procedure of the claim instance belongs to the Group covered until the Maximum. The derived state GroupNoLimit is derived when the medical procedure of the Claim instance belongs to the group covered with no limit. The ModelScope tool compares the medical procedure with the medical procedures in the GroupNoLimit and results in the derived state if the medical procedure has been found in the group. Submit Claim is an event that connects all of these objects. A Claim instance is sorted by one of the rules: CoverageMax and CoverageNoLimit. The states that can be eached by the capability C3 are "Claim.paidToMax" or "Claim.paidNoLimit".

4.3 The Protocol Models Are Simulated

Simulation of protocol models can be done both mentally and with the ModelScope tool [13,18]. The mental execution is already powerful. The simulator has to see the objects that recognize the same event and mentally imagine that these objects proceed together when they are both in the state to accept this event.

The mental simulation of Fig. 2 shows that the proposed capabilities are not easy to manage.

Simulation of protocol models for capabilities C2 and C3

– Suppose that each capability (C2 and C3) is assigned to a different role (an Actor in Protocol Model).
– Suppose that the role assigned to capability C2 has made a mistake in defining a coverage counter.
– Another role, assigned to capability C3, uses the counter and will make mistakes in compensation of claims, but this role is not able to find the source of mistakes and change the counter.
– Therefore, the functionality of creating, changing, retrieving of each counter should be defined in capability C3.

Simulation of of protocol model for capabilities C3.

– The capability C3 aggregates the capability "To transfer the amount of a sorted claim to the account".
– However, no account information is available.
– The system is currently lacking in capability C4, which is necessary for accessing the customer's account and for transferring a claim payment and an insurance premium.

4.4 The New Version of the Protocol Models for Capabilities Is Redrawn

Figures 3 and 4 show the protocol model of capabilities, each of which has all life cycle operations of the business objects it contains. The life cycle events of coverage-counters are now in the protocol model C3. The protocol model for capability C4 contains an object Account. "Event Date of begin" means that at the moment when policy is activated, the permission for the account access in granted to the Insurance Enterprise. The mixin "Check for claims" searches for a "Claims in state ToNoLimit ot ToMax" and proceeds event "Transfer amount of a sorted claim" to the account in state "granted". The set of protocol models for capabilities is the protocol model for a new capability map.

Capability 1:
To define an Insurance product

Capability 2:
To sell a Policy of an Insurance Product

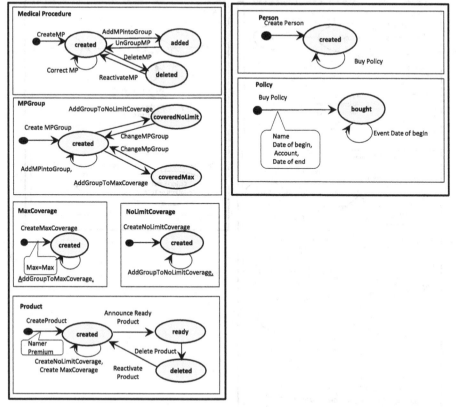

Fig. 3. Protocol model of two capabilities C1, C2 corresponding to the second version of the capability map

4.5   The New Version of the Protocol Model Is Simulated

Designers are satisfied, when only a single capability protocol model contains all the necessary life cycle events for business objects belonging to that capability. Such a capability can be assigned to a responsible role (actor) and necessary resources. Other capabilities can only derive and use the information about the existence, state, and other attributes of business objects controlled by other capabilities. The functionality composed in a capability does not depend on other capabilities, their roles, and resources.

In our case study, designers were satisfied with the location of protocol machines (functionality chunks) in protocol models for each capability shown in Figs. 3 and 4.

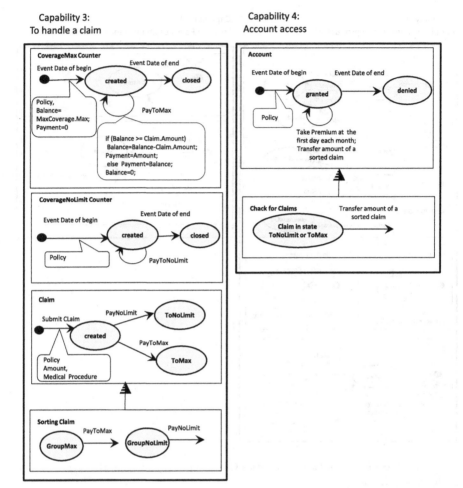

Fig. 4. Protocol models of two capabilities C3, C4 corresponding to the second version of the capability map

4.6 The New, Manageable Version of the Capability Model Is Redrawn from the Protocol Model

Using the protocol models of capabilities (Figs. 3 and 4), the new version of the capability model is redrawn in Fig. 5.

The semantics of protocol modeling makes it possible to model each capability as one protocol model, that composes all the recognized functionality chunks. The set of protocol models is the protocol model of a capability map.

For redrawing purposes, we can think of a capability as an abstraction of its protocol model, and a capability map as an abstraction of the set of protocol models for all capabilities.

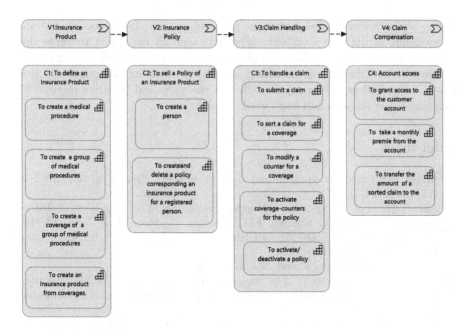

Fig. 5. Value Stream and Capability Map of an Insurance Business. Version 2. Manageable.

5 Conclusion and Future Work

In this paper, we have shown how to design the value streams and capability maps using the semantics of protocol modeling. Protocol modeling keeps the model at the level of life cycles of business objects and their synchronized behavior. It also synchronizes aspects (checks and derivations) with behaviors of businesses objects. This is the level required for the separation of capabilities in capability maps.

We have proposed an iterative method that can guide the design of value streams and the associated capabilities with protocol models. Designers can use protocol models to mentally simulate the management tasks, such as assigning roles and planning resources, with protocol models and ensure the manageability of the designed capabilities. We have shown that even mental simulation of protocol models allows us to improve the unmanageable design and to move the pieces of functionality to the capability that contains all the business object life cycle events. We have shown that missing capabilities are also identified. By simulating the protocol model with the ModeScope tool, various management activities such as resource allocation and finding the sources of process errors become even more visible [18].

An enterprise architecture typically contains multiple value streams for different stakeholders. The value streams are mapped to capabilities. Internal and external, innovative, enabling and supplemental [28], all these capability types can be separated and synchronized as protocol models. We expect that protocol modeling of different capability types will identify capability patterns that aggregate specific types of business objects. We intend to conduct several master projects in different organizations, such as government document archives, and cloud providers. The projects will test the proposed iterative method for designing value streams and supported capabilities.

References

1. Ackoff, R.L.: Systems thinking and thinking systems. Syst. Dyn. Rev. **10**(2–3), 175–188 (1994)
2. Alférez, M., et al.: Aspect-oriented model development at different levels of abstraction. In: France, R.B., Kuester, J.M., Bordbar, B., Paige, R.F. (eds.) ECMFA 2011. LNCS, vol. 6698, pp. 361–376. Springer, Heidelberg (2011). https://doi.org/10.1007/978-3-642-21470-7_25
3. Allee, V.: The Future of Knowledge. Routledge (2009)
4. D'Hondt, M., D'Hondt, T.: The tyranny of the dominant model decomposition. In: OOPSLA Workshop on Generative Techniques in the Context of Model-Driven Architecture (2002)
5. FP 7 ICT Programme Collaborative Project: CaaS - Capability as a Service for digital enterprises, no. 611351 (2023). https://caas-project.eu/definitions/
6. Gordijn, J., Akkermans, H.: E3-value: design and evaluation of e-business model. IEEE Intell. Syst. **16**(4), 11–17 (2001)
7. Hofman, C., Roubtsova, E.: A reference model for a service level agreement. In: Shishkov, B. (ed.) BMSD 2020. LNBIP, vol. 391, pp. 55–68. Springer, Cham (2020). https://doi.org/10.1007/978-3-030-52306-0_4
8. de Kinderen, S., Gaaloul, K., Proper, H.A.: Bridging value modelling to archimate via transaction modelling. Softw. Syst. Model. **13**(3), 1043–1057 (2014)
9. Kort, C., Gordijn, J.: Modeling strategic partnerships using the e3value ontology: A field study in the banking industry. In: Handbook of Ontologies for Business Interaction, pp. 310–325. IGI Global (2008)
10. Kotusev, S.: Fake and real tools for enterprise architecture: the zachman framework and business capability model. Enterp. Architect. Prof. J., pp. 1–14 (2019)
11. Koutsopoulos, G.: KYKLOS-A modeling method and tool for managing changing capabilities in organizations, Ph.D. thesis, Department of Computer and Systems Sciences, Stockholm University (2024)
12. McNeile, A., Roubtsova, E.: CSP parallel composition of aspect models. In: Proceedings of the 2008 AOSD Workshop on Aspect-Oriented Modeling, pp. 13–18 (2008)
13. McNeile, A., Roubtsova, E.: Executable protocol models as a requirements engineering tool. In: 41st Annual Simulation Symposium (ANSS-41 2008), pp. 95–102. IEEE (2008)
14. McNeile, A., Simons, N.: Protocol modelling: a modelling approach that supports reusable behavioural abstractions. Softw. Syst. Model. **5**(1), 91–107 (2006)
15. McNeile, A., Simons, N., Roubtsova, E.: Protocol modelling (2024). https://newprotocolmodelling.weebly.com/publications.html
16. McNeile, A.T., Simons, N.: State machines as mixins. J. Object Technol. **2**(6), 85–101 (2003)

17. Merriam-Webster: Social system (2023). https://www.merriam-webster.com/dictionary
18. Metamaxim: MODELSCOPE (2024). http://www.metamaxim.com/
19. OPENGROUP: TOGAF series guide, value streams (2022). https://pubs.opengroup.org/togaf-standard/business-architecture/value-streams.html
20. OPENGROUP: TOGAF - enterprise architecture methodology, version 9.1 (2023). http://www.opengroup.org/togaf/
21. Parker, W.: Buy-a-pair-give-a-pair (2023). https://www.warbyparker.com/buy-a-pair-give-a-pair
22. Roubtsova, E., Bosua, R.: Privacy as a service (PraaS): a conceptual model of GDPR to construct privacy services. In: Shishkov, B. (ed.) BMSD 2021. LNBIP, vol. 422, pp. 170–189. Springer, Cham (2021). https://doi.org/10.1007/978-3-030-79976-2_10
23. Roubtsova, E., Michell, V.: A method for modeling of KPIs enabling validation of their properties. In: Proceedings of the 5th ACM SIGCHI Annual International Workshop on Behaviour Modelling-Foundations and Applications, pp. 1–10 (2013)
24. Sandkuhl, K., Stirna, J., Persson, A., Wißotzki, M.: Enterprise Modeling: Tackling Business Challenges with the 4EM Method. Springer, Berlin, Heidelberg (2014). https://doi.org/10.1007/978-3-319-94857-7
25. The Open Group: Archimate 3.1 Specification. https://pubs.opengroup.org/architecture/archimate3-doc/. Accessed 1 Oct 2022
26. Verheul, J., Roubtsova, E.: An executable and changeable reference model for the health insurance industry. In: Proceedings of the Third Workshop on Behavioural Modelling, pp. 33–40 (2011)
27. Vernadat, F.: Enterprise modelling: research review and outlook. Comput. Ind. **122**, 103265 (2020)
28. Wißotzki, M., Sandkuhl, K.: Elements and characteristics of enterprise architecture capabilities. In: Matulevičius, R., Dumas, M. (eds.) BIR 2015. LNBIP, vol. 229, pp. 82–96. Springer, Cham (2015). https://doi.org/10.1007/978-3-319-21915-8_6
29. Wolf, B.M.: The machine that changed the world. J. Int. Bus. Stud. **22**(3), 533–538 (1991). https://doi.org/10.1057/jibs.1991.40

A Method to Align Business Capability Maps and Enterprise Data Models

Sefanja Severin[1,2](✉) ⓘ, Ella Roubtsova[1] ⓘ, Ben Roelens[1,3] ⓘ, and Stef Joosten[1,4] ⓘ

[1] Open Universiteit, Valkenburgerweg 177, 6419 AT Heerlen, The Netherlands
{sefanja.severin,ella.roubtsova,ben.roelens,stef.joosten}@ou.nl
[2] Stedin Groep, Blaak 8, 3011 TA Rotterdam, The Netherlands
[3] Ghent University, Tweekerkenstraat 2, 9000 Ghent, Belgium
[4] Ordina, Ringwade 1, 3439 LM Nieuwegein, The Netherlands

Abstract. The business capability map has gained close attention from organizations as an essential tool for communication between business and IT. However, its integration with the enterprise data model is hampered by semantic issues that complicate stakeholder communication. This study, based on an analysis of TOGAF, presents a refined metamodel to resolve these issues and ensure alignment between the business capability map and the enterprise data model. The utility of the metamodel was demonstrated through a case study of Dutch energy system operators. The findings not only enhance model consistency and stakeholder communication but also provide a foundation for future research, suggesting the integration of additional elements into the metamodel to broaden its scope and utility.

Keywords: TOGAF · enterprise architecture modeling · business capability map · enterprise data model · business object

1 Introduction

Over the past few decades, organizations have struggled to align business and IT to improve their performance [18]. An important inhibitor of alignment is the lack of business understanding by IT. For such understanding, enterprise architecture management has produced a number of boundary objects [16], that is, objects that "have different meanings in different social worlds but their structure is common enough to more than one world to make them recognizable, a means of translation" [27, p. 393]. A boundary object with increased interest from organizations is the business capability map [1]. Another artifact, also intended as a boundary object but with less success due to its highly abstract character [24], is the enterprise data model [10]. This study proposes a method for aligning these models, thereby increasing their potential to create coherence between the intersecting social worlds of business and IT.

B. Shishkov (Ed.): BMSD 2024, LNBIP 523, pp. 48–64, 2024.
https://doi.org/10.1007/978-3-031-64073-5_4

1.1   Business Capability Map

The business capability map provides a complete overview of all the capabilities of an organization. *Business capability* can be defined as "a particular ability that a business may possess or exchange to achieve a specific purpose" [30, Sect. 4.28]. An example is the ability to recruit workers or send invoices. By not specifying *how* workers are recruited or *how* invoices are sent, business capabilities provide an abstraction of details, such as people, processes, and technology, allowing them to be understood by diverse communities.

Business capability maps do not cover the entire spectrum of business modeling. Other business models describe organizational structures, regulations, and business processes, among others. Still, practitioners consider the business capability map as the focal point of business architecture [9] because of its ability to relate many viewpoints. For example, by relating regulations and business processes to business capabilities, it is easy to determine which regulations impact which business processes.

1.2   Enterprise Data Model

The enterprise data model (also referred to as *information map* [9, 29]) provides a complete overview of objects managed by the organization, such as *recruitment, customer invoice*, etc. As such, it establishes a common vocabulary, which promotes interoperability across an organization's information system landscape and enables data-driven decision-making.

Although business capability maps can be used as references to create, for example, service-oriented archtictures [13], enterprise data models are more useful for paradigms that prioritize objects over actions, such as resource-oriented architectures [23], object-oriented programming [33], model-driven development [3], and database design. In fact, the enterprise data model can be considered essential for software development, as it "sets forth the foundation for all data and data-related projects" [10, p. 104].

1.3   Reasons for Model Alignment

Our conceptualization of the world is driven by our goals and enables communication to realize them. For example, when looking for food, we conceptualize the world as being composed of edible and non-edible items, allowing food gatherers to cooperate. If we characterize the business capability map as a goal model and the enterprise data model as a conceptualization of the world, it becomes apparent that neither model exists independently.

More practically, the enterprise data model does not generally appeal to a business audience because of its highly abstract character, despite its potential business benefits [24]. If properly aligned, business capabilities provide a context for the elements of the enterprise data model, explaining *why* an object is managed. This should increase its appeal, and thereby, its quality and utility.

Conversely, the business capability map can benefit from alignment with the enterprise data model. By aligning the models, the knowledge in the enterprise data model can be used to refine the business capability map and to precisely define *what* is managed by a business capability. Furthermore, aligning these models may increase their completeness and pertinence and enable a more holistic view of the organization, allowing stakeholders to relate perspectives.

When considering software design, aligned models may be better suited to support the requirements definition and design stages of the software development life cycle. For example, during requirements definition, business capabilities can be used as high-level requirements, while the enterprise data model provides a matching vocabulary to express lower-level requirements. During the design stage, business capabilities can be used to identify the main software components, while the enterprise data model helps identify the information exchange between those components.

Figure 1 shows a simplified example of alignment in which the correspondence between elements from different models is highlighted using colors.

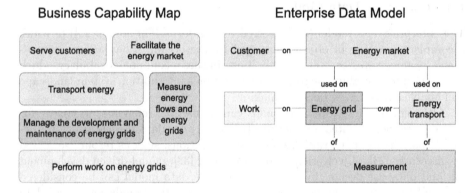

Fig. 1. Simplified example of alignment between a business capability map and an enterprise data model (Color figure online)

1.4   Research Question

Despite the popularity of business capability maps in practice [1], a limited number of capability frameworks have been developed in the academic literature [15]. Offerman et al. [22] identified two business capability frameworks in the literature: one by Brits et al. [8], with limited empirical evidence for its application, and one by TOGAF [30], which is related to the BIZBOK Guide [9]. Given its frequent use in practice, this study uses TOGAF as the main reference.

The TOGAF Series Guides identify the business capability map as one of four core elements of business architecture, along with the value stream map, information map, and organization map. The information map in TOGAF has the same content as the enterprise data model; only its name is different. The TOGAF Enterprise Metamodel defines the elements and relationships of these maps. The TOGAF Series Guides provide guidelines to relate the business capability map and information map, but do not offer a method to check their consistency. To address this gap, the following research question is formulated:

Research question: How can the TOGAF Enterprise Metamodel be refined to ensure consistency between the business capability map and the enterprise data model?

To answer this question, we perform a semantic analysis of the TOGAF metamodel and propose a refined metamodel with rules and guidelines that ensure consistency between the business capability map and the enterprise data model. The practical applicability of the metamodel was evaluated against NBility [21], an industry reference model of Dutch energy system operators.

1.5 Outline of the Paper

Sect. 2 explains the TOGAF Enterprise Metamodel, which defines the elements of the business capability map and enterprise data model (or information map). Section 3 provides insights from semantic analysis. Section 4 presents the refined metamodel, along with its consistency rules and guidelines. Section 5 evaluates the refined metamodel in a practical case. Section 6 concludes the paper and discusses opportunities for future research.

2 TOGAF Enterprise Metamodel

The business capability map and the information map are collections of *business capabilities* and *business information* concepts, respectively. These appear in the TOGAF Enterprise Metamodel, as shown in the M2 layer of Fig. 2. The figure does not contain multiplicities for relationships because TOGAF does not define them.

By instantiating the concepts in the M2 layer we arrive at the M1 layer. For example, *business capability* (M2) is instantiated as the *ability to perform work on energy grids* (M1), which is instantiated as a single demonstration of this ability by performing grid reconstruction work on Broadway (M0). The M0 layer is the lowest layer and describes individual things in the real world. The research question in this study concerns the *business capability* and *business information* concepts in the M2 layer.

3 Semantic Analysis

This section analyzes TOGAF's explicit and implicit definitions of *business capability*, *business information*, and their relationship. A good understanding of these concepts is required to refine the TOGAF Enterprise Metamodel with rules and guidelines. Figure 3 shows how these concepts relate to the other concepts discussed in this section.

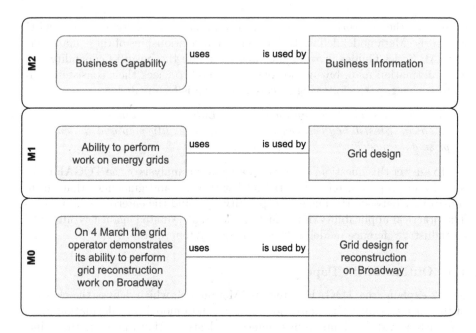

Fig. 2. The TOGAF Enterprise Metamodel is at the M2 layer.

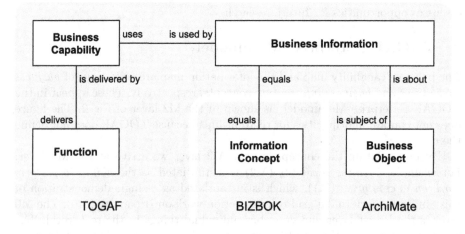

Fig. 3. Overview of concepts discussed in the semantic analysis

3.1 Analysis of *Business Capability*

An analysis of *business capability* can be found in other studies: Wißotzki [34] explored the notion of *capability* in the academic literature, Azevedo et al. [4] analyzed *business capability* using Unified Foundational Ontology (UFO), and Roubtsova and Michell [25] clarified the definitions of *affordance* and *capability* using behavioral models. However, the analysis in this section is different, as it aims to clarify the distinction between *business capability* and *function* in TOGAF.

TOGAF defines *business capability* as "a particular ability that a business may possess or exchange to achieve a specific purpose" [30, Architecture Content, Sect. 2.4]. TOGAF also defines *function*, namely as "a set of business behaviors based on a chosen set of criteria" [30, Architecture Content, Sect. 2.4]. The distinction between these concepts is difficult to understand, as TOGAF uses them interchangeably, for example, in its description of a diagram consisting of *functions*: "The purpose of the Functional Decomposition diagram is to show on a single page the *capabilities* [emphasis added] of an organization that are relevant to the consideration of an architecture" [30, Sect. 3.6.3]. Berrisford concludes that "the function and capability concepts are widely confused" [7].

This confusion appears to be an aspect of the TOGAF Enterprise Metamodel. For example, it defines the *uses* relationship between *business capability* and *business information*. However, the issue with this relationship is that an *ability* cannot *use* something, whereas a function can. Additionally, the TOGAF metamodel states that a function *delivers* a business capability. This can be true of a piano-practicing function that delivers a piano-playing ability. However, it is clear from the text of TOGAF that this is not the intended meaning of the *delivers* relationship. Berrisford clarifies: "TOGAF inherits Business Function from Information Engineering and the like, but inherits Capability from Capability-Based Planning. It hasn't quite got the nerve or the will to modify their two vocabularies until they are integrated" [6, p. 16].

Capability is a central concept in several enterprise architecture frameworks such as the Department of Defense Architecture Framework (DoDAF), UK Ministry of Defence Architecture Framework (MODAF), and NATO Architecture Framework (NAF) [26]. For example, the USA uses a two-theater defense model in which the highest-level capability is the ability to handle two major conflicts simultaneously in different parts of the world. Note that this capability specifies the number, size, timing, and location of conflicts, all of which relate to a *particular ability* to perform the defense *function*. Thus, *business capability* can be considered a *particular* ability to perform a function [35]. To clarify, another capability could be the ability to handle *three* major conflicts, which is yet another particular ability to perform the same defense function. This suggests a many-to-one relationship between capabilities and functions. If we allow capabilities to be defined without regard for the functional decomposition of an organization, they may even be related many-to-many.

Considering *business capability* and *function* this way creates a separation of concerns between strategy and business architecture. This corresponds with ArchiMate, where business capabilities are situated in the Strategy Layer, while business functions are placed inside the Business Layer [31].

If we apply this refined understanding of the distinction between *business capability* and *function* to the capability examples provided by TOGAF, such as Partner Management [28], we can conclude that the business capability map in TOGAF comprises functions.

3.2   Analysis of *Business Information*

TOGAF defines an information map as "a collection of information concepts and their relationships to one another" [30]. *Information concept* is not part of the TOGAF Enterprise Metamodel but is defined by the related BIZBOK Guide as a "way in which to represent business terms and semantics within the context of business architecture" [9, p. 784]. It is similar in meaning to TOGAF's *business information*, which "represents a concept and its semantics used within the business" [30, Architecture Content, Sect. 2.4]. TOGAF uses *business information* and *information concept* interchangeably.

The TOGAF Series Guide to Information Mapping defines the *is about* relationship between *information concept* (or *business information*) and ArchiMate's [31] *business object*: "this relationship links information concepts that are metadata about business objects to the corresponding business object; e.g., it links *information* about customers to those *customers*" [29]. This reveals that TOGAF understands *business information* not as defined, namely as a concept, but as knowledge or facts *about* instances of a concept.

3.3   Analysis of the Relationship Between *Business Capability* and *Business Information*

The TOGAF Series Guide to Business Capabilities states: "The naming convention involves expressing the business capability in a noun-verb format, whereby each outcome (input, output, or deliverable) is described as a noun and each activity that is associated with producing, controlling, or monitoring the outcome is described as a verb; e.g., 'Catalog Products' or 'Payment Processing'. The noun part of the business capability is a unique business object— a single, persistent thing that is of interest to the business. The advantage of making a business object the focal point of the business capability is that it simplifies the process of identifying the information objects that are tied to and used by the business capability" [28]. This description shows that *business capability* and *business information* (referred to as *information object*) are only indirectly related through *business object*.

Let us consider an energy system operator. The TOGAF metamodel allows us to express that the operator's capability to develop and maintain energy grids modifies information about energy grids, which, in turn, is used by the capability to transport energy. This is a rather roundabout way of expressing what is going on, namely, that the first capability manages the energy grids to be used by the latter. Information exchange often plays a part in this, but not always and not necessarily.

Many examples of business capability maps in the related BIZBOK Guide [9] contain information management capabilities such as "Partner Information Management", alongside capabilities such as "Partner Definition". This pattern suggests that only the information management capabilities have a modification relationship with business information elements. Therefore, although the "Partner Definition" capability manages partners in the real world, it does not manage information about these partners. Instead, the "Partner Information Management" capability is responsible for managing this information. As a result there is a missing relationship between the "Partner Definition" capability and partner information. This example illustrates how linking *business capability* to *business information*, rather than *business object*, can negatively impact consistency.

Note that if control over a business object and information about that object are split between capabilities, these capabilities should be tightly coupled to manage information accuracy. This illustrates that managing *business information* should be considered one of many implementation aspects of a capability, not a capability itself.

4   Refined Metamodel with Rules and Guidelines

This section considers the TOGAF Enterprise Metamodel, analyzed in the previous section, as a starting point for defining the refined metamodel in Fig. 4, along with its consistency rules and guidelines in Table 1.

4.1   The Use of *Business Function* Over *Business Capability*

A goal of the business capability map is to provide a stable reference. Functions are more stable than business capabilities because whenever a function changes, the corresponding business capability changes, whereas the reverse is not true. For example, a business may change its strategy by replacing its capability to manage the distribution of two million goods with one that can manage three million goods. This strategy change does not affect the definition of the distribution-management function. The only change was the *ability* to perform the function. Therefore, in the refined metamodel, we use *function* over *business capability*. To prevent confusion with other function types, such as the *application function* defined by the related enterprise modeling language ArchiMate [31], we rename this concept as *business function*.

4.2   The Use of *Business Object* Over *Business Information*

A good metamodel allows for an accurate representation of the subject domain. Although information is required to run a business, the primary concern of any business is the management of real-world objects, such as energy grids. Managing information regarding these grids is only a means and not the primary goal. Describing the world through information about it creates unnecessary detours and hinders understanding, thus undermining the purpose of the models. It also complicates conversations about data quality [12], in particular, data accuracy: the degree to which data represent real-world objects.

The tendency to focus on information rather than things of primary interest to the business is perhaps rooted in the origins of enterprise architecture management, namely *information* technology (IT). This fixation on information weakens the model's potential to bridge the gap between business and IT. Therefore, we use *business object* over *business information* in the refined metamodel.

4.3   Refined Metamodel

Fig. 4 shows the refined metamodel. The definitions of the elements and relationships in the metamodel are as follows:

- **business function**: "collection of business behavior based on a chosen set of criteria such as required business resources and/or competencies [...] managed or performed as a whole" [31, Sect. 8.3.2];
- **business object**: "concept used within a particular business domain" [31, Sect. 8.4.1];
- **controls**: changes and prevents changes to the state of a concept;
- **modifies**: changes the state of a concept;
- **composed of**: "consists of one or more other concepts" [31, Sect. 5.1.1];
- **contextualizes**: influences the definition of a concept [32];
- **associated to**: "unspecified relationship" [31, Sect. 5.2.4].

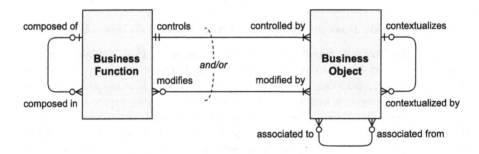

Fig. 4. Refined metamodel

The metamodel has a *contextualizes* relationship. Contextualization is an abstraction mechanism similar to generalization, aggregation, and composition [2]. A context is a set of objects and their names, meaning that objects can have different names in different contexts. In enterprise data models, the elements at the highest level of abstraction are typically called *subject areas* [10], which refers to their role as the context for lower-level elements. In our metamodel, we choose to be agnostic to the level of abstraction and, therefore, do not label the top-level objects as subject areas.

The metamodel defines multiplicities using crow's foot notation, in which a ring represents *zero*, a dash represents *one* and a crow's foot represents *many* (or *infinite*). In pairs, they represent the minimum and maximum multiplicities. For example, the figure shows that each business function is composed of zero to many business functions, and that each business object is controlled by exactly one business function. The relationships and their multiplicities are justified in the next section, which provides the rationale for each consistency rule and guideline.

4.4 Consistency Rules and Guidelines

Fig. 4 shows the metamodel, which is the basis for formulating consistency rules and guidelines. The metamodel already contains a set of rules in the form of multiplicities that are not zero to many. These rules are reformulated in natural language in Table 1, together with additional rules and guidelines for use as a checklist. The rules are rigid, and the guidelines are recommendations. Rules refer to an element that is composed of or contextualizes other elements as their *abstraction*. The number of times an element is (recursively) composed or contextualized by another element determines its *level of abstraction*. The rationales for these rules and guidelines are as follows.

Table 1. Consistency rules and guidelines.

	Rules
R1	Each business function is composed in at most one business function
R2	Each business object is contextualized by at most one business object
R3	Each composition and contextualization relationship is not part of a cycle
R4	At each level of abstraction, the business functions are mutually exclusive
R5	At each level of abstraction, the business functions are collectively exhaustive
R6	At each level of abstraction, the business objects are mutually exclusive
R7	At each level of abstraction, the business objects are collectively exhaustive
R8	Each business function relates to a business object only if their abstractions are related or when they have no abstractions
R9	Each business object is associated to a business object only if it is at the same level of abstraction
R10	Each business function controls and/or modifies at least one business object
R11	Each business object is controlled by exactly one business function
	Guidelines
G1	Each business function controls and/or modifies exactly one business object
G2	Each business object is controlled and/or modified by exactly one business function

R1–3. Business architecture models may contain more elements than humans can process easily. Abstraction mechanisms, such as composition and contextualization, allow the elements to be grouped into bite-sized chunks. These rules ensure the formation of a nested hierarchy, as required by rules 4 to 7.

R4–7. The MECE principle [20] applies at each level of abstraction. This principle states that items in a group must be mutually exclusive (ME) and collectively exhaustive (CE), meaning that they may not have gaps or overlaps. The collection of business functions at a particular level of abstraction conforms to this principle if each atomic business activity in an organization is associated with exactly one business function. For business objects, this implies that each thing in an organization is associated with exactly one business object. For example, business objects *Customer* and *Corporate Customer* are not mutually exclusive because a particular corporate customer is associated with both business objects. If these are the only business objects used to describe an energy system operator, they also have gaps because the energy grid is not associated with either.

R8. If a business function is related to a business object, then the abstraction of the function is *by definition* related to the abstraction of the object. This rule implicitly restricts the relationships between business functions and business objects to matching levels of abstraction. This increases consistency, allowing stakeholders to easily switch perspectives.

R9. Restricting association relationships within each level of abstraction allows levels to be used independently.

R10. A business function that does not control and/or modify a business object cannot create value and must be eliminated.

R11. The *controls* relationship enables a business function to prevent state changes to business objects. This implies access control; that is, any business function that *modifies* a business object can do so only because the controlling business function allows it. Assigning each business function exclusive control over a business object creates low coupling. A business object that is not controlled by a business function is not of interest to the business and is therefore not a business object.

G1–2. At each level of abstraction, these guidelines create a similar number of business functions and business objects, and thus, a matching level of granularity. These guidelines are not rules because managing a business object may require multiple functions. A typical example is where different functions manage the same business object but at different life stages. In such cases, the definition of multiple functions is allowed if managing each life stage requires its own set of resources or competencies. Multiple functions can *modify* a business object, but only one can *control* it (Rule 11).

5   Evaluation Using a Case Study

5.1   Introduction

This section introduces a case study of Dutch energy system operators to illustrate (Sect. 5.2) and evaluate (Sect. 5.3) the practical applicability of the refined metamodel, along with its rules and guidelines. A system operator is an entity entrusted with the task of transporting natural gas or electricity. The Netherlands has two national or transmission system operators (TSOs), one for gas and one for electricity, and six regional or distribution system operators (DSOs). System operators have a monopoly in their assigned regions and are therefore heavily regulated. In addition to the transportation of energy, they are also charged with facilitating energy markets and balancing demand and supply. The transition to sustainable energy poses significant challenges for system operators and is the main driver of digital transformation.

To accelerate the energy transition, Dutch system operators created a common business capability map for their industry, NBility [21]. It is a "daughter" of the Dutch Governmental Reference Architecture (NORA) [19]. The model is updated twice a year to allow for refinements that originate from its application in domains such as organizational design, enterprise architecture, data governance, business process management, and information system design. The author of this study is a member of the NBility working group, allowing easy access to the lessons learned from practice during the definition and application of the model.

5.2   Illustration

Fig. 5, a model at the M1 layer (see Sect. 2), illustrates violations of consistency rules by previous NBility versions (left) and adjustments by the NBility working group (right) to conform to the refined metamodel with its rules and guidelines. For example, Rule 11 states that each business object is controlled by exactly one business function. Figure 5 shows the violation of this rule by business object *Facility product*, which is controlled by five business functions. To resolve this inconsistency, the working group generalized these business functions as *Manage real estate facilities*. The result is a matching level of granularity between the function and object.

Rule 8 states that each business function relates to a business object only if their abstractions are related or when they have no abstractions. Figure 5 shows that the business function *Lay down right in rem and obtain route permits* controls the business object *Right in rem or route permit*, whereas the abstraction *Support work* does not control the abstraction *Energy grid*. Rights in rem and route permits are permissions to install and maintain grid components at certain

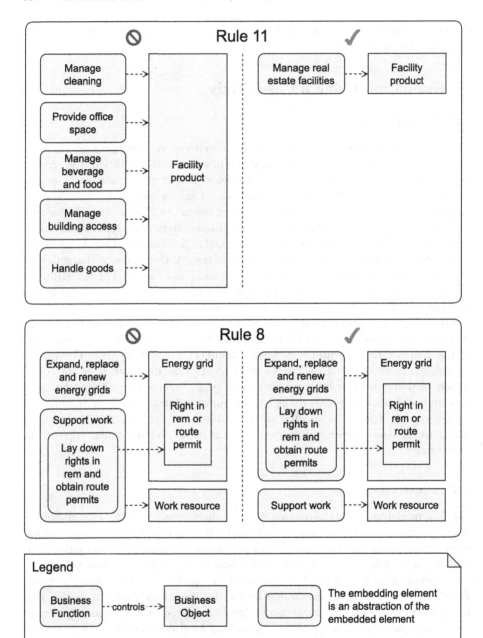

Fig. 5. Illustrations of consistency improvements by the NBility working group

locations. Although these permissions must be obtained before work execution and therefore seem to support work on the energy grid, they should be considered part of the energy grid, as they are relevant after the work has been completed and as long as the energy grid exists. This inconsistency made the working group realize that *Lay down rights in rem and obtain route permits* should not be considered part of *Support work* but of *Expand, replace and renew energy grids*. This example demonstrates that the refined metamodel not only ensures consistency but also improves each map individually.

5.3   Evaluation

Table 2 shows the consistency checks for the different versions of NBility, starting with the version that first included business objects (v2.0). Except for rules 5 and 7, the only data required to perform these checks are the NBility model itself. Rules 5 and 7 were checked during model review and use. The table shows the progression towards increased levels of compliance. The publication of version 2.3 is expected to be in 2024.

Table 2. Consistency checks for different versions of NBility

	v2.0	v2.1	v2.2	v2.3
R1	100%	100%	100%	100%
R2	100%	100%	100%	100%
R3	100%	100%	100%	100%
R4	100%	100%	100%	100%
R5	no quantified data			
R6	67%	67%	67%	100%
R7	no quantified data			
R8	94%	97%	99.5%	100%
R9	100%	100%	100%	100%
R10	91%	87%	95%	100%
R11	100%	100%	100%	100%
G1	79%	80%	90%	94%
G2	84%	89%	92%	91%

Given the successful application of the refined metamodel in the NBility case, where full compliance with the consistency rules and nearly complete adherence to the guidelines (91–94%) is achieved, it is demonstrated that the refined metamodel with its rules and guidelines can be applied in practice. Furthermore, the members of the NBility working group testify to the practical benefits of the metamodel, noting improvements not only in the consistency between maps but also in the refinement of each map individually, as one map provides close guidance for the definition of the other.

Users of the NBility model noted that consistency between the maps improved their understanding, as business objects, with their definitions, explain *what* exactly is being managed by a business function, whereas business functions explain *why* a business object is managed. For example, the aligned models helped NBility users better explain the meaning of certain business objects to data stewards. Other users reported back that the aligned models helped remove confusion about which software team had the responsibility to provide data about a certain business object, as this could now be linked to the business functions they were already responsible for.

6   Discussion and Conclusion

This study introduces an advancement in enterprise architecture by proposing a method to align business capability maps and enterprise data models, based on a semantic analysis of TOGAF concepts. The practical utility of the method is demonstrated by its application in the NBility case, which shows notable improvements in its models.

The TOGAF Series Guides provide some guidelines for model alignment; however, they are based on an indirect relationship between *business capability* and *business information*, which skips the *business object*, as indicated by our semantic analysis. We therefore propose renaming the information map and enterprise data model as *business object model*: a collection of objects relevant to the business, for which there *may* be associated data. Positioning the model as a representation of real-world business objects, rather than of information or data about those objects, may increase its chances of acting as an effective boundary object between business and IT [16].

If we consider business capabilities as goals or requirements, because they serve to achieve specific purposes, a comparison can be made with requirements engineering in the context of software development. There, the conceptual or object model (cf. enterprise data model) is checked against the goal or requirements model (cf. business capability model) [14,17]. This study transposes this concept from software development to enterprise architecture management. Similar to Lamsweerde [17], we clearly distinguish between objects in the environment and their representation in the software.

The scope, size, and complexity of the organizations involved in the case study create confidence in the general applicability of the method. However, its general applicability and effectiveness across different contexts may require further exploration, inviting either additions or increased confidence in the completeness of the rules and guidelines.

The learning curve associated with understanding and applying the refined metamodel may require effort to facilitate its adoption by practitioners. Alternatively, future studies could investigate the feasibility of automating the consistency rules using languages such as Alloy [5] and Ampersand [11].

Finally, subsequent studies could refine the metamodel to include additional elements, such as value streams and organizational units [30], thereby advancing its scope and utility.

Disclosure of Interests. The authors have no competing interests to declare that are relevant to the content of this article.

Acknowledgments. I am grateful to the members of the NBility working group for their pleasant interactions and expertise, my manager and the Stedin Group for their kind support, and my supervisors for their generous guidance throughout this research.

References

1. Aleatrati Khosroshahi, P., Hauder, M., Volkert, S., Matthes, F., Gernegroß, M.: Business capability maps: current practices and use cases for enterprise architecture management . In: Hawaii International Conference on System Sciences (2018)
2. Analyti, A., Theodorakis, M., Spyratos, N., Constantopoulos, P.: Contextualization as an independent abstraction mechanism for conceptual modeling. Inf. Syst. **32**(1), 24–60 (2007)
3. Atkinson, C., Kuhne, T.: Model-driven development: a metamodeling foundation. IEEE Softw. **20**(5), 36–41 (2003)
4. Azevedo, C.L., Iacob, M.E., Almeida, J.P.A., van Sinderen, M., Pires, L.F., Guizzardi, G.: Modeling resources and capabilities in enterprise architecture: a well-founded ontology-based proposal for ArchiMate. Inf. Syst. **54**, 235–262 (2015)
5. Babkin, E.A., Ponomarev, N.O.: Analysis of the consistency of enterprise architecture models using formal verification methods. Bus. Inform. **3**, 30–40 (2017)
6. Berrisford, G.: The functions and capabilities of activity systems (2011). http://grahamberrisford.com/AM%204%20System%20theory/DescriptionAndReality/ModellingConcepts/AM2%207%20Functionality.pdf
7. Berrisford, G.: TOGAF functions, capabilities, value streams (2017). http://grahamberrisford.com/00EAframeworks/01Fundamentals/Capabilities%20and%20Functions%20in%20TOGAF.htm
8. Brits, J., Botha, G., Herselman, M.: Conceptual framework for modeling business capabilities, Ph.D. thesis, Tshwane University of Technology (2006)
9. Business Architecture Guild: A Guide to the Business Architecture Body of Knowledge, Version 13.0 (2024)
10. DAMA International: DAMA-DMBOK: Data Management Body of Knowledge. Technics Publications, USA (2017)
11. Filet, P., van de Wetering, R., Joosten, S.: Enterprise architecture alignment. In: Sørensen, F.L., (ed.) Enterprise architecture and service-oriented architecture, Nova Southeastern University, pp. 1–40 (2020)
12. van Gils, B., Proper, H.A.: Enterprise modelling in the age of digital transformation. In: Buchmann, R.A., Karagiannis, D., Kirikova, M. (eds.) PoEM 2018. LNBIP, vol. 335, pp. 257–273. Springer, Cham (2018). https://doi.org/10.1007/978-3-030-02302-7_16
13. Homann, U.: A business-oriented foundation for service orientation. Microsoft Developer Network (2006)
14. Insfrán, E., Pastor, O., Wieringa, R.: Requirements engineering-based conceptual modelling. Requirements Eng. **7**(2), 61–72 (2002). https://doi.org/10.1007/s007660200005
15. Kotusev, S., Alwadain, A.: Modeling business capabilities in enterprise architecture practice: the case of business capability models. Inform. Syst. Manage. **41**(2), 201–223 (2024). https://doi.org/10.1080/10580530.2023.2231635

16. Kotusev, S., Kurnia, S., Dilnutt, R.: Enterprise architecture artifacts as boundary objects: An empirical analysis. Inf. Softw. Technol. **155**, 107108 (2023)
17. Lamsweerde, A.V.: Requirements Engineering: From System Goals to UML Models to Software Specifications. John Wiley and Sons, Ltd (2009)
18. Luftman, J., Lyytinen, K., Zvi, T.B.: Enhancing the measurement of information technology (IT) business alignment and its influence on company performance. J. Inform. Technol. **32**(1), 26–46 (2017). https://doi.org/10.1057/jit.2015.23
19. Ministerie van Binnenlandse Zaken en Koninkrijksrelaties: Nederlandse overheid referentie architectuur (NORA) (2023). https://www.noraonline.nl
20. Minto, B.: The pyramid principle: logic in writing and thinking. Pearson Education, Harlow (2009)
21. Netbheer Nederland: Nbility 2.2 (2023). https://www.edsn.nl/nbility-model/
22. Offerman, T., Stettina, C.J., Plaat, A.: Business capabilities: a systematic literature review and a research agenda. In: 2017 International Conference on Engineering, Technology and Innovation (ICE/ITMC), pp. 383–393. IEEE (2017)
23. Overdick, H.: The resource-oriented architecture. In: 2007 IEEE Congress on Services, Services 2007, pp. 340–347. IEEE (2007)
24. Peels, F., Bons, R., Plomp, M.: The business value of enterprise data models (2016)
25. Roubtsova, E., Michell, V.: Behaviour models clarify definitions of affordance and capability. In: Proceedings of the 2014 Workshop on Behaviour Modelling-Foundations and Applications, pp. 1–10 (2014)
26. Sandkuhl, K., Stirna, J. (eds.): Capability Management in Digital Enterprises. Springer, Cham (2018). https://doi.org/10.1007/978-3-319-90424-5
27. Star, S.L., Griesemer, J.R.: Institutional ecology, translations' and boundary objects: amateurs and professionals in Berkeley's museum of vertebrate zoology, 1907–39. Soc. Stud. Sci. **19**(3), 387–420 (1989)
28. The Open Group: TOGAF® series guide: business capabilities, version 2 (2022). https://www.opengroup.org/library/g211
29. The Open Group: TOGAF® series guide: information mapping (2022). https://www.opengroup.org/library/g190
30. The Open Group: TOGAF® standard, 10th edition (2022). https://www.opengroup.org/library/c220
31. The Open Group: ArchiMate® 3.2 specification (2023). https://pubs.opengroup.org/architecture/archimate3-doc/
32. Theodorakis, M., Analyti, A., Constantopoulos, P., Spyratos, N.: Context in information bases. In: Proceedings. 3rd IFCIS International Conference on Cooperative Information Systems (Cat. No. 98EX122), pp. 260–270. IEEE (1998)
33. Wegner, P.: Concepts and paradigms of object-oriented programming. ACM Sigplan Oops Messenger **1**(1), 7–87 (1990)
34. Wißotzki, M.: The notion of capability in literature. In: Sandkuhl, K., Stirna, J. (eds.) Capability Management in Digital Enterprises, pp. 27–39. Springer, Cham (2018). https://doi.org/10.1007/978-3-319-90424-5_2
35. Zdravkovic, J., Stirna, J., Grabis, J.: Capability consideration in business and enterprise architecture frameworks. In: Sandkuhl, K., Stirna, J. (eds.) Capability Management in Digital Enterprises, pp. 41–56. Springer, Cham (2018). https://doi.org/10.1007/978-3-319-90424-5_3

Assigning Declarative Semantics to Some UML Activity Diagrams and BPMN Diagrams

Bert de Brock$^{(\boxtimes)}$ (iD)

Faculty of Economics and Business, University of Groningen, PO Box 800,
9700 AV Groningen, The Netherlands
E.O.de.Brock@rug.nl

Abstract. *Research problem and research questions*: There exist several diagram techniques to represent (business) processes, such as Activity Diagrams and BPMN-diagrams. But what is their formal semantics? Do they have a mathematical *declarative* semantics? We intend to provide such a semantics.

Contribution: We define a mapping from UTIL, a universal *textual* instruction language template with a formal, declarative semantics, to Activity Diagrams and another mapping from UTIL to BPMN. In this way, we give the generated BPMN and Activity Diagrams a formal, declarative semantics as well. It also provides a basis to study those diagrams and to compare them on a semantic level. It gives an alternative perspective on those diagrams as well.

Keywords: Textual Instruction Languages · Graphical Instruction Languages · Activity Diagrams · BPMN Diagrams · Declarative Semantics

1 Introduction

There exist several alternative diagram techniques to represent (business) processes: Activity Diagrams, BPMN-diagrams, Sequence Diagrams, etc. But do they have a formal, declarative semantics? Do they have a formal syntax, e.g., a grammar?

We try to find answers to these questions. We do so as follows: In [1], we defined a grammar and a formal, declarative semantics for a universal *textual* instruction language template (UTIL). In [2], we defined a mapping from UTIL to Sequence Diagrams and, for validation purposes, also to English. The current paper introduces a mapping Fa from UTIL to Activity Diagrams and a mapping Fb from UTIL to BPMN. See Fig. 1.

© The Author(s), under exclusive license to Springer Nature Switzerland AG 2024
B. Shishkov (Ed.): BMSD 2024, LNBIP 523, pp. 65–82, 2024.
https://doi.org/10.1007/978-3-031-64073-5_5

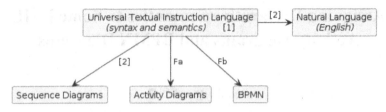

Fig. 1. Previous work and current paper

The mappings are defined inductively (i.e., syntax-directed), following the grammar of UTIL. In doing so, we give the generated diagrams a formal, declarative semantics. This also provides a basis to study those diagrams and to compare them on a semantic level.

Moreover, it gives an alternative perspective on those diagrams.

1.1 Related Work Versus Our Work

In much of the literature in this area, the theory is given only by means of concrete examples, e.g., in terms of orders, products, customers, sales, etc. No general theory in terms of A and B or x and y, so to say. It is 'theory-by-example' instead of 'theory-with-example'. Typical instances are [3–5]. We do present a general theory (notably in the Sect. 3–5), not only examples. This provides a basis to study those diagrams.

In the literature that has some form of generalization, it often stays unclear what the boundaries of those constructs are or which *combinations* of constructs are (im)possible (say, specified via a grammar). As if we would introduce a programming language by writing (in isolation) that it contains the following constructs: **if** <condition>, **until** <condition>, **while** <condition>, **else** <statement>, **repeat** <statement>, **then** <statement>, **do** <statement>, **end**, and **begin**. Instead, we will present a grammar, clearly indicating which (combinations of) constructs are possible.

Moreover, the semantics of the constructs is usually only given informally in natural language, or at best via some kind of operational semantics. For instance, the specification of UML in [6] states under Scope (page 1): *"The semantics define, in a technology-independent manner, how the UML concepts are to be realized by computers"*. This is not a *declarative* semantics but at best an *operational* semantics.

Regarding BPMN, Dijkman et al. [7] note that *"the actual semantics is only described in narrative form using sometimes inconsistent terminology"*. And as Leopold et al. [8] write *"Due to the extensive symbol set, a complete formalization of BPMN would introduce unnecessary complexity"*. Also Petri-Nets are imperative [9]. See [10, 11] for BPMN and [12] for BPMN's extensive symbol set.

Regarding semantic comparisons of those diagrams: Various papers analyse (and sometimes compare) several business process modelling languages on an ontological level [13–15] but not on a semantic, mathematical level, as we do. Activity Diagrams and BPMN-diagrams don't seem to have a mathematical *declarative* semantics.

For quick informal sketches in a discussion, such BPMN and activity diagrams are fine without an exact semantics. However, as a vehicle for precise specifications, that is not sufficient. For the language UTIL, [1] gives a formal, declarative semantics.

In [16], Russell et al. describe 43 relevant and widely used workflow control patterns, e.g., the XOR-split, XOR–join, AND-split, AND–join, OR-split, and OR-join. We show how to express those examples in UTIL.

1.2 Paper Outline

The rest of this paper works out all the details and is organized as follows. Section 2 recalls the underlying universal textual instruction language template UTIL, with Basic Building Blocks that should be specified separately per domain and application area. It also presents an example with specific set of Basic Building Blocks, resulting in an imperative programming language.

Section 3 is central and contains the general rules to map UTIL-expressions to Activity Diagrams and to BPMN, and illustrates them with a running example. Section 4 recalls the declarative semantics for UTIL-instructions from [1]. Section 5 provides the declarative semantics for those BPMN and UML Diagrams. Section 6 discusses the possibilities to explicitly assign *actors* to individual instructions. Section 7 contains a summary and conclusions. Finally, Sect. 8 mentions some possible future work.

2 UTIL: A Universal Textual Instruction Language Template

We recall that instruction languages concentrate on the dynamics, not on the statics. Section 2.1 contains a grammar for the language UTIL. As an illustration, Sect. 2.2 gives an example of a UTIL-expression illustrating many of the UTIL-constructs, while Sect. 2.3 presents a class of Basic Building Blocks with which we get an (imperative) programming language.

2.1 Grammar for UTIL

Based on [1], we present a generic grammar to specify instruction patterns, starting from arbitrary 'Basic Building Blocks'. As usual, the non-terminals of the grammar will be of the form <...>, while terminals are written in **bold**. The start symbol is <I> (for 'Instruction'). The non-terminal <PN> stands for 'procedure/process name'. The grammar rules (and their common names) are:

<I> ::= <BBB>	/* Basic Building Block
| <I>; <I>	/* Sequential composition
| **if** <condition> **then** <I> **end**	/* Conditional
| **if** <condition> **then** <I> **else** <I> **end**	/* Alternative
| **repeat** <I> **until** <condition>	/* Loop (one or more times)
| **while** <condition> **do** <I> **end**	/* Loop (zero or more times)
| **begin** <I> , <I> **end**	/* Arbitrary order (AND-split and -join)
| **maybe** <I> **end**	/* Option
| **either** <I> **or** <I> **end**	/* Choice (XOR-split and -join)
| **skip**	/* Syntactic construct for: 'Do nothing'
| **perform** <PN>	/* Call (a.k.a. 'Include')
<D> ::= **define** <PN> **as** <I> **end**	/* Definition/Declaration

The symbol ';' can be read as '**when ready, then do**'. We note that *Option, Choice*, and *Arbitrary order* introduce non-determinism. We refer to [17] for detailed explanations and to Sect. 4 for a formal, declarative semantics of the syntactic constructions.

One of the constructs **while** and **repeat** is redundant because we can rewrite them into each other by means of the following equivalences:

(E01)   **while** C **do** S **end** ≡ **if** C **then repeat** S **until not** C **end**
(E02)   **repeat** S **until** C ≡ S; **while not** C **do** S **end**

To avoid nested **either-or**-expressions, we could change the **either-or**-rule into

<I> ::= **either** <I> { **or** <I> } **end**

where the curly brackets denote 'one or more times'. It represents the general XOR-split and -join. The general OR-split and -join can be expressed as follows:

begin if C1 **then** S1 **end, if** C2 **then** S2 **end**, ..., **if** Cn **then** Sn **end end**

The UTIL-constructs *Sequential composition* (';'), **if-then, if-then-else, repeat-until, while-do**, *Declaration*, and *Call* are also known in programming languages.

You can get a *recursive definition* if the procedure calls itself, as shown in [17] with the *Towers of Hanoi*.

2.2 UTIL-Expressions: An Example

The following generic example of a UTIL-expression illustrates many of the constructs:

Example 1: A generic UTIL-expression	
T1;	Do task T1
if C1 **then** T2 **else** T3 **end**;	If condition C1 holds then do task T2 else do task T3
T4;	Do task T4
begin T5, T6 **end**;	In any order: do task T5, do task T6
repeat T7 **until** C2;	Repeat task T7 until condition C2 holds
either T8 **or** T9 **end**;	Do either task T8 or task T9
perform P	Call 'subtask' P

Note: Some authors make a distinction between a *task* (being atomic) and an *activity* (being non-atomic). However we do not want to make such a distinction and call all of them a *task*.

2.3 Basic Building Blocks: An Example

In fact, our grammar fragment is not yet finished: The grammar rules for the non-terminal <BBB> must be specified separately. They are *domain specific* or even *application specific*. For example, BBBs could be *assignment statements*, i.e., BBBs of the form

<variable> := <expression>

In this way we get an (imperative) programming language. It contains procedure *declarations* (**define** <PN> **as** <I> **end**) and procedure *calls* (**perform** <PN>). Our generalization leads us from *Structured Programming* to *Structured (Process) Modelling*.

The non-deterministic construct ' <I>, <I>' (for arbitrary order) might be appropriate for a programming language, but the non-deterministic constructs '**maybe** <I> **end**' and '**either** <I> **or** <I> **end**' might be left out for a programming language.

Examples of *application specific* basic instructions are *Register Student, Delete Request, Update Order*, and *Retrieve Stock Overview*. Or, more detailed, *Register Student with name x, address y, and birth date z*, for instance.

3 Mapping UTIL to Activity Diagrams and to BPMN

In this section, we map UTIL-expressions to Activity Diagrams and to BPMN. We define two mappings: a mapping function Fa from UTIL to Activity Diagrams and another mapping function Fb from UTIL to BPMN. So, in summary:

Fa: UTIL → Activity Diagrams
Fb: UTIL → BPMN

We use the drawing *generation* tools Plantuml (plantuml.com) to generate Activity Diagrams [18] and BPMN Sketch Miner (bpmn-sketch-miner.ai/doc) to generate BPMN-diagrams [19]. A drawing *generation* tool has text as input and a diagram as output:

For clarity, we classify and treat the grammar rules in the following five groups:

(1) for Basic Building Blocks (i.e., basic tasks)	(1 case)
(2) for two tasks, with or without mutual ordering	(2 cases)
(3) for conditional tasks, with or without condition and with or without alternative	(4 cases)
(4) for loops (one or more times, or zero or more times)	(2 cases)
(5) for *Declaration* and *Call* of sub-tasks	(2 cases)

70   B. de Brock

See the (correspondingly numbered) Tables 1, 2, 3, 4 and 5. We neglect the auxiliary construct **skip**. Below, the mapping functions Fa and Fb are defined inductively, following the syntax of UTIL. Fa(S) stands for the _Activity Diagram_ of task S, Fb(S) stands for the _BPMN Diagram_ of task S. We draw the diagrams vertically, not horizontally. So, processes go from the top down.

Table 1. Basic Building Block (1 case)

Type	Textual expression	Activity diagram	BPMN diagram
Basic task	T	T	T

Table 2. Two tasks with or without mutual ordering (2 cases)

Ordering?	Textual expression	Activity diagram	BPMN diagram
Yes	S1; S2	Fa(S1) → Fa(S2)	Fb(S1) → Fb(S2)
No	begin S1, S2 end	Fa(S1) Fa(S2)	Fb(S1) Fb(S2)

For reasons of space, Table 3 combines the UTIL-expression and the Activity diagram in one column.

Table 3. Task with or without explicit *condition* and with or without *alternative* (4 cases)

Explicit Condition?	Alternative?	Textual expression Activity diagram	BPMN diagram
Yes	Yes	**if C then S1 else S2 end** yes〈C?〉no Fa(S1) Fa(S2)	❌ C? yes no Fb(S1) Fb(S2) ❌
Yes	No	**if C then S1 end** 〈C?〉no yes Fa(S1)	❌ C? yes no Fb(S1) ❌
No	Yes	**either S1 or S2 end** Fa(S1) Fa(S2)	❌ Fb(S1) Fb(S2) ❌
No	No	**maybe S1 end** Fa(S1)	❌ Fb(S1) ❌

The BPMN-diagram of the **while**-loop in Table 4 is based on equivalence (E01):

(E01) **while C do S end ≡ if C then repeat S until not C end**

Table 4. Loop (2 cases)

Type	Textual expression	Activity diagram	BPMN diagram
one or more times	**repeat** S **until** C	Fa(S) — C? no	Fb(S) — C? (no/C?)
zero or more times	**while** C **do** S **end**	C? no/yes — Fa(S)	C? (no/yes) — Fb(S) — C? (yes/no)

For the mapping of **perform** P to an Activity Diagram, Table 5 makes use of the so-called *rake-symbol* (shown on the right): ⊓⊓

Table 5. Declaration and call of a (sub)task (2 cases)

Type	Textual expression	Activity diagram	BPMN diagram
Declaration	**define** P **as** S **end**	P — Fa(S)	*BPMN does not have a separate declaration possibility*
Call	**perform** P	⊓⊓ P	P ⊞

We propose that BPMN should get a separate process declaration possibility as well.

Applying our mapping rules to Example 1, we get the corresponding mapping results as shown in Figs. 2A and 2B.

In the case of Activity Diagrams and BPMN Diagrams, the final mapping result is often preceded by a start circle and followed by a final circle, as shown in Figs. 3A and 3B.

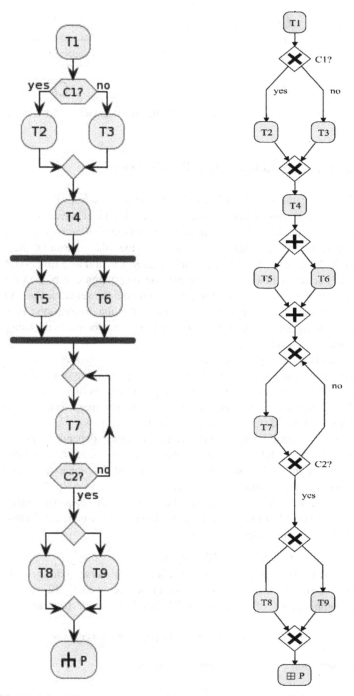

Fig. 2A. Activity Diagram for Example 1   **Fig. 2B.** BPMN Diagram for Example 1

74   B. de Brock

Fig. 3A. Begin and end of an Activity Diagram

Fig. 3B. Begin and end of a BPMN Diagram

4   Declarative Semantics for UTIL-Instructions

We recall the declarative semantics for UTIL-instructions from [1]: We consider the semantics of an individual action to be the state transition it achieved, i.e., from an 'old' state to a 'new' state. Therefore we model the semantics of an *individual action* as a *state transition*, i.e., a pair of states (s; s′); we call s the 'old' state and s′ the 'new' state.

We are inclined to model the semantics of an instruction as a function that assigns to any ('old') state a ('new') state. However, an instruction can be non-deterministic (e.g., 'Either do A or do B'). Therefore, we will model the semantics of an *instruction* as a *relation*, namely *the set of possible transitions* that that instruction can achieve. We note that 'executing a non-deterministic instruction' corresponds to choosing one of the possible 'new' states as the next state.

To link instructions and conditions to semantics, an 'interpretation function' m is needed. For an instruction e, m(e) can be read as the *meaning* of e, where m(e) is the transition relation representing the set of all of possible transitions that instruction e can achieve. For a condition c, m(c) is a function that assigns to each state x a value 1 (for 'c is true in state x') or 0 (for 'c is false in state x').

For a *basic* instruction e, m(e) must get an application-dependent specification. For each state, the 'new' state(s) must be specified. E.g., for the *Register Student* example, the 'new' state might be the 'old' state plus that info of that one extra student (or stays the 'old' state if some constraint is not met).

For all grammar rules of UTIL, and therefore for all *composite* instructions, [1] defines m(e) inductively in terms of the constituents of instruction e. Below, we recall some of them, using the following notations:

- $\underline{id(U)} \stackrel{\text{def}}{=} \{ (s;s) \mid s \in U \}$, called the **identity** on U,

  where U is the set of possible states (a.k.a. *the universe of discourse*)
- R1 $\square$ R2 denotes the *composition* of relation R1 followed by R2, i.e., consisting of all the 'combinations' of transitions in R1 'interlinked with' transitions in R2:

  $$\underline{R1 \,\square\, R2} \stackrel{\text{def}}{=} \{ (x;z) \mid \exists y \in dom(R2): (x;y) \in R1 \text{ and } (y;z) \in R2 \}$$

- For an instruction e and a condition c, we define:

  $\underline{m(e) \, \mathbb{X} \, m(c)} \stackrel{\text{def}}{=} \{ (x;y) \in m(e) \mid m(c)(x) = 1 \}$, the e-transitions where c starts true

  $\underline{m(e) \, \mathbb{X} \, m(c)} \stackrel{\text{def}}{=} \{ (x;y) \in m(e) \mid m(c)(x) = 0 \}$, the e-transitions where c starts false

The meaning of the instructions in terms of the meaning of their constituents:

m(**skip**)	$\stackrel{\text{def}}{=}$ id(U)	
m(e1; e2)	$\stackrel{\text{def}}{=}$ m(e1) □ m(e2)	/* composition of relations
m(**either** e1 **or** e2 **end**)	$\stackrel{\text{def}}{=}$ m(e1) ∪ m(e2)	/* set-theoretical union
m(**begin** e1, e2 **end**)	$\stackrel{\text{def}}{=}$ (m(e1) □ m(e2)) ∪ (m(e2) □ m(e1))	
m(**if** c1 **then** e1 **else** e2 **end**)	$\stackrel{\text{def}}{=}$ (m(e1) ⊠ m(c1)) ∪ (m(e2) ⊠ m(c1))	

Moreover, because '**if** c1 **then** e1 **end**' abbreviates '**if** c1 **then** e1 **else skip end**' and '**maybe** e1 **end**' abbreviates '**either** e1 **or skip end**', we can compute their meaning too. For instance: m(**maybe** e **end**) = m(**either** e **or skip end**) = m(e1) ∪ id(U)

Given the formal semantics, we could now formally prove several properties, e.g., whether certain transformations are meaning-preserving.

5   Declarative Semantics for Some BPMN and Activity Diagrams

Given the declarative semantics for the composed UTIL-instructions and the mappings from UTIL-instructions to Activity Diagrams and BPMN Diagrams, we are able to provide a declarative semantics for those diagrams as well. In Table 6, we present the derived formal, declarative semantics of some of the BPMN and Activity Diagram constructs treated earlier.

Table 6. Declarative semantics of some of the Activity Diagrams and BPMN Diagrams, as well as their corresponding UTIL-expressions

Sequential composition	Arbitrary order	Alternative	Choice
m(D1) □ m(D2)	(m(D1) □ m(D2)) ∪ (m(D2) □ m(D1))	(m(D1) ⊠ m(C)) ∪ (m(D2) ⊠ m(C))	m(D1) ∪ m(D2)
S1; S2	**begin** S1, S2 **end**	**if** C **then** S1 **else** S2 **end**	**either** S1 **or** S2 **end**

(D1 is the diagram corresponding to S1 and D2 is the diagram corresponding to S2.)

6 Instructions with Explicit Actors

In the case of a standard programming language (as in Sect. 2.3) there is only one actor, namely 'the computer'. But if the individual instructions are spread over two or more actors, we might need to indicate the *actor (role)* to fulfil that task. Also for a condition, it should be indicated which actor must do the condition check if there are several actors.

An actor can be anything that can 'act', e.g., a human being, a team, a system, a software application, a sensor, etc. It could also be a department or another organizational entity to take care of a task (e.g., 'quality control'). And in describing biological processes, the actor could be a biological cell, for instance.

6.1 Indicating Actors in UTIL

In UTIL, an instruction ('task for actor') and a condition can have the following form:

<actor> : <task>   <actor> : <condition>

The grammar for the new start symbol <T+A> (for 'Task for Actor') can then be as follows, where the grammatical additions are underlined:

<T+A> ::= <u><actor>:</u> <BBB> | <T+A>; <T+A> | **skip**
   if <u><actor>:</u> <condition> **then** <T+A> [**else** <T+A>] **end**
   repeat <T+A> **until** <u><actor>:</u> <condition>
   while <u><actor>:</u> <condition> **do** <T+A> **end**
   <u><actor>:</u> **maybe** <T+A> **end** | <u><actor>:</u> **either** <T+A> **or** <T+A> **end**
   begin <T+A>, <T+A> **end** | <u><actor>:</u> **perform** <PN>
<D> ::= **define** <PN> **as** <T+A> **end**

We note that adding actors might be done in a later (incremental) development stage.

As an illustration (and further explanation), suppose that in Example 1 the instructions are spread over three actors (A1, A2, and A3) as follows:

Example 2: Our generic UTIL-expression with explicit actors

A1:T1;	Actor A1 must do task T1
if A1:C1	Actor A1 must check condition C1; if C1 holds
then A1:T2 **else** A1:T3 **end**;	then A1 must do task T2 else A1 must do task T3
A2:T4;	Actor A2 must do task T4
begin A1:T5, A2:T6 **end**;	In any order: Actor A1 must do task T5, A2 must do T6
repeat A2:T7 **until** A2:C2;	Actor A2 must repeat task T7 until condition C2 holds
A3: **either** A3:T8 **or** A3:T9 **end**;	Actor A3 must do either task T8 or task T9
A3: **perform** P	Actor A3 must do 'subtask' P

6.2   Diagrams with Actors (in Situ)

For BPMN and Activity Diagrams, the Basic Building Blocks and conditions could be adapted accordingly, as shown in general in Fig. 4.

Figures 5A and 5B show the results for Example 2.

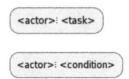

Fig. 4. Indicating the actor to do the task or condition check

6.3   Diagrams with Swim Lanes

However, there is a nicer way to represent diagrams with actors. To clearly visualize in BPMN and Activity Diagrams, which actor must do what, we can make a separate column for each actor involved, pull each task and condition (horizontally) to its proper column, and then remove the actor from the tasks and conditions. Those columns are also known as *swim lanes*. For each diagram, Table 7 shows a *Basic Building Block with actor* in a swim lane.

Applying this (together with our mapping rules) to Example 2, we get the corresponding BPMN and Activity Diagram with swim lanes as shown in Figs. 6A and 6B.

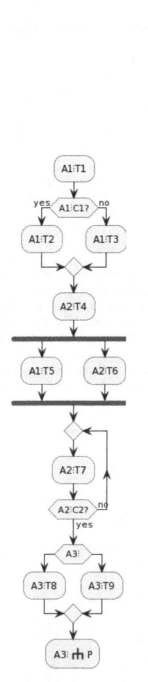

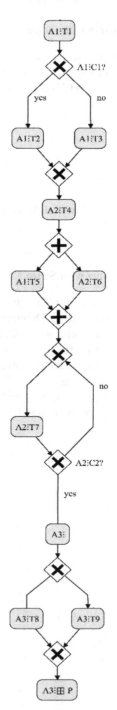

Fig. 5A. Activity Diagram for Example 2   **Fig. 5B.** BPMN Diagram for Example 2

Table 7. Basic Building Blocks with actors in a swim lane

UTIL- expr.	Activity diagram	BPMN- diagram
A: T	A T	A --- T

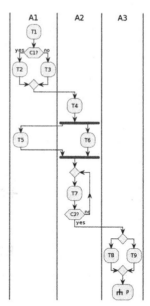

Fig. 6A. Activity Diagram
(with swim lanes) for
Example 2

7 Summary and Conclusions

We distinguished two types of basic building blocks (BBBs) regarding actions:

      1. T   /* Task T must be done
      2. A: T   /* Actor A must do task T

A task is typically formulated as an *imperative verb phrase*, while an object/message/information/'thing' M is often formulated as a *noun phrase*, maybe preceded by an *(in)definite article*. On top of those BBBs, we specified constructors to express composite action patterns. E.g., the construct

A0: either A1: T1 or A2: T2 end

expresses that actor A0 must decide whether actor A1 must do task T1 or actor A2 must do task T2. (A0 might be a 'boss', while A1 and A2 might be subordinates.)

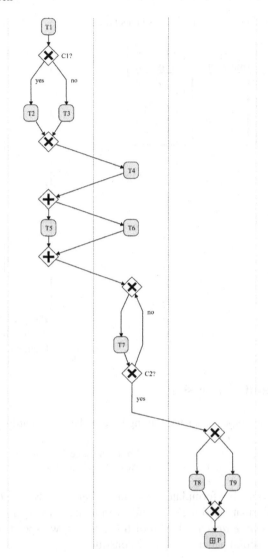

Fig. 6B. BPMN Diagram (with swim lanes) for Example 2

We defined mappings from the Universal Textual Instruction Language template UTIL to Activity Diagrams and to BPMN, with and without swim lanes. Earlier work already defined a mapping Fs from UTIL to Sequence Diagrams and a mapping Fn to natural language (English in that case). In summary:

Fa: UTIL → Activity Diagrams
Fb: UTIL → BPMN
Fs: UTIL → Sequence Diagrams
Fn: UTIL → NL (English)

Since UTIL has a formal, declarative semantics [1], we were able to give the generated diagrams a formal, declarative semantics as well (e.g., see Table 6). This provides a basis to study those diagrams and to compare them on a semantic level as well.

We also proposed that BPMN should get a separate *process declaration* possibility (see the gap in Table 5).

8 Future Work

The work presented in this paper provides a basis to compare the diagrams on a semantic level, because it indirectly shows the correspondence between Activity Diagrams and BPMN Diagrams. It opens the way for further fruitful research, for instance, to work out semantic comparisons between those diagrams. Since many UTIL-constructs are similar to programming language constructs, our mappings relate Activity Diagrams and BPMN Diagrams to programming language constructs as well. It leads us from *Structured Programming* to *Structured (Process) Modelling*.

Several research questions emerge, e.g., to what extend can they provably express the same things? Another nice exercise would be to express all 43 workflow control patterns mentioned in [16] in UTIL. For instance, as mentioned in Sect. 2.1, the general OR-split and -join can be expressed in UTIL as

begin if C1 **then** S1 **end, if** C2 **then** S2 **end,** ..., **if** Cn **then** Sn **end end**

As another example, a general OR-split and -join not driven by conditions but decided by (human) actors, can be expressed in UTIL as

begin A1: **maybe** B1: S1 **end,** A2: **maybe** B2: S2 **end,** ..., An: **maybe** Bn: Sn **end end**

expressing that actor A1 decides whether actor B1 might do S1, actor A2 decides whether actor B2 might do S2, ..., and actor An decides whether actor Bn might do Sn. (As is usual with variables, those differently mentioned actors could be the same.)

Given the formal semantics, we could now formally prove several properties, e.g., whether certain diagrams have the same meaning.

Acknowledgments. The author wants to thank the anonymous reviewers for their useful suggestions.

References

1. de Brock, B.: Declarative semantics of actions and instructions. In: Shishkov, B. (eds) BMSD 2020. LNBIP, vol. 391, pp. 297–308. Springer, Cham (2020). https://doi.org/10.1007/978-3-030-52306-0_20. Accessed 8 Apr 2024
2. de Brock, B.: Developing Information Systems Accurately – A Wholistic Approach. Springer, Cham (2023). https://doi.org/10.1007/978-3-031-16862-8. Accessed 8 Apr 2024

3. Engels, G., Forster, A., Heckel, E., Thone, S.: Process Modeling Using UML. Ch. 5 in [20] (2005). https://www.cs.le.ac.uk/people/rh122/papers/2005/EFHT05PAIS.pdf. Accessed 8 Apr 2024

4. Larman, C.: Applying UML and Patterns. Addison Wesley Professional (2004)

5. Nizioł, M., Wisniewski, P., Kluza, K., Ligeza, A.: Characteristic and comparison of UML, BPMN and EPC based on process models of a training company. Ann. Comput. Sci. Inf. Syst. **26**, 193–200 (2021)

6. UML: https://www.omg.org/spec/UML/2.5.1/PDF. version 2.5.1, by OMG, December 2017. Accessed 8 Apr 2024

7. Dijkman, R.M., et al.: Semantics and analysis of business process models in BPMN. Inf. Softw. Technol. **50**(12), 1281–1294 (2008)

8. Leopold, H., et al.: Supporting process model validation through natural language generation. IEEE Trans. Softw. Eng. **40**(8), 818–840 (2014)

9. Fahland, D., et al.: Declarative versus imperative process modeling languages: the issue of understandability. In: Halpin, T., et al. (eds.) Enterprise, Business-Process and Information Systems Modeling. BPMDS EMMSAD 2009 2009. LNBIP, vol. 29. Springer, Heidelberg (2009). https://doi.org/10.1007/978-3-642-01862-6_29. Accessed 8 Apr 2024

10. BPMN: http://www.bpmn.org. version 2.0, by OMG, December 2010. Accessed 8 Apr 2024

11. Dumas, M., et al.: Fundamentals of Business Process Management. Springer, Heidelberg (2018). https://doi.org/10.1007/978-3-662-56509-4. Accessed 8 Apr 2024

12. BPMN Quick guide: https://www.bpmnquickguide.com/view-bpmn-quick-guide/. Accessed 8 Apr 2024

13. Adamo, G., Di Francescomarino, C., Ghidini, C.: Digging into business process meta-models: a first ontological analysis. In: Dustdar, S., Yu, E., Salinesi, C., Rieu, D., Pant, V. (eds.) CAiSE 2020. LNCS, vol. 12127, pp. 384–400. Springer, Cham (2020). https://doi.org/10.1007/978-3-030-49435-3_24

14. Suchánek, M., Pergl, R.: Mapping UFO-B to BPMN, BORM, and UML activity diagram. In: Pergl, R., Babkin, E., Lock, R., Malyzhenkov, P., Merunka, V. (eds.) EOMAS 2019. LNBIP, vol. 366, pp. 82–98. Springer, Cham (2019). https://doi.org/10.1007/978-3-030-35646-0_7

15. Recker, J., Indulska, M., Rosemann, M., Green, P.: Do process modelling techniques get better? A comparative ontological analysis of BPMN. In:16th Australasian Conference on Information Systems, pp. 175–184. Australian Computer Society (2005)

16. Russell, N., ter Hofstede, A.H.M., van der Aalst, W.M.P., Mulyar, N.: Workflow control-flow patterns: a revised view. Technical report 06–22 BPM Center (2006). https://www.workflowp atterns.com/documentation/documents/BPM-06-22.pdf. Accessed 8 Apr 2024

17. de Brock, B.: From business modeling to software design. In: Shishkov, B. (eds) BMSD 2020. LNBIP, vol. 391, pp. 103–122. Springer, Cham (2020). https://doi.org/10.1007/978-3-030-52306-0_7. Accessed 8 Apr 2024

18. Activity diagrams via Plantuml. https://plantuml.com/activity-diagram-beta. Accessed 8 Apr 2024

19. BPMN diagrams via BPMN Sketch Miner. https://www.bpmn-sketch-miner.ai/doc/index.html. Accessed 8 Apr 2024

20. Dumas, M., van der Aalst, W.M.P., ter Hofstede, A.H.M.: Process-Aware Information Systems. Wiley, New York (2005)

A Systematic Approach to Derive Conceptual Models from BPMN Models

Ricardo Lopes[1]([✉]), João Araújo[1]([✉]), Denis Silva da Silveira[2]([✉]),
and Alberto Sardinha[3]([✉])

[1] NOVA LINCS, NOVA School of Science and Technology, Caparica, Portugal
{rvc.lopes,joao.araujo}@fct.unl.pt
[2] Universidade Federal de Pernambuco (UFPE), Recife, Brazil
dsilveira@ufpe.br
[3] Pontifícia Universidade Católica do Rio de Janeiro (PUC-Rio), Rio de Janeiro,
Brazil
sardinha@inf.puc-rio.br

Abstract. In the digital systems industry, there is a critical intersection between business process modeling and software engineering. This means that companies need to coordinate and align both business process models and conceptual models. However, responsibilities are often divided within the companies, with individuals having expertise in only one of these areas. This division makes the transition from business process models, typically represented as BPMN diagrams, to Conceptual Models, represented as UML Class Diagrams, a challenging task. The difficulty arises from the intrinsic differences between the two notations. This paper proposes an approach to address this problem by developing a software system that leverages the capabilities of OpenAI's ChatGPT to extract contextual information from BPMN diagrams and generate corresponding UML Class Diagrams. This approach provides a systematic method for transforming business process models into software-based conceptual models. Furthermore, it demonstrates the potential of Artificial Intelligence in automating the complex task of software engineering when combined with business process management.

Keywords: Business Process Model Notation (BPMN) · Conceptual Model · Large Language Models · Model Driven Development

1 Introduction

BPMN serves as the industry standard for crafting business process models [8, 20]. Within the realm of digital systems, depicted through UML Class Diagrams, there's a growing demand to transition seamlessly between these notations [2,6]. However, manual processes are prone to errors, impeding this translation.

The challenge lies in bridging the gap between business process modeling and software engineering, two fields with inherently different focuses and requirements. Business process modeling often involves understanding social theories

B. Shishkov (Ed.): BMSD 2024, LNBIP 523, pp. 83–96, 2024.
https://doi.org/10.1007/978-3-031-64073-5_6

and analyzing organizational behaviors to create accurate models. On the other hand, software engineering requires expertise in computational domains like scalability and resource management to develop effective systems. Connecting these domains requires a deep understanding of both, necessitating collaboration between business analysts and software engineers [3, 20].

While there has been considerable research on BPMN to UML Class Diagram transformations, the proposed methods often compromise on critical quality aspects necessary for practical application.

Recent advancements in Artificial Intelligence (AI) and the success of Large Language Model (LLM)s offer an opportunity to extract context from data effectively [19]. We aim to use these advancements to enhance existing BPMN to UML Class Diagram transformation solutions.

Our proposed software system takes an Extensible Markup Language (XML) representation of a BPMN diagram as input and generates a complete UML Class Diagram without the need for additional user input. We will leverage OpenAI's ChatGPT, extracting contextual information for the transformation with the intention of aligning the Conceptual Diagram with the business process. This Diagram can serve as a foundation to guide software development.

Our paper marks the initial phase of a novel approach to transforming business processes into software systems. It introduces a systematic method for smoothly converting business process models into software-based conceptual models, thereby reducing the need for user expertise. Additionally, it investigates whether AI can streamline the complex task of software engineering when combined with business process management. This synergy lays the groundwork for further progress in both fields.

The remainder of this paper is structured as follows. Section 2 provides essential contextual information on domains pertinent to the research, such as Business Processes, Conceptual Models, and Model Transformations. Section 3 presents a critical analysis of existing literature pertaining to the research topic, accompanied by comparisons among the reviewed materials. This section offers insights into the aspects of the theme that have been researched and those that require further exploration, thereby guiding the development of the subsequent sections. Section 4 outlines the development of the transformation, encompassing preliminary steps, transformation rules, and the approach employed for execution. Section 5 showcases an example of the transformation's execution. In Sect. 6, we discuss the challenges encountered during the research process. Finally, in Sect. 7, we evaluate the results of our research and present conclusions drawn from the work conducted.

2 Background

This background section begins with a discussion of BPMN (Subsect. 2.1), continues by providing an overview of our understanding of conceptual models (Subsect. 2.2), and concludes with a brief summary of model transformations (Subsect. 2.3).

2.1 BPMN

The BPMN, recognized globally as a language for modeling business processes, provides organizations with a graphical representation of their operational sequences and interactions, facilitating effective comprehension and communication of internal business procedures. Initially developed by the Business Process Management Initiative (BPMI) and now maintained by the Object Management Group (OMG), BPMN has undergone significant evolution over the years. With the introduction of BPMN 2.0 in 2011, notable enhancements were made, enabling support for complex modeling use cases, such as event-driven processes [7]. Today, BPMN stands as a mature and widely accepted notation, empowering organizations to enhance processes, optimize operations, and achieve efficiency and agility [8].

Within this context, these models are established using a metamodel that employs the UML notation [12], recognized as the standard for software engineering modeling. Organized into multiple layers, BPMN's *Core* layer is particularly significant, housing essential elements like *Process*, *Choreography*, and *Collaboration*, pivotal for constructing BPMN diagrams [7]. This study centers on the process metamodel, as depicted by a fragment in Fig. 1, with our transformation patterns directly referencing this metamodel.

The partial BPMN metamodel depicted in Fig. 1 illustrates that the metaclass *Process* inherits traits from *FlowElementsContainer*, encompassing various *FlowNodes* (*Activity*, *Event*, and *Gateway*) interconnected by *SequenceFlows* [7]. *SequenceFlows* indicate the sequence of activities within a process, linking *Tasks*, *Gateways*, and *Events* to one another.

2.2 Conceptual Models

The conceptual models provide abstract representations or simplified descriptions of systems, concepts, or ideas [1]. They are used to break down complex concepts into manageable visual components, aiding understanding.

There are various types of conceptual models, such as mind maps [9,10], feature models [14], among others. This paper focuses on conceptual software models represented by UML Class Diagrams [12]. These diagrams illustrate the static structure of a software system, including classes, attributes, relationships, and interfaces. Unlike specific programming languages or technologies, UML Class Diagrams provide high-level views of software systems and can guide code generation. Figure 2 presents a snippet of its metamodel, which comprises two primary elements: the *classifiers* (and their internal structure) and the *relationships* among the classes.

A classifier (*Classifier*) can either be a class (*Class*) or an association (*Association*). A class (*Class*) serves as a descriptor for a set of objects with behavior, structure, and similar relationships [12]. Classes consist of properties (*Property*) that define their state and elements that define their behavior (*Operation*). Basic data types describe a set of values without identity, typically corresponding to

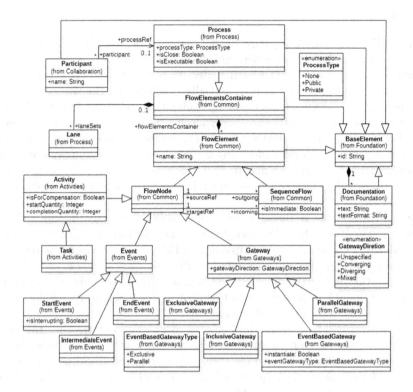

Fig. 1. Fragment of the BPMN metamodel [7].

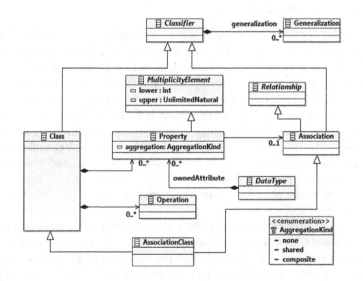

Fig. 2. Fragment of the Class Diagram metamodel [12].

numbers, strings, dates, and times. In addition, class diagrams delineate various relationships, including association, aggregation, and composition, as well as dependencies, inheritance, and realization [12].

2.3   Model Transformations

The model transformations involve automatically manipulating input models to generate output models that conform to a specific specification and serve a particular purpose. This procedure finds extensive application across software engineering, system design, and scientific modeling domains. The goals of model transformation include refining models for greater detail, adapting them to different use cases, creating reusable templates, and transforming source models into target models while preserving essential information [5].

In a model-to-model transformation, a transformation language is applied to the metamodel of an input model, converting it into a target metamodel. LLMs, such as ChatGPT, are trained on extensive textual datasets and excel in Natural Language Processing (NLP) [17]. They demonstrate proficiency in creative writing, conversational abilities, and technical skills like code generation. However, LLMs encounter reliability and accuracy issues. They often present statements as facts, even when they might be incorrect. Over-reliance on LLMs can also result in skill degradation [18]. It's imperative to rigorously test LLMs for specific use cases and validate their outputs.

3   Related Work

The study by [16] aims to use Query View Transform (QVT) [11] to derive a UML Class Diagram from a BPMN diagram. The approach relies on class and method names within the process flow for automatic transformations. However, it does not address class attributes or various BPMN elements such as *Error Events*, *Timer Events*, and *Data Inputs/Outputs*.

In [13], the goal is to enhance the relationship between Informations System (IS), Computing Independent Model (CIM), and Business Process (BP). They propose an Model Driven Architecture (MDA) compliant approach called DESTINY to automate the generation of an IS Analysis model from a Business Process Management (BPM) described in BPMN notation. However the grammatical rules employed by DESTINY may potentially introduce errors and inaccuracies, *e.g.*, when software architects with limited BP knowledge are involved.

The BPM2CD method, as proposed in [4], involves transforming BPMN diagrams into UML Class Diagrams with manual intervention from a knowledgeable Business Analyst (BA). The BA identifies pertinent nouns in BPM activities, which are then translated into classes. Subsequently, the BA establishes a repository of Concept Categories (*e.g.*, *"Roles of people"* or *"Recording of finances"*) and maps examples from the BP. The result is a comprehensive UML Class Diagram; however, the manual nature of the process demands highly qualified BAs and developers, introducing the potential for errors.

The TMBC method, as proposed by [15], automatically transforms BPMN diagrams into UML Class Diagrams by applying rules to specific BPMN elements. It excludes certain elements and generates associations based on *Pool/Lane* placement and process flow. Although efficient, some transformations may not be optimal. Additionally, it lacks attributes and formal association handling.

We analyzed the papers based on three performance indicators: (i) The output is a complete UML Class Diagram; (ii) The transformation rules do not limit the construction of BPMN; (iii) The transformation does not need extra input from the user. Paper [16] meets criterion (iii), [13] meets criterion (i), [4] meets criteria (i) and (ii), and [15] meets criteria (ii) and (iii). One of our research objectives is to develop a transformation method that satisfies all three objectives.

4   The Proposed Method

4.1   Preliminary Steps

Recognizing that we were using ChatGPT for our transformation, we deemed it beneficial to simplify the diagram representation. This would not only enhance the diagram's comprehensibility to the LLM but also reduce the character count in our inputs, thereby trimming processing time and costs. To achieve this, we extracted an XML representation of diagrams from the open-source tool *draw.io*. Subsequently, we parsed the XML to retain only essential information in an easily readable format.

To ascertain if ChatGPT could directly transform a BPMN diagram into a UML Class Diagram, we conducted a straightforward experiment. We provided ChatGPT with the XML code of a BPMN diagram and prompted it to generate the equivalent XML code for a UML Class Diagram. Our findings revealed that ChatGPT 3.5 lacks the capability to produce valid transformations or construct logically structured UML Class Diagrams.

Furthermore, we conducted additional experiments aimed at completing incomplete UML Class Diagrams. Since our transformation process requires a comprehensive diagram as output, we deliberately removed information from a UML Class Diagram. Subsequently, we supplied the equivalent BPMN diagram to ChatGPT and prompted it to fill in the missing parts of the UML Class Diagram. Each experiment was repeated three times to ensure consistency in ChatGPT's responses.

These experiments are depicted in the accompanying Fig. 3 and are explained below.

Experiment 1 (*Remove Client to Driver Association*): In this experiment, we assessed whether ChatGPT could fill in incomplete conceptual models. We removed the directed association from the *"Client"* class to the *"Driver"* class and requested ChatGPT to establish the type and direction of the relationship between them.

The expected outcome was *"Directed Association* - Driver to Client". The generated outputs were: *"Directed Association* - Driver to Client", *"Directed Association* - Driver to Client", and *"Directed Association* - Driver to Client". As intended, ChatGPT successfully identified the association along with its source and target.

Experiment 2 (*Remove Vehicle/Client Multiplicity*): Multiplicity in UML Class Diagram relationships is arguably the most intricate aspect of the transformation, as it is deeply intertwined with the context of the classes involved. Therefore, we removed the multiplicity in the relationship between the *"Vehicle"* and "Client" classes and tasked ChatGPT with completing it. We expected the output to be *"Vehicle* - 1..*, *Client* - 0..*"*. However, the generated outputs were: *"Vehicle* - 0..*, *Client* - 0..1", *"Vehicle* - 1..*, *Client* - 0..1", and *"Vehicle* - 1..*, *Client* - 0..1". Although ChatGPT failed to capture the context implying that multiple clients can rent a car simultaneously, the other assertions were mostly accurate.

Based on these experiments, we concluded that ChatGPT is suitable for simple completion tasks, and thus, we devised transformation rules with these capabilities in mind.

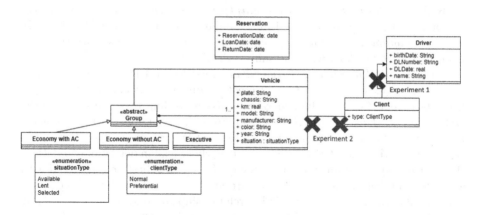

Fig. 3. Diagram Completion Experiments

4.2 Transformation Rules

Here we define the transformation rules, where both the process and rationale for each rule will be elucidated. Rules will consist of a standard segment, which pertains to the transformation without the assistance of an LLM. Some rules will also include an LLM segment, detailing how the LLM supports the transformation rule. The basic structure for the rules is inspired by those found in [15], albeit with adjustments made to accommodate the introduction of the LLM.

Rule 1 - *All Lanes and Pools become classes*: In BPMN, *Lanes* and *Pools* denote roles and subjects within the system that carry out tasks essential for completing the business process. Consequently, they are represented in software development as classes responsible for executing operations. *Pools* and *Lanes* in the BPMN diagram will be depicted as classes, bearing the same name with an appended suffix "*Actor*".

Rule 2 - *Tasks become operations*: In BPMN, a *Task* describes an action that must be performed to complete the business process. In software architecture, these *Tasks* equate to operations that exist in classes. The method derived from the *Task* is then situated within the class derived from the *Pool/Lane* housing the *Task*.

Rule 3 - *All Data Objects become classes*: *Data Objects* are used to represent when a task requires or manipulates data. From a software architecture viewpoint, these can be seen as the parameters and return types of operations, respectively. Consequently, each *Data Object* is converted into a *Class* with the same name. These *Classes* function as "*Data Classes*", primarily data types and pertinent internal behaviors within the system. Additionally, *Data Objects* generate attributes within the *Class* derived from the *Pool/Lane* they reside in denoted by "List<*NameOfDataObject*>*NameOfDataObject+List*".

Rule 4 - *Data Stores become empty classes*: *Data Stores* are sequences of raw data that are to be stored in some database, such as JSON objects. In a *Class Diagram*, *Data Stores* are represented as an empty class with the same name as the *Data Store*, with the suffix "*Data*".

Rule 5 - *Relationships between classes*: Every BPMN element turned into a *Class* (except for *Pools*) will create a directed association relationship from its parent *Class* to the generated *Class* according to the following hierarchy: *Pool* $\rightarrow$ *Lane* $\rightarrow$ *DataObject/DataStore*. This establishes how elements higher up in the system hierarchy can use the *Classes* generated by lower-level elements. **LLM:** The LLM aspect is particularly crucial in determining relationships, primarily in establishing multiplicity. This task is best accomplished with an understanding of the system structure and context of the business process. Additionally, the LLM provides further relationships beyond those stipulated by the rules, requiring contextual comprehension, such as the association between a "*Reservation*" class and a "*User*" class.

Rule 6 - *Operations parameters and return types*: In BPMN *Tasks* can require and manipulate *Data Objects*. When a *Task* manipulates a *Data Object*, its operation will return the type generated by that *Data Object*. Similarly, if a *Task* requires *Data Objects*, the parameters of its operation will be of types generated by those *Data Objects*. In instances where *Tasks* lack sufficient information to determine these properties, a "N/A" string will be substituted for the parameter/return type. **LLM:** The LLM aspect aids in completing the fields marked with "N/A".

Rule 7 - *Message Flows*: *Message Flows* indicate that one agent is communicating with another, enabling *Classes* generated in different *Pools* to be related. Therefore, *Message Flows* establish association relationships directed

from the *Class* derived from the source of the *Message Flow* to the *Class* derived
from the target of the *Message Flow*.

4.3   The Transformation Approach

This section explains the approach conceived to perform the transformation. An
Object-oriented approach was selected, entailing the creation of data types for
BPMN and UML elements, alongside a *"Transformation"* class responsible for
applying the rules to these elements. To better manipulate and store BPMN and
UML elements, we established the system structure, the simplified representa-
tion of which is depicted in Fig. 4. We opted to maintain a *"loose"* definition of
BPMN elements, considering their potential structural variations, while UML
Class Diagram elements are more precisely defined within the system. This decision aimed to streamline the logic in the transformation process and facilitate
visualization of the UML Class Diagram.

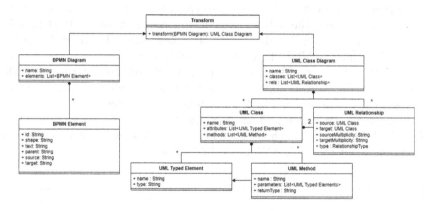

Fig. 4. System Structure Classes

The transformation process is illustrated in Fig. 5 and comprises three main
stages. In the *"Pre-Processing"* stage, essential information is extracted from
the XML code representing the BPMN diagram, creating a *"BPMNDiagram"*
class composed of many *"BPMNElements"*. Subsequently, the *"BPMNDiagram"*
class undergoes the *"Transformation"* stage, where the rules defined in 4.2 are
applied to the BPMN elements. This process generates an incomplete UML
Class Diagram, which is refined through interaction with ChatGPT, following
the guidelines specified in Subsect. 4.2, resulting in an instance of the *"UML-
ClassDiagram"* class. Finally, this class is passed to the *"Visualization"* stage,
where XML code is generated from the diagram, enabling visualization and further editing by the user in the *draw.io* tool.

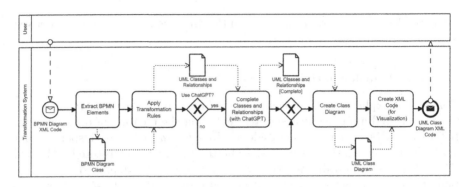

Fig. 5. Transformation Process

5 Proof of Concept

For this proof of concept, we utilized a benchmark BPMN diagram, depicted in Fig. 6, and processed it through our system. The result, excluding the ChatGPT stage, is presented in Fig. 7. Subsequently, the diagram produced by the system, incorporating the ChatGPT stage, is displayed in Fig. 8.

ChatGPT completed the classes with internally relevant attributes, added multiplicity to the relationships, and created two new relationships, one from the *"Customer"* class to the *"AttendantActor"* class, which could define that attendants heed a customer, and one from the *"Reservation"* class to the *"VehicleLoaningActor"* class, which could represent the reservation itself containing information about the vehicle loaning establishment.

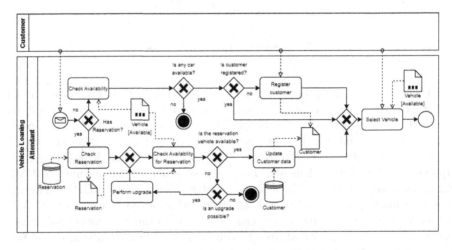

Fig. 6. Proof Of Concept - Benchmark BPMN diagram

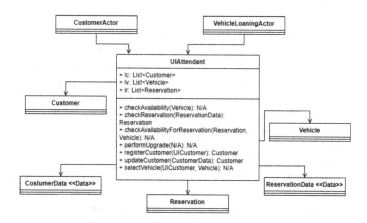

Fig. 7. Proof Of Concept - Result without ChatGPT

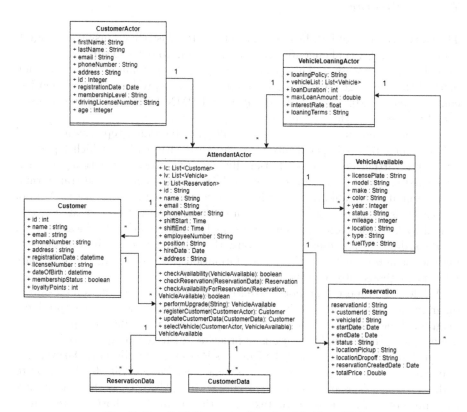

Fig. 8. Proof Of Concept - Result with ChatGPT

6   Challenges

The primary challenges encountered in this research revolve around integrating an LLM solution into a software system. With OpenAI's API, there is no provision for maintaining a model with context that the users can interact with repeatedly. Consequently, each time the system prompts ChatGPT for information, all BPMN and UML Class Diagram data must be resent to the model. This accumulates token costs over time. While theoretically, this could be circumvented by batching all desired requests and parsing the reply, it introduces excessive complexity for both the system and the model.

Another challenge, particularly noticeable with ChatGPT 3.5, is the occasional failure to follow instructions perfectly. This can lead to instances where the model's output structure deviates from the requested format, making it unreadable by the system. While GPT-4 addresses this issue to some extent with significantly improved instruction following, the increased cost exacerbates the original challenge.

7   Conclusions

The transformation of BPMN diagrams into UML Class Diagrams poses a significant and complex challenge for enterprises seeking to develop software systems from business processes. This paper introduces an automatic transformation method that leverages AI assistance in an attempt to produce a comprehensive, context-aware UML Class Diagram from a BPMN Diagram, offering a user-friendly solution to this challenge.

The proposed method involves refining the diagram's representation and defining rules tailored specifically to collaborate with a LLM, which OpenAI's ChatGPT further enhances. Additionally, a software transformation system is developed to facilitate the processing of diagrams and execute the transformation automatically, making the method practical and accessible to users. A proof of concept is presented, demonstrating how the transformation process converts a small BPMN diagram representing a vehicle rental facility's business process.

Regarding future research directions, the initial focus will be on completing the visualization stage of the transformation process and adding internally relevant methods into the classes using ChatGPT.

While our proposed method currently generates a somewhat context-aware diagram, we aim to enhance it further by developing a method that produces diagrams inherently based on the context provided by the business process. To achieve this, we will explore various approaches, including adapting rule behaviors to align with the context of the Business Process and improving the system's management of relationships beyond associations. Efforts will also be made to address challenges associated with working with LLMs, such as the cost of multiple prompts with the same context, and the organizing ChatGPT responses for easier parsing.

Acknowledgements. We gratefully acknowledge the funding support provided by CNPq (Grant No. 421085/2023-1), FACEPE/APQ (Grant No. 0867-6.02/22), and NOVA LINCS (UIDB/04516/2020) with the financial support of FCT.IP for this research.

References

1. Norman, D.A.: Some Observations on Mental Models, pp. 241–244. Morgan Kaufmann Publishers Inc., San Francisco (1987). ISBN: 0934613249
2. Eriksson, H.E., Penker, M.: Business Modeling With UML: Business Patterns at Work, 1st edn. Wiley, Hobokrn (2000). ISBN 0471295515
3. Martínez, A., Pastor, O., Estrada, H.: Closing the gap between organizational modeling and information system modeling. In: WER, pp. 93–108 (2003)
4. Rungworawut, W., Senivongse, T.: From business world to software world: deriving class diagrams from business process models. In: Proceedings of the 5th WSEAS International Conference on Applied Informatics and Communications. WSEAS, pp. 233–238. Citeseer (2005)
5. Singh, Y., Sood, M.: Models and transformations in MDA. In: 2009 First International Conference on Computational Intelligence, Communication Systems and Networks, pp. 253–258. IEEE (2009)
6. Mili, H., Tremblay, G., Jaoude, G.B., Lefebvre, É., Elabed, L., El Boussaidi, G.: Business process modeling languages: sorting through the alphabet soup. ACM Comput. Surv. **43**(1), 1–56 (2010)
7. OMG-BPMN. Business process model and notation (bpmn), version 2.0 (2011). https://www.omg.org/spec/BPMN/2.0/About-BPMN/
8. Chinosi, M., Trombetta, A.: BPMN: an introduction to the standard. Comput. Stand. Interfaces **34**(1), 124–134 (2012). ISSN 0920-5489
9. Wanderley, F., da Silveira, D.S., Araújo, J., Moreira, A.: Transforming creative requirements into conceptual models. In: IEEE 7th International Conference on Research Challenges in Information Science (RCIS). IEEE (2013). https://doi.org/10.1109/RCIS.2013.6577704
10. Wanderley, F., Silveira, D., Araujo, J., Moreira, A., Guerra, E.: Experimental evaluation of conceptual modelling through mind maps and model driven engineering. In: Murgante, B., et al. (eds.) ICCSA 2014. LNCS, vol. 8583, pp. 200–214. Springer, Cham (2014). https://doi.org/10.1007/978-3-319-09156-3_15
11. OMG-MOF. Mof query/view/transformation (2016). https://www.omg.org/spec/QVT/1.3/About-QVT
12. OMG-UML. Unified modeling language (2.5.1). Technical report, Object Management Group (2017). https://www.omg.org/spec/UML/About-UML/
13. Khlif, W., Elleuch, N., Alotabi, E., Ben-Abdallah, H.: Designing bp-is aligned models: an mda-based transformation methodology (2018)
14. da Silveira, D.S., Loiola, E.M., Araújo, J., Moreira, A., Fernandes, P.: Towards a reusable business process modelling approach. Int. J. Bus. Process Integrat. Manag. **10**(2), 104–114 (2020). https://doi.org/10.1504/IJBPIM.2020.117150. https://www.inderscienceonline.com/doi/abs/10.1504/IJBPIM.2020.117150
15. Boesing, H.F., Matos, S.N., Andrade, V.C., Gueiber, E.: Using MDA to transform business processes from analysis classes. In: 16th Brazilian Symposium on Software Components, Architectures, and Reuse, pp. 50–59 (2022)

16. Habri, M.A., Esbai, R., Lamlili El Mazoui Nadori, Y.: BPMN to UML class diagram using QVT. In: Ben Ahmed, M., Teodorescu, H.-N.L., Mazri, T., Subashini, P., Boudhir, A.A. (eds.) Networking, Intelligent Systems and Security. SIST, vol. 237, pp. 593–602. Springer, Singapore (2022). https://doi.org/10.1007/978-981-16-3637-0_42

17. Le Scao, T., et al.: What language model to train if you have one million gpu hours? arXiv preprint arXiv:2210.15424 (2022)

18. Liyanage, U.P., Ranaweera, N.D.: Ethical considerations and potential risks in the deployment of large language models in diverse societal contexts. J. Comput. Social Dyn. 8(11), 15–25 (2023)

19. Lu, S., Bigoulaeva, I., Sachdeva, R., Madabushi, H.T., Gurevych, I.: Are emergent abilities in large language models just in-context learning? (2023)

20. Mateus, D., da Silveira, D.S., Araújo, J.: A systematic approach to derive user stories and gherkin scenarios from bpmn models. In: Shishkov, B. (ed.) Business Modeling and Software Design, pp. 235–244. Springer, Cham (2023). https://doi.org/10.1007/978-3-031-36757-1_15. ISBN 978-3-031-36757-1

An Analysis of Kinds of Skills and Knowledge in Information System Development

Coen Suurmond$^{(\boxtimes)}$ (iD)

Cesuur B.V., Velp, The Netherlands
coen@cesuur.info

Abstract. Methods are important in information system development (ISD), but skills and knowledge of the participants in the project matter as well. The paper focuses on projects in the business environment, and the part of ISD that bridges the gap between the social world of the business organisation and the formal world of software development. In the theoretical part, research is discussed from quite diverse disciplines. The common factor is that all theories are in some way related to the creating, presenting and developing of new structures that will change the social environment. A case is presented for an application and analysis of the theoretical concepts, paying special attention to the importance of managing differing worldviews and different kinds of knowledge in a project.

The paper shows how a design process is a complex of multiple interdependent learning cycles (a concept from Soft Systems Methodology), where different knowledge domains and different kinds of knowledge are involved. Different kinds of artefacts are involved in the coordination between the different learning cycles. An important group of artefacts has a life cycle that start as an empty shell with a suggestive name, evolving in subsequent cycles into formally and fully specified IT concepts. In the transition from the social world of business to the formal world of IT, social skills and knowledge about human behaviour is crucial in information system development.

Keywords: Information system Development · Design Cycle · Knowledge · Artefacts · Phronesis

1 Introduction

In the early 80s I was struck by the title of an article by Van Rees about information system development (ISD): 'De methode doet het niet' [1]. In Dutch, it is a nice ambiguous title because it carries two meanings: "The method does not work" and "The method does not do the work". The article tells us that in case of ISD gone wrong you should not blame the method for failing to deliver. It is the person who does (not) do it, not the method. In the decades since, when reading or hearing examples of successfully applied methods, the message conveyed by that title frequently comes to mind: to what extent was it the method that brought about the results, and to what extent were the results due to the skills of the analysts applying the method? How much tacit knowledge, how

B. Shishkov (Ed.): BMSD 2024, LNBIP 523, pp. 97–111, 2024.
https://doi.org/10.1007/978-3-031-64073-5_7

many implicit assumptions are hidden in the method? When methods in information system development (ISD) are discussed, the suggestion is often that any competent person would achieve successful results when using the method under discussion (or, by inversion of the argument, that the same person using a different method would achieve a lesser result). But I am wondering: is the role of a method in ISD to rigorously prescribe "how to do it", or is its role more that of a toolbox of models and heuristic guidelines to be skilfully applied in a given context by a competent analyst? In this paper I want to analyse the question what kind of skills and knowledge are required in ISD as a necessary complement to applying methods.

The primary domain of the paper is the development of business information systems, although most of the arguments will most likely apply to public organisations as well. In previous work I discussed the fundamental difference between the social world of business and organisations (governed by social sign system, especially natural language) and the formal world of IT systems (logical machines governed by formal sign systems). The development of a business information system could therefore be viewed as constituted of three elements. One element is the building of the logical machine (software development). Another element is the deployment of IT system in the organisation (implementation). The element this paper focuses on is about finding the specifications of the logical machine that will serve the purposes of the business organisation. The latter element is about bridging the gap between the social world of business and the formal world of the IT system. This element can be fully isolated in ISD (cf. De Brock [2]), or be "embedded" in software development (as in some agile methods). No matter how the ISD project is organised, no matter who, how, when or where the formal specifications of the software are determined, an IT system is a system governed by formal rules [3]. This leads to the question to be discussed in this paper: *what kind(s) of knowledge and what kind(s) of skills are involved in the transition from the social world of the organisation to the formal world of IT systems?*

The paper is structured as follows. In the next section some relevant background notions about business and IT systems will be briefly explored. The main theoretical part is Sect. 3, where research will be discussed about skills, knowledge, design, experimenting with models, and the role of artefacts in human cognition. The relevance of these theories for ISD will be discussed, drawing conclusions about the kind of knowledge and skills that are involved in developing a proper IT system for the business organisation. Section 4 presents an illustrative case from industry, showing how the kinds of knowledge and skills discussed in Sect. 3 present themselves during an actual project. Section 5 discusses the theories and the case in the wider context of ISD, followed by the concluding section.

2   About Business, Business Organisations and IT Systems

The domain of the paper is the development of business information systems. The environment in which such systems are used is not fully predictable (although the behaviour of the system as such should be), for users can exploit the system in creative and unexpected ways in order to achieve their goals (also, negatively, to frustrate other people's goals). It is not about IT used for automation in controlled, stable and predictable environments.

Secondly, it is about environments where processes are not strictly hierarchical but often to some degree reciprocal and interdependent, and where multiple user communities are involved. Interdependency means a reciprocal relation between processes, for example while the planning process initially is triggering production runs, later on (actual) production runs might also trigger the planning process. Or when the planner asks a production supervisor: "could you manage to achieve X by 15:00?", and the supervisor answers "Yes, provided that you can arrange Y and Z for me". Heterogeneity of the user community is about hierarchical levels (execution of primary processes, supervising, controlling, managing, strategizing) as well as about different business domains (sales, production, planning, quality assurance, finance).

It is useful to recapitulate briefly the view on business and its information systems based on the theory of the firm [4, 5] and on business contracts [6, 7]. The rationale of a firm is in doing business on its markets, business relations are important in avoiding excessive transaction costs and business contracts are relational contracts embedded in a social context of regulations, conventions and expectations). Organisational processes are subservient to those business transactions, and business information systems are subservient to the organisational processes. Hence, doing business, executing organisational processes, is embedded in the social world and natural language (which includes 'legalese' or language used by professionals of the law). IT systems are logical machines, rigidly executing logical instructions on pre-categorised inputs and behaving like a state-transition machine.

3   Theoretical Background

3.1   General

The theoretical background is based on the work of three different researchers in three different domains: Bent Flyvbjerg, who is a leading expert in the field of megaprojects; Simon Kretz, who is an architect, urban designer, lecturer and design researcher, and Barend van Heusden who is a researcher in the domain of the relation between cognition and semiotics and who has recently published about the role of the artefact as fourth type of sign. All three authors can be viewed as reflective practitioners as analysed by Schön [8], combining practical work with reflection and research. All are involved in researching creative cognition processes in the social world, rather than explaining away such processes as just a product of some intangible and inexplicable act of creativity. This makes their theories relevant for the subject of this paper, the role of skills and knowledge in ISD.

The three authors will each be discussed in a separate section, followed by two sections that relate these theories with requirements engineering and information system development. I will argue that the combination of the three theories can explain and enrich the central concept of the Learning Cycle in Soft Systems Methodology [9]. The theories also exemplify why (and to what extent) instrumental rationality should be complemented by practical skills in working in the social world while developing information systems.

3.2 Flyvbjerg – Megaprojects as Trait-Making Projects

Megaprojects. "Megaprojects are large-scale, complex ventures that typically cost \$1 billion or more, take many years to develop and build, involve multiple public and private stakeholders, are transformational and impact millions of people [...] Conventional project managers should not lead megaprojects. Megaprojects require reflective practitioners [...] as leaders who have developed deep domain experience in this specific field" [10]. "The iron law of megaprojects: over budget, over time, under benefits, over and over again" [10]. "Generally [...] such projects tend to 'break' sooner or later, for instance when reality catches up with optimistic, or manipulated, estimates of schedule, costs or benefits, and delays, cost overruns, and so on follow. Projects are then often paused and reorganized [...] in an attempt to 'fix' problems and deliver some version of the initially planned project with a semblance of success. [...] The break-fix model is wasteful and leads to misallocation of resources [...] for the simple reason that under this model decisions to go ahead with projects are based on misinformation rather than on information" [11]. IS projects, like megaprojects, are often transformational, have many different kinds of stakeholders involved, and are often over time, over budget and under benefits. That makes it worthwhile to learn from Flyvbjerg's research into megaprojects.

Rationality and Power. Flyvbjerg wrote in his book Making Social Science Matter: "social and political thinking becomes problematic if it does not contain a well-developed conception of power" [12]. His thinking about rationality and power was formed by his research of an ambitious inner-city renovation project in Aalborg, documented in his book Rationality and Power: "The Aalborg Project, designed to substantially restructure and democratically improve the downtown environment, was transformed by power and Realrationalität into environmental degradation and social distortion." [13]. In his analysis, Flyvbjerg focuses in his analysis on Foucault's question "How is power exercised?", viewing power not as something that "is" and that is "located in persons or in a structure" (as our hierarchical organisations suggests) but as a processual concept in context. Power is about force relations, as can be exemplified when someone needs the cooperation of another person. Here, power is not just a matter of formalised (hierarchical) relations and established rules, it is also about the willingness of the other person to behave cooperatively. Withholding cooperative behaviour can take many forms, e.g. passively doing only what is explicitly asked, not coming forward with relevant information or downright refusal. Power does not have to be reduced to raw interests either. People have values, opinions, and interests, their cooperation in discussions, organisational processes and projects will be affected by them. In analogy to the twin concepts of politics and Realpolitik Flyvbjerg coins the concept of "Realrationalität" next to the concept of formal rationality. Flyvbjerg is critical about Habermas' theory of communicative action, because it leaves out the role of power. He writes: "Philosophy and science often present rationality as independent of context; for example, in universal philosophical, ethical, or scientific imperatives, a current example being the theory of communicative rationality and discourse ethics of Habermas. If these imperatives are followed, the result is supposed to be rational and generally acceptable actions. Our study of politics, administration, and planning in Aalborg shows rationality to be a discourse of power. Rationality is context-dependent, the context often being power. [...] Communication is more typically characterized by nonrational rhetoric and maintenance of interests than by freedom from domination and consensus seeking".

Knowledge in Projects: Episteme – Techne – Phronesis. In the work of Flyvbjerg on the management of megaprojects phronesis is a key concept. At the very beginning of his book Making Social Science Matter, he wrote "Phronesis goes beyond analytical, scientific knowledge (episteme) and technical knowledge or know how (techne) and involves judgements and decisions made in the manner of a virtuoso social and political actor. I will argue that phronesis is commonly involved in social practice" [13]. In his most recent book, How Big Thing Get Done, Flyvbjerg mentions phronesis in several of his heuristics for better project leadership, emphasising the role of practical experience in doing projects. In this book he describes this Aristotelian concept as "the "practical wisdom" that allows us to see what is good for people and to make it happen" [14].

The concept of phronesis cannot be considered without the related concepts of episteme and techne, as discussed together by Aristotle in book VI of his Nicomachean Ethics. The three concepts represent three kinds of knowing [15]. Episteme is about general knowledge ("belief about things that are universal and necessary"); techne is about making things ("All art is concerned with coming into being, i.e. with contriving and considering how something may come into being [...] and where origin is in the maker and not in the thing made"); and phronesis is about understanding the human world ("practical wisdom, then, must be a reasoned true state of capacity to act with regard to human goods"). Phronesis comes to expression when people need to take action, it is about considering and assessing the situation in relation to purposeful behaviour [16–18]. Because there is no adequate English translation of this Aristotelian concept, the term phronesis will we used in this paper.

3.3 Kretz: The Cosmos of Design

Simon Kretz views design as "an instrument of change, a means of gaining insight and a resource for a structuring of practical theory" [19]. "Design not only solves obvious problems, but it is also used to challenge the existing reality. Problems often only even become visible through design. Design is thus not only a shaping force, but a seeking and inquiring activity. In this regard, the goal of design is new insights, new knowledge". Kretz's home patch is our environment of buildings and urban spaces, and he "was able to compile over ten years of practical and research experience in the architecture department at ETH Zurich". His analysis, however, is not restricted to architecture but about design in general, witnessed by his Introduction to Cosmos of Design: "What is presented here is a systematic representation of the thought and cognitive processes of design, an explanatory model. The goal of the model is to improve the understanding of design, to provide a theoretical basis and to finally make it applicable to everyday design and teaching". In the domain of ISD, his work on design as a complex cognitive process can shed new light on the use of models as a cornerstone of requirements engineering.

In discussing Gänshirt's design cycle Kretz agrees with Ganshirt's observation that "the three named spheres of activity that characterize the 'design cycle' (perception – mental consideration of inner ideas – expression of those ideas) can sometimes be distinguished very clearly in the consecutive working steps, but often they are so tightly interwoven that the individual elements can scarcely be isolated any longer and fuse into a single action – the act of designing" [20]. Partial sketches and immature designs as intermediate results function not only as stepping stones to the resulting 'final' design, but have also an essential function in challenging both reality and the customer's wishes.

Based on the analysis of Kretz and Gänshirt one could represent the design cycle as a succession of challenges, applicable both to the design cycle as a whole and to all kinds of subcycles resulting in partial design artefacts. The first challenge is when the designer is 'pondering', mentally forming and considering their inner ideas. In this phase, the designer is kind of mentally experimenting with ideas, which can vary from a very general floating of abstract ideas to precise mental calculations (think of a chess grand master). It is about the mental process of developing ideas, "perceiving" and assessing intermediate results, aborting lines of thinking and starting new lines. The second challenge is the expression of inner ideas in a sufficiently precise and accessible partial artefact (texts, schemas, scale models, whatever). Partial means that the artefact is focussing on certain aspects, leaving out irrelevant aspects. The level of precision must be sufficient to make possible problems clear, which is a prerequisite in the process of seeking and acquiring knowledge about the domain, the problem, and its possible solutions. Once the first challenges are met and a coherent artefact is established, the third step is challenging existing and projected reality. The artefact provides a sound base for experimenting with scenarios. New insights and knowledge can be sought and acquired by discussion and experimenting, and the next loop can begin.

In his PhD thesis Kretz differentiates between design in a narrow sense and an expanded sense [21]. Design in a narrow sense is about individual problems. In an expanded sense it is about a collection of design problems and about a longer time frame. It is about reflecting on experiences to derive patterns and models and in building a theory of practice. An example of the latter aspect that is well known in the IT community is the work on patterns by Christopher Alexander [22]. In this paper the focus will be on the analysis of design in a narrow sense, simultaneously seeking knowledge and proposing solutions.

3.4   Van Heusden

In his analysis of semiosis (the semiotic, or sense-making process) Barend van Heusden [23, 24] recently presented the artefact as a fourth type of sign, to be added to the commonly used triplet of sign types of icon, index and symbol. The artefact is a concrete expression of a process of creation. The sense of this sign type is in the (imagined) making process, and the artefact is understood as something that allows one to make something. Artefacts abound in human culture; we are surrounded by them – everywhere and always. They take many forms, from food and clothes and utensils to sophisticated technology, and language. Or think of works of art, computers, or scale models of buildings-to-be. Design artefacts ask the 'reader': What do you think of it? Could you live with it? Could you live in it? Does it make sense to you? The artefact is a sign, and as such it is always *about something*: this 'something' being what can be done with the artefact, how it can be used. Or, in more abstract terms: creative human activity. Different from symbols and indices, that signify concepts and structures respectively, artefacts signify this creative activity. Or, as Aristotle has it, the artefact's "origin is in the maker and not in the thing made". As with other signs, however, the sense of artefacts is not fixed. It will change when a different way of using the artefact is imagined, when it is 'interpreted' differently. An oak tree in the woods is not an artefact, yet a Bonsai tree is. As always with signs, it is important to emphasise that something works as a sign from the very moment it is interpreted as such – signs exist only and in so far as they are involved in the semiosis or sense making process. Thus, a scale model in the design process of a building is meant to highlight the structure of the building-to-be, the same model in the reception area after realisation of the building gives the visitor an impression of the building-as-is, and later on the same model can be used in a shop for model making materials to give the prospective buyer an impression of what can be done with the materials.

In terms of the Gänshirt Design Cycle an intermediate design artefact is a concrete expression of an idea, and as such a stepping stone for further conceptualisation, analysis and discussion, leading to a next iteration of developing ideas for the design-to-be. In terms of Kretz's Cosmos of Design an intermediate artefact in the design process is a tool for gaining new knowledge about the world by experimentation.

3.5 Comparison to Some Approaches in Information System Development

In Soft Systems Methodology (SSM), the Learning Cycle has many resemblances with the ideas discussed above. The title of the concise practical handbook on SSM by Checkland and Poulter is *Learning* for Action. It is not about textbook knowledge, but about human skills. In the foreword of this book, Ray Ison wrote "One of Checkland and Poulter's main messages is that it is only by taking part in SSM practice that you will really understand and enjoy the benefits" [9]. Models are an essential part of the Learning Cycle, being necessary artefacts for structuring discussion about reality, facilitating the process of seeking and acquiring knowledge (sometimes existing, sometimes new). The role of experience, the role of creating artefacts and discussing their possible meanings, and experimenting with conceived solutions by means of intermediate models are elements that are found in SSM as well as in the theories discussed in the sections above. Which is why it is worth investigating how these theories can help to understand and to guide the processes within the Learning Cycle of SSM.

In his recent publications Bert de Brock clearly separates the worlds of requirements engineering (RE) and software engineering (SE). In between the two worlds stands the Conceptual Model (CM), consisting of the conceptual data model and the process model. The CM of the system-to-be fully specifies its state space and its state transitions [25]. Hence the CM leaves no functional behaviour open to interpretation and no (undocumented) choice during SE. This implies that the behaviour of the system-to-be can be fully analysed and validated, SE is not forced to make assumptions and to make choices about functional behaviour. My preferred designation for the end product of RE is Information Machine (IM), because it specifies a logical machine processing information. Like a physical machine, the logical machine might be (creatively) configured and used in ways not foreseen at the time of design, validation and development.

De Brock emphasises that the end product of RE – the conceptual model – is a formalised specification satisfying rigorous standards of precision. Like software, the CM essentially belongs to the domain of logic and mathematics, and accordingly requires a precise specification language. RE as a process towards that rigorous end product, however, is a trajectory in the human world (often meandering from vague and possibly contradictory or impossible user wishes via partial results to the end product (which requires social skills). Van Rees made a similar distinction, when he observed that in the physical world of construction, designing is the field of the architect (where "the method does not work", but the design process is guided by heuristics, patterns and experience). Which is then followed by the work of the constructor (where highly structured processes, anchored in methods, should be required) [1]. In his work, De Brock acknowledges the importance of the experience and social skills of the requirements engineer for the RE process, as well as the logical and mathematical skills is specifying the CM. In Flyvbjerg's terms: the requirements engineer must have both technical and phronetic skills.

3.6   Trait Taking or Trait-Making

In discussing the transformational character of projects, Flyvbjerg makes use of Hirschman's distinction between projects that are "trait-making" vs "trait-taking" [26]. Trait-making is about changing social structures, trait-taking "fit into and follow pre-existing structures and do not attempt to modify them" [10]. According to Flyvbjerg, trait-making projects are fundamentally different from trait-taking projects, which explains why "megaprojects [...] are not just magnified versions of smaller projects" [10]. Trait-making project require phronetic skills.

Doing an IS project can disrupt existing structures, introduce new views, and establish new patterns of behaviour. This has implications for both project management and for finding out requirements. Project management has to deal with organisational transitions and power relations. Requirements engineering has to deal with unstable, changing social practices.

In the context of seeking knowledge in the RE process, the trait-making/trait-taking distinction determines the kind of knowledge you are looking for. In case of trait-taking, there is an existing situation that can be explored, and the domain experts are supposed to know "all about it". The elicitation of requirements is meant to bring that knowledge out. Such projects could be viewed as automation processes where new technology is implemented to do the same things in essentially the same way, but 'better' in one or more respects. In trait-making projects, on the other hand, patterns of behaviour in the world of the user-community will fundamentally change. Elicitation of *existing* knowledge is not sufficient anymore and experimenting with models about the new world is required, to find out what works under what conditions.

In my experience, the transition of information processes from informal to formal often has an element of trait-making that is not sufficiently recognised in IT projects. The way people work with information in business processes often changes (more pre-codified, less free form) and this has an impact on and disrupts existing patterns of behaviour. This aspect should be dealt with in the RE process, requiring a shift from a technical to a phronetic focus.

3.7 Summary of This Section

To summarise and conclude this section: while the **result** of a design process should be a precise specification as a starting point for the constructor (in ISD: for software development), the **process** of designing is often anything but a precise methodological trajectory. It is rather an intertwined combination of investigating, of creating intermediate artefacts and of experimenting with those artefacts. The design process involves three different kinds of knowledge. Episteme is general knowledge about organisations, business processes and business domains, techne is about practical knowledge and skills in creating physical or logical artefacts (that do not "talk back") and phronesis is about practical knowledge and skills in creating solutions in the social world of organisations (where people are not passive objects but actively react and adapt to questions, initiatives and circumstances). Actually, while knowledge has a passive connotation as describing a state of "being-in-the-know" (which fits the category of general knowledge), for techne and phronesis the capability to apply the knowledge in a concrete context is what really matters.

This substantiates the statement of Jaap van Rees in his article 1982: in the analysis and design process it is not the method that 'does it', but the person who "does it" on the basis of insight, knowledge, experience, resourcefulness and inventiveness. Flyvbjerg adds depth to this insight by drawing attention to and analysing different kinds of knowledge involved. He also shows why things go wrong when phronesis is ignored. Kretz discusses how change, research and knowledge acquisition are interrelated and hardly separable aspects in design processes, and thus adds an essential component to the SSM Learning Cycle. Van Heusden, finally, shows how artefacts work as signs, created deliberately and subsequently interpreted ('made sense of') in context by the participants in the design process (including the original maker of the artefact, who might develop alternative interpretations of their own artefact).

4   Case: A Redesign of a Legacy System for Slaughter Lines

4.1   Introduction

In the slaughter line the carcasses are moved along the work places by an overhead conveyor chain. At some points in the line the carcass is inspected for specific anomalies. The result of inspections can be physically marked on the carcass, logged, or both. Most work on the carcass is repetitive and requires no information. Some work is incidental and caused by anomalies found during inspection of a carcass. When needed, carcasses can be moved to a side track for more time-consuming incidental work.

At the end of the line, just before the carcass is moved into the cooling down process, the carcass is weighed and classified. This determines the base price to be paid to the farmer. Anomalies on the carcass registered in the slaughter line can lower the base price. Weight and classification are determined by calibrated equipment. The government has tasked an independent organisation with inspections and classification, as well as supervising the slaughtering process (which includes certified registration of mandatory carcass data). The slaughterhouse can capture additional data required for its own purposes, such as internal selection, feedback to its farmers and supply management.

Over time, the amount of information collected in the process has grown significantly, due to commercial interests as well as food safety regulations. The pace of a typical line has also increased from 300 carcasses/hr to 650 (which means less than 6 s per carcass for each work place along the line).

Information in the line can be transferred by physical markings and/or recorded by IT systems. Each method has its advantages and drawbacks. Direct recording in IT systems allows for immediate central visibility and for automated decisions in the line. Physical markings have greater visibility in the line, allowing recognition and visual checks from a distance, and do not require sophisticated synchronisation at the working place.

4.2 The Legacy System

The first version of the slaughter line system was developed back in 1987 with the introduction of a new European regulation for carcass classification in slaughterhouses. Our initial system had interactions with the human user, with peripheral equipment (scale and product detectors), and other systems (classification, carcass sorting system, and office systems).

The most important challenge in developing the first version of our system was reliable synchronisation between the systems and equipment distributed over about 6 to 12 slots of the conveyor. It took quite some trial and error and generated a lot of practical knowledge for our developer, both regarding real time behaviour of systems and equipment, as well as physical behaviour of transport system, carcasses and detectors. Indeed, creating a reliable system for detecting and keeping track of carcasses in the physical world is the work of a specialist. An essential part of such knowledge is gained through experience and cannot be acquired from documentation alone. This very specific domain knowledge had over the decades accumulated in one highly valued specialist in our company.

While the initial system was predominantly a data capturing system in a technically heterogeneous but functionally simple environment, this changed over the years in several ways. More data was to be captured, and physical routing functions were added to our system. Additional equipment had to be integrated, and additional regulations had to be satisfied. This resulted in a need to re-engineer our system. Another need was to decrease the dependency on a single specialist, preferably not just by 'cloning' his knowledge. The redesign was an internal project, connected with a customer project where the redesigned software would be deployed.

4.3 Redesign with Separation of Knowledge Domains

Objectives. The primary objectives of redesigning the system were firstly a rigorous cleaning up of its structure and secondly a radical separation of knowledge domains. We wanted the new system to be structured along the domains of real-time interactions with the physical world, functional information management, and interactions with the human world of users and ergonomics. Such a structure would allow experts in the respective domains to focus on their task, and the overall structure should be clean enough to be understandable by all. Although we did not use those terms at the time, we distinguished the knowledge domains of techne, general rules, and phronesis. It is interesting to note that making such a distinction is by itself a phronetic act: it is about understanding the way people work and are (in-)sensitive to the problems belonging to a certain domain.

At the beginning of the redevelopment, we formulated a simple slogan for the three constituent parts of the new system: the technical system knows everything about space and time (but nothing about content), the information management system knows every-thing about content (but nothing about space and time), and a coordinating system ties the two systems together (indeed, we did not separate human interactions in that slogan).

Technical Part. A main track of the project was the stripping of the legacy system to its bare technical functions of interacting with movements and events in the physical world. Keeping track of the carcasses is the core of this system. Interaction with the coordination system required mechanisms for referencing carcass IDs, positions in the line, and types of actions. In practice several identification mechanisms are available, such as a number on a tin plate in the ear, RFID in the hook, a sequence number on the skin. Different systems use different ways of identifying the carcass. However, each of these mechanisms had its drawbacks, and neither was completely reliable. Also, we did not want our core system to be dependent on external mechanisms. Hence, we decided to make it the responsibility of the core system to issue a unique token for each newly detected carcass, existing IDs could be attached as property values in the information system. Hence, missing values and non-uniqueness could be allowed for the existing IDs (which occasionally could happen). In interacting with other systems, we could use each of the alternative IDs. This decision might look simple, but it solved a lot of legacy problems.

For position references we could use an existing mechanism based on a signal from the power unit of the conveyors. This mechanism was proven to be both precise and reli-able. All actions in the physical system are triggered by the carcass reaching a position. Examples of actions are sending a message, starting or ending an input zone, or setting or resetting a switch or a signal lamp. All exchanges of messages between the technical system and the coordination system were based on three references (token, position, message type) plus relevant parameters (very few and very simple).

The technical system described above can be viewed as an "information machine" providing a set of basic functions: identifying new carcasses on the line, following them, and interchanging messages with the coordination system on predefined points using predefined messages. A critical non-functional requirement was a guaranteed cycle time of 100ms max. This means that each hard-wired input and output and each message will be serviced within that cycle time, this upper boundary is determined by the pace and required precision of the physical events.

Information Management Part and Coordination Part. The availability of this tech-nical "information machine" allows the information management part of the system to be developed as a rather straightforward information system for a business process. It is mostly about simple functional specifications for input and output on well-defined work places.

However, the path to that simple set of functions was not exactly easy. We had to find out many details about work processes and circumstances in the line. In most cases, while the general idea was clear, details could be hard to come by. Typically, when you start to question someone about the fine details of a particular work process, the answer is often that although they themselves do not know exactly how it works, they are sure other people will know. The funny thing is, the people they refer to frequently give the same answer. Hence, although everyone assumes that the knowledge you ask for is certainly available, you cannot find anyone who really knows. Which means that such knowledge about the work in the line has to be generated by an iterative process of observing, talking, writing, modelling, validating. Talking to different people with different perspectives on the work in the slaughter line is essentially a phronetic process. Knowing your interlocutors and their jobs helps a great deal in phrasing your questions, interpreting the answers, observing and reacting in the right way, and to separate the wheat from the chaff in a conversation.

Slaughter Line User Interaction Part. Based on an information analysis, the information to be captured and presented can be specified for each work place along the slaughter line, which is quite straightforward as a functional issue. Decisions about the method to use (IT system, pencil marks, coloured ribbons) possibly depend on possibly required visibility on the carcass itself, as well as the fitness of the physical work space for IT equipment. General requirements are that (1) the worker must have both carcass and information in view at the same time, (2) adding information to the carcass must be doable without taking the eyes off the carcass, and (3) the worker must not be restricted in his movements by equipment. In the past, we had developed several solutions for input and output, varying from screens with a small keypad, various cases with big coloured mushroom buttons and an LCD display, and signal lamps. Physical markings on the carcass that needed to be available in the IT system would be captured at the weighing position.

Based on earlier work we developed a standardised set of devices for handling input and output. Some were based on configurable touch screens, emulating the color-coded big "mushroom buttons" in use for the meat inspectors. Other devices are based on hard wired I/O (think of physical buttons and signal lamps). Regardless of the type of device, they are all controlled by the same pattern: (a) the physical control system detects the beginning of an input or output zone and sends a message to the information control system; and (b) the information control system reacts by sending information to the device. At the end of the zone a similar pattern is applied: (a) the physical control system detects the end-position of the zone, sends a message, and (b) the information control system reads the device.

As all hard-wired inputs and outputs are connected to the hardware of the physical control system, this system has to provide input/output functions. This means that conceptually the physical control system consists of (a) one self-contained system for keeping track of the conveyor and the carcasses, (b) zero, one or more self-contained instances of input/output devices for individual work places along the line, and (c) a common message handler for communication with the information control system and dispatch of the messages to the functional block responsible for that message type on that position.

5 Discussion

5.1 Kinds of Knowledge Involved in the Case

In the slaughter line system different knowledge domains were distinguished, with a predominant kind of knowledge in each domain. In the domain of the physical world techne is predominant, it is about the behaviour of physical elements of the conveyor system with its power units, detectors, switches, and the tracking of the physical position of the carcasses. In the domain of information management general rules are predominant, specifying functions how information about carcasses is received, processed and made available to the parts of the system interacting with the technical part and/or the user. In the domain of user interaction phronesis is prevalent, because it is about understanding the job and the working environment of the user.

It is in the approach to the project of redesigning the slaughter line system where phronesis is of overriding importance, and in multiple ways. One way is its role in creating a common ground between the participants in the project. Another way is in designing a system where knowledge domains and hence kinds of knowledge are neatly separated in its constituent parts. Both ways are about recognising the differences between knowledge domains, kinds of knowledge, kinds of personal expertise, and finding ways of combining them in a fruitful way.

5.2 Role of Artefacts in the Design Cycle

Different artefacts played different roles in the design of the new system. It started with a very high level 'sketchy model' of the system parts, to convey the general idea of one part about physical space, one about information management, and one about the coordination between the two. This was the general model we started with and which was unchanged at the end of the project. A lower-level kind of artefacts were used for fleshing out the technical implementation of the coordination mechanism, representing the function of the 'errand-boy' between the system parts. A third group of artefacts was about the different references to be used in the system: identification of carcasses, of physical positions in the line, and of message types. Different kinds of artefacts had different roles and different life-cycles in the project. While the high-level model was fixed at the beginning, the other artefacts were refined step by step from general idea to a precise specification.

A common factor in all artefacts was their role in trait-making. Both for the software developers and for the customers the approach to the problem was new, and we needed those artefacts to convey from the start the meaning of the different components of the system (hence the use of a colloquial term as 'errand-boy' for the messaging mechanism). As explained by Kretz, artefacts are used as a presentation of a design, to experiment with, and to gain knowledge.

6 Conclusion

The paper was triggered by the title of the article "De method doet het niet" or "The method does not (do the) work" by Van Rees. This led to an analysis of the skills and knowledge required in information systems development for a business organisation, especially with regard to the transition from the social world of the organisation to the formal world of IT systems. The theoretical work of Flyvbjerg (about trait-making projects and about power relations in projects), Kretz (about design) and Van Heusden (about the artefact as sign) was discussed. In an illustrative case of redesigning a legacy system various project issues about differing worldviews, different knowledge domains, and social (power) relations were discussed. The conscious application of artefacts in the design cycle (with an increasing degree of specificity) was presented as a flexible and effective way of moving towards delivering a product that would satisfy very different kinds of requirements: functionality, reliability, robustness as 'hard requirements', operational usability and separation of knowledge domains as 'soft requirements'.

Phronesis, an often neglected element in information system development, was in several ways an important factor. First of all, in the internal project to align worldviews of participants and to develop a common ground between them. Phronesis is also important in interacting with the customers, to gain knowledge, to validate solutions, and later on for implementation and maintenance. Dealing with heterogeneous groups of stakeholders, representing different functional domains/worldviews/knowledge domains, is partly about objective facts, partly about interpretation of procedural issues, and partly about power relations. Even in discussing objective facts phronesis is involved, because rational arguments work best when chosen and presented in a way that resonates with your conversation partner.

The status and the role of artefacts in ISD is an element that should be explored further in several ways. Firstly, as an element in the design cycle, starting as a general idea and ending in a formally specified concept. But another important aspect is that such artefacts can have multiple meanings in different domains. In the transition from the social world to the formal world artefacts may start as a natural language concept and end as a fully specified concept with formal relations to other concepts in a data model. Still, the name of such a database artefact will have connotations with the natural language concept. A sales order in business is a social construct designating an agreement between business partners, subject to human interpretation and law. A sales order in the database is a reduced version of that social construct, leaving out many tacit assumptions that belong to the business world. A third venue for exploration might be the status of modelling artefacts in UML and business process models. It is my conjecture that from the view of software engineering many of such artefacts are in fact empty shells lacking precise specification. The labels attached to such modelling artefacts suggest a precise meaning which in fact they do not have. This can lead to ambiguity and misinterpretation during software engineering.

To conclude, the assertion in Van Rees' title that it is the analyst and not the method that does the work, is corroborated by the theories and the case discussed in the paper. In ISD, the transition from the social world of business to the formal world of IT is a design process, where the logical machine is specified. Therefore, methods for this trajectory should not be recipes to be followed step-by-step, but rather a combination of documentary conventions and heuristic guidelines for work-in-progress, in combination with a rigorously specified end product (which will be the input for the software engineers).

References

1. Van Rees, J.: De Methode Doet Het Niet. Reprinted in: Van Rees, J., Wisse, P.: De Informatie-Architect. Kluwer, Deventer 1995 (original article 1982)
2. de Brock, B.: Advantages of a formal specification of a case. In: Shishkov, B. (ed.) BMSD 2022. LNBIP, vol. 453, pp. 158–181. Springer, Cham (2022). https://doi.org/10.1007/978-3-031-11510-3_10
3. Tanenbaum, A.S.: Structured Computer Organization. Prentice Hall International, London (1976)
4. Coase, R.H.: The nature of the firm. In: Williamson, O.E., Winter, S.G. (eds.) The Nature of the Firm: Origins, Evolution, and Development, pp. 18–33. Oxford University Press, Oxford (1993)
5. Kay, J.: Foundations of Corporate Success. Oxford University Press, Oxford (1993)
6. Macneil, I.R.: The New Social Contract. Yale University Press, New Haven (1980)
7. Campbell, D. (ed.): The Relational Theory of Contract: Selected Works of Ian Macneil. Sweet & Maxwell, London (2001)
8. Schön, D.A.: The Reflective Practitioner. Ashgate, Aldershot (1983)
9. Checkland, P., Poulter, J.: Learning for Action. Wiley, Chisester (2006)
10. Flyvbjerg, B.: The iron law of megaproject management. In: Flyvbjerg, B. (ed.): The Oxford Handbook of Megaproject Management. Oxford University Press, Oxford (2017)
11. Flyvbjerg, B.: Introduction. In: Flyvbjerg, B. (ed.): Megaproject Planning and Management: Essential Readings. Edward Elgar Publishing, Cheltenham (2014)
12. Flyvbjerg, B.: Making Social Science Matter. Cambridge University Press, Cambridge (2001)
13. Flyvbjerg, B.: Rationality and Power. University of Chicago Press, Chicago (1998)
14. Flyvbjerg, B.: How Big Things Get Done. Macmillan, London (2023)
15. Barnes, J. (ed.): The Complete Works of Aristotle. Princeton University Press, Princeton (1984)
16. OUP: The Oxford English Dictionary. Oxford University Press, Oxford (1989)
17. Diggle, J., Fraser, B.L., James, P., Simkin, O.B., Thompson, A.A., Westripp, S.J. (eds.): The Cambridge Greek Lexicon. Cambridge University Press, Cambridge (2021)
18. Liddell, H.G., Scott, R. (eds.): Greek-English Lexicon. Clarendon Press, Oxford (1843, 1996)
19. Kretz, S.: The Cosmos of Design. Verlag der Buchhandlung Walter König, Köln (2020)
20. Ganshirt, C.: Tools for Ideas. Birkhäuser, Basel (2021)
21. Kretz, S.: Der Kosmos des Entwerfens. file:///C:/Users/csuurmond/Downloads/KOSMOS_DES_ENTWERFENS_Simon_Kretz-1.pdf. Accessed 12 Feb 2024
22. Alexander, C.: A Pattern Language. Oxford University Press, Oxford (1978)
23. Van Heusden, B.P.: Signs in tine. In: Biglari, A. (ed.) Open Semiotics, Volume 2 Culture and Society. L'Harmattan, Paris (2023)
24. Van Heusden, B.P.: Theoretische Cultuurwetenschap - Een Inleiding. Uitgeverij Passage, Groningen (2024)
25. De Brock, B.: Developing Information Systems Accurately. Springer, Cham (2023). https://doi.org/10.1007/978-3-031-16862-8
26. Hirschman, A.O.: Development Projects Observed. Brookings Institution Press, Washington (2015, 1967)

VR-SDLC: A Context-Enhanced Life Cycle Visualization of Software-or-Systems Development in Virtual Reality

Roy Oberhauser(✉) ⓘ

Computer Science Department, Aalen University, Aalen, Germany
`roy.oberhauser@hs-aalen.de`

Abstract. As systems grow in complexity, so does their associated lifecycle and with it the need to manage the various elements, relations, and activities involved in the Software (or Systems) Development Life Cycle (SDLC). Various notations for system, software, or process modeling have been specified, such as the Systems Modeling Language (SysML), Unified Modeling Language (UML), and Business Process Model and Notation (BPMN) respectively, yet due to their target system and two-dimensional (2D) diagram focus, they are ill suited for visualizing a comprehensive contextualized view of the entire systems engineering or software engineering lifecycle. To address lifecycle modeling, the Lifecycle Modeling Language (LML) utilizes a relatively simple ontology and three primary diagrams while supporting extensibility. Yet lifecycle comprehension, analysis, collaboration, and contextual insights remain constrained by current 2D limitations. This paper contributes our Virtual Reality (VR) solution concept VR-SDLC for contextualized holistic visualization of SDLC elements, relations, and diagrams. Our prototype implementation utilizing LML demonstrates its feasibility, while a case study exhibits its potential.

Keywords: Virtual Reality · Systems Lifecycle · Software Development Life Cycle · Systems Engineering · Software Engineering · Systems Modeling · Lifecycle Modeling Language (LML) · Visualization

1 Introduction

Software Engineering (SE) and Systems Engineering (SysE) involves lifecycles, yet such lifecycles are rarely if ever formally modeled beyond some higher-level abstraction, nor are technical instantiations, e.g., as processes, concretely used (perhaps because they are subject to frequent variation). Typically engineering, and particularly system or software[1] design, involves modeling the target system-of-interest, where supporting methodologies or notations such as Model-Driven methods (MDX) are well-known and have reached some level of maturity. However, the lifecycle itself is not typically modeled, thus much

---

[1] For this article, "systems" development/engineering can be replaced with "software" when hardware development is out-of-scope for some endeavor.

B. Shishkov (Ed.): BMSD 2024, LNBIP 523, pp. 112–129, 2024.
https://doi.org/10.1007/978-3-031-64073-5_8

of what is planned and executed during the associated lifecycle is not readily accessible to stakeholders in a contextual manner. But with regard to quality, not only the system itself, but the associated processes, methods, techniques, activities, and artifacts utilized during SysE and SE have associated expectations and conformance requirements that play an essential role in achieving some set of qualities (safety, security, reliability, etc.). For example, maturity models (e.g., CMMI), standards (e.g., IEC 61508), guidelines (e.g., MISRA), etc., often focus on preventative process-centric measures to address construction or systemic error risks, since - especially for software-intensive systems - comprehensive verification and validation (V&V) of the final system alone is not viable. Thus, various stakeholders must access, analyze, and collaborate on lifecycle elements. And while the target system and its associated model to be developed can be complex, the lifecycle and surrounding SysE system or environment can often necessarily be even more complex. However, any work performed is often "hidden" in various artifacts and activities by actors, yet not necessarily (easily) tracked and retained. This, in turn, can affect efficiency, effectiveness, traceability, V&V, and compliance. For instance, Automotive SPICE exemplifies such expectations within the automotive industry.

But realizing lifecycle modeling necessitates an appropriate modeling language. The Lifecycle Modeling Language (LML) [1] positions itself as a systems engineer's language for integrating all lifecycle disciplines (program management, systems engineering, testing, deployment, and maintenance) into a single framework, such that all stakeholders can model and understand systems. It can be easily translated [2] to other common notations and languages, such as BPMN [3], UML [4], SysML [5], etc., and can be used to support holistic traceability through the lifecycle, be it artifacts or activities. Yet when one considers the various disciplines, lifecycle elements, actors, and relations involved in a SysE or SE endeavor (which can be viewed as an open system), its actual complexity (and possibly reactive over-simplification) can make true comprehension across stakeholders challenging. It is interesting to note that the Systems Engineering Vision 2025 from INCOSE foresees systems modeling using immersive technology to share system understanding across stakeholders [6]. Towards supporting stakeholder comprehension and insight, the intent of this paper is to investigate and explore an immersion capability for SDLC utilizing LML.

Our VR-related prior work includes: VR-EA [7] supporting Enterprise Architecture (EA) Archimate models in VR; VR-EAT [8] integrating the tool Atlas for visualizing dynamically-generated EA diagrams; VR-EA+TCK [9] integrating Knowledge Management Systems (KMS) and Enterprise Content Management Systems (ECMS); VR-EvoEA+BP [10] for context-enhanced enterprise models with animated evolution and business process (BP) dynamics; and VR-BPMN [11], VR-SysML [12], and VR-UML [13] visualizing BPMN, SysML, and UML models respectively.

This paper contributes VR-SDLC, our nexus-based VR solution concept for a context-enhanced visualization of lifecycle models for SysE and SE lifecycles. It comprehensively portrays lifecycle model elements, relations, and diagrams enhanced with context and exemplified with LML models. Furthermore, multiple lifecycle projects can be portrayed concurrently to support cross-project or program portfolio analysis and optimizations. Its hypermodeling capability (depiction with other models such as

SysML/UML in VR) showcases how both a target model and its lifecycle can be portrayed concurrently in VR. Our realization demonstrates its feasibility, while a case study using sample LML models exhibits its potential.

The paper is structured as follows: Sect. 2 discusses related work; Sect. 3 gives a background on LML; our solution concept is described in Sect. 4; Sect. 5 details our realization; our evaluation is in Sect. 6, followed by a conclusion.

2 Related Work

With regard to development lifecycle process standards, ISO offers the ISO/IEC/IEEE 15288 [14] for systems or 12207 [15] for software. However, these exist in natural language and do not provide a machine-processable technical implementation nor modeling language for their process models. Dori [16] laments ambiguous aspects of the 15288 lifecycle standard and how a modeling approach might address these. SysML 1.x lacked an official complete ontology, while SysML version 2.0 is still in beta and thus has limited support.

Work related to lifecycle tool integration includes the Open Services for Lifecycle Collaboration (OSLC) [17], which focuses on specifications for the integration of software development tooling. It can be used for Application Lifecycle Management (ALM), Product Lifecycle Management (PLM), and IT Operations and utilizes the Resource Description Framework (RDF), Linked Data, and REST. It does not address system lifecycle modeling.

As to modeling the system lifecycle, LML, introduced in the previous section and described further in the next section, positions itself as a lifecycle modeling language. In the area of automation systems, the Object-Process Methodology (OPM) [18] is a conceptual approach, language, and methodology for both the modeling and knowledge representation of such automation systems. Relating objects to processes, it offers graphical, hierarchical, interrelated diagrams, and on their basis a textual model can be generated. Yet OPM also positions itself as being domain-independent. Work regarding SysML-centric approaches includes Bajaj et al. [19], who describe MBSE++, their vision for model-based SysE across the system lifecycle with a unified Total System Model framework that utilizes SysML in conjunction with other models; they present a vision, challenges, and potential use cases exemplified with browser-based 2D visualizations on the Syndeia platform. For managing the lifecycles of the models themselves, Fisher et al. [20] focus on models as configuration items and repository support, mentioning Model Lifecycle Management (MLM) and MLM Systems (MLMS) to support a MLM processes for this context. They argue that Product Lifecycle Management (PLM) tools often lack good integration with MDE tools, while Application Lifecycle Management (ALM) are more SW-focused and lack system development capabilities. Here as well no lifecycle modeling language is addressed. Bork et al. [21] provide a survey comparing 11 (mostly visual) modeling language specifications, including LML, UML, BPMN, and OPM.

Regarding visualization, while typical VR use cases during engineering include modeling, simulation, and operation of the target system, we found no related work regarding the use of VR for visualizing the lifecycle of SysE or SE.

3   Background on the Lifecycle Modeling Language

LML [1] was selected as a basis modeling language for the SDLC for several reasons: 1) it's positioned specifically as a lifecycle modeling language, 2) it's maturity (since 2013 to version 1.4 in 2022), 3) it's relative simplicity and extensibility, 4) it's based on an ontology, 4) it's fundamental tenet that each entity has at least one corresponding visualization, and 5) the accessibility of a concrete format and sample model datasets for testing our solution concept.

LML uses common vocabulary to define modeling elements (e.g., entity, attribute, schedule, cost, relationship). Primary visual modeling constructs are the box (representing a part of the system) and the directed arrow (depicting relationships between elements, like "consists of," "derived from," or "costs"), to make it easy for various stakeholders to grasp. The LML ontology consists of 20 entities in total. The 12 primary (8 children) entities are Action, Artifact, Asset (Resource), Characteristic (Measure), Connection (Conduit, Logical), Cost, Decision, Input/Output, Location (Orbital, Physical, Virtual), Risk, Statement (Requirement), and Time. How the principal entities relate to each other and support traceability is shown in Fig. 1.

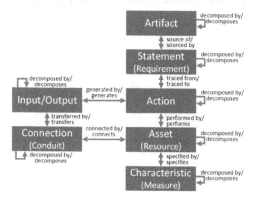

Fig. 1. Principal LML entities/relationships supporting traceability (adapted from [1]).

As to visualization, LML defines a logical construct using visualization models in four areas (primary entities) [22]:

- Functional models (Action, Input/Output),
- Physical models (Asset/Resource, Connection),
- Documentation entities (Artifact, Statement/Requirement), and
- Parametric and program entities (Time, Risk, Cost, Characteristic/Measure, Location).

LML defines three key diagram types: Action (behavioral), Asset (physical), and Spider (traceability). While other diagrams are offered, these three express essential elements for systems engineering. While LML offers a metamodel, it lacks a visual metamodel, a coordinate system (for precisely specifying the height and width of modeling constructs), variables for specifying color or shape, yet it does offer horizontal and vertical position variables [21]. LML tools can also dynamically generate diagrams, which can help to ensure their veracity given a data-centric model. Since LML diagrams can be auto-generated by tooling, it moves SysE towards Data-Driven SysE (DDSE) rather than remaining focused on Model-Based SysE (MBSE) [2].

As to available mappings to other popular notations such as SysML and BPMN, a mapping of SysML to LML is addressed in Appendix A of the LML Specification [1]. As LML is extensible, Equation and Port were added to provide SysML visualizations. Any lifecycle modeling will involve modeling processes. While BPMN is popular and supports highly complex process models, version 2.0.2 has 116 elements. In contrast, LML retains a simple ontology and graphical notation. Mapping between BPMN and LML Action Diagrams is described by Stevie [23].

Innoslate by Spec Innovations [27] is a cloud tool offering model-based SysE supporting LML and other modeling languages. It integrates requirements, testing, V&V, system modeling, simulation, project management, and issue tracking. Via its web-based user interface, various LML and other (e.g., SysML) diagrams can be generated as shown as a dashboard of widgets in Fig. 2 or as separate diagrams as shown in Fig. 3.

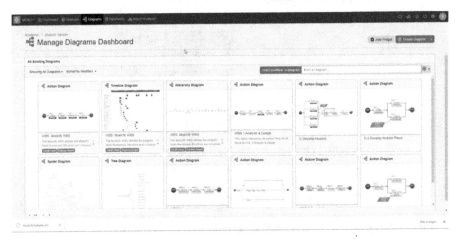

Fig. 2. Innoslate diagram dashboard screenshot for Musicify Sample project.

4 Solution Concept

Our solution approach leverages VR for visualizing the various lifecycle and system models and their interrelationships simultaneously, mapped to a spatial structural model that can be immersively explored and experienced. The comprehensive integration of context as a first principle for lifecycles supports analysis and comprehension of the "big picture" for structurally and hierarchically complex and interconnected lifecycle elements, models, diagrams, and artifacts. It provides a 3D visualization for the entire lifecycle model, viewable and filterable from different perspectives by diverse stakeholders, such as system/software architects/engineers, requirements analysts, test engineers, operators, auditors, logisticians, and project/program managers.

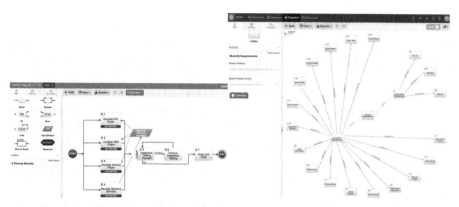

Fig. 3. LML Action (left) and Spider (right) diagram screenshots in edit mode in Innoslate.

4.1 Grounding in VR-Related Research

Our reasoning for applying VR in our solution concept is based on prior VR research in areas we view as related to modeling, analysis, and collaboration, some of which are highlighted here. In their systematic meta-analysis, Akpan & Shanker [24] showed VR and three-dimensional (3D) offer significant advantages in the area of Discrete Event Modeling (DES), including model development, analysis, and Verification and Validation (V&V), with the most consistent conclusions being the positive effects of 3D/VR model analysis and V&V. Of 23 articles examining 3D analysis, 95% concluded using 3D was more potent and lead to better analysis than 2D, e.g., when evaluating a model's behavior or performing a what-if analysis. They also found a consensus that 3D/VR can present results convincingly and understandably for decision-makers. 74% of 19 papers concluded that 3D/VR significantly improves the model development task (supporting teams and improving precision and clarity). To investigate VR's suitability for analytical tasks for an Information Architecture (IA), Narasimha et al. [25] used a card sorting collaboration experiment. They found that VR was at least as good as in-person card sorting, and that VR did not perform worse than video screen-share or VR; in fact, for certain variables VR was even better than both conventional and video-based conditions. Qualitative data evaluating awareness indicated that during collaborative interaction, participants were aware of their task, others, and their context, while collaborating similarly to an in-person setting. Additionally, the qualitative data showed evidence of positive views towards VR. The outcomes suggest that both a sense of presence and collaboration (equivalent to an in-person setting) is possible within VR. Another survey of Immersive Analytics (IA) by Fonnet & Prie [26] analyzed 177 papers. They found concurring evidence that for graph and spatial data analysis, IA provides benefits vs. non-IA when the scene complexity exceeds the 2D display, while for multi-dimensional data, the advantages are more task-dependent. They remark that while IA enables exploration of large-scale data worlds, context-aware navigation techniques are insufficiently exploited - although they are critical for users. We thus conclude that the immersive VR experience has significant potential for comprehensively depicting 3D models, supporting awareness, analysis, stakeholder inclusion, collaboration, and contextualization.

4.2   VR-SDLC Solution Concept

The contribution of our paper is a VR solution concept for the contextual visualization of the SE or SysE lifecycle models, including associated diagrams and heterogeneous models. Our solution concept is abstract, extensible, and leverages available lifecycle modeling construct providers (e.g., LML). We are not endorsing any particular language, scheme, methodology, product, or tool, but rather utilizing them to investigate the feasibility of utilizing VR for conveying SDLC with contextual aspects. The modeling constructs are typically extensible, should additional elements or diagrams be required. For complex systems and their lifecycle, VR's visual, immersive medium provides a collaborative opportunity for portraying lifecycle aspects in a contextually-relevant manner for diverse stakeholders.

SysE, SE, and EA are broad topics, yet having many facets and potentially overlapping commonalities. SysE and SE typically rely on and are executed in an organization such as an enterprise, which in turn has an EA. We thus developed various solutions concepts as shown in our solution map in Fig. 3. Our generalized VR Modeling Framework (VR-MF), described in [7], provides a domain-independent hypermodeling framework addressing key aspects for modeling in VR: visualization, navigation, interaction, and data retrieval. On this basis, VR-EA [7] provides specialized direct support and mapping for EA models in VR, including both ArchiMate as well as BPMN via VR-BPMN [11], while VR-ProcessMine [28] supports process mining in VR. VR-EAT [8] extends this to our enterprise repository integration solution, exemplified with Atlas integration, visualization of IT blueprints, and interaction capabilities. VR-EA+TCK [9] expands this further by integrating KMS and ECMS capabilities in VR. And VR-EvoEA+BP [10] adds VR support for animating enterprise evolution and (even non-BPMN) business processes. Our VR-based solutions specific to SE and SysE include: VR-SDLC (the focus of this paper, shown in blue), which could leverage our VR-V&V [29], VR-TestCoverage [30], VR-GitCity [31] and VR-Git [32] as well as our modeling solutions including VR-UML [13], VR-SysML [12], and VR-SysML+Traceability [33]. In supporting SDLC lifecycles with VR, we foresee future opportunities to leverage the aforementioned solution concepts in the enterprise and organizational space (e.g., knowledge, processes, infrastructure, architecture, artifacts) towards more comprehensive and holistic solutions in the (SE and SysE) engineering, development, and operations space as well.

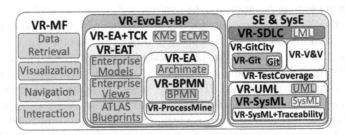

Fig. 4. VR solution concept map showing VR-SDLC (blue) in relation to our other concepts.

To achieve these objectives, our solution concept necessitates data integration and VR visualization, navigation, and interaction capabilities, addressed as follows:

Lifecycle Data Integration. As a representative tool and repository for lifecycle data integration, Innoslate provides diverse lifecycle-related data in a coherent repository and meta-model based on LML. The Innoslate cloud-based tool provides a 2D browser interface and offers sample LML projects that can be exported in its XML format.

Visualization. Since many possible relations between digital elements are possible, a spherical nexus was chosen to visualize all elements and relations for a project lifecycle. To provide some initial ordering, layering within the sphere is available as a grouping mechanism based on similar element types using the color assigned to that type, resulting in a sphere with colored layers (intra-layer element placement is random). A default (customizable) node color scheme is used. To assist with orientation and make interaction more intuitive by providing a context for what a model represents, labeled glass boxes readable from any angle contain a nexus based on some model. As 2D-based views and diagrams remain a primary form of SysE and SE documentation, they are visualized via 3D hyperplanes in proximity to its nexus for contextual support. In summary, hitherto intangible digital elements "or digital twins" are thus made visible and related to one another across the lifecycle spectrum.

Navigation. To support immersive navigation in VR while reducing the likelihood of potential VR sickness symptoms, two navigation modes are supported in the solution concept: the default uses gliding controls, enabling users to fly through the VR space and get an overview of the entire model from any angle they wish. Alternatively, teleporting permits a user to select a destination and be instantly placed there (i.e., moving the camera to that position), potentially reducing the probability of VR sickness when moving through a virtual space.

Interaction. Interaction in VR is supported primarily via the VR controllers and our VR-Tablet concept. Views consisting of diagrams are stacked as hyperplanes (with sub-diagrams placed below), with corresponding objects highlighted in the Nexus or diagram. Our VR-Tablet paradigm provides: interaction support, detailed information regarding a selected element, and can support browser-based multimedia content, browsing, filtering, and searching for nexus nodes.

5   Realization

The logical architecture of our VR-SDLC prototype realization is shown in Fig. 5, consists of the following modules: the Data Hub (with a GUI, an LML Adapter and Transformer, and a Database), and the Unity VR modules: General, Tablet, and LML-specific modules (ActionDiagrams, SpiderNexus, AssetDiagrams, and Connectors).

The Data Hub GUI, realized with PythonQT, simplifies data import via drag-and-drop. Our Python-based adapter and transformer converts the XML exported from Innoslate. The main elements of the XML structure are: innoslate (the root element), schema, schemaClass, schemaRelation, xmlTargetRelation, database, entity

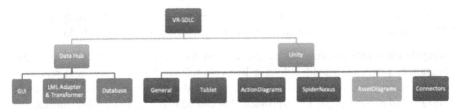

Fig. 5. VR-SDLC Logical Architecture.

(name, description, schemaClassId, numbering, creation/change timestamp, etc.), simulationData (Action Diagram structure), relationship (between two entities: sourceId, schemaRelationId, targetId). This is mapped to our JSON format, which is stored in the Neo4j graph database, which provides a flexible basis for supporting contextualization via its graph structure and Cypher Query Language. Figure 6 exemplifies relations between Action Diagram elements viewed in the Neo4j database browser.

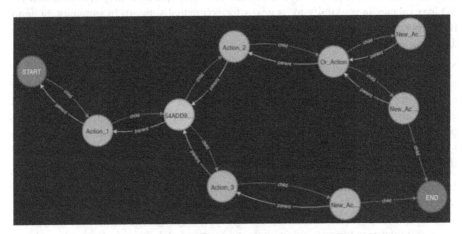

Fig. 6. Elements of an Action Diagram viewed in Neo4j Browser.

From the three primary diagram types specified in LML, our prototype realization currently supports the equivalent of Spider and Action diagrams in VR. The *Spider* diagram is mandatory for traceability, depicting how entities relate to one another. To realize the essence of what Spider diagrams convey in VR, we instead utilize a spherical nexus to visualize the relations between entities. The *Action* diagram - the only diagram type unique to LML - is used to express functional sequencing in a simplified way (vs. flow charts, UML/SysML Activity Diagrams, or BPMN) with a notation that supports comprehension by other stakeholders. Control node types consist of SERIAL, LOOP, PARALLEL, OR, START, END, and SNYC. We realized Action diagrams in VR as a 3D model of the diagram and its elements on a hyperplane. *Asset* diagrams provide a physical representation of design elements. They consist of Asset, Resource as a subclass of Asset, and Conduits. Due to time and resource constraints, however, our prototype does not yet support Asset diagrams. For visualization realization purposes, they can be viewed as a simplified variant of the Action diagram, and thus we do not foresee any technical hindrances.

As to support for additional (non-primary) diagram types, our demonstrated support for many diagram types and notations in VR was enumerated with Fig. 4 in the prior section, and we thus can envision support for the wide variety of the optional and common diagram visualizations recommended for use with LML [22] (VR-UML, VR-SysML, VR-BPMN).

6 Evaluation

An empirical evaluation is out-of-scope for this paper but included in future work. For the evaluation of our solution concept with our prototype realization, we refer to the design science method and principles [34], in particular, a viable artifact, problem relevance, and design evaluation (utility, quality, efficacy). For this case study, we focus on supporting lifecycle comprehension, analysis, and contextualization. In particular, with regard to scenarios involving diverse project lifecycle instantiations (SysE and SE), heterogeneous side-by-side models (e.g., with SysML), and cross-project or program management aspects.

To verify support for differing lifecycles, the following LML sample project datasets from the Innoslate tool were used:

Autonomous Vehicle: a SysE sample representing the development of an autonomous vehicle for SAE International Level 5 full automation. It consists of 199 nodes and 886 links, including 39 Statements, 37 Requirements, 33 Tasks, 16 Actions, 11 Assets, 18 Dependencies, 12 Time Elements, and 8 Input-Outputs. It contains 11 Action Diagrams.

FireSAT Satellite: a space satellite system that performs early detection and warning for forest fires. This SysE sample is from the Applied Space Systems Engineering book. It consists of 347 nodes and 1270 links, including 4 Statements, 44 Requirements, 33 Tasks, 63 Actions, 90 Assets, 3 Resources, 7 Artifacts, 15 Test Cases, 11 Characteristics, 12 Time elements, 9 Input-Outputs, 17 Conduits, 3 Equations, and 18 Cost elements. It contains 27 Action Diagrams.

Musicify Streaming Service: a hypothetical music streaming service as a software-centric (SE) reference example for software engineers. It consists of 189 nodes and 722 links, including 3 Statements, 20 Requirements, 2 Artifacts, 32 Tasks, 36 Actions, 25 Assets, 10 Conduits, 13 Time Elements, 6 Cost Elements, 15 Dependencies, 1 Resource, and 22 Test Cases. It contains 19 Action Diagrams.

SPECTER Lunar Rover: a SysE sample inspired by NASA's Break the Ice Challenge for a system for excavation and delivery of icy regolith under extreme lunar conditions. It consists of 152 nodes and 558 links, including 1 Statement, 17 Requirements, 51 Tasks, 12 Actions, 13 Assets, 4 Conduits, 4 Issues, 3 Artifacts, 17 Time elements, etc. It contains 26 Action Diagrams.

6.1 Multi-project and Program Management Analysis Support Scenario

Figure 7 demonstrates the ability to load and compare multiple LML lifecycles simultaneously, each in a transparent cube containing a nexus of interconnected nodes representing its lifecycle elements. Each nexus is centered on a common axis, thus the larger the nexus (illusion of being shifted forward), the greater the number of nodes; in this case FireSAT (second from left) is the largest with 347 nodes. To provide order, each nexus is layered by colored node type. Thus, one can visually readily determine that FireSAT has more Assets (red nodes) than the other projects. The stats for each project are displayed as a type-colored legend near the nexus box. Furthermore, via the VR-Tablet a user can toggle show all diagrams across all projects (Fig. 8), which are placed on an axis in front of each nexus (to avoid collisions, they are currently spaced apart, but we intend to further optimize proximity placement). Thus, a user can quickly determine which, if any, diagrams are even available. Via the VR-Tablet, the available diagrams are scrollable by name, and can be selected and shown.

Hence, cross-project coordination or program management analysis (e.g., quality assurance) can be readily undertaken, e.g., to consider lifecycle optimizations or improvements in efficiency or effectiveness measures. While at first glance it may seem cognitively complex, which in fact such lifecycles are, yet VR-SDLC offers an immersive overview of the reality that can then be adjusted and filtered for the interests of the stakeholder involved.

Fig. 7. Multiple LML projects loaded as VR-SDLC nexuses.

6.2 Contextualization Scenario

This scenario focuses on providing stakeholders with contextual support. Each nexus provides insight to the entire contextual information available to a given project, provided primarily via the links between nodes as shown in Fig. 9.

For the context of a given element, if any element in a nexus is selected as shown in Fig. 10, only links to first-degree nexus neighbors remain colored, other nodes and links are ghosted. This highlights its direct context, while leaving hints at the overall context. Here, the node "Obtain Music Information" of type Requirement is selected, with the VR-Tablet providing additional details (colored by type) about data associated with the element. The first-degree neighbors and *relations* for this element are: *decomposes* the

Fig. 8. VR-SDLC showing all diagrams available for multiple LML projects.

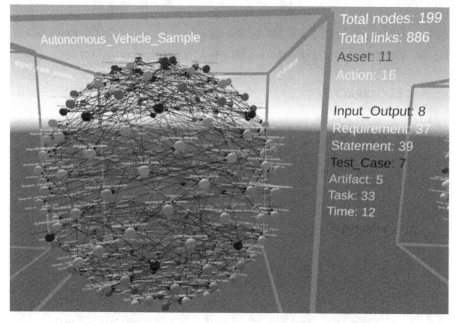

Fig. 9. VR-SDLC depicting LML Autonomous Vehicle Sample nexus.

Statement Functional_Requirements (pink), is *satisfied_by* the Asset Storage_Service (red), and is *verified_by* the Test Case Music_Information (black).

For diagrams, context relative to other diagrams is provided if associations to sub- or super- diagrams exist (as illustrated in Fig. 11 for a set of diagrams and Fig. 12 for a single Task). Also, when selecting an element in either the nexus or diagram, only the links in the nexus to first-degree neighbors remain colored, all other nexus nodes and links are ghosted, and only the diagrams associated with that node are shown. This can be seen in Fig. 13, where the Task Musicify WBS was selected.

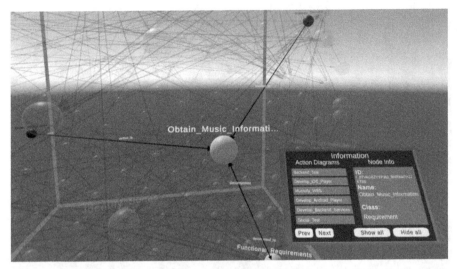

Fig. 10. VR-SDLC depicting selection in LML Musicify Sample nexus. (Color figure online)

Fig. 11. VR-SDLC expanded contextual hierarchy of LML Action diagrams.

In contrast, in a browser using 2D diagrams, this contextual information can be difficult to attain. For instance, in the Innoslate tool, when one double-clicks one element, then the view typically changes to the subdiagram. One can place diagrams side-by-side (see Fig. 14), but it is not visually obvious (but rather possible via numbering) to extract how the elements and diagrams possibly relate.

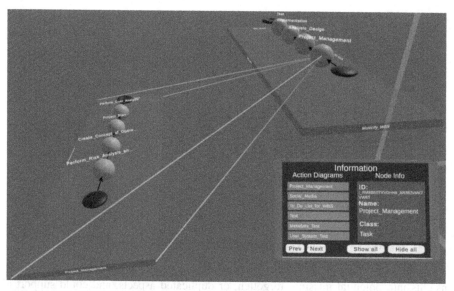

Fig. 12. VR-SDLC showing an LML Action subdiagram for the Project_Management Task.

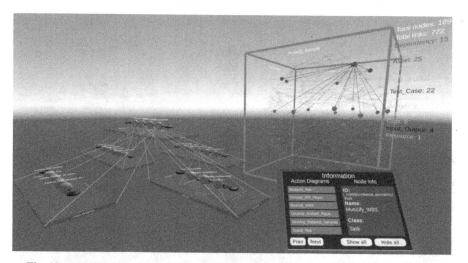

Fig. 13. VR-SDLC Contextualization of Actions in Nexus and multiple LML Diagrams.

6.3 Heterogeneous Hypermodeling Support Scenario

Immersive heterogeneous multi-model analysis is supported by loading multiple models in VR as shown in Fig. 15, where SysML diagrams (as hyperplanes) are loaded via VR-SysML [12] near the LML models. In previous work, we have demonstrated loading heterogenous models in VR, such as our VR-UML [13], VR-EA for ArchiMate [7], and VR-BPMN [11] solutions models. The unlimited space in VR offers the ability to be cognizant of the various models available and how they relate, and can offer new

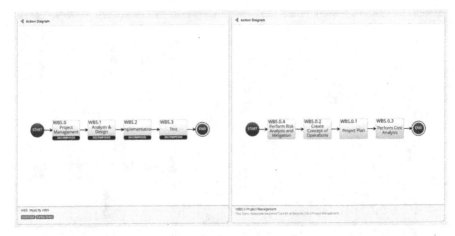

Fig. 14. LML Action Diagrams placed side-by-side as widgets in Innoslate.

insights into potential missing, forgotten, or duplicated aspects, and could support a more comprehensive traceability.

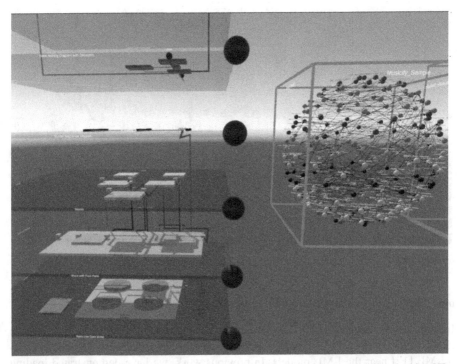

Fig. 15. Example heterogeneous multi-model visualization and analysis capability showing VR-SysML diagrams (as hyperplanes) near LML models.

Furthermore, integration with our EA-centric VR-EA+TCK [9] is readily feasible, and would enable a much more comprehensive and holistic insight for stakeholders, taking into account the entire organization (as the enterprise) with all its related elements and systems, such as KMS and ECMS. Furthermore, a time-based lifecycle or target system evolution with a process-mining view as demonstrated in VR-EvoEA+BP [10] could be applied at the project-level to the SDLC lifecycle as well. Integration with VR-BPMN [11] models is also feasible, if such process models were available to the lifecycle or if the available mapping of LML to BPMN were desired. We thus see further opportunities for multi-model integration with VR-SDLC.

7 Conclusion

Current modeling notations for lifecycle and system/software models are available, yet are typically 2D diagram-focused and run into inherent visual limitations, lacking the ability to comprehensively visualize the lifecycle, to do this contextually, and to visually integrate the lifecycle with its target models. VR-SDLC contributes a solution concept for an immersive visualization experience of SysE and SE lifecycle models, supporting diverse stakeholders with context-enhanced insights into the lifecycle. Via its nexus-based approach, VR-SDLC comprehensively portrays lifecycle model elements, relations, and diagrams while enhancing them with context. The solution concept was demonstrated with our prototype realization that showed support for diverse LML model lifecycles. Multiple lifecycle projects can be portrayed concurrently to support inter-project or program portfolio analysis and optimizations. Its hypermodeling capability was demonstrated with VR-SysML, showcasing how both a target model in SysML and its lifecycle in LML can be portrayed concurrently in VR. The VR-SDLC solution concept is abstract and flexible, and alternative modeling languages, data formats or integrations, and additional modeling elements or diagram types could be readily supported. VR-SDLC could be used to enhance or extend existing very capable 2D lifecycle and modeling tools such as Innoslate.

The benefits of our solution approach include comprehensive lifecycle model visualization, supporting comprehension, analysis, and contextualization. This includes heterogeneous side-by-side lifecycle models lifecycle with the target models, enabling the tailoring, traceability, and verification of lifecycle activities to the target model (e.g., UML/SysML) situation. Furthermore, the ability to load various lifecycle models in VR simultaneously supports cross-project or program management analysis. By portraying the lifecycle contextually and comprehensively, more inclusive and intuitive stakeholder collaboration and contextual insights are supported.

Future work includes realizing support for Asset Diagrams, model modification in VR, OSLC support, automated model verification, and a comprehensive empirical study.

Acknowledgements. The authors would like to thank Sasche Roelofs and Jonas Kling for their assistance with the design, implementation, evaluation, and figures. Further, we would like to thank Spec Innovations for providing academic access to their Innoslate tool and the accompanying sample data sets.

References

1. Lifecycle Modeling Language Steering Committee: Lifecycle Modeling Language (LML) Specification, Version 1.4, October 2022. https://www.lifecyclemodeling.org
2. Vaneman, W.K., Sellers, J.J., Dam, S.H.: Essential LML: lifecycle modeling language (LML): a thinking tool for capturing, connecting and communicating complex systems. SPEC Innovations (2018)
3. Object Management Group: BPMN Specification 2.0.2 (2014)
4. Object Management Group: Unified modeling language version 2.5.1 (2017)
5. Object Management Group: Systems modeling language version 1.6 (2019)
6. International Council on Systems Engineering (INCOSE): Systems Engineering Vision 2025. INCOSE (2014). https://web.archive.org/web/20190308160903. http://www.incose.org/docs/default-source/aboutse/se-vision-2025.pdf. Accessed 19 Mar 2024
7. Oberhauser, R., Pogolski, C.: VR-EA: virtual reality visualization of enterprise architecture models with ArchiMate and BPMN. In: Shishkov, B. (ed.) BMSD 2019. LNBIP, vol. 356, pp. 170–187. Springer, Cham (2019). https://doi.org/10.1007/978-3-030-24854-3_11
8. Oberhauser, R., Sousa, P., Michel, F.: VR-EAT: visualization of enterprise architecture tool diagrams in virtual reality. In: Shishkov, B. (ed.) BMSD 2020. LNBIP, vol. 391, pp. 221–239. Springer, Cham (2020). https://doi.org/10.1007/978-3-030-52306-0_14
9. Oberhauser, R., Baehre, M., Sousa, P.: VR-EA+TCK: visualizing enterprise architecture, content, and knowledge in virtual reality. In: Shishkov, B. (eds.) BMSD 2022. LNBIP, vol. 453, pp. 122–140. Springer, Cham (2022). https://doi.org/10.1007/978-3-031-11510-3_8
10. Oberhauser, R., Baehre, M., Sousa, P.: VR-EvoEA+BP: using virtual reality to visualize enterprise context dynamics related to enterprise evolution and business processes. In: Shishkov, B. (eds.) BMSD 2023. LNBIP, vol. 483, pp. 110–128. Springer, Cham (2023). https://doi.org/10.1007/978-3-031-36757-1_7
11. Oberhauser, R., Pogolski, C., Matic, A.: VR-BPMN: visualizing BPMN models in virtual reality. In: Shishkov, B. (ed.) BMSD 2018. LNBIP, vol. 319, pp. 83–97. Springer, Cham (2018). https://doi.org/10.1007/978-3-319-94214-8_6
12. Oberhauser, R.: VR-SysML: SysML model visualization and immersion in virtual reality. In: Proceedings of the International Conference of Modern Systems Engineering Solutions (MODERN SYSTEMS 2022), pp. 61–66. IARIA (2022)
13. Oberhauser, R.: VR-UML: the unified modeling language in virtual reality – an immersive modeling experience. In: Shishkov, B. (eds.) BMSD 2021. LNBIP, vol. 422, pp. 40–58. Springer, Cham (2021). https://doi.org/10.1007/978-3-030-79976-2_3
14. ISO/IEC/IEEE: ISO/IEC/IEEE 15288:2023 - Systems and software engineering — System life cycle processes (2023)
15. ISO/IEC/IEEE: ISO/IEC/IEEE 12207:2017 - Systems and software engineering — Software life cycle processes (2017)
16. Dori, D.: Model-based standards authoring: ISO 15288 as a case in point. Syst. Eng. **27**(2), 302–314 (2023). https://doi.org/10.1002/sys.21721
17. OASIS Standard: OSLC Core Version 3.0. Part 1: Overview (2021)
18. ISO: ISO/PAS 19450:2024 Automation systems and integration – Object- Process Methodology (2024)
19. Bajaj, M., Zwemer, D., Yntema, R., Phung, A., Kumar, A., Dwivedi, A., Waikar, M.: MBSE++—foundations for extended model-based systems engineering across system lifecycle. In: INCOSE International Symposium, vol. 26, no. 1, pp. 2429–2445 (2016)
20. Fisher, A., et al.: Model lifecycle management for MBSE. In: INCOSE International Symposium, vol. 24, pp. 207–229 (2014). https://doi.org/10.1002/j.2334-5837.2014.tb03145.x

21. Bork, D., Karagiannis, D., Pittl, B.: A survey of modeling language specification techniques. Inf. Syst. **87**, 101425 (2020). https://doi.org/10.1016/j.is.2019.101425
22. Vaneman, W.K.: Enhancing model-based systems engineering with the lifecycle modeling language. In: 2016 Annual IEEE Systems Conference (SysCon), pp. 1–7. IEEE (2016). https://doi.org/10.1109/SYSCON.2016.7490581
23. Stevie, L.: Business process model notation and the lifecycle modeling language (2023). https://www.lifecyclemodeling.org/updates/bpmn-and-lml. Accessed 19 Mar 2024
24. Akpan, I.J., Shanker, M.: The confirmed realities and myths about the benefits and costs of 3D visualization and virtual reality in discrete event modeling and simulation: a descriptive meta-analysis of evidence from research and practice. Comput. Ind. Eng. **112**, 197–211 (2017)
25. Narasimha, S., Dixon, E., Bertrand, J.W., Madathil, K.C.: An empirical study to investigate the efficacy of collaborative immersive virtual reality systems for designing information architecture of software systems. Appl. Ergon. **80**, 175–186 (2019)
26. Fonnet, A., Prie, Y.: Survey of immersive analytics. IEEE Trans. Vis. Comput. Graph. **27**(3), 2101–2122 (2019)
27. Innoslate. https://specinnovations.com/innoslate
28. Oberhauser, R.: VR-ProcessMine: immersive process mining visualization and analysis in virtual reality. In: The Fourteenth International Conference on Information, Process, and Knowledge Management (eKNOW 2022), pp. 29–36. IARIA (2022)
29. Oberhauser, R.: VR-V&V: immersive verification and validation support for traceability exemplified with ReqIF, ArchiMate, and test coverage. Int. J. Adv. Syst. Meas. **16**(3 & 4), 103–115 (2023)
30. Oberhauser, R.: VR-TestCoverage: test coverage visualization and immersion in virtual reality. In: Proceedings of the Fourteenth International Conference on Advances in System Testing and Validation Lifecycle (VALID 2022), pp. 1–6. IARIA (2022)
31. Oberhauser, R.: VR-GitCity: immersively visualizing Git repository evolution using a city metaphor in virtual reality. Int. J. Adv. Softw. **16**(3 & 4), 141–150 (2023)
32. Oberhauser, R.: VR-Git: Git repository visualization and immersion in virtual reality. In: Proceedings of the Seventeenth International Conference on Software Engineering Advances (ICSEA 2022), pp. 9–14. IARIA (2022)
33. Oberhauser, R.: VR-SysML+Traceability: immersive requirements traceability and test traceability with SysML to support verification and validation in virtual reality. Int. J. Adv. Softw. **16**(1 & 2), 23–35 (2023)
34. Hevner, A.R., March, S.T., Park, J., Ram, S.: Design science in information systems research. MIS Q. **28**(1), 75–105 (2004)

Smart Contracts as Data Quality Consensus Enforcers in Data Markets

Timothy Heideman[1,2], Indika Kumara[1,2(✉)] (iD), Willem-Jan Van Den Heuvel[1,2], and Damian Andrew Tamburri[1,3]

[1] Jheronimus Academy of Data Science, Sint Janssingel 92,
5211 DA 's-Hertogenbosch, Netherlands
{t.j.heideman,i.p.k.weerasinghadewage,
w.j.a.m.vdnHeuvel}@tilburguniversity.edu
[2] Tilburg University, Warandelaan 2, 5037 AB Tilburg, Netherlands
[3] Eindhoven University of Technology, 5612 AZ Eindhoven, Netherlands
d.a.tamburri@tue.nl

Abstract. Data markets offer a way for organizations to trade data products with each other. Data in data products typically ranges from carefully formatted raw data to comprehensive insights for business decision-making. However, the lack of trust between data sellers and buyers makes transactions in the data markets challenging. The agreements regarding the quality of the data offered and consumed must be established and automatically enforced. This work proposes a smart contract-based framework to enable peer-to-peer value exchange in data markets while enforcing consensus between data sellers and buyers on data quality. We developed the framework using the design science research methodology and implemented it using Solidity. The implementation was deployed and tested on the Ethereum blockchain platform. Moreover, we used semi-structured interviews with experts to validate and refine the proposed data transaction protocol.

Keywords: Data Market · Smart Contracts · Data Contracts · Data Sharing · Blockchain

1 Introduction

Data has been established as a valuable commodity that is being collected, processed, and sold by organizations and individuals for re-use by other parties [2,9,25]. While many open data sources exist, parties might be more inclined to purchase data from a third-party supplier due to higher data quality [28]. There are additional benefits to acquiring data from a third party, such as access to data that might not be readily available or would be expensive to collect. Such data from suppliers might also have undergone cleaning and curating, resulting in a data product that the buyer can use immediately.

Data marketplaces offer a way for organizations to trade their data. Data sellers can cater to a wide range of buyers in these marketplaces by providing products whose data ranges from raw data to comprehensive insights for business decision-making [25]. The commercial success of these data markets, however,

B. Shishkov (Ed.): BMSD 2024, LNBIP 523, pp. 130–148, 2024.
https://doi.org/10.1007/978-3-031-64073-5_9

is hampered by challenges, such as the limited pre-purchase information, lack of individual pricing models, the asymmetry between sellers and buyers of data, and Arrow's paradox [10,25]. The latter describes a scenario in which buyers need access to data to evaluate a data product's quality before deciding upon their purchase [1]. However, still, sellers are only willing to give the required access *after* said data product has been purchased.

Several literature reviews on the data market exist [10,17,25]. They analyzed existing data market platforms (e.g., private, consortiums, and independent), stakeholder roles (e.g., data sellers/providers, data buyers/consumers, and market brokers), and application domains. While many data platforms exist on the Web, they predominantly serve provider interests, offering one-sided information and neglecting consumer data needs, which impedes effective data exchange [13]. To be successful, data platforms must converge on integrating data offerings and consumer needs [13] and cater to diverse consumer preferences [25]. For example, some consumers prioritize reliability and standardization, while others seek novel insights for decision-making. These different needs can be better served through tailored agreements in peer-to-peer transactions. However, the quality and value assessment of data by potential buyers necessitates pre-purchase access, contradicting the premise of selling information [17,25]. This dilemma underscores the challenge of establishing trust and value in data transactions, which is critical for the future trajectory of data marketplaces.

To mitigate this problem, a data market can provide the capability to validate the quality of the data exchanged between parties who do not necessarily trust one another [10]. This enables the buyer to have information regarding the data quality of a dataset without having accessed it. At the same time, the data seller does not have to grant access to the buyer. Therefore, such data markets can enable the sale between these two parties who might not trust one another. However, most current data markets offer very little pre-purchase information or independent data testability [17,25].

Thus, in this paper, we aim to answer the question: *How can the consensus among parties regarding data quality validation be transparently enforced in peer-to-peer data transactions in data marketplaces?*. We propose a data transaction protocol that utilizes smart contracts and blockchain technology [19] to enable organizations to perform efficient data transactions and establish trust in the quality of the shared data. Due to its decentralized nature, security, and consensus mechanisms, blockchain technology helps address the traditional marketplace issues, including Arrow's paradox [8,10,13]. In particular, smart contracts enable the automated execution of actions upon certain conditions being met without trust, acting as an independent third party [3,27]. We implemented the proposed solution using the Solidity smart contract language and the Ethereum blockchain platform. We then conducted a semi-structured interview with experts to validate its usefulness and completeness. This paper is structured as follows. Section 2 describes the research methodology. Section 3 presents our smart-contract-based approach in detail. Section 4 describes the prototype implementation and the interview-based validation of the proposed solution. Finally, Sect. 5 reviews the related work, and Sect. 6 concludes the paper.

2 Research Methodology

This study uses Design Science Research Methodology (DSRM), which focuses on creating artifacts designed to solve specific problems [21]. We selected DSRM as we aim to create a methodology (i.e., the artifact) that can address the problem of enforcing consensus regarding data quality assessment in peer-to-peer data exchanges between organizations in data marketplaces. Following the DSRM process, we consulted the literature to identify the problem of achieving consensus among participants in data transactions and to design a smart contract-based solution to address the identified problem. We created a prototype implementation to demonstrate the feasibility of the proposed solution. A set of interviews with experts were conducted to validate the solution's practicality and utility.

2.1 Relevance of Blockchain Technology

To illustrate how smart contracts can enforce consensus and secure value exchange in peer-to-peer data transactions between organizations, we use a scenario where two parties want to engage in peer-to-peer data transactions. To achieve this, they first communicate the terms of sale, such as the price of the data and the required data quality. Together, they set up a data quality SLA (Service-Level Agreement) and define what processes will be followed when expectations are not met [18]. The parties then decide how to measure non-conformance to the agreed data quality requirements and the acceptability thresholds for each requirement. Since the data quality requirements are formalized and belong to one of the standard dimensions (e.g., accuracy and completeness), they can be objectively measured [12]. The parties write quality control code that they can both use to test whether the data meets the quality requirements. The parties decide upon the time expected to resolve the issue and, lastly, appoint a third-party mediator to resolve the dispute if the resolution times are not met.

It is important to establish whether blockchain technology is appropriate to help alleviate the problems related to transparently enforcing the consensus of data quality validation. For this purpose, we use the above scenario and follow Pedersen et al.'s ten-step decision path [20] for selecting the blockchain technology for a specific use case (see Figure 1).

Is there a need for a shared common database?: Yes. A shared database can be used as an immutable store for the smart data contracts that will represent the terms the parties have agreed upon.

Are multiple parties involved?: Yes. The parties involved are the data buyer, the data seller, and the mediator, who can step in if needed.

Do involved parties have conflicting interests/trust issues?: Yes. The data buyer wants the data but is not incentivized to pay for it once it receives the data. Similarly, the data seller is incentivized to demand payment, regardless of the quality of the data they deliver.

Parties can/want to avoid a trusted third party?: Yes. Having mentioned the issues of transacting through data market platforms, both parties want to engage in a peer-to-peer transaction.

Do rules governing system access differ between participants?: Yes. The mediator's unique role and the differing roles between the data buyer and seller make system access rules different.

Do transacting rules remain largely unchanged?: Yes. The parties' transacting rules should not be changed once established.

Is there a need for an objective, immutable log?: Yes. Immutable storage can store the terms of data-sharing contracts and enable the resolution of disputes by a third-party mediator. In addition, all transaction-related data that might be needed for mediation by a third party will be immutably stored in the shared database.

Is there a need for public access?: No. The peer-to-peer transaction details do not need to be made public outside of the business network in which the organizations operate.

Where is consensus determined? Inter-organizational or intra-organizational: In our motivation scenario, the consensus is determined between organizations. Thus, the inter-organizational case is applicable, needing a *permissioned public blockchain* [20]. However, if greater privacy and governance control are desired, groups of organizations might choose to use a *permissioned private blockchain* instead.

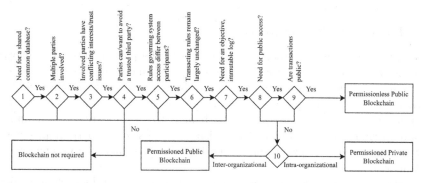

Fig. 1. Overview of the Blockchain decision path [20]

Based on these answers, we conclude that blockchain-based smart contracts have the potential to be a good solution to address our research problem.

2.2 Interview Protocol

We conducted semi-structured interviews while encouraging interviewees to express themselves freely. We followed the best practices of conducting such interviews [14]. To report on the interview findings, the evaluation structure of DSRM was used [23]. The goal of the interviews is to assess the proposed solution based on the following evaluation criteria:

1. *Completeness*: Is anything missing from the framework's design?
2. *Simplicity*: How does the simplicity or complexity of the framework affect its adoption?

3. *Understandability*: Is the framework comprehensible in its context?
4. *Operational Feasibility*: What are the possible challenges to integrating the framework in practice?
5. *Usefulness*: Are the identified issues addressed by the framework?

We conducted interviews virtually using Microsoft Teams, with the audio automatically transcribed. To protect the interviewees' privacy, their identities have been coded to the format 'E-#' as shown in Table 1.

Table 1. Overview of expert interviews

Interview	Type	Organization	ID	Years of Experience
1	Data Management	Software Company	E-1	12
2	Web3 Developer	Blockchain Company	E-2	11
3	Co-founder	Blockchain Company	E-3	7
4	Blockchain Consultant and Author	Innovation Foundation	E-4	30+
5	CIO	International Bank	E-5	10

2.3   Participant Recruitment Process

We applied purposive sampling [11] to identify the participants with relevant expertise and varied viewpoints. We chose this technique as our study's goal is not to make population-wide generalizations but to gather insights that will help further improve the proposed framework. According to Etikan et al. [11], this sampling technique provides particular benefit to the researcher with limited resources, time, or workforce at their disposal. We selected participants based on their knowledge and professional experience in blockchain, data management, and smart contracts.

Participants were recruited by exploring spaces active in blockchain or data management. Channels used for outreach were email and phone for parties who made themselves reachable through public information, such as research labs and publishers of literature. The potential for outreach was larger in anonymous channels on communication platforms such as Discord and Telegram. Two Discord community servers totaling 1100 members provided an opportunity for outreach. Two telegram groups focused on blockchain development and Web 3.0, totaling slightly over 9000 members combined, were also used to perform outreach. Unfortunately, the response rate in these communities was extremely low, and interview turnout was even lower.

The interviews started by asking the interviewees about their relevant background and inviting them to talk about their experiences. Then, they were presented with the proposed framework and asked to provide feedback. Interviews lasted 25 to 45 min, and their transcripts were immediately created while scrubbing personal or proprietary information. To extract the insights from the interview transcripts, we systematically applied thematic analysis [6].

2.4   Replication Package

The replication package of our study is available online[1]. It includes the implementation of smart contracts, interview transcripts, and the approval of ERB (Ethical Review Board) for conducting interviews.

3   Smart Contracts-Based Approach for Enforcing Consensus in Data Transactions

We propose a smart contract-based solution to facilitate peer-to-peer data transactions between organizations in data markets. Figure 2 provides a high-level overview of our smart contract-based solution. The subsequent sections will discuss it in detail.

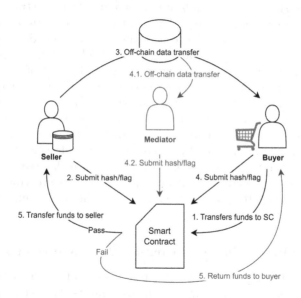

Fig. 2. A high-level overview of the data transaction process involving a smart contract and, if needed, mediator

3.1   Roles of Smart Contracts

As discussed in Sect. 2.1, a data market needs a permissioned (private or public) blockchain. The smart contracts used in such blockchain environments need to secure value exchange between parties. The data buyer should be protected against losing money when the data delivered does not meet the agreed-upon

---

[1] https://doi.org/10.5281/zenodo.11114114.

standards as recorded in the data quality SLA. The data seller should be protected from not receiving their funds when the delivered data meets all the objective quality standards defined in the SLA.

The smart contract acts as an escrow service and an immutable store of quality control procedures. This means the buyer transfers the agreed-upon sum to the smart contract, which then only pays it out if the negotiated terms on data quality are met. The smart contract enables both buyer and seller to engage in a data sale where following the negotiated terms on data quality is a requirement to complete the monetary transfer between the parties. This allows buyers and sellers to engage in data transactions knowing that the contract enforces adherence to the agreed quality standards and protects both buyer and seller by acting as an escrow service, discouraging misbehavior [15]. Parties are protected from stalemates as a neutral mediator is available in a dispute.

The smart contract secures the value exchange by acting as an escrow service. Payment to the smart contract indicates a commitment to the transaction to the seller. The smart contract requires a hash and a flag from both parties to release the payment. The retrieved and executed quality control code is stored in the smart contract. The hash is generated by applying a hash function to the quality control code. This proves the handling and acknowledgment of the agreed-upon quality control procedure. Executing the code on the data should result in a flag or completeness result, indicating whether the data has met the required standard. After being sent the data, which the seller has verified to meet the quality standard, the buyer completes the same quality control procedure and submits their hash and flag to the smart contract, releasing the payment to the seller. Adhering to this protocol enforces consensus between the parties by ensuring both parties perform the same quality control procedure. Therefore, there can be no dispute regarding the quality of the data, which is needed to deal with Arrow's paradox [1].

3.2   Roles of Players in Smart Contract Mediated Data Transactions

Data Seller. The data seller (or the data provider) offers the data to be sold. They are responsible for ensuring that the data meets the specifications agreed upon with the data buyer. The data seller interacts with the smart contract by requesting the quality control code required to verify the data quality before delivery. Furthermore, the data seller submits the result of executing the quality control code and a hash value of the code. The data seller interacts with the data buyer when transferring the data to the buyer in an off-chain manner. The smart contract releases payment to the data seller when both parties achieve consensus regarding the quality of the delivered data and the steps required to reach that conclusion. In the event of a dispute, the data buyer interacts with the data seller to try and achieve consensus by ensuring both parties submit identical hashes and results, proving they have done the same work. Failing to do so within the agreed-upon time limit notifies a selected third-party mediator who will communicate with the data buyer and the data seller and interact with the smart contract to arbitrate and resolve the dispute.

Data Buyer. The data buyer (or the data consumer) is the party interested in obtaining the data product(s) the data seller offers. The data buyer must ensure that the data received from the data seller meets the specifications agreed upon with the data seller. The data buyer interacts with the smart contract by sending funds over to the smart contract, which acts as an escrow service and signals commitment to the transaction to the data seller. Upon receiving the data from the data seller, the data buyer requests the quality control code stored in the smart contract and uses it to verify the quality of the data. Then, they submit their hash and quality control results to the smart contract. If the received data does not meet the agreed-upon specifications as verified using the quality control code, sending the result and hash to the smart contract will lead to the smart contracting detecting a lack of consensus. They will enter dispute mode, where parties can re-submit their hashes within a defined period before the mediator is requested to resolve the dispute. In the case of such a dispute, the data seller and buyer should strive to identify the cause of the issue to achieve consensus so that the transaction can be resolved.

Third-Party Mediator. The mediator is vital in resolving disputes between the data buyer and seller. Their involvement is required only when parties fail to adhere to the protocols required by the smart contract and fail to achieve consensus on their own. They interact with the buyer and seller to obtain the exchanged data. They interact with the smart contract by requesting the quality control code to check the data received and exchanged between the parties. The mediator submits the hash and results as an outcome of the quality control process to the smart contract, breaking the stalemate and resolving the dispute.

3.3   Smart Contract Mediated Data Transaction Workflow

The contract must be created before any data transactions can be made. Once parties have formulated their agreements about the terms of sale and the quality requirements for creating a data quality SLA, either party will write the quality control code used to verify conformance to the requirements. The buyer deploys the smart contract. Following the agreement with the seller, the relevant parameters are processed. The parameters include:

- The agreed price of the data product to be delivered is expressed in the currency utilized by the smart contract.
- The quality control code (as a string value).
- The amount of time the buyer and seller have given themselves to resolve the dispute independently.
- and the addresses of all involved parties, including the mediator (are used to identify the parties and their roles).

Once the contract is deployed, parties verify that it represents their agreements, and the transaction process can commence. The BPMN (Business Process Model and Notation) process model in Fig. 3 illustrates the transaction process.

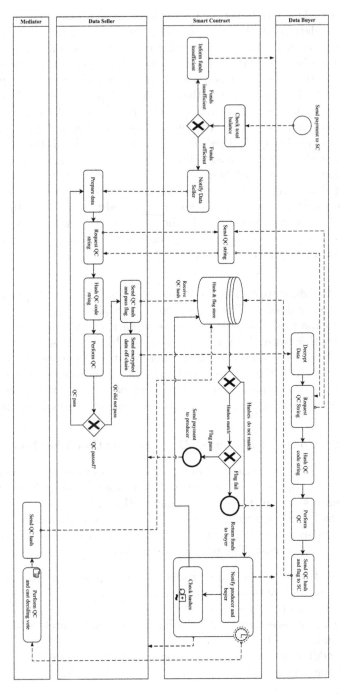

Fig. 3. The BPMN model for data transfer utilizing a smart contract to enforce consensus between participants. QC: data control code

The transaction is initiated with the buyer transferring the required amount to the seller, which is rejected if it does not meet the required amount. This prompts the seller to prepare the data, retrieve the quality control code, and execute and hash it. If in order, the seller sends the hash and flag to the smart contract. The data is then sent off-chain to the data buyer. The buyer then requests the quality control code and performs the same steps, submitting the hash and flag to the smart contract. If the protocol was followed, both should match, meaning there is a consensus between the parties regarding the process and result, and funds are released to the seller by the smart contract. If the hashes or flags do not match, a timer starts, and parties have the agreed-upon time to resolve the issue and resubmit their hashes and flags until they can reach a consensus. Suppose this is not achieved within the allotted time. In that case, the smart contract notifies the third-party mediator who will obtain the data, perform the same quality control procedure, and submit the resulting hash and flag, releasing the fund to either the buyer or seller, depending on the outcome.

Adopting this process encourages data sellers to ensure their delivery of data products aligns with the pre-established quality standards. Non-compliance could deny the data seller's payment. On the other hand, transferring funds to the smart contract before any data is sent shows commitment to the transaction with the data seller. Parties might disagree regarding the quality of the result. To circumvent any possible ambiguities regarding the verification methods employed by each party, the process mandates using the quality control code immutably stored inside the smart contract on the blockchain. This approach fosters both transparency and trust among the parties. The escrow service performed by the smart contract, combined with the role of the independent mediator, ensures that parties have a fair resolution of the transaction in case of a dispute. If the data buyer submits incorrect claims of failing quality control, the data seller is assured of payment after a mediator verifies the data quality. Conversely, the data buyer is protected against paying for non-complying data. In case of a dispute, the mediator might conclude the data as non-complying, and the smart contracts will release the funds held in escrow back to the buyer.

Based on the data transaction process, Algorithm 1 expresses the functionality of the smart contract, highlighting the initialization of variables, functions, and conditions dictating the actions of the smart contract.

4   Evaluation

In this section, we first present the prototype implementation of our smart-contract-based approach and the estimation of Gas costs for running the proposed smart contract using the prototype. Next, we discuss the findings from the semi-structured interviews.

4.1   Proof of Concept

To verify the feasibility of the proposed solution, we developed and tested a proof of concept of the smart contract. The code was written in Solidity[2] and

---

[2] https://soliditylang.org/.

Algorithm 1. DataTransactionAuditor smart contract

1: **procedure** INITIALIZE(dataQualityCode, dataSeller, mediator, minAmount, deadlineHours)
2:     $dataQualityCode \leftarrow dataQualityCode$
3:     $dataSeller \leftarrow dataSeller$
4:     $dataBuyer \leftarrow msg.sender$
5:     $mediator \leftarrow mediator$
6:     $minAmount \leftarrow minAmount$
7:     $deadlineHours \leftarrow deadlineHours$
8: **end procedure**

9: **procedure** CREATETRANSACTION
10:     **if** $msg.value \geq minAmount$ and $msg.sender == dataBuyer$ **then**
11:         Hold payment in smart contract
12:         Create a new transaction with initial values
13:     **end if**
14: **end procedure**

15: **procedure** SUBMITHASHES(transactionId, codeHash, resultFlag)
16:     Store $codeHash$ and $resultFlag$ for the invoking party (dataBuyer or dataSeller)
17:     **if** Both parties submitted hashes and flags **then**
18:         **if** hashes and flags match **then**
19:             **if** resultFlag is true **then**
20:                 Release payment to dataSeller
21:             **else**
22:                 Refund payment to dataBuyer
23:             **end if**
24:         **else**
25:             **if** disputeDeadline is not set **then**
26:                 Start dispute timer
27:             **end if**
28:         **end if**
29:     **end if**
30: **end procedure**

31: **procedure** MEDIATORSUBMITHASHES(transactionId, codeHash, resultFlag)
32:     **if** $codeHash$ matches with either buyer's or seller's hash and their corresponding flag matches $resultFlag$ **then**
33:         **if** resultFlag is true **then**
34:             Release payment to dataSeller
35:         **else**
36:             Refund payment to dataBuyer
37:         **end if**
38:     **end if**
39: **end procedure**

can be found in our online appendix (see Sect. 2.4). We used Remix IDE[3] to test the contract. Remix allows for deploying smart contracts written in Solidity in a simulated environment. These environments run the Ethereum Virtual Machine (EVM), the runtime environment required to execute smart contracts on the Ethereum network. The smart contract can, therefore, be deployed on both the public Ethereum network and Ethereum Enterprise, the private permissioned blockchain variant. An EVM runs on every active node in the Ethereum network. Remix IDE offers several virtual environments to test, each containing mul-

---

[3] https://remix.ethereum.org/.

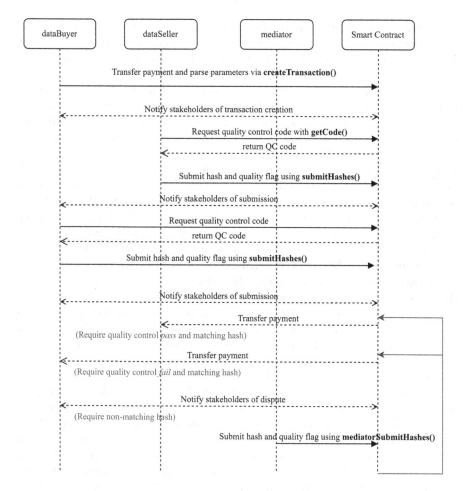

Fig. 4. The smart contract code implementation of the transaction process

tiple addresses charged with 100 ETH (Ether), a digital currency. Remix IDE, therefore, allows for unrestricted testing and evaluation of the smart contract's functionality. It also provides detailed transaction logs, debugging of function calls, and input transaction parameters.

As shown in Fig. 4, the data buyer deploys the contract in agreement with the data seller, filling in the parameters according to specifications. The smart contract is now deployed and contains the addresses of the *dataSeller*, *dataBuyer*, and *mediator*. The contract also has stored *minAmount*, the minimum payment required by the *dataSeller* in Wei (the smallest denomination of ETH), needed for the transaction to be created. Also, it has been recorded what number of *deadlineHours* both parties have given themselves before the mediator is notified.

The *dataSeller* can now transact ETH to the smart contract, which will be accepted if the amount is equal to or higher than *minAmount* using *createTransaction()*. The transaction is reverted otherwise or if an address other than the buyer tries to transfer funds to the smart contract. With the smart contract having received sufficient funds, a unique *transactionId* is created, and it emits an event notifying all stakeholders, including the data seller, of a new pending transaction.

The data seller prepares the requested data for delivery. The seller can now call the public view function *getCode()* to retrieve the code parties agreed to use to verify the dataset's quality. The execution of this code and its positive outcome should signify that the data is up to the pre-established standard agreed upon by both parties. The seller now hashes the retrieved code off-chain using a hashing algorithm decided upon with the buyer. An example of such a hashing algorithm would be SHA-256, which is compatible with the bytes32 format requirement used by this implementation. Anticipating the possibility of deployment on the public Ethereum network and recognizing that solidity does support hashing functions, processing strings can be costly for large strings and becomes more expensive with every added byte of data sent in a transaction. It is, therefore, recommended that the data that needs to be transacted once a contract is deployed be minimized. Assuming the data seller's quality control passes on the data set, they prepare to send the data to the buyer. The seller and *only* the seller can now call *submitHashes* and parses the relevant *transactionId*, the *codeHash* and the outcome of running the code on the data. In this case, that outcome is represented by *true* or *false* representing a pass or fail, respectively. Only the buyer or seller can use this function. Any other addresses that try to call this function will have their transaction reverted.

At this point, the data will be transferred off-chain to the data buyer. They will perform the same operations as the data seller concerning retrieving the quality control code, hashing the code block, and observing the outcome of executing the code. They are now able to submit their *codeHash* and *resultFlag* using *submitHashes()*. If the hashes and flags match with a passing flag, the transaction is completed by transferring the funds associated with the *transactionId* to the data seller. If the hashes match with a failing flag, the buyer is refunded their funds. In either case, *isResolved* is set to *true*, and further transactions to the contract about that particular *transactionId* are rejected. If the hashes or flags do not match, the contract notifies stakeholders of the conflict through the emission of an event and sets the deadline for the dispute to be resolved by both buyer and seller.

Parties can attempt to achieve consensus by resubmitting their hashes and flags using *submitHashes* until they match, indicating consensus has been achieved. If a hash is submitted after the deadline has passed, the third party will be notified, and the contract will not accept any more submissions from either the buyer or seller. The mediator will now communicate with the buyer and seller off-chain to obtain the data and will use the public view function *dataQualityCode()* to perform the same procedure as the buyer and seller. The resulting hash and flag can be submitted to the contract by the mediator only using *mediatorSubmitHashes*. If it matches either party's hash and flag, the pass flag value will decide whether the buyer is refunded or if the seller is paid and the transaction *isResolved*.

Table 2. Gas costs of Solidity functions in USD on May 12th, 2023

Method Name	Txn Gas	Exec. Gas	Avg. Exec. (USD)	Fast Exec. (USD)
deploy	1,856,203	1,667,993	$43.13	$177.87
createTransaction	158,534	137,470	$3.55	$15.19
submitHashes	81,616	59,772	$1.55	$7.82
resolve transaction	115,134	93,290	$2.41	$11.03
mediatorSubmitHashes	68,455	46,599	$1.20	$6.56
getCode		16758	$0.43	$1.61

4.2 Cost Estimation

All functions in the smart contract implementation were successfully tested. When conducting transactions on the public Ethereum and Ethereum Enterprise network, a unit of measure called Gas is used to represent the computational effort required to process a transaction. We used the Gas prices of Ethereum Gas Stations to estimate the Gas use and the costs of deploying the smart contract on the public Ethereum network. The prices for average and fast transactions were taken on the 12th of May, 2023. The price for average execution (under 5 min) was 14.3 Gwei, and the price for fast execution (under 2 min) was 53 Gwei. With a closing price of 1,808.02 on the 12th of May, 2023, 1 Gwei would equal 0.00000180802 USD. The estimated costs of running the transacting functions of the smart contract on the public Ethereum network are displayed in Table 2. For this test, an 186-byte string was parsed as the parameter for the quality control code. Deploying smart contact was the most expensive operation, while the access quality control code was the least costly.

4.3 Interview Results

The interview transcripts were analyzed for evidence of support or opposition towards the evaluation characteristics using the DSRM evaluation reporting structure [23]. Participants' opinions gathered during the semi-structured interviews were classified as positive or negative regarding the evaluation characteristics of completeness, simplicity, understandability, operational feasibility, and usefulness. Table 3 summarizes the interview results.

The completeness was evaluated through the experts' ability to identify if something was missing from our framework. One expert noticed the lack of automated refund logic outside the scenarios discussed. While not specific to our framework, another expert expressed the need to define how the code would be implemented on both sides, stating code interpreter or hardware issues. There were no particular comments regarding the improvement of the simplicity of the framework. Participants found the framework simple enough that little to no extra clarification was often needed. The framework was generally claimed to be well-understood by the experts stating, *"I can see you probably streamlined this*

Table 3. Evaluation results

Evaluation Characteristic	Case evidence (No. comments)	Prominent comments
Completeness	✓x 5	E-1: *"I think this is the most thorough proposal I've seen of, like, what does a successful data contract look like?"*
	✗x 2	E-2: *"One vulnerability is if the [mediator] could be influenced in any way, and that would be in the advantage of one side or the other."*
Simplicity	✓x 2	E-4: *"But for me, this is really good, simplified, I can follow it."*
	✗x 1	E-2: *"You'd have to probably really earmark the industries that you want to double down on, and probably you would need variations of the same protocol depending on [the] industry and you would, for it to blossom, you obviously need it adopted."*
Understandability	✓x 4	E-3: *"I can see you probably streamlined this a lot already, so, you know, it's very easy for me to understand, you know?"*
	✗x 1	E-5: *"so it's the full code implementation that you get from the contract and there. Yeah. And that's for me a little bit hard to understand "*
Operational feasibility	✓x 3	E-3: *"I think this is very scalable, this is pretty simple."*
	✗x 3	E-2: *"...historically speaking, there's usually an imbalance of power. So the terms of what quality is and how to interact are determined by one partner as opposed to this kind of, like, you know, uh, transparent collaborative."*
Usefulness	✓x 4	E-4: *"Yeah, it's a yes...This is a good, uh, set up for [companies who want access to data]. And it's not too much. It's not too complicated."*
	✗x 1	E-4: *"But again, this model is far from reality. ... People have to believe that this can also work in their own in reality."*

✓indicates evidence of support towards the evaluation characteristic in a comment
✗ indicates evidence of opposition towards the evaluation characteristic in a comment

a lot already, so, you know, it's very easy for me to understand, you know?" (E-3), *"From an academic standpoint, I like this, and in theory, it all makes sense to me."* (E-1).

The perceived simplicity helped the experts draw parallels between their professional experience, resulting in various opinions regarding the operational feasibility. A participant stated how the framework is very transparent and collaborative, which, while desirable, *"it didn't reflect the world that I've come from, so it's a very futuristic view."* (E-2). This comment is a strong indicator of the operational challenges of the framework on the basis that it requires transparency and collaboration from the involved parties, which cannot always be expected from practical business scenarios. On the other hand, a participant saw very little friction in putting the framework to use *"I think this is very scalable, this is pretty simple"*(E-3). Another operational feasibility concern seemed to mainly stem from defining the agreements between the parties *"I think the problems that still arise are around actually defining that QC."*. Another expert suggested parties should go beyond that definition and reduce the risk of losing consensus by agreeing on implementing the quality control code at the hardware level *"..that is code, but that is on an abstraction level. What is totally different is what is dealt with on the processor level ... that needs to be done in the same way. Otherwise, the outcome of the process is totally different."* (E-5).

From the interviews, it becomes apparent that the main concerns voiced by the experts concern parties agreeing and creating consensus on all the aspects of the transaction, which requires identical performance from both parties. Therefore, ignoring costs, it is attractive to move as many actions of the transaction on-chain as possible. Considering the experts' feedback, the framework was adjusted to clearly describe under which conditions any funds should automatically be returned to the buyer (i.e., no incoming data within seven days of the initial deposit of funds.)

5   Related Work

This section reviews the data market studies that use smart contracts. SDTE [7] is a blockchain-based data trading platform that allows data sellers to provide access to the analysis of their raw data to data buyers and brokers without disclosing raw data contents. ViSDM [8] is a decentralized crowdsourcing marketplace where the crowd collects and trades the data to the data consumers. It uses smart contracts to implement market operations such as negotiating and distributing data prices, managing the data asset catalog, and making payments. Serrano [22] proposed using blockchain technology to implement three levels (data abstraction, value-added services, and authenticity) of data validation and verification in data markets. Charles and Delgado [4] employed blockchain technology to share or trade health data in data markets transparently so that patients can control and get visibility into the uses of their health data. PeB-DaMa [16] used a consortium blockchain-based model to support trading Car data. It focuses on data pricing strategies and optimizing data trading and welfare in the market. SPDS [26] utilized blockchain technology to support auditing usage of smart gird data and smart contracts to implement various data access and usage policies. ProvNet [5] used the networked blockchain model to store data provenance information while avoiding revealing raw data contents. Finally, Song et al. [24] conducted a systematic literature review on blockchain-based models for data sharing and exchange, including data markets. They noticed the blockchain had been used in scenarios such as implementing fine-grained data access control, making the shared data readily available, and improving data interoperability through enforcing data governance policies and standards.

Compared with the above studies, we developed a smart contract-based data transaction protocol to enable data sellers and buyers (or brokers) to establish and enforce the data quality SLAs transparently. Smart contracts, being transparent and unchangeable, guarantee the execution of agreements and the safe distribution of funds, promoting self-governance and confidence in the absence of external meddling. Moreover, a blockchain-based system can address the information asymmetry by making consumers' needs more visible to providers or enabling the negotiation of the terms of sale. It can also prevent Arrow's paradox by adjusting the terms of sale to a system where an asynchronous exchange of value takes place, and data quality is guaranteed.

6   Conclusion and Future Work

We presented an approach using blockchain technology and smart contracts to facilitate efficient and secure peer-to-peer transactions in data marketplaces. We presented a smart contract-based protocol for exchanging data between data sellers and buyers while enforcing the consensus regarding the quality of the delivered data. Smart contracts can reduce the risks associated with deploying data to a third-party platform and the risk of purchasing data that does not meet the pre-established quality requirements. The proof of concept demonstrated the functionality of the proposed solution. Moreover, while the proposed framework was generally well-received by experts, concerns were raised regarding its operational feasibility. In future work, we plan to study the proposed framework's scalability and performance in relation to its capability to support the current transaction volumes of traditional data marketplaces. Furthermore, we plan to extend the proposed data transaction validation process to prevent revealing sensitive information about buyers and sellers. Moreover, we will study alternative blockchain platforms and techniques for minimizing the Gas cost of using a specific platform.

Acknowledgments. This project has been financially supported by the Dutch Research Council (NWO) as part of the CHAIN project within the program 'Responsible Innovation. Designing for public values in a digital world.'

References

1. Arrow, K.J.: Economic Welfare and the Allocation of Resources for Invention, pp. 219–236. Macmillan Education UK, London (1972)
2. Busby, E., Hammoud, T., Rose, J., Prashad, R.: The evolution of online user data. The Boston Consulting Group (2012)
3. Buterin, V., et al.: A next-generation smart contract and decentralized application platform. White Paper **3**(37), 2–1 (2014)
4. Charles, W.M., Delgado, B.M.: Health datasets as assets: Blockchain-based valuation and transaction methods. Blockchain in Healthcare Today **5** (2022)
5. Chenli, C., Tang, W., Gomulka, F., Jung, T.: Provnet: networked bi-directional blockchain for data sharing with verifiable provenance. J.Parall. Distrib. Comput. **166**, 32–44 (2022)

6. Clarke, V., Braun, V., Hayfield, N.: Thematic analysis. Qual. psychol.: a practical guide to research methods **222**(2015), 248 (2015)
7. Dai, W., Dai, C., Choo, K.K.R., Cui, C., Zou, D., Jin, H.: Sdte: a secure blockchain-based data trading ecosystem. IEEE Trans. Inf. Forensics Secur. **15**, 725–737 (2020)
8. Daliparthi, V.S.S.A., Momen, N., Tutschku, K., De Prado, M.: Visdm 1.0: Vision sovereignty data marketplace a decentralized platform for crowdsourcing data collection and trading. In: Proceedings of the 2023 ACM Conference on Information Technology for Social Good, p. 374–383. GoodIT '23, Association for Computing Machinery, New York, NY, USA (2023)
9. Demchenko, Y., Los, W., de Laat, C., et al.: Data as economic goods: definitions, properties, challenges, enabling technologies for future data markets. ITU J.: ICT Disc. **2**(23) (2018)
10. Driessen, S.W., Monsieur, G., Van den Heuvel, W.J.: Data market design: a systematic literature review. IEEE Access **10**, 33123–33153 (2022)
11. Etikan, I., Musa, S.A., Alkassim, R.S., et al.: Comparison of convenience sampling and purposive sampling. Am. J. Theor. Appl. Stat. **5**(1), 1–4 (2016)
12. Gualo, F., Rodriguez, M., Verdugo, J., Caballero, I., Piattini, M.: Data quality certification using iso/iec 25012: industrial experiences. J. Syst. Softw. **176**, 110938 (2021)
13. Hayashi, T., Ohsawa, Y.: Teeda: an interactive platform for matching data providers and users in the data marketplace. Information **11**(4), 218 (2020)
14. Hove, S.E., Anda, B.: Experiences from conducting semi-structured interviews in empirical software engineering research. In: 11th IEEE International Software Metrics Symposium (METRICS'05), pp. 10–pp. IEEE (2005)
15. Hu, X., Lin, Z., Whinston, A.B., Zhang, H.: Hope or hype: on the viability of escrow services as trusted third parties in online auction environments. Inf. Syst. Res. **15**(3), 236–249 (2004)
16. Ingrid Bauer-Hänsel, Qianyu Liu, C.J.T., Schwabe, G.: Designing a blockchain-based data market and pricing data to optimize data trading and welfare. Int. J. Electron. Comm. **28**(1), 3–30 (2024)
17. Liang, F., Yu, W., An, D., Yang, Q., Fu, X., Zhao, W.: A survey on big data market: pricing, trading and protection. IEEE Access **6**, 15132–15154 (2018)
18. Loshin, D.: Observing data quality service level agreements. Tech. rep. (2009)
19. Nakamoto, S.: Bitcoin: A peer-to-peer electronic cash system. Decentralized business review, p. 21260 (2008)
20. Pedersen, A.B., Risius, M., Beck, R., et al.: A ten-step decision path to determine when to use blockchain technologies. MIS Q. Exec. **18**(2), 99–115 (2019)
21. Peffers, K., Tuunanen, T., Rothenberger, M.A., Chatterjee, S.: A design science research methodology for information systems research. J. Manag. Inf. Syst. **24**(3), 45–77 (2007)
22. Serrano, W.: Verification and validation for data marketplaces via a blockchain and smart contracts. Blockchain: Res. Appl. **3**(4), 100100 (2022)
23. Shrestha, A., Cater-Steel, A., Toleman, M.: How to communicate evaluation work in design science research? an exemplar case study. ACIS (2014)
24. Song, R., Xiao, B., Song, Y., Guo, S., Yang, Y.: A survey of blockchain-based schemes for data sharing and exchange. IEEE Trans. on Big Data **9**(6), 1477–1495 (2023)
25. Stahl, F., Schomm, F., Vomfell, L., Vossen, G.: Marketplaces for digital data: Quo vadis? Tech. rep., ERCIS Working Paper (2015)
26. Wang, Y., et al.: Spds: a secure and auditable private data sharing scheme for smart grid based on blockchain. IEEE Trans. Industr. Inf. **17**(11), 7688–7699 (2021)

27. Zheng, Z., et al.: An overview on smart contracts: challenges, advances and plat-forms. Futur. Gener. Comput. Syst. **105**, 475–491 (2020)
28. Zhu, Y., Buchmann, A.: Evaluating and selecting web sources as external infor-mation resources of a data warehouse. In: Proceedings of the Third International Conference on Web Information Systems Engineering, 2002. WISE 2002, pp. 149–160. IEEE (2002)

From Mutualism to Amensalism: A Case Study of Blockchain and Digital Identity Wallets

Tamara Roth[1,2(✉)] ⓘ, Alexander Rieger[1,2] ⓘ, and Alexandra Hoess[2] ⓘ

[1] Sam M. Walton College of Business, University of Arkansas, 220 N McIlroy Ave #301, Fayetteville, AR 72701, USA
{TRoth,ARieger}@walton.uark.edu

[2] Interdisciplinary Centre for Security, Reliability, and Trust, University of Luxembourg, 29 Av. John F. Kennedy, 1855 Kirchberg, Luxembourg
alexandra.hoess@uni.lu

Abstract. Innovation with emerging technologies is often challenging. They are still evolving and many are surrounded by unbalanced claims and hyperbole, which give rise to ambiguity and complicate adoption. These difficulties become even more pronounced when organizations attempt to introduce two loosely coupled emerging technologies. Building on a six-year case-study of the European Blockchain Partnership that attempted to simultaneously introduce blockchain and digital identity wallets, we flesh out the evolution their relationship. Our analysis surfaces a complex material-discursive process that first only discursively and later also materially de-coupled the two technologies along three population ecology principles for species interaction: technological mutualism, technological commensalism, and technological amensalism. Our study contributes an information systems perspective on the enactment and evolution of loosely coupled emerging technologies. Moreover, we use insights from population ecology to better explain and understand the underlying mechanisms.

Keywords: Organizing Vision Theory · Emerging IT · Loose Coupling · Mutualism · Commensalism · Amensalism

1 Introduction

Organizations are in constant need for innovation to keep up with the dynamic changes in their environments [1]. This need turns some into voracious consumers of emerging information technologies (IT). These technologies come to the marketplace with high promises but in an "[often] immature state, puzzling as to [their] benefits, future prospects, and long-term form" [2]. This ambiguity makes emerging IT malleable and leaves room for interpretation regarding their application in an organizational context [3, 4]. Organizations typically use this room to envision how the technology could address pertinent business problematics [5, 6]. Over time, the ensuing sense-making processes may surface important organizational needs and spotlight specific expectations in a so-called organizing vision (OV), i.e., "a focal community idea for the application of information technology in organizations" [2].

© The Author(s), under exclusive license to Springer Nature Switzerland AG 2024
B. Shishkov (Ed.): BMSD 2024, LNBIP 523, pp. 149–165, 2024.
https://doi.org/10.1007/978-3-031-64073-5_10

Earlier OVs are often incoherent and replete with variegated discursive frames and value-laden buzzwords. This makes it difficult for organizations to assess their true potential [4, 7]. At the same time, the resulting frame diversity allows organization across multiple industries to engage with the IT [3, 4] and can also facilitate a discursive connection to other (emerging) technologies. Parameswaran et al. (2023), for instance, explore complementary frames for emerging technologies that are tightly coupled, i.e., codependent, using the example of RFID tags and RFID readers [8]. Such co-dependent technologies have typically not been developed as a "single-whole" innovation, such as enterprise resource planning systems with their various modularized components [8]. Instead, they are each adopted in two different adopter communities where their joint adoption boosts value creation but where on their own, each IT would have little value [9, 10]. The early stages of this co-dependence are influenced by internal-external influencers who introduce resonant discursive elements into the enacting organization and inform the respective innovation communities about the material outcomes in the organization [8].

Little is known, however, about how these processes play out when the emerging ITs are 'loosely coupled' and each can create substantial value on their own. While singular studies exist that elaborate on the transition pathways of innovations with a similar trajectory, the focal innovations typically have a higher degree of materiality than many of the emerging innovations [11, 12]. We thus engage in a theory-building effort and ask the following research question:

How can organizations in enactment fields discursively and materially navigate loose coupling between emerging ITs?

To build our theory, we conduct an inductive longitudinal case study of the European Blockchain Services Infrastructure (EBSI) [13, 14], which brought together two loosely coupled emerging ITs: blockchain technology and digital identity wallets. Since all three authors of this work were involved with EBSI in different functions over the last six years, we could gain particularly rich insights into how the EBSI project made sense of initially overlapping frames between the organizing visions for the two technologies and materialized these frames. We could also observe the further development of this joint materialization once it became clear that blockchain was not required for the success of digital identity wallets and certain members of the wallet innovation community began to advocate for separation.

Our findings from the project are twofold. First, we find that loosely coupled, emerging ITs require continuous sense-making and materialization processes to maintain discursive resonance and preserve material complementarity. Second, we find that these technologies will retain "evidence of separateness and identity" [9] and their individual development, which can affect their co-development. Especially when resonance is difficult to achieve or the community discourses change drastically, the initial mutually beneficial relationship (mutualism) can evolve to benefit only one technology (commensalism) and even actively harm one technology to ensure the survival of the other (amensalism). We translate these findings into a conceptual model for the material-discursive co-enactment of loosely coupled ITs, adding an information systems perspective to innovation with complementary technologies that have a higher degree of material malleability.

The rest of the paper is structured as follows. The theoretical background section provides an overview of the key concepts. The research method section then presents details on our case study, data collection and analysis. In the next section, we present the insights from our case study before we synthesize our insights into a conceptual model in the discussion section. After discussing theoretical contributions and practical implications, we present boundary conditions and conclude with a summary of key insights.

2 Theoretical Background

2.1 Sense-Making of IT Organizing Visions

Organizing visions are typically created by innovation communities and aim to provide an explanation for the use and function of emerging information technologies beyond rational-economic considerations [15, 16]. They provide a joint account of "the innovation's existence and purpose relative to its broader social, technical, and economic context" [2]. Their goal is to reduce uncertainty concerning an emerging IT through extensive innovation community sense-making. This sense-making gauges the emerging IT's potential to address specific business problematics and envisions various other uses based on the IT's alleged technical capabilities [3, 4]. The resulting interpretations often imbue the organizing vision with wishful and unbalanced claims that manifest in variegated discursive frames, i.e., linguistic constructs that produce specific meaning, and value-laden buzzwords [4]. While these frames and buzzwords can help the IT achieve contagion, they limit the organizing vision's coherence and can be a source of confusion [3, 5, 17].

Organizations interested in enacting emerging technologies thus need to engage in their own sense-making processes to cut through the thicket of discursive frames and buzzwords [4]. The goals of this organization-level sense-making are typically the same as those of community-level sense-making: (1) interpretation, i.e., gauging the usefulness of specific discursive frames; (2) legitimation, i.e., demonstrating the capability of the emerging IT to address pertinent business problematics; and (3) mobilization, i.e., gaining support and momentum for further diffusion of the IT organizing vision [2, 7, 8]. Organization-level sense-making often benefits from early material enactment of the organizing vision, which helps organizations determine if specific discursive frames should be retained or discarded [3, 18]. This materialization of the discourse can transpire in different forms, ranging from text, media, and intonations to artifacts and implementations. In whichever form, it is relevant to better understand the practical implications of the produced meaning [19].

Organizational sense-making processes are often accompanied by sense-giving, sense-taking, and sense-breaking processes [20]. Sense-giving pushes specific discursive frames that align with interpretations of trusted sense-givers [3, 21, 22]. Sense-taking imports discursive frames relevant to achieving desired organizational outcomes [20, 22, 23]. Sense-breaking, in turn, allows to remove dissonant elements when the selected frames do not resonate with the wider organizational context [4].

2.2 Loose Coupling and Population Ecology Principles of Species Interaction

Organizing visions are typically created for single-whole innovations. However, they can also be constructed for two ITs when they have a high degree of (perceived) complementarity [8]. A good example are co-dependent technologies, such as RFID chips and readers that are tightly coupled and depend on co-enactment in different user communities [8–10]. However, joint organizing visions may also emerge for independent and loosely coupled technologies that can be enacted separately [24–26].

Loose coupling is often defined as "elements [of a system] that are responsive but retain evidence of separateness and identity [where they] affect each other [...] suddenly (rather than continuously), occasionally (rather than constantly), negligibly (rather than significantly), indirectly (rather than directly), and eventually (rather than immediately)" [9]. It can also be defined according to the responsiveness and distinctiveness of the elements. Where elements are responsive but not distinct, the system is tightly coupled. Where they are distinct but not responsive, the system is considered decoupled. Only where systems are both responsive and distinct, they are loosely coupled [9, 25]. Loose coupling is possible on a material level, which is typically not influenced by community discourse, but also on a discursive level, which often derives inspiration from the innovation community [9, 10].

Loosely coupled technologies often behave in a way that mirrors basic population ecology principles for species interaction, that is, how certain factors influence their interaction [27, 28] and [29]. For instance, when two technologies benefit from being combined, the relationship can be described as technological mutualism [27, 28, 30]. When only one technology benefits but the other is unaffected, the relationship can be described as technological commensalism. This often happens when a host technology functions as a springboard for the commensal technology [27, 28, 31]. Technology amensalism emerges when one technology is actively inhibited, for instance due to bad reputation, but the other technology is not [32, 33].

2.3 The Co-Evolution of Blockchain Technology and Digital Identity Wallets

Two technologies that are particularly suited for the study of co-enactment of two loosely coupled emerging technologies are blockchain and digital identity wallets. Blockchains are distributed databases that allow a network of so-called blockchain nodes to keep a synchronized state of the database [34, 35]. The basic ordering element of the database are blocks that are connected via cryptographic hash functions, which allows for the transparent tracing of transactions [36–38]. Digital identity wallets, in turn, allow users to collect secure digital credentials, and selectively present the identity attributes in these credentials [39–42].

Originally, the two technologies emerged from a similar technological 'niche' shaped by libertarian ideals [11, 43]. This niche positioned blockchain as the only technology that could deliver the 'trust' infrastructures and revocation registries required to verify the authenticity and validity of digital identity attributes [11, 42–44]. Over time, however, it became clear that blockchain may have been a good starting point but is no essential component [11, 42]. Digital credentials, for instance, do not need to be stored on a blockchain to be verifiable and to ensure their integrity [42, 45, 46]. These shared beginnings combined with later parting make blockchain and digital identity wallets appealing candidates to address our research question.

3 Research Method

3.1 Case Selection

To investigate how organizations discursively and materially navigate loose coupling in the co-enactment of emerging ITs – including changes in their relationship – we conduct a case-study of the European Blockchain Partnership (EBP). The EBP was established in 2018 between the European Commission and the EU's member states (plus Liechtenstein and Norway) with the objective of establishing a blockchain-based infrastructure – the European Blockchain Services Infrastructure (EBSI) – for delivering cross-border public services.

Soon after its creation, the EBP created a working group focused on using EBSI to support the issuance and verification of digital credentials. This group developed an identity framework that other groups could use to issue various credentials, such as digital (university) diplomas and social security passes. EBSI's digital diploma use case received particular attention when the EBP launched an early-adopter program in the beginning of 2021. Since the project involves both blockchain and digital identity wallets, it offered particularly rich insights into the enactment of loosely coupled emerging ITs.

3.2 Data Collection

For our case study, we collected data from three different sources [13]: interviews, documentation, and participant observations. Interviews were our primary source of evidence and we conducted them in three waves to "minimize the elapsed time between the events of interest and the collection of data" [47]. Specifically, we conducted a first set of 7 interviews with EBP members, member state governments, and technology partners (incl. infrastructure operators) in the fall of 2020 to explore the EBP's view on blockchain and digital identity wallets. These interviews suggested mounting (discursive) tensions from the loose coupling of the two technologies. Over time, these tensions intensified and dominated EBSI's development. To surface the EBP's sense-making and response to these tensions, we interviewed another 21 EBP members and partners in the summer and fall of 2022 (wave 2), a third set of six interviews in the spring of 2023 (wave 3) (Table 1).

Our informants included European Commission representatives, delegates from national and local governments, technology providers, and universities (Table 1). We sampled our informants based on their involvement with EBSI in general and the diploma use case in particular [47]. We focused on interviewees who were highly "knowledgeable about" the case [47].

All our interviews were semi-structured and followed a logical sequence [47]. We first asked our informants why and how they became involved with the EBP. We then segued to questions about their initial expectations of the interplay between blockchain and digital identity wallets and how they perceived the EBP's implementation process. Our last (set of) questions prodded our informants to critically reflect on how their perception of the mutual relevance of blockchain and digital identity wallets evolved over time. We audio-recorded and transcribed all interviews. They took 56 min on average.

Table 1. Overview of the conducted interviews.

	Number of interviewed experts			
	European Commission	National & local governments	Technology partners	Piloting Organizations
Wave 1 Fall 2020	1	3	3	–
Wave 2 Fall & Summer 2022	5	8	5	3
Wave 3 Spring 2023	–	2	3	1

We complemented these interviews with internal and publicly available project documents [13]. The internal documents ranged from meeting presentations over legal assessments and internal project reports to technical documentation. The publicly available documentation included blog posts & other marketing material, press releases, public presentations, and public reports (Table 2).

Table 2. Overview of the collected project documents.

	Types of documents	Total number of pages
Internal documents	Internal presentations, legal assessments, internal project reports, technical documentation	210+ pages
Public documents	Blog posts & other marketing material, press releases, public presentations, public reports	160+ pages

Our third source of evidence were participant observations. All authors of this study were actively involved with the EBP in different roles and regularly attended EBP meetings dedicated to different aspects of EBSI. More specifically, the second author of this work became involved with the EBP in October 2018 as a national representative for EBP's technical advisory group and occasionally attended meetings dedicated to the identity framework and the digital diploma use case. From March 2021 to March 2024, both the first and second author were involved with one of the national early-adopter projects for the digital diplomas use case. The third author of this work joined the project in November 2021 and then regularly attended meetings of the EBP's technical, policy and use case group. Moreover, they participated in strategic negotiation meetings regarding the future of blockchain and digital identity wallets.

Throughout these meetings, the observing authors took notes and collected presentations and protocols for later analysis. Overall, our participant observations provided us with rich insights into how the EBP made sense of a joint organizing vision for blockchain and digital identity wallets and materialized a loose coupling between these technologies.

3.3 Data Analysis

Following our data collection, we retraced how the EBP made sense of the joint organizing vision for blockchain and digital identity wallets and materialized selected complementary frames. We also analyzed how this discursive-material complementarity developed over the course of the project. For this purpose, we performed a three-stage coding process [48, 49].

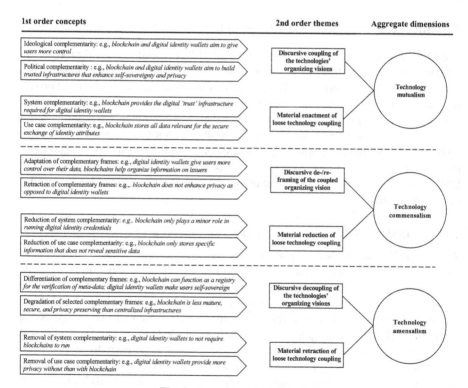

Fig. 1. Emerging data structure.

In a first, open coding round, we focused on theme discovery in the interviews and project documents and assigned initial codes to statements we considered relevant. We were especially interested in themes related to discursive sense-making of complementary frames and their materialization but maintained an open mind. Based on the identified themes, we then performed a second, axial coding round. This second round

helped us to refine our codes and aggregate them into overarching constructs and identify interdependencies between these constructs [48, 49]. The constructs that emerged
over the second coding round showed differences in both the discursive sense-making
and material enactment over time and surfaced marked differences in the relationship
between the two focal technologies.

We then refined these constructs and their interdependencies by iterating between
our codes and the pertinent theories on loose coupling [9, 24, 25] and population ecology
principles of species interaction [22–24]. As a last step, we conducted selective coding
to fill-in the gaps of our theoretical insights. Throughout the axial and selective coding
process, we triangulated our interview transcripts and project documents with our participant observations to enhance construct validity and generalizability of our research [14,
50]. Overall, our coding process produced more than 2300 codes, which we managed
using the MAXQDA software kit. Figure 1 summarizes our findings of the qualitative
coding in a data structure.

4   Emerging Theoretical Framework

The EBP's engagement with blockchain and digital identity wallets can be bracketed into
three phases. While the first phase was dominated by attempts to frame and materialize a
coupled organizing vision (mutualism phase), challenges along the development process
soon required discursive and material de-coupling to maintain legitimacy (commensalism phase). In a third phase, digital identity wallets were introduced into a revision of
the European Union's regulation on electronic identification, authentication and trust
services (eIDAS), which afforded a high degree of legitimization and mobilization. But
the revised regulation cut the connection to blockchain, inevitably demanding that the
EBP respond to a competing, de-coupled organizing vision for digital identity wallets
(amensalism phase).

4.1   Establishing Mutualism Between the Two Emerging ITs

When the EBP was founded in April 2018, its first activities were focused on identifying
cross-border public services that could be supported by a blockchain-based infrastructure. Throughout this process of finding resonant discursive frames, several member
states began to promote a coupled organizing vision between blockchain and digital
identity wallets that had been developed by the so-called Internet Identity Workshop
community. This coupled organizing vision painted blockchain and digital identity wallets as uniquely complementary technologies that would allow users to regain control
over their digital identities and establish 'self-sovereign identities'. Resonance was especially high with those member states that felt that the EU's current eIDAS framework
was difficult to implement. Blockchain and digital identity wallets provided a welcome
departure from this framework – not least because they aligned well with political priorities of the van-der-Leyen presidency, such as data privacy and digital sovereignty. One
EBP member state representative explains this perceived technological mutualism:

> "We really believe[d] that the ledgers and the network supported by a blockchain
> can play a very important role to protect the privacy of citizens and to enable the
> self-sovereign identity of the user."

In April 2019, the early sense-making efforts resulted in the creation of a EBP working group for the development of a new digital identity framework based on blockchain and digital identity wallets. Drawing on the organizing vision promoted by the Internet Identity Workshop community, the new framework was nicknamed the European Self-Sovereign Identity Framework (ESSIF). The plan was for ESSIF to inform and support various EBSI services focused on the issuance and verification of identity documents. During its early days, the ESSIF working group was *"enthusiastic about blockchain as a technology"* and perceived a high degree of complementarity between the two technologies. Over the course of the next year, the ESSIF working group set out to materialize this perceived complementarily in a conceptual architecture. This architecture anchored blockchain as a core 'trust' infrastructure that would store various data required for the secure issuance and verification of identity attributes. For instance, this data included cryptographic identifiers for issuers, issuer accreditation organizations, and credential holders, as well as data in or about the credentials. A European Commission representative explains:

> *"We thought that aside of using blockchain for storing information about accreditation organizations, which accredits the issuers to issue specific credentials, we can also store some additional information such as decentralized digital identifiers of natural persons."*

4.2 Handling Commensalism Between the Two Emerging ITs

By early 2021, the EBP had decided to implement ESSIF in EBSI and pilot it for the exchange of digital university diplomas. However, the piloting phase soon surfaced problems with the coupled organizing vision that led to a phase of technological commensalism, in which increased functionality and budget were directed towards digital identity wallets. Increased functionality resulted especially from difficulties reconciling the storage of personal information such as digital credentials and identifiers on the blockchain with the requirements of the EU's General Data Protection Regulation (GDPR). This dissonance first dawned on the ESSIF working group when they began to develop specifications for the information that should be stored on EBSI. This specification exercise included a survey of how other projects approached the implementation of 'self-sovereign identities', which revealed that digital credentials did not need to be stored on a blockchain. On the contrary, such storage would contradict one of the core principles of self-sovereign identities, namely the protection of the user's privacy. One EBP member state representative reflects:

> *"We did consider saving a hash of the [credential] on the blockchain. But we soon discarded this idea for many reasons. One of them is that well [...] who knows if in 20 years someone could obtain the original information from a hash. [...] So, we decided to remove that information from the blockchain"*

To reduce the resulting dissonance, the EBP revised EBSI's architecture so that digital credentials would only be stored in digital identity wallets, but not on EBSI. To salvage the rest of the vision, the ESSIF working group doubled down on those data for which they perceived continued complementarity, including identifiers for credential issuers and holders. But the storage of holder identifiers was again problematic from a privacy perspective, which became evident during a formal GDPR assessment. The assessment unequivocally concluded that a natural person's identifiers should also not be stored on a blockchain. The ESSIF working group was now again forced to engage in a material dissonance reduction process that *made "the blockchain layer become thinner and thinner. Much more things are [now] happening outside the blockchain network because of privacy issues".* The resulting ESSIF architecture only used EBSI as a registry for trusted issuer information and put digital identity wallets center-stage. One European Commission representative recounts:

> *"We went through a long, long, long battle with the data protection officers and lawyers and policymakers. And we've understood if we would allow to store the decentralized identifiers of natural persons on the ledger, on EBSI, the EBSI service wouldn't be GDPR-compliant. [But] we don't really need to store it on the ledger. We can keep it on the wallet side, and that's the new version of conformance."*

These material compromises inevitably led to problems with how EBSI had been marketed to the member states. The European Commission responded with a marketing campaign that promoted an adapted organizing vision that better reflected the material reality. EBSI officially became a trusted issuer registry.

4.3 Navigating Amensalism Between the Two Emerging ITs

In parallel to the EBP's efforts, the European Commission had announced plans to rework the eIDAS identity framework and regulation in October 2020. Eight months later, in June 2021, the European Commission revealed a proposal for a new framework and regulation. The proposal had a substantial part dedicated to the use of digital identity wallets but did not mention blockchain as a preferred technology for implementing trust infrastructures. The proposal hit the EBP hard. Some chose to maintain a positive attitude and promoted the interpretation that blockchain was not explicitly excluded. Other EBP members were more skeptical as they sensed open resentment against blockchain by the eIDAS expert groups. These groups saw blockchain as an inferior alternative to the eIDAS trust registries already in place. A national EBP representative explains:

> *"I would say that especially the people that created eIDAS are not all positive about blockchain […] The IT people who really developed it, they can show that there is a system that is working. They are not necessarily convinced why we would need something new."*

As the eIDAS revision moved through the EU's legislative process, the uncertainty around blockchain's future role for digital identity wallets intensified, plunging the EBP into a phase of technological amensalism, where digital identity wallets benefitted from having a 'host' technology that helped demonstrate their viability but blockchain suffered from the relationship. In February 2022, the European Commission then published a first outline for the reference architecture framework under eIDAS 2.0. However, blockchain was again not mentioned. Instead, the European Commission argued that the regulation should be technology neutral, which provoked a sense-breaking process and the destruction of the EBP's coupled organizing vision. One national EBP representative explains:

> "Do I need a blockchain for a digital identity? [...] The eIDAS revision has given a lot of space to this discussion. Because there is a clear will to break away from [blockchain] and the revision is also supposed to be technology-neutral, [...], there is no further talk about blockchain."

To cope with the looming break-down of the coupled organizing vision, the EBP engaged into a soul-searching process and feverish attempted to find a new organizing vision for blockchain and EBSI. At this stage, the EBP questioned digital identity wallets altogether. Some even perceived them as a "child that has outgrown its parent [blockchain]'s home." As a first measure, the EBP again reframed EBSI's presentation, dropping all mentioning of 'self-sovereign identity' in favor of a framing EBSI as a multi-purpose registry for trustworthy information. Furthermore, the EBP doubled down on other use cases that did not require digital identity wallets, such as product traceability. A European Commission explains:

> "At the end, EBSI is ultimately used as a source of trust. That's the main purpose of blockchain: to build resilient lists that allow everyone from everywhere to get the required data to verify some other information."

5   Discussion

We now elaborate on the insights we gained from our analysis and describe the observed discursive and material processes in the co-enactment of blockchain and digital identity wallets from an initially mutualistic to a commensalistic and later amensalistic relationship. We also explain how these relationship changes influenced the loose coupling of the two technologies.

5.1   Tentative Model

Our core contribution is a conceptual model of the discursive-material processes underlying the co-enactment of loosely coupled emerging ITs (Fig. 2). The model builds on theories about the creation and diffusion of (co-dependent) organizing visions [2–4, 8], loose coupling of organizational systems [9, 24], and population ecology principles of species interaction transferred to technology-technology and technology-system interaction [27, 28, 32, 33].

The co-enactment will usually start with a sense-giving process by the innovation communities responsible for the creation of organizing visions for two single-whole emerging technologies. Sometimes, these innovation communities are grounded in the same technological 'niche', which can increase the degree of complementary discursive frames [8]. Blockchain technology and digital identity wallets, for instance came from the same libertarian niche that imbued their organizing visions with various complementary frames, such as self-sovereignty and privacy [11, 44].

Once organizations in enactment fields detect complementarities between selected discursive frames in both organizing visions, they can engage in a process of discursive sense-taking that more systematically extracts and discursively couples complementary frames [8], creating a relationship of technology mutualism [28]. In a next step, they can then materially enact these coupled frames [7]. Where this enactment does not resonate well with the wider organizational context, the frames either need to be adapted (where possible) or retracted. Otherwise, unsuccessful coupling frames may raise questions about the technologies' complementarity [4]. The enactment process may also be complicated by the continued development of the organizing visions for each of the individual technologies, especially when other enacting organizations chose different adaptation or retraction strategies.

Since it may often be difficult to enact all (purported) complementarities, the technologies may naturally become more loosely coupled over time. For instance, blockchain became a 'host' technology for digital identity wallets during the second phase of the EBSI project, turning their relationship from technology mutualism to technology commensalism. The commensal technology, in this case digital identity wallets, profited from the 'host' technology blockchain, while the host remained unaffected [28, 31]. Condensed into a conjecture, we can state:

Conjecture 1: Loosely coupled emerging technologies will become commensalistic if complementary frames are difficult to enact in the wider organizational environment.

Should the re-framed joint organizing vision still prove difficult to reconcile with the wider organizational context despite looser coupling and a clear host-commensal distinction, organizations can enter a discursive sense-breaking process. Such sense-breaking can be exacerbated when, for instance, one innovation community actively opposes the loose coupling and counteracts complementarities with the commensal technology. This happened during the EBSI project when the eIDAS working groups actively opposed coupling digital identity wallets with blockchain. In response, the EBP reduced the technologies' loose coupling to a minimum and blockchain once again became a single-whole technology in search of a use case. On a discursive level, the relationship between the technologies changed to technology amensalism, where one technology is negatively affected while the other remains neutral [32, 33]. Materially, the relationship remained commensalistic. Condensed into a conjecture, we can state:

Conjecture 2: Organizations in enactment fields cannot resolve an amensalistic relationship between loosely coupled emerging technologies as long as one of the innovation communities works against the coupling.

5.2 Theoretical Contributions

This research contributes to the literature on the enactment of emerging ITs by unpacking the discursive-material processes that initiate (loose) coupling between such technologies in a joint organizing vision and influence the evolution of their relationship during their co-enactment. While organizing visions are a widely studied topic in information systems [2–4, 16], studies on the co-enactment of two complementary, emerging ITs are scarce [8]. Moreover, loose coupling has been primarily researched between organizational processes and technologies but not between organizing visions. Our analysis of the EBSI project thus not only demonstrates the challenges involved in enacting a coupled organizing vision for two emerging ITs, but also elaborates on the difficulties navigating loose coupling between two immature technologies prone to change.

More specifically, we add to literature on organizing visions [2–4] by demonstrating how organizational sense-making [21, 22] and population ecology [27, 28, 30] lenses can be integrated to describe and navigate the implementation of loosely coupled emerging ITs. In particular, we surface three coupling types - technology mutualism, technology commensalism, and technology amensalism - that highly depend on the degree of discursive and material complementarity between the emerging ITs. We also describe how the coupling type may change for the worse in response to enactment challenges and discursive opposition to the coupling in the organizing visions of the individual technologies. Where such changes occur, enacting organizations can respond with discursive and material changes to salvage the remaining complementarities or to emphasize the distinctiveness of one of the technologies as a single-whole innovations to guarantee its survival. But our research also indicates that once the process of decoupling is initiated, it may be difficult to stop and reverse.

5.3 Practical Implications

Our findings suggest that managers interested in emerging information technologies should be careful when it comes to investing into bundles of such technologies - especially when they are only loosely coupled. While such a shotgun marriage can be beneficial in legitimizing the bundled technologies and increasing their mobilization potential, it can quickly degenerate once the honeymoon phase is over, and it becomes apparent that initially perceived complementarities are hard to realize. In these instances, organizations need to engage in discursive and material 'marriage counseling' to set aside differences and ensure a shared bedrock of resonance.

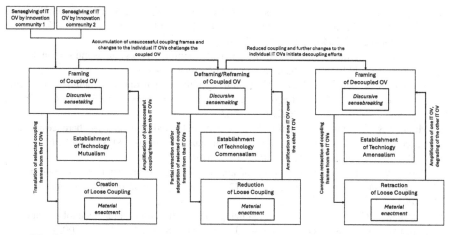

Fig. 2. Conceptual Model for the Co-enactment of Loosely Coupled Emerging ITs.

However, these counseling activities may not always be successful. Emerging ITs are often still evolving, and sometimes, they may be appropriated by new conversants in the innovation community that are not interested in maintaining the originally envisioned coupling. In these cases, organizations need to act decisively and question if they want and need to keep both technologies. These decisions can be difficult, but they are essential for giving the technology that remains a more promising way forward.

6 Conclusion

Based on insights from the European Blockchain Partnership, our study derives a model for the co-enactment of loosely coupled emerging ITs that possess a lower level of materiality than typical technical innovations. Our model illustrates the challenges involved in co-enacting such ITs and demonstrates how insights from population ecology can help better explain and understand the underlying material-discursive processes that initiate the loose coupling and drive the evolution of their relationship in an organizational context.

Acknowledgements. This research was funded in part by the Luxembourg National Research Fund (FNR) and PayPal, PEARL grant reference 13342933/Gilbert Fridgen, grant reference NCER22/IS/16570468/NCER-FT, and grant reference 14783405, as well as Luxembourg's Ministry for Digitalisation. For the purpose of open access, and in fulfillment of the obligations arising from the grant agreement, the authors have applied a Creative Commons Attribution 4.0 International (CC BY 4.0) license to any Author Accepted Manuscript version arising from this submission.

Disclosure of Interests. The authors have no competing interests to declare.

References

1. Gaspary, E., Moura, G.L.D., Wegner, D.: How does the organisational structure influence a work environment for innovation? Int. J. Entrep. Innov. Manag. **24**(2–3), 132–153 (2020). https://doi.org/10.1504/IJEIM.2020.105770
2. Swanson, E., Ramiller, N.: The organizing vision in information systems innovation. Organ. Sci. **8**(5), 458–474 (1997). https://doi.org/10.1287/orsc.8.5.458
3. Miranda, S.M., Kim, I., Summers, J.D.: Jamming with social media: how cognitive structuring of organizing vision facets affects IT innovation diffusion. MIS Q. **39**(3), 591–614 (2015). https://doi.org/10.25300/MISQ/2016/40.2.02
4. Miranda, S.M., Wang, D.D., Tian, C.A.: Discursive fields and the diversity-coherence paradox: an ecological perspective on the blockchain community discourse. MIS Q. **46**(3), 1421–1452 (2022). https://doi.org/10.25300/MISQ/2022/15736
5. Currie, W.L.: The organizing vision of application service provision: a process-oriented analysis. Inf. Organ. **14**(4), 237–267 (2004). https://doi.org/10.1016/j.infoandorg.2004.07.001
6. Ramiller, N.C., Swanson, E.B.: Organizing visions for information technology and the information systems executive response. J. Manag. Inf. Syst. **20**(1), 13–50 (2003)

7. Davidson, E.J., Østerlund, C.S., Flaherty, M.G.: Drift and shift in the organizing vision career for personal health records: an investigation of innovation discourse dynamics. Inf. Organ. **25**(4), 191–221 (2015). https://doi.org/10.1016/j.infoandorg.2015.08.001

8. Parameswaran, S., Kishore, R., Yang, X., Liu, Z.: Theorizing about the early-stage diffusion of codependent IT innovations. J. Assoc. Inf. Syst. **24**(2), 379–429 (2023). https://doi.org/10.17705/1jais.00789

9. Orton, J.D., Weick, K.E.: Loosely coupled systems: a reconceptualization. Acad. Manag. Rev. **15**(2), 203–223 (1990). https://doi.org/10.2307/258154

10. Øvrelid, E., Bygstad, B.: Exploring loose coupling in system interaction. Selected Papers of the IRIS, Issue Nr. 7 (2016). https://aisel.aisnet.org/iris2016/5. Accessed Jan 2016

11. Sedlmeir, J., Barbereau, T.J., Huber, J., Weigl, L., Roth, T.: Transition pathways towards design principles of self-sovereign identity. In: ICIS 2022 Proceedings (2022). https://aisel.aisnet.org/icis2022/is_implement/is_implement/4. Accessed 29 Mar 2024

12. Geels, F.W., Schot, J.: Typology of sociotechnical transition pathways. Res. Policy **36**(3), 399–417 (2007). https://doi.org/10.1016/j.respol.2007.01.003

13. Yin, R.K.: Case Study Research: Design and Methods, 6th edn. SAGE Publications, Inc. (2017). https://us.sagepub.com/en-us/nam/case-study-research-and-applications/book250150

14. Eisenhardt, K.M.: What is the Eisenhardt method, really? Strateg. Organ. **19**(1), 147–160 (2021). https://doi.org/10.1177/1476127020982866

15. Agarwal, R., Prasad, J.: The role of innovation characteristics and perceived voluntariness in the acceptance of information technologies. Decis. Sci. **28**(3), 557–582 (1997). https://doi.org/10.1111/j.1540-5915.1997.tb01322.x

16. Kim, I., Miranda, S.: 20 years old but still a teenager? A review of organizing vision theory and suggested directions. In: PACIS 2018 Proceedings, June 2018. https://aisel.aisnet.org/pacis2018/23

17. Wang, P., Ramiller, N.C.: Community learning in information technology innovation. MIS Q., 709–734 (2009). https://doi.org/10.2307/20650324

18. Hardy, C., Maguire, S.: Organizing risk: discourse, power, and 'riskification'. AMR **41**(1), 80–108 (2016). https://doi.org/10.5465/amr.2013.0106

19. Orlikowski, W.J., Scott, S.V.: What happens when evaluation goes online? Exploring apparatuses of valuation in the travel sector. Organ. Sci. **25**(3), 868–891 (2014). https://doi.org/10.1287/orsc.2013.0877

20. Maitlis, S., Christianson, M.: Sensemaking in organizations: taking stock and moving forward. ANNALS **8**(1), 57–125 (2014). https://doi.org/10.5465/19416520.2014.873177

21. Gioia, D.A., Chittipeddi, K.: Sensemaking and sensegiving in strategic change initiation. Strateg. Manag. J. **12**(6), 433–448 (1991). https://doi.org/10.1002/smj.4250120604

22. Weick, K.E., Sutcliffe, K.M., Obstfeld, D.: Organizing and the process of sensemaking. Organ. Sci. **16**(4), 409–421 (2005). https://doi.org/10.1287/orsc.1050.0133

23. Weick, K.E.: Sensemaking as an organizational dimension of global change. In: Cooperrider, D.L., Dutton, J.E. (eds.) Organizational Dimensions of Global Change: No Limits to Cooperation, pp. 39–56. SAGE Publications, Inc. (1999). https://sk.sagepub.com/books/organizational-dimensions-of-global-change

24. Berente, N., Yoo, Y.: Institutional contradictions and loose coupling: postimplementation of NASA's enterprise information system. Inf. Syst. Res. **23**(2), 376–396 (2012). https://doi.org/10.1287/isre.1110.0373

25. Mitchell, V.L., Zmud, R.W.: The effects of coupling IT and work process strategies in redesign projects. Organ. Sci. **10**(4), 424–438 (1999)

26. Nambisan, S., Luo, Y.: Toward a loose coupling view of digital globalization. J. Int. Bus. Stud. **52**(8), 1646–1663 (2021). https://doi.org/10.1057/s41267-021-00446-x

27. Coccia, M., Watts, J.: A theory of the evolution of technology: technological parasitism and the implications for innovation magement. J. Eng. Technol. Manag. **55**, 101552 (2020). https://doi.org/10.1016/j.jengtecman.2019.11.003

28. Coccia, M.: Classification of innovation considering technological interaction (2018). https://papers.ssrn.com/abstract=3218945. Accessed 20 Apr. 2024

29. Gastaldi, L., Appio, F.P., Trabucchi, D., Buganza, T., Corso, M.: From mutualism to commensalism: assessing the evolving relationship between complementors and digital platforms. Inf. Syst. J., 1–47 (2023). https://doi.org/10.1111/isj.12491

30. Barnett, W.P.: The organizational ecology of a technological system. Adm. Sci. Q. **35**(1), 31–60 (1990). https://doi.org/10.2307/2393550

31. Pistorius, C.W.I., Utterback, J.M.: Multi-mode interaction among technologies. Res. Policy **26**(1), 67–84 (1997). https://doi.org/10.1016/S0048-7333(96)00916-X

32. Sandén, B.A., Hillman, K.M.: A framework for analysis of multi-mode interaction among technologies with examples from the history of alternative transport fuels in Sweden. Res. Policy **40**(3), 403–414 (2011). https://doi.org/10.1016/j.respol.2010.12.005

33. Zhang, G., McAdams, D.A., Shankar, V., Darani, M.M.: Modeling the evolution of system technology performance when component and system technology performances interact: commensalism and amensalism. Technol. Forecast. Soc. Change **125**, 116–124 (2017). https://doi.org/10.1016/j.techfore.2017.08.004

34. Ellinger, E.W., Gregory, R.W., Mini, T., Widjaja, T., Henfridsson, O.: Skin the the game: the transformational potential of decentralized autonomous organizations. MIS Q. (Forthcom.) (2023). https://doi.org/10.25300/MISQ/2023/17690

35. Halaburda, H., Levina, N., Semi, M.: Digitization of transaction terms as a shift parameter within TCE: strong smart contract as a new mode of transaction governance. MIS Q. (Forthcom.) (2023). https://doi.org/10.25300/MISQ/2023/17818

36. Beck, R., Müller-Bloch, C., King, J.L.: Governance in the blockchain economy: a framework and research agenda. J. Assoc. Inf. Syst. **19**(10), 1020–1034 (2018). https://doi.org/10.17705/1jais.00518

37. Chong, A., Lim, E., Hua, X., Zheng, S., Tan, C.-W.: Business on chain: a comparative case study of five blockchain-inspired business models. J. Assoc. Inf. Syst. **20**(9) (2019). https://doi.org/10.17705/1jais.00568

38. Ziolkowski, R., Miscione, G., Schwabe, G.: Decision problems in blockchain governance: old wine in new bottles or walking in someone else's shoes? J. Manag. Inf. Syst. **37**(2), 316–348 (2020). https://doi.org/10.1080/07421222.2020.1759974

39. Glöckler, J., Sedlmeir, J., Frank, M., Fridgen, G.: A systematic review of identity and access management requirements in enterprises and potential contributions of self-sovereign identity. Bus. Inf. Syst. Eng. (2023). https://doi.org/10.1007/s12599-023-00830-x

40. Lacity, M., Carmel, E.: Self-sovereign identity and verifiable credentials in your digital wallet. MIS Q. Exec. **21**(3) (2022). https://aisel.aisnet.org/misqe/vol21/iss3/6

41. Rieger, A., Roth, T., Sedlmeir, J., Fridgen, G., Young, A.G.: Organizational identity management policies. J. Assoc. Inf. Syst. (Forthcom.) (2024)

42. Sedlmeir, J., Smethurst, R., Rieger, A., Fridgen, G.: Digital identities and verifiable credentials. Bus. Inf. Syst. Eng. **63**(5), 603–613 (2021). https://doi.org/10.1007/s12599-021-00722-y

43. Hoess, A., Rieger, A., Roth, T., Fridgen, G., Young, A.: Managing fashionable organizing visions: evidence from the European blockchain services infrastructure. In: ECIS 2023 Proceedings (2023). https://aisel.aisnet.org/ecis2023_rp/337

44. Lacity, M.C.: Blockchain: from bitcoin to the internet of value and beyond. J. Inf. Technol. **37**(4), 326–340 (2022). https://doi.org/10.1177/02683962221086300

45. Kudra, A., Rieger, A., Roth, T., Sedlmeir, J., Fridgen, G., Young, A.G.: Digital identity wallets. University of Arkansas Working Paper (2024)

46. Rieger, A., Roth, T., Sedlmeir, J., Weigl, L., Fridgen, G.: Not yet another digital identity. Nat. Hum. Behav. **6**(1), 3 (2022). https://doi.org/10.1038/s41562-021-01243-0

47. Huber, G.P., Power, D.J.: Retrospective reports of strategic-level managers: guidelines for increasing their accuracy. Strateg. Manag. J. **6**(2), Article no. 2 (1985). https://doi.org/10.1002/smj.4250060206

48. Corbin, J.M., Strauss, A.: Grounded theory research: procedures, canons, and evaluative criteria. Qual. Sociol. **13**(1), 3–21 (1990). https://doi.org/10.1007/BF00988593

49. Saldaña, J.: The Coding Manual for Qualitative Researchers, Fourth. SAGE Publications Ltd. (2021). https://uk.sagepub.com/en-gb/eur/the-coding-manual-for-qualitative-researchers/book273583. Accessed 20 Apr 2024

50. Eisenhardt, K.M., Graebner, M.E., Sonenshein, S.: Grand challenges and inductive methods: rigor without rigor mortis. AMJ **59**(4), 1113–1123 (2016). https://doi.org/10.5465/amj.2016.4004

A Review on Privacy and Monetization Aspects Within BCI and XR-BCI Ecosystems

Tuomo Lahtinen[1,2]([✉]) [iD], Andrei Costin[1,2] [iD], Guillermo Suarez-Tangil[3] [iD], and Narges Yousefnezhad[1] [iD]

[1] Binare.io, Jyväskylä, Finland
{tuomo.lahtinen,andrei.costin,narges.yousefnezhad}@binare.io
[2] University of Jyväskylä, Jyväskylä, Finland
{tutalaht,ancostin}@jyu.fi
[3] IMDEA Network Institute, Leganés, Spain
guillermo.suarez-tangil@imdea.org
https://binare.io/, https://jyu.fi/it/

Abstract. The use of BCI and XR-BCI devices is yet to become more widespread among the general population. These devices could pose a significant risk to the users' privacy, as they enable the revelation of users' emotions, beliefs, and other potentially highly sensitive details. When this information is obtained, it is possible to both invade users' privacy as never before as well as monetize data very precisely through neuromarketing.

This work presents a review of the privacy and monetization of BCI and XR-BCI. It was discovered that many companies collect a considerable amount of data without knowing or revealing the actual purpose of the collection. This data includes sensitive information about health. One of the future risks is that emotions and generic raw brain-wave data are leaked to advertisers through neuromarketing, which is considered a valuable asset for advertisers, e.g., to reveal a person's willingness to buy something. We urge the need to evaluate the current privacy policies and terms of service of BCIs and XR-BCIs against existing frameworks such as the General Data Protection Regulation (GDPR).

1 Introduction

Brain-Computer Interface (BCI) technology continues to advance and recent research has highlighted significant improvements in the quality of collected and processed brain data. For example, recent advance in BCI allows reconstructing speech [45], images [7], and music tracks [5] from the raw brain data. This progress not only heralds a new era of understanding and interaction with the human brain, mind, and its entire thought and memory processes. It also opens avenues for the convergence of BCI with eXtended Reality (XR) and the Internet of Things (IoT), among other things. In the near future, XR and IoT devices can likely be seamlessly controlled by mere thoughts. Nevertheless, the widespread adoption of XR-BCI is contingent upon the convergence of technological advancements with effective monetization strategies. These strategies are

B. Shishkov (Ed.): BMSD 2024, LNBIP 523, pp. 166–185, 2024.
https://doi.org/10.1007/978-3-031-64073-5_11

expected to generate a return on the investments made into related technologies and R&D. The fusion of XR and BCI presents a multitude of opportunities for manufacturers to capitalize on this cutting-edge technology. By leveraging the wealth of brain data obtained through BCI, manufacturers can tailor XR experiences to individual users, offering personalized content and immersive environments. Moreover, the monetization potential extends beyond product sales, encompassing subscription models, premium content, and targeted advertising based on neural activity.

Data has emerged as a valuable asset in the contemporary digital era, driving innovation and influencing the global economy. A significant proportion of revenue generated by some Big Tech companies is derived from advertising, which is dependent on the user data collected by these companies, and eventually resold to other organizations in various forms (e.g., raw, anonymized, aggregated, personalized). For example, Meta generated almost all of its revenue (97%) through advertising [15]. Generally, Big Tech companies are not willing to sell their data [8] but sell data-based services such as the possibility to set advertisements for specific target groups [8,36].

Neurotechnology is seen as the next artificial intelligence (AI) frontier for Big Tech and there is an effort to make BCIs accessible to a wider audience [26]. Also, past events demonstrate that Big Tech companies are acquiring and pursuing data ownership. The Google-operated Project Nightingale, for instance, was designed to collect and analyse personal health data, affecting millions of individuals across the United States [40]. The issue of mental health data has also attracted negative attention, with concerns that Big Tech companies may exploit and monetize mental health data in the same way as they do other data [32]. Cerebral and Teladoc admitted/fined that they provided patient health-related app data to third parties, including Google, Meta, TikTok, and Snapchat [6]. At the opposite end of the spectrum are hacking cases that target mental health and mind-related data of mental health organizations, such as Vastaamo [51]. In this case, non-BCI mental data was hacked. The patients were blackmailed, leading to the establishment of a government hotline to aid the thousands of victims, bankruptcy and foreclosure of Vastaamo, suspended sentence to Vastaamo's then-CEO, and an international suspect hunt leading to capture in France and extradition to Finland of the main suspect Aleksanteri Kivimäki [51]. This case demonstrates clearly the multi-layer complexities arising from breaches and abuses involving brain and mental-health data, and this is not an event considering the ever-connected and fully digitized brain wave data coming from BCIs. Medical data may include sensitive details e.g., it is possible to diagnose Alzheimer's disease using electroencephalography (EEG) [1,13]. The inherent challenge lies in identifying when such data is accessed. BCI systems rely on user data for their functionality, making them vulnerable to exploitation regardless of their original purpose [21].

This paper examines the multifaceted realm of data monetization, exploring its implications, opportunities, and challenges in the context of the digital landscape. In particular, the development of the XR-BCI technology is leading to a transformative shift in how data is collected and leveraged for monetization purposes. As we navigate this evolving landscape, it becomes imperative to understand the potential of XR-BCI in data monetization and critically examine the ethical and privacy considerations inherent in such endeavors. Moreover, amidst this exploration, we underscore the crucial role of transparent privacy and terms of use notifications in safeguarding user rights and fostering trust in data-driven ecosystems. To the best of our knowledge, with this paper, we contribute the first study that performs an in-depth review of the Privacy Policies (PP) and monetization provisions in Terms of Services (ToS) related to a wide range of state-of-the-art BCI, XR, XR-BCI technology, and service providers.

With this paper, we mainly aim to address the following Research Questions (RQ):

- RQ1: How would XR-BCI devices be monetized in the future and what risks does this bring to the end-users?
- RQ2: How do XR and BCI vendors display data collection practices in their privacy policies, as well as in Terms of Service notifications? Are privacy policies transparent and uniform across the technology spectrum, or are they fragmented and omit information that could potentially harm or pose an issue to the privacy of the users?

We will address the first research question (RQ1) in greater detail in Sect. 2. XR-BCI devices are primarily utilized for research purposes. Consequently, we are analyzing the existing literature and prospects for XR-BCI through BCI. The second research question (RQ2) is addressed in greater detail in Sect. 3. In this section, we present our privacy policy analysis and the main findings, which we believe cover the most relevant XR and BCI manufacturers. Section 4 discusses in greater depth the issues we have identified as being of particular importance in the context of XR-BCI and neuromarketing.

2   Data Monetization Policies

Digital technologies continue to change the marketing landscape through data and its applications [37]. Data monetization plays an important role when companies collect data from customers and users. The purpose of collecting data is to directly or indirectly generate revenue for the company, increase the value of the company, and provide a richer and wider service base to customers. Nowadays, there is a lot of data available and different monetization strategies are proposed by researchers. Parviainen et al. [36] noted that data value increased significantly when companies started to offer services and rentals instead of just products. Although brain data has been discussed in the research literature [36], data monetization policies are ill-defined and it is still unclear what general strategies will drive this industry nor how this can reshape the landscape of online marketing.

To address this gap, this section presents a general overview of prospective monetization strategies (Sect. 2.1). We later instantiate these strategies around monetization from the perspective of BCI and XR-BCI (Sect. 2.2 and Sect. 2.3). These subsections delve into neuromarketing and how it disrupts the marketing landscape, particularly in comparison to traditional marketing techniques.

Additionally, it identifies some key factors that could drive the transition of XR-BCI into mass markets.

2.1 General Data Monetization Strategies

Monetization strategies are primarily focused on generating profit, rather than protecting privacy. In some cases, the engaged user is perceived as an asset, because without the user, data is not available [8]. The user becomes an asset at the point of consent to data collection. This is a strategy employed by Big Tech companies, which seek to engage users (apply privacy policies) for their services and products to obtain the legal right and consent to collect data. According to Baglione et al. [4] users are likely to choose a free version over a paid one, even if a small fee increases privacy and removes ads. The research assessed user preferences for free/paid Facebook accounts, but the results can be generalized to other services and platforms. The payment for ad-free or increased privacy is perceived as a form of pay-for-privacy, yet users appear reluctant to select this option when freemium is available [11].

Several approaches to monetizing data include selling data, analyses, or data-based services [36]. Data can be sold as raw data, but when data is parsed, cataloged, or enriched, the value of the data increases significantly [19, 36]. Selling analyses focus on handling the data and extracting the required information from it (quality of data increases). This type of data is easier to understand than raw data, but the data buyer may prefer raw data rather than analyzed data because analyzed data has fewer use cases. Data-based services are a way to give users partial access to raw data, for example, to target Facebook ads to specific interest groups [36].

The primary findings of the study conducted by Zhang et al. [53] indicate that lower-value companies tend to sell more data comparing those with higher value. Additionally, these lower-value companies often possess fewer competitive strategies when facing larger companies [53]. For example, Big Tech companies do not want to sell their data directly as selling data-based services generates continuous revenue for the company. The number of users and engaged users are seen as a measure of power among Big Tech and more users often means more personal data is collected [8], therefore more revenue can be generated.

Challenges in developing data-driven business models are often related to data characteristics, privacy, and security. When data is collected, the quality of the data is a critical aspect when thinking about data-driven business models, as to increase the value of the data it needs to be accurate, complete, consistent, timely, etc. Data privacy and security are important, and laws and regulations are in place to protect customers' rights. However, companies must address issues such as protecting data from theft and errors through various security measures [36].

2.2 BCI and XR-BCI Data Monetization

In the current landscape, XR-BCI finds its primary applications in the critical fields of medical care and robot control. However, with advancements on the horizon, future domains are poised to embrace XR-BCI technology, spanning diverse sectors such as gaming, smart home integration, and military operations. According to Mhaidli et al. [25], marketers are keen to emphasize the array of advantages XR presents, citing its ability to immerse users, leverage interactive functionalities, and faithfully reproduce products digitally, thus paving the way for innovative marketing strategies across various industries.

XR-BCI will likely play a significant role in the growth of the metaverse in the future [52]. Highlighting the metaverse as a future platform is crucial, as XR-BCI is likely to be employed in this kind of platform, as well as in health-related solutions. Data monetization represents a means of deriving benefits from the creation of XR-BCI devices or services operating within the XR-BCI, thereby generating revenue for the company. Chen et al. [12] posit that the metaverse publisher will control the metaverse and the information that exists in it. This implies that the publisher will collect a vast quantity of user data that can be monetized and sold. However, this process is difficult to control [12]. XR-BCI devices are the most probable candidates for acting as terminals to enter the metaverse. This suggests that XR-BCI devices are part of the metaverse and share data monetization strategies with it. As more brain data is collected, BCIs will potentially contribute to the metaverse, creating a new type of data for monetization. This is discussed in more detail in the neuromarketing Sect. 2.3.

2.3 Neuromarketing

The term neuromarketing is currently defined in a fragmented manner, with no clear consensus on the meaning. However, by examining the importance of understanding the consumer through the lens of psychology and neuroscience, the term can be better defined [42]. Consumer neuroscience can be divided into two categories. The first category concerns the understanding of consumer behavior, while the second category encompasses the theoretical contributions that mark the initial stages of the conceptual evolution of the field [16]. The future of neuromarketing is contingent upon the ability of companies to create value through this marketing discipline. However, as Duque-Hurtado et al. [16] observe, the challenge in expanding the understanding of neuromarketing is that the majority of research in this field is conducted privately. In this study, neuromarketing is defined as a marketing concept that employs brain data to inform the targeting of products or services to individuals. By analyzing brain data, marketers can tailor their approach to align with a person's mood, emotions, willingness, and interests, among other factors in a real-time [9,46].

In a study on neuromarketing, Ariely et al. [2] sought to determine whether this field is merely a source of hype or a genuine area of hope. Nearly fifteen years later, there are indications that neuromarketing is on the verge of becoming a reality, with BCI devices playing a pivotal role in this process. The rationale behind the use of neuromarketing is twofold. Firstly, it is hoped that it will yield new information that can not be obtained through other marketing strategies. Secondly, it is believed that neuromarketing will provide insights into so-called hidden information. Another anticipated benefit of neuromarketing is that it offers a more cost-effective approach to marketing [2]. It is challenging to assess the efficacy of traditional marketing and advertising strategies, as they do not consider the consumer's willingness and emotions. Neuromarketing could assist in uncovering this hidden information, including potential willingness and emotions [28].

The issue of revealing hidden information is a topic of great interest. The question arises as to whether consumers are willing to provide this information and whether this is an ethical practice. Stanton et al. [42] listed several studies suggesting that predicting users' choices and purchase decisions using fMRI (functional Magnetic Resonance Imaging) or EEG is possible. Neuromarketing is considered safe because only the subjects were exposed to the brain scan, and people still have the right to choose whether or not to wear a BCI device. Furthermore, the justification for neuromarketing is based on the assumption that consumers would have purchased the product in question even in the absence of neuromarketing, as indicated by the brain data. Another rationale for neuromarketing is that it enables companies to identify the most suitable product for consumers. However, there is a potential ethical issue if two products are equally satisfying to the customer, but the advertising campaign persuades the customer to purchase the more expensive option [42]. Other monetization methods may include actions such as user tracking, behavior analysis, virtual advertising embedded in the physical world, or attempts to influence people's behavior (e.g. guiding their actions). These methods have the potential to exacerbate the privacy concerns associated with XR devices [39].

> **Privacy frameworks:** The integration of BCI into XR devices raises additional concerns due to the current and future capabilities of BCI. Frameworks such as the GDPR and the Privacy Act 2020 are designed to ensure the privacy of users. In the future, a strict BCI and XR-BCI evaluation could be conducted to determine their alignment with these frameworks i.e. is there any specification for neural data? Also, laws could help to increase privacy such as the Colorado bill with the law that extends privacy rights to include neural data, recognizing it as sensitive information [27]

Marketing Examples. As neuromarketing emerges, it is imperative to consider potential future scenarios. In light of this, it is essential to pose questions to neuromarketing practitioners and researchers also:

1. Is it ethical to collect brain data for advertising purposes (e.g. by analyzing emotions, mood, and other individual characteristics such as gender, religion, or political preference)? Are BCI users prepared to justify this practice?
2. For example, if you think of a car, will BCI neuromarketing "force you" to see car commercials?
3. Can brain data be used for direct or subtle consumer manipulation?

The three cases presented below demonstrate how neuromarketing could be employed in a real-time. The third case presented a scenario where a malicious entity employed marketing techniques to manipulate XR users into voting in a manner that was aligned with the attacker's intentions. This kind of political target marketing is mentioned by Värbu et al. [47] and in this example case, the idea was implanted into the user's brain using a traditional roadside board inside the extended reality.

Case 1: A person is playing a game using an XR-BCI headset. The game goes rather badly and the player fails to complete the level. The BCI now receives brain data showing that the player's mood is angry and disappointed. Personal adverts are adjusted to match the player's current mood. The player's mood and personal data suggest that the player will engage in retail therapy, which was found to be effective in improving mood in temporary negative mood states [3]. New ads will be updated to appear on various platforms such as social media, blogs, websites, etc. to encourage angry players to conduct online shopping.

Case 2: A person plays a game using an XR-BCI headset. During the game, the person gets hungry and thinks of food. After finishing the game, the person sees food advertisements with good offers with free home delivery. The person decides to buy because it is an easy and quick option.

Case 3 (Traditional marketing inside XR, not neuromarketing): A person using the XR-BCI headset walks down the city street and sees a roadside commercial about a famous politician. This person does not have a significant political leaning ahead of the upcoming elections. When the election comes, the person votes for the candidate he/she saw in the roadside commercial. In this case, the commercial does not exist, it was virtually overlaid on the billboard. This virtual advert could hypothetically be displayed by a legitimate targeted political campaign that can detect and replace advertisements based on a higher bidder, or by unlawful actors that have *"sensed"* this voter is undecided without authorization and is trying to influence the elections.

3 Analysis of Privacy Policies

Privacy Policies and Terms of Service are essential legal documents that outline users' and service providers' rights and responsibilities in any user-provided settings and are especially relevant in the digital realm. Privacy policies delineate the manner in which an organization collects, stores, utilizes, and protects the personal information of its users. This encompasses data such as names, email addresses, browsing history, and payment details, but other data can also be collected such as raw brain data or results from brain data analysis.

Nowadays, some regulatory frameworks govern data collection and storage, e.g., the General Data Protection Regulation (GDPR). While the increased transparency may be perceived as a positive development, superficial or malevolent treatment of such regulatory frameworks may lead to a false sense of privacy and security for the users. Furthermore, the increase in privacy notifications that fulfill the requirements of the law may add transparency, but they will not give freedom or the possibility for the web user to make decisions that would increase individual privacy [14]. For example, users can still encounter privacy breaches through consumer agreements, despite the security measures in place [38].

The complexity of privacy policies increases [14], which may make users less willing to read and understand them fully end-to-end and all their implications. As Steinfeld 's [43] website study observed, if a privacy policy is not displayed by default and the user must actively open it, the default is to ignore it. Also, Obar & Oeldorf-Hirsch 's [33] research supports the argument that users bypass privacy policies. Furthermore, if the user does open it, they will likely only glance it through [14,33]. This may be attributed to the length and complexities of the texts within privacy policies and terms of services. Based on the average reading speed of individuals, it would take some time to read and fully comprehend those documents. The privacy policy and terms of service are both lengthy documents. Research suggests that the privacy policy takes approximately 30 min to read while the terms of service take approximately 15 min [33].

3.1   Review Preparations

As final users do not tend to scrutinize privacy policies, in this review, we analyzed the privacy policies of established companies with potential access to brain activity. Our review process is comprised of multiple phases, as summarized in Fig. 1. We start with the identification of suitable BCI and XR manufacturers as described in Sect. 3.2. Following this, the privacy policies were analyzed in order to ascertain details about data collection, third-party involvement, the privacy of minors, and any potential references to neural data collection. Upon completion of the analysis, the findings were processed, validated, and compared with the monetization review conducted for this paper i.e. extracting results as discussed in Sect. 3.2.

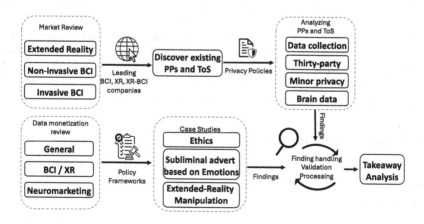

Fig. 1. Method used to review privacy aspects within BCI and XR ecosystems.

The companies selected for this analysis are categorized into three groups: those involved in extended reality (XR), non-invasive BCI, and invasive BCI technologies. The selection criteria encompassed companies engaged in the manufacture or development of XR headsets, non-invasive BCI devices, or invasive BCI devices. In reality, some companies fit under two different categories. A detailed listing of the chosen companies is provided in Table 1.

Table 1. List of BCI, XR, XR-BCI companies under review in this paper.

Extended Reality	Non-invasive BCI	Invasive BCI
Sony [41]	NeuroSky [31]	Neuralink [30]
Meta [24]	Muse [29]	Synchron [44]
Varjo [49,50]	Emotiv [17]	
	OpenBCI [35]	
	BrainAccess [10]	

The extended reality (XR) category encompasses three companies engaged in the development and sale of XR technology. Sony, for instance, produces VR glasses for gaming. Meta, a prominent entity, not only develops metaverse technologies but also participates in numerous XR/BCI-based research projects [22,23]. Additionally, Varjo stands out for its focus on crafting XR glasses tailored for professional applications. It is also noteworthy that Varjo is engaged in the development of XR-BCI devices in collaboration with Open-BCI [48].

The non-invasive BCI category comprises five different companies. These include NeuroSky, Muse, Emotiv, and BrainAccess, each of which is dedicated to the creation of EEG-based lightweight BCI devices intended for individual use. Furthermore, OpenBCI is distinguished by its commitment to the development of open-source EEG-based BCI devices tailored for research purposes.

The invasive BCI category is comprised of mainly two rival companies, Neuralink and Synchron. Both have obtained clinical approval for their devices, enabling testing with patients, which both companies have started recently. These companies specialize in the design of products intended to address the needs of individuals facing limitations in their daily activities.

3.2   Results of the Review

This section presents our main findings from the privacy policies we analyzed. The findings are presented below per company:

EmotivBCI [17]

- *Data collection.* Emotiv collects various types of personal information directly from users, including contact information, financial account information, and user account information. Additionally, they collect personal information from third parties and automatically when users use their services.

- *Third-party sharing.* Emotiv shares personal information with vendors, third-party service providers, and agents for various purposes, including billing, marketing, and compliance. **They also share pseudonymized EEG Data and Experiment Data with third parties for research purposes, potentially without explicit consent from users for each instance.**
- *Data retention.* Emotiv stores personal information for as long as necessary to provide services, comply with legal obligations, and for scientific or historical research purposes.
- *Policy updates.* Emotiv reserves the right to **modify its privacy policy at any time**, and users are encouraged to **periodically review the policy.**
- *Minors' privacy.* Their services are not intended for children under the age of 16 and they do not **knowingly collect** personal information from children.

NeuroSky [31]

- *Data Collection.* Personal information may be collected during various activities including purchasing products, registering products, participating in forums, downloading software updates, registering for events, or participating in online surveys.
- *Personal Information.* Personal information is used to provide customer service, access to products and services, and send product announcements, software updates, special offers, and event notifications.
- *Information Sharing.* NeuroSky does not sell, rent, or exchange personally identifiable information without user consent, but **it may share information with third-party service providers who perform services on behalf of NeuroSky.**
- *Disclosure Exceptions.* NeuroSky mentions potential scenarios where personal information might be disclosed, such as legal processes, defending legal claims, or as otherwise required by law. However, it **does not specify how user privacy will be protected in such situations.**
- *Minors' privacy.* Their website is intended for users 18 years and older, but it also provides guidance for parents if they believe their minor child has submitted personal information.
- *Third-party Sites.* Linked sites are outside its control and responsibility.
- *Sales of Assets.* In case of a sale or transfer of NeuroSky assets, **user databases containing personally identifiable information may be transferred to third parties.** While it promises to notify users of such events, it's unclear how users can manage their data in such circumstances.
- *Changes to Privacy Policy.* It reserves the right to **change the privacy policy without explicitly informing users.**
- *Cookies.* NeuroSky uses cookies to identify web browsers and track user activities on the website. While it states that cookies do not reveal personally identifiable information, it does not provide clear instructions on how users can manage or disable cookies

- *Up to date.* The Privacy policy was updated last time in 2009 and it is short (**out-dated**).

Muse BCI [29]

- *Data Collection.* Muse collects various types of data including Sensor, Processed, Activity, Preference, and Transmission Data. The collected data is used for providing real-time feedback during sessions, generating reports, customer support, research purposes, technical troubleshooting, performance management, and product enhancement.
- *Location Data.* Muse collects Location Data to enable Bluetooth connectivity on Android devices but claims not to store this data
- *Data Sharing.* **Users' data is shared with third parties involved in research or product improvement**, but details about the criteria for selecting these third parties and ensuring data privacy are not provided.
- *Observer Monitoring.* Muse Connect allows observers to monitor participants' sessions with the consent of the participants. When participants consent to data sharing, **Muse BCI shares their Activity Data, Processed Data, Email, Name, and Profile picture with the observer.**
- *Minors' privacy.* Muse products are directed to persons aged 16 or over, and Muse does not **knowingly collect** personal information from children under 16.
- *Data Retention.* User data will be stored for extended periods, even after the user's account becomes inactive. The length of time data is retained and the purposes for which it is retained are not clearly defined.
- *Transfer of personal data.* User data may be transferred to multiple countries, each with different privacy laws and regulations, raising concerns about data protection and security during transfer.

OpenBCI [35]

- *Collection of Personal data.* OpenBCI collects various types of personal information from users, including contact information, financial information, technical device information, and user content.
- *Third-party partners.* OpenBCI works with third-party partners and processors such as Google, Facebook, and Shopify. While these partnerships may enhance the services provided, **users should be informed about how their data is shared with these entities and for what purposes.**
- *Cookies.* OpenBCI collects information via cookies, which are used for tracking user activities and preferences.
- *Data Protection.* It claims to implement security measures to protect user data against unauthorized access or breaches.
- *Data transfer.* Personal data can be transferred to countries outside the European Union, indicating compliance with data protection regulations.
- *Privacy rights.* It acknowledges users' privacy rights, including the right to object to data processing and opt-out mechanisms.

- *Minor's privacy.* It does not **knowingly collect** personal information from children under the age of 16, demonstrating a commitment to protecting children's privacy.

BrainAccess [10]

- *Storage of Personal Information.* BrainAccess collects personally-identifying information such as name, email, phone number, and address when users visit the site, register, fill out forms, or subscribe to newsletters. Users' personal information might be used for providing services, managing accounts, providing support, and sending promotional material.
- *Sharing personal information.* It does not disclose users' personal information except in certain circumstances, such as to comply with the law or protect legal rights.
- *Data sharing:* Non-personally identifying information may be shared with third parties for marketing and other uses.
- *Direct marketing.* BrainAccess may use users' contact information for direct marketing purposes without prior consent if they are current or former clients.
- *Minors' privacy.* Its site and services are not designed for children under the age of 16 and BrainAccess does not **knowingly collect** information from them.

Neuralink [30]

- *Collection of personal information.* Neuralink collects various types of personal information, including health and medical information, personal contact information, biographical and demographic information, and communication information.
- *Information automatically collected.* Neuralink uses cookies and similar technologies to collect information automatically about users' use of the website, such as IP address, browser type, pages viewed, and time spent on pages.
- *Sharing of personal information.* It **shares personal information with various entities**, including service providers, healthcare providers, research partners, and professional advisors.
- *User consent.* It collects, uses, and discloses personal information with user consent or as permitted or required by law.
- *Data retention.* Neuralink retains personal information for as long as necessary to fulfill the purposes for which it was collected and processed.
- *Security measures.* It claims to have implemented safeguards to help secure users' personal information. However, users should be informed about the specific security measures in place and any potential risks to their data security.
- *Minors' privacy.* Neuralink does not **knowingly collect** personal information from anyone under the age of 18.

Synchron BCI [44]

- *Collection of personal information.* Synchron collects various types of personal information, including contact information, internet and network identifiers, and information provided in correspondence. Additionally, in the context of clinical trials, Synchron may collect biographical, demographic, and health-related information from users.
- *Cookies.* Synchron uses cookies, pixel tags, and similar technologies to collect information about users' service use.
- *Sharing of personal information.* **Shares personal information with various entities and providers** for purposes such as service provision, research and development, and legal compliance.
- *Security measures.* It claims to have implemented safeguards to help keep users' personal information safe, including administrative, data security, and physical safeguards.
- *Data retention.* Synchron retains users' personal information for as long as necessary to fulfill the purposes for which it was collected and processed.
- *Third-party sites.* Linked sites are outside its control and responsibility.

Meta Platforms Technologies Privacy Policy/VR [24]

- *Mandatory account data.* Meta account needs information name, contact information, password, and date of birth. Meta Horizon profile (for VR) stores information about the profile name, profile picture, username, avatar, list of followers, and interactions with games and apps.
- *Data collection VR.* While interacting with the VR app some information is collected (e.g. physical characteristics and movements) (e.g. **Mandatory data:** Headset/controllers position and orientation, and audio data, and **Volunteer data:** Hand and body tracking, eye tracking, natural facial expressions, fit adjustment), meta VR Product activity (e.g. payment credentials, event, purchases, downloaded apps, frequency and duration of your activities), content, fitness information (e.g. calories, time active, goals and achievements), gameplay and statistics, environmental information and dimensions (e.g. room size, etc.), camera and audio information (improve VR world by processing data in device), voice interactions, device information (e.g. device attributes, logs, crash reports, 3-party app use), and information from partners and third parties.
- *Data share.* **All public marked data, horizon profile (e.g., avatar, username, profile, connected people, and interactions)**, is shared with third parties to ensure the delivery of the requested service.
- *Third-party.* Meta does not govern how third-party apps utilize, retain, or distribute data when users opt to share data with those apps during their interactions. It is crucial to acknowledge that when users activate features such as eye-tracking, or when certain physical attributes are not mandatory, but the user needs to enable them as apps may require these for optimal functionality, Meta is also collecting this enabled data.

- *Purpose of data collection.* Meta collects data to provide services, including advertisements and commercial content. This data is also used to promote safety, security, and integrity, as well as to communicate with users. Finally, the data is used to improve services by innovating and researching.
- *Parent responsibility/Minors' privacy.* Meta's platforms are not for children under 13 without parents' consent. Account for children between 10 and 12 is the parent's responsibility, and this account is to be treated the same way as any other account.

Sony PS VR2/Sony's general privacy policy [41]

- *Automatic Information Collection.* Sony mentions the automatic collection of various data types, including device identifiers, network identifiers, location information, gameplay details, and errors. This extensive data collection may raise concerns about the level of user surveillance and the potential for intrusive monitoring of user activities
- *Information sharing.* **Sony may share user information with various third parties**, including service providers, partners, advertising partners, and government authorities. While some sharing may be necessary for providing services, the broad scope of sharing raises questions about the extent to which user data is exposed to external parties.
- *Marketing.* Sony employs user information for personalized marketing communications and targeted advertising. While personalized content can enhance user experience, it also raises privacy concerns regarding the tracking and profiling the users for advertising purposes without explicit consent.
- *Data transfer.* User data may be transferred to and processed in different countries, potentially subjecting it to varying privacy regulations. This lack of control over data transfers raises concerns about data protection standards and user privacy rights in different jurisdictions.
- *Data retention.* Sony may store the user information for extended periods, even after the termination of user accounts, for purposes such as legal compliance and dispute resolution. Extended data retention practices raise concerns about the potential misuse or unauthorized access to stored user data.
- *Limited control.* Users may have limited control over the collection, use, and sharing of their data, particularly in cases where data processing is considered necessary for service delivery.

Varjo XR-3 and VR-3 [49,50]

- *Data Collection.* Varjo collects various categories of personal data, including basic customer and user information, IP addresses, login information, subscription details, usage data, technical data, feedback, and communications.
- *Marketing.* Varjo processes personal data for marketing and sales purposes, including sending newsletters, targeted marketing, customer analysis, and offering products and services.
- *Third-party Sharing.* **Varjo shares personal data with connected parties, group companies, vendors, third-party service providers, and authorized third parties.**

- *Data Transfer.* Personal data may be transferred outside the EU/EEA, raising concerns about data protection standards and regulatory compliance in other authorities.
- *Data Retention.* Varjo stores personal data for as long as necessary.
- *User Rights.* Users have rights to access, correct, erase, restrict processing, object to processing, withdraw consent, opt-out of marketing, and request data portability.

4   Discussion over Main Results

We discuss the issues we see in *privacy policies* and *collection practices*, and how those affect neuromarketing in the future.

Issues with Privacy Policies: The analysis of the privacy policies of numerous companies reveals that a considerable amount of data is being collected, including network identifiers, health-related data, and usage data. The purpose for the extensive collection of information is unclear, as well as how this affects the protection of children. There are guidelines regarding the privacy of minors, with the majority of users between the ages of 16 and 18 opening an account. Meta has the lowest age requirement for users, with individuals aged 13 permitted to open accounts and commence utilization of Meta's services, with the consent of the parent or guardian. The age may be lowered to 10. While some platforms define an age boundary, it is unclear how companies ensure that this is fulfilled. For instance, according to Hargittai et al. [20], parents are willing to assist their children with account creation. In fact, 78 percent of children aged 14 and 47 percent of children aged 10 have received assistance from their parents. However, the protection of minors is regulated by tight privacy regulations for children, such as the US Children's Online Privacy Protection Act (COPPA) of 1998 [18].

Based on our analysis of current privacy policies and our experience with the use of this technology, we derive the following insight:

> **Minors, misfits in current privacy policies:** Current efforts made by companies are far from sufficient to permit fine-grained and actionable parental controls. Current collection practices depict a different reality around the age target. This creates a void in the protection of children's online privacy and their brain online exposure. We advocate for privacy policies to be reviewed to align with the technological and usage realities.

Emotiv recommends that users periodically review their privacy policy. However, this is prone to issues — reviewing policy is demanding, and changes are generally overlooked. To fix this, Emotiv should give some notification of the changes they have made to the privacy policy. Furthermore, NeuroSky reserves the right to modify its privacy policy without explicitly notifying users of this action. This policy is also outdated, according to the NeuroSky webpage, as the privacy policy was last updated in 2009. To address the mentioned issue, it is recommended that users be made aware of any changes to the PP, such as the Privacy Act 2020 in New Zealand [34].

Issues with Data Collection Practices: One of the most common procedures is data sharing with a third party. Some companies also note that data can be transferred, for example, outside the EU, and in this case, data protection regulations will change after transfer. It is also noteworthy that when companies announce sharing data with third parties, it is often not clear which entities will gain access to the data.

Notably, none of the companies under review stated that neural data (brain data) is used for marketing purposes. However, there are instances where data-sharing practices remain unclear. For instance, BrainAccess states that it shares non-personally identifying information for marketing purposes, yet it is unclear whether brain data falls within this category. Similarly, Emotiv is sharing pseudonymized EEG Data and Experiment Data with third parties for research purposes. Additionally, invasive BCI devices (Neuralink or Synchron) are employed for health purposes, with the associated health data being shared with select entities. Devices manufactured by these companies are also the most capable of producing high-quality data containing the most sensitive data. Team EMB [46] has presented a blog text that outlines potential avenues for future marketing strategies for Neuralink. As such, we derive the following insight.

> **Risk of leaking emotions to advertisers through neuromarketing:** To seamlessly incorporate neuromarketing into campaigns, marketers require access to state-of-the-art tools and technologies, encompassing data gathered from EEG headsets, eye-tracking devices, and neuroimaging equipment. This data, which we have examined in light of certain policies, is leveraged for service enhancement. However, sensory data of this nature holds significant relevance in neuromarketing, potentially unveiling extremely sensitive information like emotions to advertisements [46].

5   Conclusion

In this work, we have presented a systematic method for reviewing privacy assurances offered and monetization aspects within BCI and XR-BCI ecosystems. Our review is done through the lenses of data collection practices self-declared in privacy policies and terms of service, as well as through the review of the academic literature in the area of neuromarketing. From our review, we observed concerning issues in how privacy policies discuss the usage of brain data, as well as issues in correct data collection practices. In particular, we have discussed genuine risks behind the leakage of emotions and generic raw brain-wave data to advertisers, and the lack of controls in this emerging technology in the face of its rapid and yet-to-be-regulated development. We also derived key takeaways that offer actionable insights that aim to improve the privacy of minors. Finally, we offered a data monetization review that discusses the existing policy frameworks and contextualizes their limitations through three case studies that discussed: i) the ethical implications behind using brain data for advertising; ii) the use of emotions for the subliminal advertisement based on emotions; and iii) risks to the advertisement ecosystem in the (mis)use of extended-reality (XR) (e.g., political manipulation), especially when coupled with BCI as in XR-BCI.

We posit that significant work needs (technology-wise, regulation-wise, legal-wise) to be done to ensure the security, safety, and privacy of individuals using nascent BCI and XR-BCI technologies that equip popular headsets with brain-computer interfaces. The insights we offer in this work will have a profound transformation on the research agenda of the business modeling and software design community.

Acknowledgment. (Part of) This work was supported by the European Commission under the Horizon Europe Programme, as part of the project LAZARUS (https://lazarus-he.eu/) (Grant Agreement no. 101070303). The content of this article does not reflect the official opinion of the European Union. Responsibility for the information and views expressed therein lies entirely with the authors. (Part of this work was) Funded by the European Union (Grant Agreement Nr. 101120962, RESCALE Project). Views and opinions expressed are however those of the author(s) only and do not necessarily reflect those of the European Union or the Health and Digital Executive Agency. Neither the European Union nor the granting authority can be held responsible for them. (Part of) This project was also supported by TED2021-132900A-I00 from the Spanish Ministry of Science and Innovation, and Guillermo Suarez-Tangil has been appointed as 2019 Ramon y Cajal fellow (RYC-2020-029401-I) both funded by MCIN/AEI/10.13039/501100011033 — with funds from the EU NextGenerationEU/PRTR and ESF Investing in your future respectively.

References

1. Adeli, H., Ghosh-Dastidar, S., Dadmehr, N.: A spatio-temporal wavelet-chaos methodology for EEG-based diagnosis of Alzheimer's disease. Neurosci. Lett. **444**(2), 190–194 (2008)
2. Ariely, D., Berns, G.S.: Neuromarketing: the hope and hype of neuroimaging in business. Nat. Rev. Neurosci. **11**, 284–292 (2010)
3. Atalay, A.S., Meloy, M.G.: Retail therapy: a strategic effort to improve mood. Psychol. Mark. **28**, 638–659 (2011)
4. Baglione, S.L., Tucci, L.A., Woock, P.: Would you pay for a facebook account to protect your privacy? J. Social Media Soc. (2020). https://www.thejsms.org/index.php/JSMS/article/download/693/405
5. Bellier, L., et al.: Music can be reconstructed from human auditory cortex activity using nonlinear decoding models. PLoS Biol. **21**, e3002176 (2023)
6. Belmonte, A.: The mental health app data privacy problem is getting worse (2024). https://finance.yahoo.com/news/the-mental-health-app-data-privacy-problem-is-getting-worse-161425472.html. Accessed 15 Feb 2024

7. Benchetrit, Y., Banville, H., King, J.R.: Brain decoding: toward real-time reconstruction of visual perception. arXiv:2310.19812 (2023)
8. Birch, K., Cochrane, D., Ward, C.: Data as asset? the measurement, governance, and valuation of digital personal data by big tech. Big Data Soc. (2021)
9. Bonaci, T., Calo, R., Chizeck, H.J.: App stores for the brain: privacy & security in brain-computer interfaces. In: 2014 IEEE International Symposium on Ethics in Science, Technology and Engineering, pp. 1–7. IEEE (2014)
10. Brainaccess: Privacy policy. https://www.brainaccess.ai/privacy-policy/. Accessed 15 Apr 2024
11. Bryce, C.: Who invited the pay-for-privacy economy? (2019). https://medium.com/swlh/post-privacy-who-invited-the-pay-for-privacy-economy-626aecaf53e9. Accessed 20 Apr 2024
12. Chen, Z., Wu, J., Gan, W., Qi, Z.: Metaverse security and privacy: an overview. In: 2022 IEEE International Conference on Big Data (Big Data). IEEE (2022)
13. Dauwels, J., Vialatte, F., Cichocki, A.: Diagnosis of Alzheimer's disease from EEG signals: where are we standing? Curr. Alzheimer Res. 7(6), 487–505 (2010)
14. Degeling, M., Utz, C., Lentzsch, C., Hosseini, H., Schaub, F., Holz, T.: We value your privacy... now take some cookies: measuring the GDPR's impact on web privacy. arXiv preprint arXiv:1808.05096 (2018)
15. Dixon, S.J.: Annual revenue generated by meta platforms from 2009 to 2023 (2024). https://www.statista.com/statistics/268604/annual-revenue-of-facebook/. Accessed 17 Apr 2024
16. Duque-Hurtado, P., Samboni-Rodriguez, V., Castro-Garcia, M., Montoya-Restrepo, L.A., Montoya-Restrepo, I.A.: Neuromarketing: its current status and research perspectives. Estudios gerenciales (2020)
17. EMOTIV Inc. Emotiv privacy policy (2023). https://id.emotivcloud.com/eoidc/privacy/privacy_policy/. Accessed 15 Apr 2024
18. Commission, F.T.: children's online privacy protection rule (2013). https://www.ftc.gov/system/files/2012-31341.pdf. Accessed 21 Apr 2024
19. Faroukhi, A.Z., El Alaoui, I., Gahi, Y., Amine, A.: Big data monetization throughout big data value chain: a comprehensive review. J. Big Data 7, 1–22 (2020)
20. Hargittai, E., Schultz, J., Palfrey, J., et al.: Why parents help their children lie to facebook about age: unintended consequences of the 'children's online privacy protection act'. First Monday (2011)
21. Landau, O., Puzis, R., Nissim, N.: Mind your mind: EEG-based brain-computer interfaces and their security in cyber space. ACM Comput. Surv. (CSUR) 53(1), 1–38 (2020)
22. Meta: Toward a real-time decoding of images from brain activity (2023). https://ai.meta.com/blog/brain-ai-image-decoding-meg-magnetoencephalography/. Accessed 20 Apr 2024
23. Meta: Research from meta—ar/vr (2024). https://research.facebook.com/publications/research-area/augmented-reality-virtual-reality/. Accessed 20 Apr 2024
24. Meta: Supplemental meta platforms technologies privacy policy (2024). https://www.meta.com/fi/en/legal/privacy-policy/. Accessed 15 Apr 2024
25. Mhaidli, A., Rajaram, S., Fidan, S., Herakovic, G., Schaub, F.: Shockvertising, malware, and a lack of accountability: exploring consumer risks of virtual reality advertisements and marketing experiences. IEEE Secur. Priv. 22(01), 43–52 (2024)
26. Mills, M.: Big tech sees neurotechnology as its next ai frontier (2024). https://finance.yahoo.com/news/big-tech-sees-neurotechnology-as-its-next-ai-frontier-100022978.html. Accessed 14 May 2024

27. Moens, J.: Your brain waves are up for sale. a new law wants to change that. (2024). https://www.nytimes.com/2024/04/17/science/colorado-brain-data-privacy.html. Accessed 21 Apr 2024
28. Morin, C.: Neuromarketing: the new science of consumer behavior. Society (2011)
29. Muse: Legal muse. https://choosemuse.com/pages/legal. Accessed 15 Apr 2024
30. Neuralink: Neuralink privacy policy (2024). https://neuralink.com/privacy-policy/. Accessed 15 Apr 2024
31. NeuroSky: Privacy policy (2009). https://neurosky.com/privacy-policy/. Accessed 15 Apr 2024
32. Nosthoff, A.V., Maschewski, F., Couldry, N.: Big tech is exploiting the mental health crisis to monetize your data (2023). https://eprints.lse.ac.uk/120934/. Accessed 15 Apr 2024
33. Obar, J.A., Oeldorf-Hirsch, A.: The biggest lie on the internet: ignoring the privacy policies and terms of service policies of social networking services. Inf. Commun. Soc. 23(1), 128–147 (2020)
34. Office of the Privacy Commissioner: Do i need to notify customers of changes to our privacy policy? (2020). https://privacy.org.nz/tools/knowledge-base/view/473. Accessed 21 Apr 2024
35. OpenBCI: Privacy & security (2021). https://docs.openbci.com/FAQ/Privacy/. Accessed 15 Apr 2024
36. Parvinen, P., Pöyry, E., Gustafsson, R., Laitila, M., Rossi, M.: Advancing data monetization and the creation of data-based business models. Commun. Assoc. Inf. Syst. (2020)
37. Quach, S., Thaichon, P., Martin, K.D., Weaven, S., Palmatier, R.W.: Digital technologies: tensions in privacy and data. J. Acad. Mark. Sci. 50, 1299–1323 (2022)
38. Reilly, C.M.: Brain-machine interfaces as commodities: exchanging mind for matter. Linacre Q. 87(4), 387–398 (2020)
39. Roesner, F., Kohno, T.: Security and privacy for augmented reality: our 10-year retrospective. In: VR4Sec: 1st International Workshop on Security for XR and XR for Security (2021)
40. Schneble, C.O., Elger, B.S., Shaw, D.M.: Google's project nightingale highlights the necessity of data science ethics review. EMBO Mol. Med. 12(3), e12053 (2020)
41. Sony Interactive Entertainment LLC: Privacy policy (2024). https://www.playstation.com/en-us/legal/privacy-policy/. Accessed 15 Apr 2024
42. Stanton, S.J., Sinnott-Armstrong, W., Huettel, S.A.: Neuromarketing: ethical implications of its use and potential misuse. J. Bus. Ethics 144, 799–811 (2017)
43. Steinfeld, N.: i agree to the terms and conditions: (how) do users read privacy policies online? an eye-tracking experiment. Comput. Hum. Behav. 55, 992–1000 (2016)
44. Synchron: synchron privacy policy (2023). https://www.synchronbci.com/Synchron-Privacy-Policy.aspx. Accessed 15 Apr 2024
45. Tang, J., LeBel, A., Jain, S., Huth, A.G.: Semantic reconstruction of continuous language from non-invasive brain recordings. Nat. Neurosci. 26, 858–866 (2023)
46. Team EMB: the future of neuralink and marketing possibilities (2024). https://blog.emb.global/neuralink-and-marketing/#q-how-does-neuralink-collect-neural-data-for-marketing. Accessed 21 Apr 2024
47. Värbu, K., Muhammad, N., Muhammad, Y.: Past, present, and future of EEG-based BCI applications. Sensors 22(9), 3331 (2022)
48. Varjo: openbci and varjo partner to bring neurotechnology to spatial computing (2022). https://varjo.com/company-news/openbci-and-varjo-partner-to-bring-neurotechnology-to-spatial-computing/. Accessed 20 Apr 2024

49. Varjo HQ: terms of service for varjo xr-3 and vr-3 (2022). https://varjo.com/terms-of-service-for-varjo-xr-3-and-vr-3/. Accessed 15 Apr 2024
50. Varjo HQ: Privacy policy (2023). https://varjo.com/privacy-policy/. Accessed 15 Apr 2024
51. Wikipedia: vastaamo data breach (2024). https://en.wikipedia.org/wiki/Vastaamo_data_breach. Accessed 20 Apr 2024
52. Xu, Z., Chen, G., Zhang, R.: Boosters of the metaverse: a review of augmented reality-based brain-computer interface. Brain-Apparatus Commun. J. Bacomics 3(1), 2305962 (2024)
53. Zhang, X., Yue, W.T., Yu, Y., Zhang, X.: How to monetize data: an economic analysis of data monetization strategies under competition. Decis. Supp. Syst. 173, 114012 (2023)

Researching Multi-Site Artificial Neural Networks' Activation Rates and Activation Cycles

Marcus Grum[(✉)] [iD]

Junior Chair of Business Information Systems, Esp. AI-based Appl. Sys.,
University of Potsdam, Potsdam 14482, Germany
marcus.grum@uni-potsdam.de

Abstract. With the further development of more and more production
machines into cyber-physical systems, and their greater integration with
artificial intelligence (AI) techniques, the coordination of intelligent systems is a highly relevant target factor for the operation and improvement
of networked processes, such as they can be found in cross-organizational
production contexts spanning multiple distributed locations. This work
aims to extend prior research on managing their artificial knowledge
transfers as coordination instrument by examining effects of different
activation types (respective activation rates and cycles) on by Artificial Neural Network (ANN)-instructed production machines. For this, it
provides a new integration type of ANN-based cyber-physical production
system as a tool to research artificial knowledge transfers: In a design-
science-oriented way, a prototype of a simulation system is constructed
as Open Source information system which will be used in on-building
research to (I) enable research on ANN activation types in production
networks, (II) illustrate ANN-based production networks disrupted by
activation types and clarify the need for harmonizing them, and (III)
demonstrate conceptual management interventions. This simulator shall
establish the importance of site-specific coordination mechanisms and
novel forms of management interventions as drivers of efficient artificial
knowledge transfer.

Keywords: Artificial Neural Networks · Cyber-Physical Systems ·
Symbiotic Knowledge Management · Artificial Knowledge Transfer ·
Experiments · Simulation

1 Introduction

Traditionally, production machines are considered as more or less static tools
being programmed with software and hardware routines, which are used to realize value-adding production steps in order to finalize workpiece carriers [1]. Aside
analogous and digital signals that are generated because of physical sensory
information, production machines can be accompanied with Digital Twins in

B. Shishkov (Ed.): BMSD 2024, LNBIP 523, pp. 186–206, 2024.
https://doi.org/10.1007/978-3-031-64073-5_12

Industry 4.0 [2] and Internet of Things [3] contexts to capture beneficial aspects, such as flexibility [4], reliability [5], individualization [6]. Due to their conceptualization as cyber-physical systems [7], these kinds of tools enable embedded or remote signal processing, autonomous communication as well as more sophisticated intelligent task realization [8]. Although isolated prototype concepts start bringing several facets of Artificial Intelligence (AI) to such machines [9, 10], common AI usage has not yet been standardized in application systems. Hence, AI-based knowledge flows at production machines are rather inefficient [11].

These missing standards are particularly problematic if AI is introduced to networks of production machines, such as in organization-wide networks of CPS or cross-organization-wide interacting CPS networks [12]. The controlling of multi-site production facilities via Artificial Neural Networks (ANN)–each machine and site can be represented as individual *cognitive production network* [13]–is challenging because of different characteristics: Activation patterns might vary at machine-, site- and vendor-specific levels for instance as well as follow organization-specific routines and processes. So, AI-based knowledge flows in overarching, interwoven cognitive production networks might become destructive [14] and inefficient [15] in the entire network's context. Reasons can be found at different activation rates and activation cycles, so that, in a worse case, correctly working outcomes of ANN activated are overwritten or lost in disharmonious ANN-sub-structures. If it was possible to bring isolated, machine-specific or site-specific ANN networks in harmony, one can expect joint multi-site ANN-based systems to have (a) more efficient knowledge transfers as individual machines and facilities can adapt to the specific knowledge conversion, (b) destructive activations of sub-systems can be reduced, so that for instance waste, energy and time consumption can be reduced in cross-organization production chains, and (c) ANN-based networks become controllable in a way that management interventions can be applied to improve artificial knowledge transfers in advance.

This article works out the prototype of a concept about multi-site ANN-based application systems as a research instrument in form of a simulation system. This shall be the basis for on-building research, that clarifies inefficient and destructive ANN-based knowledge flows and corresponding improvement of knowledge transfers by management intervention in selected production scenarios. Thus, the following research will address the improvement of ANN knowledge transfers and focuses on the following research question:

"How can different activation types of rate and cycle combinations in multi-site Artificial Neural Networks be researched?"

The research does not intend to provide a sophisticated empirical proof of improved ANN knowledge transfers because of managed multi-site ANNs and corresponding experiments. It rather intends to clarify the basis of such an instrument in production contexts that will be demonstrated and verified in on-building empirical research, experiments and simulation runs designed in this research.

The research approach is intended to be design-oriented in accordance with the Design-Science-Research Methodology (DSRM) [16]. Thus, the second section provides the foundation of multi-site ANN simulation system construction. It further clarifies the research gap and addresses why a simulation platform is needed. Requirements are presented that need to be reflected by the prototype thereafter. These clarify what functionality such a simulation platform shall provide. The design is then presented in the third section, so that it becomes clear how this functionality shall be provided by a simulation platform. Its usefulness demonstration will be conceptualized with the aid of experiments in section four and concluded in the broader research context in the last section.

2   Theoretical Foundation

The theoretical foundation for the research presented here refers to ANN-based systems that are located at multiple sites. For demonstration purposes, these are exemplified in Industry 4.0 contexts, such as ANN-based production machinery being integrated in production processes spanning different production sites. Thus, the characterization of neuronally constructed systems is addressed in the first sub-section and the engineering of ANN-based Industry 4.0 machinery in the second sub-section. As this research aims for researching ANN's activation rates and activation cycles, the tool of system analysis and corresponding states characteristics, that are commonly used to describe periodicity of systems, are addressed in sub-section three. On the basis of these concepts, the research gap is concretized on the one hand, and on the other hand the experimental setup and the necessary research instruments can be designed in the following sections.

2.1   Neuronal System Modeling and Artificial Knowledge Transfers

Artificial Knowledge Transfers. A knowledge transfer can be interpreted as conversion of different types of knowledge being bound to various kinds of knowledge carriers [17]. While the first form of knowledge refers to well documentable *explicit knowledge* [18], that can be handed among any kind of process participant easily (e.g. a book, data file or pixel information), the second form of knowledge is hard to document as it is knowledge-bearer-bound (e.g. experience). It is referred to as *tacit knowledge* [18] and can be found at human level as well as AI-based system level [15]. Among further interpretations, this knowledge can be interpreted as *neuronal pattern* consisting of a sequence of neural activations [15], which either can be found in the human brain on a biological level or they can be generated by virtually simulated brains based on artificial neural networks [19].

Neuronal System Modeling. By modeling neuronal patterns, e.g. with the aid of the Neuronal Modeling and Description Language (short: NMDL) [20], the following is enabled [13]: Either the activity of ANN-based systems can become transparent and made explainable as *artificial knowledge transfers* since the neural injection of explicit knowledge in ANN becomes clear and artificial knowledge objects are identified automatically (activation data-centered approach). Here, the processual behavior of ANN-based systems evolves due to unknown artificial knowledge transfers. Alternatively, AI-based systems can be transparently constructed and algorithmically interpreted (AI system engineering approach). Here, ANN structures follow predefined artificial knowledge transfers. In hybrid approaches, data-centered and engineering approaches can meet to enable the debugging of ANN systems: An evolving procedural behavior and predefined artificial knowledge transfers can be compared and fed back to real-world requirements. However, these approaches have been demonstrated in organization-wide interwoven ANN-based systems which have had the same activation rates and start times [13].

Interim-Conclusion. Although ANN-based systems and respective artificial knowledge flows have been demonstrated at organization-wide levels, there is no research about interacting ANN-based systems that follow different activation rates and activation cycles. So far, neuronal modeled systems have been interwoven and activated as one system only, which is equivalent to one artificial brain. A research gap becomes apparent, here.

2.2 ANN-Based Cyber-Physical Production Systems

Cyber-Physical Systems. Following Ashton [21], the physical meaning of classical production components is enhanced by embedded systems with structures similar to the Internet such that their physical meaning is supplemented by a virtual representation. Since those computational elements are collaborating to control their respective physical and virtual entities, they are hereinafter referred to as cyber-physical systems (CPS) [22]. According to their schematic structure [23], they provide the following: At least one *communicator* realizes the connection to other CPSs using internet protocols, e.g. for exchanging AI knowledge bases. *Sensors* perceive data from the environment and a CPS generates an understanding of its preferably certain states within the environment (e.g. by AI-based recognition). *Actuators* carry out the interactions with the physical environment so that a feedback loop can be closed, such as by AI generated instructions. *Processors* realize beside other tasks the decisions of the CPS. Here, different kinds of AI-based and non-AI-based decision strategies can coexist in one CPS to follow its strategy autonomously.

Cyber-Physical Production Systems. However, connecting several CPS to one Cyber-Physical Production Systems (CPPS) [7], each CPS in the production setting possesses individual abilities to act with, or perceive information from the environment and its surrounding CPS, which is more than simply receiving messages via its communication channels. Based on its location, individual limitations restrict its actions and time dependent states (e.g. their current production phase) influence its availability to interact with other CPS and realize production routines in cooperation. Facing the complexity of CPPS, a conceptual design of worldwide distributed CPPS are provided by Bender et al. [12]. However, the corresponding simulation realization has not been realized, yet.

ANN-based CPPS. Interwoven and by ANN instructed cognitive production networks of four different CPS types (one robot arm, two feeder, one conveyor) already have been realized in organization-wide context [13]. These lead to productive routines and realized cost savings and waste reduction for instance. However, these were located at one production facility, realized productions of one company and consisted of CPS purchased from vendor only.

Interim-Conclusion. Although conceptual ideas and fragments are available for worldwide CPPS systems on the one hand and ANN-instructed CPPS on the other hand, a multi-site CPPS that is based on ANN instructions or rather global, neuronally instructed production chains having multiple production facilities have not been realized, yet. A research gap becomes apparent, here. Since this article contributes the research stream of [13], please find here comparisons regarding existing simulation platforms, the question of "buy or build?" is related with the transportation of proved concepts to CPS of different vendors.

2.3 System Analysis and System States

System Analysis. System analysis can be described as a systematic method for the model-based analysis of complex objects of investigation [24]. Here, the structure as well as the external and internal functionalities of an object of investigation (OoI) and its components are examined and evaluated in order to define requirements for a solution design. In this research, the OoI refers to ANN-based cognitive production networks of neuronally instructed production chains spanning multiple production facilities (cf. Sect. 2.2) and respective neuronal knowledge patterns (cf. Sect. 2.1) as well as the ANN-based induced production behavior. Particularly in cases of phenomena based on complex mechanisms, where the causes of phenomena were not based on isolated causal chains or relationships between a few variables (here analytical methods lead to great success), system analysis shows strengths with its consideration of system elements in an interdependent context [25]. Typically, examples refer to in growth and equilibrium processes, meshed control loops, complex decision sequences or socio-cultural development processes.

State Characterization. With the aid of *chaos theory*, system analyses e.g. intends to describe *periodicity* of dynamic systems. Intuitively, the state of a system describes enough about the system to determine its future behavior in the absence of any disregarded influences affecting the system. From particular interest is the state of *equilibrium*, which means that the behavior of dynamic systems does not change over time without external influence [26]. In this research, each production site is considered as dynamic ANN-based system (due to recurrent ANN structures and humans in the loop), which will be examined as combined dynamic system of interwoven cognitive production networks inhowfar their activation will result in a *joint equilibrium*. In this context, the joint equilibrium means that their production behavior does not change over time without external influence and a production routine evolves. It will be examined inhowfar this equilibrium is productive in regard with rejected goods, waste, time consumed, etc., too. By now, the following kinds of equilibrium-related state descriptions are distinguished for dynamic systems [26–28]:

a) Systems are *unstable* or *chaotic* if respective systems are deflected slightly and do not return to its original reference position, but the deflection increases. In this research, a deflection means a deviation from the originally learned ANN tasks and corresponding artificial knowledge flows that evolve a working production routine at reference activation rates and cycles. Often, the systems' respective knowledge flows reinforce themselves. This self-reinforcement can be referred to as positive feedback and leads to apparently *arbitrary* changes in the production context simulated.

b) A dynamic system is *stable* if the system returns to its initial state after a deflection or fault. For instance, although the production network is faced with deflected activation types, the intended production process can be realized due to efficient knowledge flows among ANN-based systems.

c) The system is *labile* if it changes state at the slightest disturbance. For instance, any kind of activation type change results in alternative production processes.

d) The dynamic system is *metastable* if it returns to a more stable equilibrium state after a sufficiently large deflection or disturbance. For instance, the production network comes up with improved production routines if different activation types are used.

e) If a metastable system has two equilibrium states, it is also referred to as *bistable*. Many dynamical systems exhibit the coexistence of several stable states, which is also known as *multistability* [29].

f) The dynamic system is *indifferent stable* if it comes to rest in a new state after every deflection or disturbance. For instance, the production network comes up with alternative production routines if different activation types are used. It needs to be questioned if the alternative is productive, too.

As the different forms of equilibrium (stable, labile, metastable, bistable, multistable and indifferent) can be related to a production behavior recurrent at regular interval, these are referred to as *periodic* systems from hereon and differentiated from *chaotic* systems.

Stability in Neuron Dynamics. Biological and artificial neuronal networks have been studied in regard with stability since decades. For instance, it is supposed that the biological origin of bistable visual perception draws back to neuron cells activity, which induces switches between different perception states [30,31]. On the level of single neurons, multistability is represented by the coexistence of basic firing patterns, like silence, spiking, regular, and chaotic bursting [32]. On the level of group of neurons, the physiology of neural systems has been examined: Here, dynamical concepts were focused, such as time delay [33], phase locking patterns [34], or delayed recurrent neural loops [35]. However, studies mostly refer to mathematical analyses, but not system analysis methods and by ANN-instructed machines in simulations. Further, they do not cover decentralized AI realization strategies and corresponding Industry 4.0 capable infrastructures.

Interim-Conclusion. Per se, there is no state description that enables the characterization of combined dynamic systems which considers different kinds of ANN activation rates and activation cycles. System analyses enables the individual analysis of any kind of sub-system but not the activation type-related state characterization so far. For instance, the system-specific ANN activation rates can have *coupled* or *decoupled* starting times. Further, from an analytical perspective, they can refer to the *same* or *different* rates, while the latter can refer to *divisible* versus *indivisible* rates, *duplicable* versus *unduplicable* or *irregular* rates. Although simulation of spiking neural networks have been analyzed in regard with balancing states, the activation type related evolving behavior of ANN-based systems, such as in production contexts, has not been focused, yet. A research gap becomes apparent, here.

3   Design

In regard with the DSRM [16], the design presents research problem solution in form of artifacts, which will demonstrate their usefulness in the demonstration section. As was identified in section two, these artifacts refer to (a) the production site design, (b) the scenario design, (c) the task design, (d) the AI system design and, (e) the simulation system design. Each will be presented in an individual sub-section.

Since the production sites were ought to be instructed by AI and the *Concept of Neuronal Modeling* [13], the individual artifacts were designed with the aid of the Neuronal Modeling and Description Language (short: NMDL) from its repository [20]. Due to its practice focus, requirements for corresponding artifacts (see Table 1) have been synthesized from literature and validated with researches and production machinery manufacturers. So, they have functioned as quality gates for artifacts presented here and they can stand as quality gates for subsequent research.

3.1   Production Site Design

In the beginning, the hardware for the experimental investigation has been designed and set up. Therefore, the distributed production facilities and machine interactions are designed. The result is the physical construction of a distributed Industry 4.0 production plant structure that can simulate global production chains. According to Fig. 1, this consists of the following production facilities: (1) an AI-based logistics center for shipping goods in Pretoria, (2) an AI-based logistics center for receiving goods in Bochum and (3) further production facilities for AI-based goods processing in Potsdam. Based on the NMDL's *Organizational Overview*, in the figure, one can see the individual organizational units and its technical sub-elements. So, the technical designation of physical devices and their composition and use in the scenario design is prepared.

On the physical production structure shown in the figure, the AiRaci-based system *AiRaci-CPS1* with the human worker named *AiRaci-Worker1* simulates

Table 1. Requirement collection

ID	Requirement Description
1.	Req. (Digitization): The production machines of a production site need to be digitized so that a Digital Twins is created per machine [36]. Analog electric signals need to be transformed to digital signals, so that these can be processed by computers embedded at the machines and routing them through standard output sockets [37].
2.	Req. *(IoT-Integration)*: The production machines as technical device needs to be integrated in the IoT structure [38], so that a communication by the machines and further dialog partners can be realized. These partners can refer to further production machines, alternative devices and human process participants.
3.	Req. *(CPS-Capabilities)*: The production machine needs to provide components of sensors, actuators, processors and communicators, so that CPS capabilities can be realized [7].
4.	Req. *(AI-based Instruction)*: As the machine design has not a purpose in itself, it needs to follow a production routine, so that a workpiece carrier is constructed step by step. In accordance with the AI-based instruction mechanism [13], the machine's controlling is not realized by static software code but adaptive, flexible and efficient AI instructions.
5.	Req. *(AI Infrastructure)*: As the machines of each production site are instructed by AI [9], the machines are integrated in an AI supportive infrastructure. In accordance with AI architectures [39], the machines correspond to the shop floor level (*cps level*) representing nodes with low computing power for AI processing. More powerful computing nodes for fast AI processing can be at the *local cloud level*. The most powerful and costly computing nodes can be rent ad-hoc via AI cloud services (*public cloud level*). Example hardware services are provided by Amazon, Google, Microsoft, etc.
6.	Req. *(AI Platform)*: Since individual machines and productions sites shall be considered as production network, these need to be integrated with one end-to-end platform for cyber-physical systems, that enables the efficient application of knowledge of ANN [40]. For this, it needs to enable the flexible, node-independent (a) situational ANN application, (b) ANN training and validation as well as (c) ANN refinement, etc., which is realized as Over-The-Air deployment. Further, arbitrary programming libraries, such as TensorFlow or PyBrain, need to be provided, so that specialized AI functions are supported. Lastly, it needs to support AI experiments, which means the parameterized machine initialization having a machine-specific selective *AI activation rate* as well as a selective *AI activation cycle*.

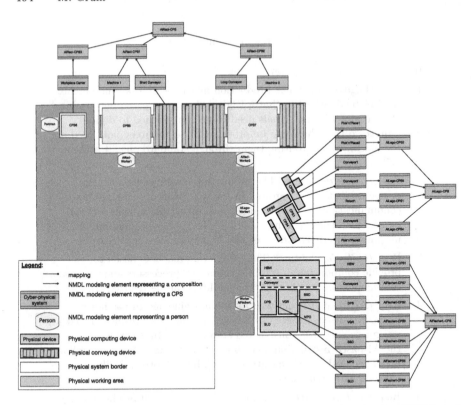

Fig. 1. The Organizational Overview of NMDL and layout of multi-site ANN-based cyber-physical production systems.

the first production facility for dispatching goods. The second production site simulates the AiRaci-based system *AiRaci-CPS2* with the human worker *AiRaci-Worker2* for receiving goods. The production facilities for further goods processing simulate the LEGO-based system structure of *AiLego-CPS1*, *AiLego-CPS2*, *AiLego-CPS3* and *AiLego-CPS4* with the human worker named *AiLego-Worker1* as well as the fischertechnik-based system structure of *AiFischertechnik-CPS1* to *AiFischertechnik-CPS7* with the human worker named *AiFischertechnik-Worker1*. The workpiece carrier called *AiRaci-CPS3* can now be passed back and forth between the AI-based production facilities, e.g. with the help of the short and long conveyors or the human letter carrier (see Postman in the figure). Each production facility continues to produce the workpiece carrier step by step according to the designed scenario.

The corresponding physical devices can be seen in Fig. 2. For replicating these kinds of physical production components, please let us know.

3.2 Scenario Design

For driving the physical production machines presented in Sect. 3.1, the software for the experimental investigation as well the implementation of produc-

Fig. 2. The physical layout of multi-site ANN-based cyber-physical production systems.

tion sequences has been realized. First, scenarios for global production chains are designed and relevant parameters are operationalized. The *ProcessView* of the NMDL represents the underlying production processes and the interaction of the physical production facilities (see Fig. 3) introduced in Fig. 1.

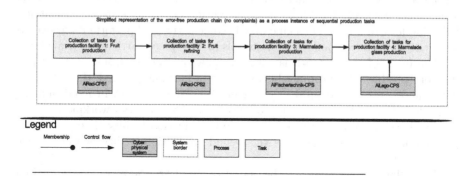

Fig. 3. The ProcessView of NMDL on the production process of multi-site ANN.

The figure shows that fruit is first produced in the first AiRaci production facility. It is then refined in the second AiRaci production facility. The refined fruit is then processed into jam in the fischertechnik production facility. In the fourth Lego production facility, the marmalade is packaged and marmalade jars are labeled so that they can be sold in retail stores. The scenario modeling of an error-free production chain thus represents a process instance of sequential production tasks with four production facilities.

Since all systems are modeled with the neural process design tool CoNM and are instructed based on AI, the focus is on observing the synchronization and activation cycles of the two AiRaci production facilities, which are at the beginning of the production chain. If neuronal information is already lost here in the first production facilities due to inefficient synchronization and activation cycles, this has an impact on subsequent cognitive production systems. These two production sites are therefore the focus of the investigation and Fig. 4 shows the detailed sequence of these two production sites.

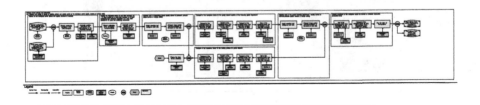

Fig. 4. The ProcessView of NMDL on the process of production tasks at the two AiRaci production sites.

The figure shows the time at which an AI-instructed CPS must become active in order to perform the production task shown in green. This relates to activation cycles and rates, which go hand in hand: In the interaction of various AI-instructed CPS, a workpiece carrier is thus produced piece by piece. At the same time, however, the CPSs involved must also be able to implement idle behavior–for example, no machine may become active and perform its respective activities to produce goods if no materials or workpiece carriers are available.

The focus of the research is therefore now on the disruption state of production (productive and idling behavior are in harmony), where the activation cycles and rates of two production facilities do not go hand in hand and, for example, *Machine1* of the first production facility produces workpieces faster and sends them to *Machine2* of the second production facility than the second production facility can process or the second production facility slows down the first.

The following parameters to be operationalized are therefore determined for the two machines named *Machine1* of the first production facility and *Machine2* of the second production facility: On the one hand, the start times of the cyclical AI deployments as *activation cycle* according to the respective tasks in the characteristics a) coupled and b) decoupled (delayed/premature). On the other hand, the repetition duration of the AI applications as *activation rate* according to the respective, same tasks in the specifications a) equal b) different.

3.3   Task Design

For clarifying the respective AI tasks of Fig. 4 called "AI-based image classification and documentation of the result on the hard disk", the NMDL's ActivityView specifies the following two:

First, an AI-based classification task that relates to the analysis of fruit images of the varieties a) bananas, b) oranges and c) apples, which contain m pixels in the x-axis and n pixels in the y-axis and have RGB values. Figure 5 shows the task of the two AI-based machines and conceptualizes the incoming data to be collected and the outgoing data to be generated in the scenarios determined.

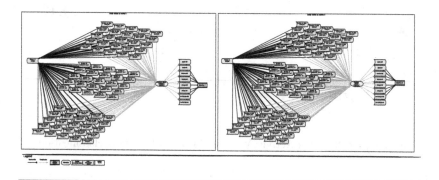

Fig. 5. The ActivityView of NMDL on AI-based picture classification of multi-site ANN

The figure shows that the RGB values of each pixel of the image to be analyzed serve as input values in the scenarios and the class combinations of the three types of fruit (bananas, oranges, apples) with the quality levels (defective and ok) must be generated as outgoing values. It must also be possible to pause the two machines, which is achieved using the two "no-fruit-pic" classes.

Since the workpiece carrier, which represents the respective fruit and represents image material, is transported back and forth between *Machine1* and *Machine2* in the scenarios by means of the short and long transport conveyor systems, Fig. 6 clarifies the second AI-based classification task that relates to the analysis of transport situations. It shows the modeling of the corresponding two AI-based transport tasks for the short conveyor bench on the left and the long conveyor belt on the right.

The figure shows which incoming sensor values from the respective transport system are used by the neural structure used here to generate the outgoing neural instructions for a) a transport movement from left to right, b) a transport movement from right to left and c) a pause. Furthermore, in both systems, the fourth neuron d) indicates an alarm situation and the fifth neuron e) indicates a complaint.

3.4   AI Application Design

First of all, the distributed production facilities created in Sect. 3.1 and situated in scenarios created in Sect. 3.2 are operated in normal mode and data is collected. For this purpose, a synthetic data set was compiled, which corresponds

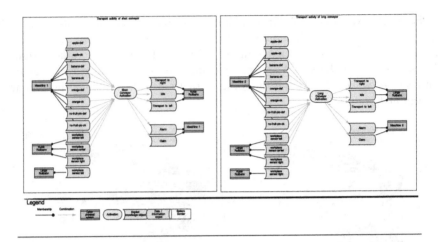

Fig. 6. The NMDL's ActivityView on AI-based transport classification.

to the conceptualization of the AI-based image analysis according to the modeling and limit scenarios (including worst-case scenarios) and is based on the (1) AI-based image classification and the shown in Fig. 5 and (2) AI-based transport classification (see Fig. 6). These datasets can be found in the repository:

- Training material for AI image classification, which is based on the collection by Kalluri (2018): *https://github.com/MarcusGrum/AI-CPS/tree/main/data/fruits-fresh-and-rotten-fruits-dataset*
- Training material for the AI transport classification of CPS1: *https://github.com/MarcusGrum/AI-CPS/blob/main/documentation/experiment05/datasets/Cps1_TrainDs.csv*
- Training material for the AI transport classification of CPS2: *https://github.com/MarcusGrum/AI-CPS/blob/main/documentation/experiment05/datasets/Cps2_TrainDs.csv*

This is followed by training to create models for the respective Industrie 4.0 production systems. The result is neural models for the machines of the distributed Industrie 4.0 production facilities, which can instruct them with neural activations based on AI-based image recognition in such a way that global production chains are realized. By comparing the incoming and outgoing values shown in Figs. 5 and 6, the interfaces between individual production facilities that are relevant for the production chain can be recognized by the names of the same name. The neuronal structures of the AI models responsible for AI-based image analysis are shown schematically in Fig. 7.

Since the neural structures were implemented with the TensorFlow programming library, the specific technical names of this programming library can be found in the figure under the respective neural layer. The trained models for AI-based image analysis have been made available in the Dockerhub as a "knowledgebase":

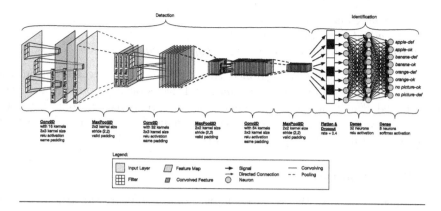

Fig. 7. The NeuronView of NMDL clarifies the AI-based picture classification.

– Relevant knowledge bases: *https://hub.docker.com/u/marcusgrum*

The neural architecture of the two transport conveyor systems has a neural connection to the respective upstream AI image analysis and is shown in Fig. 8. For this purpose, the PyBrain programming library was extended and used to implement the AI transport analysis. The extension has also been made available:

– Extended PyBrain library: *https://github.com/MarcusGrum/pybrain*

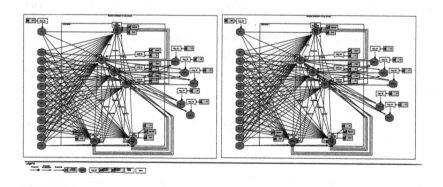

Fig. 8. The NMDL's NeuronView on AI-based transport classification of multi-site ANN.

A comparison with the conceptual scenario planning shows that the incoming neuronal values from Fig. 6 match the input neurons in Fig. 8 and that the scenarios are therefore implemented and trained at the neuronal level.

The neuronal models are used here as ANN apply requests. The mechanism responsible for this is also prepared in the repository:

- ANN request manager:
  https://github.com/MarcusGrum/AI-CPS/blob/main/code/annRequests_.../apply_annSolution.py

This means that the use of a trained AI model for image recognition on the machines named *Machine1* and *Machine2* and the associated conveyor belt systems named *ShortConveyor* and *LongConveyor* is prepared and only needs to be called up in the operationalized parameter configurations in accordance with the experimental investigation designed in the next section.

3.5   Simulation Design

The implementation of the scenarios is based on a software substructure with which the hardware of the Industry 4.0 production systems from Sect. 3.1 can be operated. This was prepared as a repository so that computing nodes or machines from different platform systems can be set up using the same software structure:

- Node-independent software structure: *https://github.com/MarcusGrum/AI-Lab*

Here, each machine is integrated as an MQTT client so that the respective AI deployment on *Machine1* and *Machine2* can be tracked throughout the entire production structure via a message broker and results are also available to other interested CPSs. So, for example, *Machine1* communicates with other CPS of the first production facility via *MessageBroker1* and *Machine2* and other production facilities of the Lego-based and Fischertechnik-based production facilities via a *MessageBroker2*, which are connected to this communication exchange via a bridged connection. In addition, the messages exchanged here can be intercepted so that times and results can be documented and used for analysis. This was prepared as a repository so that various computing nodes can implement the AI application:

- MessageBroker:
  https://github.com/MarcusGrum/AI-CPS/tree/main/code/messageBroker
- MessageClient:
  https://github.com/MarcusGrum/AI-CPS/tree/main/code/messageClient

In order to guarantee parametrized cycles and activation rates in selected experiment runs, a system-wide or cross-production site scheduling algorithm or controlling clock generator was implemented, which is integrated as an additional communication client in the communication structure. By means of its documenting and controlling role, it ensures that activations are realized at the planned (calculated) simulation times and that results, which are distributed across the communication channels, are also documented. This has been made available in the repository:

- Experiment: *https://github.com/MarcusGrum/AI-CPS/blob/main/code/experiments/experiment05.py*

In this simulation system, the communication behavior of the participating physical and virtual simulation devices shown in Fig. 9 is thus established, with the latter ensuring the correct timing of the respective experiment scenario.

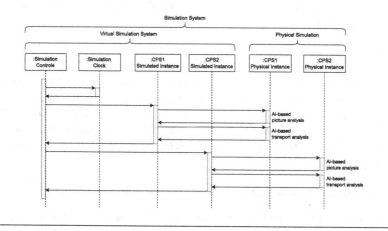

Fig. 9. The communication flow of the joint simulation system.

4   Experiment Design

For planning and carrying out the experimental investigations so that the prototype designed and implemented in the previous section can be operated with the same/different activation cycles/rates and initial hypotheses can be answered, the distributed production facilities are operated using neural instructions and performance data is collected. Figure 10 shows the design of experiments (DoE), also known as experimental design, focusing on the planning of each task as follows: Each planned task aims to describe and explain the variation of information under conditions that are thought to reflect the variation.

		Activation rates	
		same rates	different rates
Activation cycles	coupled /synchronous cycles	H1	H3
	decoupled /asynchronous cycles	H2	H4

Fig. 10. The experiment variants of multi-site ANN.

The figure shows that the planned experiments differentiate the activation cycles in the two variants "coupled" or "synchronous" and "uncoupled" or "unsynchronized" as well as the activation rates in the two variants "equal" and "different", resulting in a 2 × 2 matrix with four experiment variants. Each variant or task serves to test one of the four initial hypotheses, so that the general task can be formulated as follows:

- General experiment task:
  An AI-based production chain with at least two neuronally instructed production facilities is to be operated, whereby the activation types of the production facilities are varied with regard to the activation cycle and the activation rates and the ANN-based knowledge bases used are retained and confronted with different experiment variants in such a way that any faults that may occur due to different activation rates and cycles in production operations can be investigated.

Hypotheses: The four initial hypotheses refer to the following:

- Hypothesis 1: The synchronization of activation cycles with the same activation rates of distributed production sites promotes the trouble-free operation of production chains.
- Hypothesis 2: Decoupled activation cycles with equal activation rates of distributed production sites lead to disruptions in production chains.
- Hypothesis 3: Different activation rates in synchronized cycles of neural systems of distributed production sites lead to disruptions in production chains.
- Hypothesis 4: Different activation rates in asynchronized cycles - in the opposite sense of a standard of distributed production sites - prevent the operation of neuronally instructed production chains.

At the same time as realizing the experimental task of operating the described production facilities using neural instructions and simulated production chains, quality defects in production products and the automated documentation of production times are determined. The result is the collection of data from simulated production chains in distributed Industry 4.0 production facilities, which can be examined with regard to fault-free operation.

Assumptions: If a malfunction occurs during proper operation, it is assumed that the workpiece to be produced suffers a quality defect and must be rejected (Assumption 1). The following is also assumed:

- Assumption 2: The reference scenario and therefore the basis for training is the scenario of hypothesis 1.
- Assumption 3: Fruit workpieces are fed into the production system by the letter carrier as soon as the long conveyor system has taken over the workpiece from the short conveyor system. This ensures that there are always enough orders in the production system, but that two workpieces with competing transport movements are not placed on one and the same conveyor element.

- Assumption 4: The transports via the conveyor systems always take one simulation minute (including the calculation times of the associated neural activations for image and transport). This is particularly important with regard to shorter activation questions, as neuronal activation cannot change the physical processes in the real world.
- Assumption 5: The respective total simulation time amounts to three simulation time states or simulation cycles.

5   Conclusion

Summary. As part of a design-science-oriented research [16], this article has constructed and provided a simulation system as Open Source for examining ANN-based systems distributed at multiple machines, multiple sites and heterogeneous infrastructures. Exemplified at the example of production contexts, it so enables the simulation of global, neuronally instructed production networks having multiple production facilities. Further, an experiment design incl. activation type-related hypotheses has been worked out. It will demonstrate the simulation system and shall (I) enable research on ANN activation types in production networks, (II) illustrate ANN-based production networks disrupted by activation types and clarify the need for harmonizing them, and (III) demonstrate conceptual management interventions. As it will be in on-building research realized next, the design-oriented research cycle is finalized.

Critical Appraisal. The research question (*"How can different activation types of rate and cycle combinations in multi-site ANN be researched?"*) can be answered with regard to the design of ANN-based production chains: individual production machines are setup as ANN-based CPS (Req. 3), which is clarified by the prototype presented. They have a Digital Twin (Req. 1) and they are based on the traditional tangible resource of production machines. Intelligence is carried out with the aid of AI requests communicated via MQTT based Internet channels (Req. 2) and node-independent Docker containers providing AI expertise flexibly at diverse computing levels (Req. 5). This contributes with further examples for the domain of Production Management. These potential organization types are enabled because of the CPS capabilities, so that machines can adapt to the current context of a scenario and reflect on the machine's production tasks. By generating and providing different forms of AI instructions (Req. 4), specialized knowledge bases and data contexts are loaded from the production network so that artificial knowledge transfers are realized efficiently (Req. 6). This contributes to business process standards, since this leads to a novel form of AI processes. Being embedded in the new simulated production chain infrastructure designed, the examination of ANN activation rates and cycles is enabled by the experiment design worked out at this contribution.

Outlook. By realizing the experiments designed, effects of inefficient knowledge flows among ANN-based Industry 4.0 systems can be researched systematically. First experiment results can by found at [41]. Detailed analyses of their artificial knowledge flows will give insights to their productive behavior in networks of

ANN spanning multiple sites. Building on this, standards for AI usage spanning multiple sites can be formulated. These support effective artificial knowledge transfers of the future.

References

1. Bergweiler, S.: Smart factory systems–fostering cloud-based manufacturing based on self-monitoring cyber-physical systems, *development*, vol. 2, p. 3, 2016
2. Zanero, S.: Cyber-physical systems. Computer **50**(4), 14–16 (2017)
3. Pivoto, D. G., et al.: Cyber-physical systems architectures for industrial internet of things applications in industry 4.0: a literature review, *J. Manufact. Syst.*, vol. 58, pp. 176–192 (2021)
4. Riedl, M., Zipper, H., Meier, M., Diedrich, C.: Cyber-physical systems alter automation architectures. Annu. Rev. Control. **38**(1), 123–133 (2014)
5. Mazumder, S.K., et al.: A review of current research trends in power-electronic innovations in cyber-physical systems. IEEE J. Emerg. Sel. Top. Power Electron. **9**(5), 5146–5163 (2021)
6. Bartelt, M., Stecken, J., Kuhlenkötter, B.: Automated production of individualized products for teaching i4. 0 concepts. Procedia Manuf. **45**, 337–342 (2020)
7. Gronau, N., Grum, M., Bender, B.: Determining the optimal level of autonomy in cyber-physical production systems, In: *2016 IEEE 14th International Conference on Industrial Informatics (INDIN)*, pp. 1293–1299, 7 2016
8. Grum, M., Bender, B., Gronau, N., Alfa, A. S.: Efficient task realizations in networked production infrastructures, In: *Proceedings of the Conference on Production Systems and Logistics: CPSL 2020*, Hannover: publish-Ing., (2020)
9. Grum, M.: *Construction of a Concept of Neuronal Modeling*. Potsdam University, (2021)
10. Grum, M., Thim, C., Roling, W.M.., Schueffler, A., Kluge, A., Gronau, N.: AI Case-Based Reasoning for Artificial Neural Networks. In: Masrour, T., El Hassani, I., Barka, N. (eds.) Artificial Intelligence and Industrial Applications: Smart Operation Management, pp. 17–35. Springer Nature Switzerland, Cham (2023). https://doi.org/10.1007/978-3-031-43524-9_2
11. Grum, M., Thim, C., Gronau, N.: Aiming for knowledge-transfer-optimizing intelligent cyber-physical systems. In: Andersen, A.L. (ed.) CARV/MCPC–2021. LNME, pp. 149–157. Springer, Cham (2022). https://doi.org/10.1007/978-3-030-90700-6_16
12. Bender, B., Grum, M., Gronau, N., Alfa, A., Maharaj, B.T.: Design of a worldwide simulation system for distributed cyber-physical production networks. In: 2019 IEEE International Conference on Engineering, Technology and Innovation (ICE/ITMC), pp. 1–7. IEEE (2019)
13. Grum, M.: Construction of a Concept of Neuronal Modeling. Springer (2022)
14. Deng, J., et al.: Microglia-mediated inflammatory destruction of neuro-cardiovascular dysfunction after stroke. Front. Cell. Neurosci. **17**, 1117218 (2023)
15. Grum, M.: Managing human and artificial knowledge bearers: the creation of a symbiotic knowledge management approach. In: Business Modeling and Software Design: 10th International Symposium, BMSD 2020, Berlin, Germany, July 6-8, 2020, Proceedings 10, pp. 182–201, Springer (2020)

16. Peffers, K., et al.: The design science research process: a model for producing and presenting information systems research. In: 1st International Conference on Design Science in Information Systems and Technology (DESRIST), vol. 24, pp. 83–106 (2006)

17. Gronau, N., Grum, M.: Towards a prediction of time consumption during knowledge transfer. In: Knowledge Transfer Speed Optimizations in Product Development Contexts. Empirical Studies of Business Informatics, GITO, pp. 25 – 69 (2019)

18. Nonaka, I., Takeuchi, H.: The Knowledge-Creating Company: How Japanese Companies Create the Dynamics of Innovation. Oxford University Press (1995)

19. Bishop, C.: Neural Networks for Pattern Recognition. Clarendon Press, vol. 2, pp. 223–228 (1995)

20. Grum, M.: NMDL repository, November 2020. https://github.com/MarcusGrum/ CoNM/tree/main/meta-models/nmdl, version 1.0.0

21. Ashton, K.: That "Internet of Things" thing: in the real world things matter more than ideas. RFID J. 22(7), 97–114 (2009)

22. Khaitan, S.K.: Design techniques and applications of cyberphysical systems: a survey. IEEE Syst. J. 9(2), 350–365 (2015)

23. Veigt, M., Lappe, D., Hribernik, K.: Development of a cyber-physical logistic system (in German). Industrie Manage. 1(2013), 15–18 (2013)

24. Krallmann, H., Bobrik, A., Levina, O.: Systemanalyse im Unternehmen: Prozessorientierte Methoden der Wirtschaftsinformatik. Oldenbourg Wissenschaftsverlag Verlag (2013)

25. Fuchs-Wegner, G.: Verfahren der Analyse von Systemen. RIAS (1971)

26. Besancon, R.: The Encyclopedia of Physics. Springer, New York (2013)

27. Haase, R.: Thermodynamik. Grundzüge der Physikalischen Chemie in Einzeldarstellungen, Steinkopff (2013)

28. Heim, G., Heim, S.: Rhetos Lexikon der Physik und Philosophie (2018)

29. Pisarchik, A.N., Feudel, U.: Control of multistability. Phys. Rep. 540(4), 167–218 (2014)

30. Moreno-Bote, R., Rinzel, J., Rubin, N.: Noise-induced alternations in an attractor network model of perceptual bistability. J. Neurophysiol. 98(3), 1125–1139 (2007)

31. Gigante, G., Mattia, M., Braun, J., Del Giudice, P.: Bistable perception modeled as competing stochastic integrations at two levels. PLoS Comput. Biol. 5(7), e1000430 (2009)

32. Braun, J., Mattia, M.: Attractors and noise: twin drivers of decisions and multistability. Neuroimage 52(3), 740–751 (2010)

33. Kim, S., Park, S.H., Ryu, C.: Multistability in coupled oscillator systems with time delay. Phys. Rev. Lett. 79(15), 2911 (1997)

34. Park, S.H., Kim, S., Pyo, H.-B., Lee, S.: Multistability analysis of phase locking patterns in an excitatory coupled neural system. Phys. Rev. E 60(2), 2177 (1999)

35. Foss, J., Longtin, A., Mensour, B., Milton, J.: Multistability and delayed recurrent loops. Phys. Rev. Lett. 76(4), 708 (1996)

36. Uhlemann, T.H.-J., Schock, C., Lehmann, C., Freiberger, S., Steinhilper, R.: The digital twin: demonstrating the potential of real time data acquisition in production systems. Procedia Manuf. 9, 113–120 (2017)

37. Doyle, F., Cosgrove, J.: Steps towards digitization of manufacturing in an SME environment. Procedia Manuf. 38, 540–547 (2019)

38. Lampropoulos, G., Siakas, K., Anastasiadis, T.: Internet of Things in the context of industry 4.0: an overview. Int. J. Entrepreneurial Knowl. 7, 4–19 (2019)

39. Grum, M., Bender, B., Alfa, A.S., Gronau, N.: A decision maxim for efficient task realization within analytical network infrastructures. Decis. Support Syst. **112**, 48–59 (2018)
40. Grum, M.: Context-aware, intelligent musical instruments for improving knowledge-intensive business processes. In: International Symposium on Business Modeling and Software Design, pp. 69–88, Springer (2022)
41. Grum, M.: Managing multi-site artificial neural networks' activation rates and activation cycles. In: Business Modeling and Software Design: 14th International Symposium, BMSD 2024, Luxembourg, pp. 1–10, Springer (2024)

Reproducibility of Firmware Analysis: An Empirical Study

Narges Yousefnezhad[1]([✉])(iD) and Andrei Costin[2](iD)

[1] Binare.io, Jyväskylä, Finland
narges.yousefnezhad@binare.io
[2] University of Jyväskylä, Jyväskylä, Finland
ancostin@jyu.fi
https://binare.io/, https://jyu.fi/it/

Abstract. Firmware analysis methods are crucial for IoT security, yet their reproducibility-the ability to replicate results in subsequent research-has not been thoroughly examined. This study addresses this gap by empirically analyzing the reproducibility of three methods in two key applications of firmware analysis: third-party library identification and binary image base determination. We then evaluate the original studies on each of these methods, using two reproducibility assessment techniques, providing insights into the challenges and opportunities related to reproducibility in firmware analysis. Our findings highlight the current reproducibility status of these methods and offer guidance for improving the reliability of research in this field.

Keywords: firmware binary analysis · reproducibility · empirical research · IoT-based software

1 Introduction

In recent years, the rapid growth of embedded systems and Internet of Things (IoT) devices has greatly increased cyber threats. Firmware binaries, the essential software controlling hardware operations, are critical parts of these systems. As these firmware-based devices become more common in various industries, ensuring their security has become a top priority for cybersecurity researchers. Firmware binary analysis is crucial for this task. It helps identify vulnerabilities, detect malware, and understand the complex operations of embedded systems. This analysis includes tasks such as reverse-engineering to find the firmware's image base, which is the starting address of the executable file loaded into memory, and Software Composition Analysis (SCA) to identify embedded third-party libraries (TPL).

Growing concerns about firmware security raise questions about the effectiveness and reproducibility of analysis methods. Reproducibility, in this context, refers to the ability to replicate research results consistently across different studies. Firmware analysis is tough because firmware binaries are complex

B. Shishkov (Ed.): BMSD 2024, LNBIP 523, pp. 207–225, 2024.
https://doi.org/10.1007/978-3-031-64073-5_13

and work on different types of hardware. With firmware-based devices becoming more common in critical infrastructure and various industries, it's urgent to address vulnerabilities and reduce risks. Independent vulnerability research on firmware faces challenges like getting data, dealing with encrypted files, and working with different hardware types. Therefore, it's really important to check if established cybersecurity methods for firmware analysis can be trusted and repeated reliably. Doing a thorough research is key to understanding how well these methods work and keeping up with evolving threats.

In response to these challenges, this paper presents an empirical investigation focused on evaluating the reproducibility of specific cybersecurity methods designed for firmware analysis. While a recent study [5] has explored various aspects and issues related to reproducibility in firmware analysis, our goal is to empirically assess the reliability and effectiveness of existing methodologies on accessible firmware images. We aim to demonstrate that the descriptions of methods provided for firmware analysis often lack the quality necessary to effectively replicate reported results.

To achieve these objectives, we examine a selection of commonly used cybersecurity methods for firmware binary analysis covering both the challenges of reverse-engineering and SCA. First, to assess reproducibility from an empirical perspective, we conduct careful experimentation and analysis on these methods across various firmware binaries. Next, by evaluating the reproducibility level of the original studies on these methods, we perform a theoretical assessment of reproducibility. The main findings of this study highlight the challenges and opportunities in reproducibility within the field of firmware analysis, contributing to the ongoing discourse on cybersecurity research methodologies.

The main contributions of this paper are summarized as follow:

1. We investigate the effectiveness and reproducibility of selected cybersecurity methods for firmware binary analysis.
2. To the best of our knowledge, this research is the first empirical study focusing on identification of challenges and opportunities in reproducibility within the field of firmware analysis.
3. We employ empirical methods to aid in assessing the reproducibility of particular cybersecurity methods designed for firmware analysis.
4. Using reproducibility assessment, with this paper we demonstrate the lack of sufficient and adequate quality in method and dataset descriptions provided for selected firmware analysis studies
5. This study contributes to the ongoing discourse on cybersecurity research methodologies in particular, and on reproducibility of empirical results in general.

The rest of this paper is organized as follows. Section 2 delves into related work by focusing on the definition of reproducibility and its various types in the fields of software engineering and security. In Sect. 3, we outline our methodology for conducting the study. Section 4 presents the experiments conducted along with their evaluation. The research findings are discussed in Sect. 5. Finally,

Sects. 6 and 7 respectively offer a comprehensive discussion and conclusion regarding the outcomes of our investigation.

2   Related Work

Lately, reproducibility has emerged as a significant evaluation metric alongside other benchmarks such as speed and reliability in experimental results [3]. Reproducibility refers to a study's capacity to be replicated, either entirely or partially, by an independent research team [4]. Reproducibility is achieved when an independent group can obtain identical results using the author's provided artifacts, according to Olivier et al. [10]. As per the findings of Hernandez et al. [6], the failure to release reproducible artifacts (comprising complete source code and dataset) to the community restricts the utility of analysis platforms. The majority of publications lack reproducibility [14], while ensuring experiment reproducibility is vital in the scientific method. Reviewers in scientific journals carefully check publications for sufficient detail, particularly focusing on methodology descriptions. However, with complex software tools and datasets, relying solely on these descriptions may be inadequate for reproducibility. Limited access to such resources complicates and discourages reproducibility efforts [4].

As indicated by [12], the documentation factors – methods, data, and experiments – allow for the classification of reproducibility into three levels, quantified by numerical scores:

- Experiment
  reproducible-includes all factors, enabling independent researchers to replicate results;
- Data reproducible-requires method and data, facilitating similar findings by other researchers;
- Method reproducible-documents the method alone, allowing independent replication of results.

The current study is focused on the last degree of reproducibility, i.e., *Method reproducible*. There are also several types of reproduction studies, as outlined by Gonzalez-Barahona et al. [4]. These include: Complete new study, Procedural validation, New analysis based on the same processed dataset, New analysis based on the same raw dataset, with different parameters and methodologiesm, New study reusing only the retrieval tools.

Ensuring the reproducibility of Empirical Software Engineering (ESE) studies is integral to enhancing their credibility, providing the research community with opportunities to verify, evaluate, and enhance research outcomes [14]. Among ESE studies, those utilizing data from development repositories are especially conducive to reproducibility. These studies leverage readily shareable data and often utilize analysis tools that are either shareable or meticulously documented. Despite these favorable circumstances, many studies in this field face challenges in achieving reproducibility. Factors like unidentified data sources or software tools often hinder these studies, making them either unreproducible or difficult to replicate, even partially. [4]. The reproducibility status of empirical software engineering studies can vary significantly, ranging from easily replicable to nearly impossible to reproduce. Given the complexity of the involved processes and the multitude of details to consider, there's a pressing need for a systematic approach to assess study reproducibility. To address this need, Gonzalez and Robles [4] highlight several attributes of elements impacting reproducibility: identification of original elements, description of published information, availability for other researchers, persistence in the future, and flexibility to new environments. These attributes represent various dimensions affecting the ease of reproducing a study.

Researchers have focused on evaluating software testing techniques but haven't proposed a reproducibility-focused methodology yet, hindering both reproducibility and empirical evaluations. Despite efforts in software engineering experimentation, evaluating testing techniques remains challenging due to diverse software types and complex scope delineation [9]. It's commonplace for software developers to attempt reproducing software bugs to grasp their anomalous behaviors and rectify them. Regrettably, they frequently encounter difficulty in reproducing these bugs, resulting in flawed and unreliable software systems. Rahman et al. [13] endeavors to delve deeper into the factors contributing to the non-reproducibility of software bugs through a multi-modal study, aiming to gain a comprehensive understanding of this phenomenon. They conduct an empirical investigation utilizing 576 non-reproducible bug reports sourced from two prominent software systems (Firefox and Eclipse). They also identify 11 key factors that could potentially contribute to the non-reproducibility of reported bugs.

Recent endeavors are concentrated on establishing protocols to enhance the reproducibility of scientific studies in the system security domain. Nonetheless, the participation of embedded devices frequently adds complexity to replicating previous research. Tools like Avatar 2 can aid in reproducing earlier studies. The doctoral thesis [8] showcases the viability of record and replay for embedded devices, adapting dynamic fault detection heuristics to embedded systems using the instrumentation capabilities offered by Avatar 2's PANDA target. Additionally, conducting experiments in the field of cybersecurity poses significant challenges, particularly due to methodological issues prevalent in empirical research. Achieving reproducibility and comparability of results proves difficult due to limited access to data and privacy concerns that often preclude data sharing [1]. While this paper concentrates on experimenting with firmware analysis methods-a domain not reliant on private data (primarily firmware binary files)-implementation remains incomplete due to insufficient information regarding the implementation specifics.

Our work is closest related to very recent effort by Helmke et al. [5]. They discovered several factors that can impact the representativeness and replicability of firmware vulnerability research: whether unpacking the documents is performed, the choice between a small selection or a large-scale collection of firmware images, gathering product data versus using the operating system, and whether data is shared or links to legal but volatile sources are provided. They introduce a universally applicable framework of best practices aimed at ensuring scientifically sound firmware corpora. In contrast to our approach, they assess firmware analysis methods theoretically, without conducting an empirical study. Additionally, they utilize different evaluation metrics compared to our methodology.

3   Methodology

The identification and selection of a comprehensive paper pool are crucial steps in conducting empirical research, particularly in studies focused on cybersecurity methods for firmware analysis. This study aims to investigate the reproducibility of various cybersecurity methods applied to firmware analysis. To achieve this goal, we developed an original methodology to collect and analyze a paper pool consisting of relevant literature in the field.

3.1   Paper Pool Selection

Our selection criteria aimed to capture a broad spectrum of cybersecurity methods commonly utilized in firmware analysis, ranging from binary analysis to Image base determination approaches. We also prioritized studies that have demonstrated reproducibility or empirical validation of their findings. By focusing on reproducibility, we intend to ensure the reliability and robustness of the methods examined in our study.

3.2   Search Strategy

We executed a systematic search strategy designed to identify pertinent literature in the field of firmware analysis. The process began by reviewing foundational papers, such as those by Costin et al. [5], which aimed to improve binary analysis approaches. Building upon this foundation, we explored comprehensive survey articles and conducted thorough searches in scholarly databases using tailored keywords and phrases like "firmware analysis" and "IoT security." Our search encompassed renowned academic databases, including IEEE Xplore, ACM Digital Library, and Google Scholar, ensuring broad coverage of available literature.

3.3   Screening and Selection

Following the initial search, we screened the titles, abstracts, and keywords of retrieved papers to identify those aligning with our inclusion criteria. This comprehensive evaluation helped us exclude papers not relevant to firmware analysis methods. From the selected papers, three were chosen for implementation in our study. These included two papers employing Image base determination approaches, widely used in reverse engineering for firmware analysis, and a novel method known as ModX, developed for third-party library detection and introduced at a prestigious conference (ICSE 2022). This diverse selection aimed to provide a comprehensive overview of current methodologies.

3.4   Reproducibility Framework

As outlined in Sect. 2 and based on the classification from [12], the targeted level of reproducibility for this study is categorized as method reproducible. Our methodology was designed following the principles of Hevner's Design Science [11], which emphasizes building and evaluating artifacts to solve identified problems.

1. **Implementation**: We attempted to implement each method based on the provided algorithm descriptions from the selected papers. This involved extracting variables, data types, and functions as outlined in each algorithm.
2. **Challenges Identification**: We documented the obstacles encountered during the implementation process for each algorithm, highlighting the challenges of achieving method reproducibility.
3. **Reproducibility Attributes**: To further evaluate reproducibility, we identified several attributes associated with elements impacting reproducibility. These elements include the Data source, Retrieval methodology, Raw dataset, Extraction methodology, Study parameters, Processed dataset, Analysis methodology, and Results dataset. The attributes encompass Identification, Description, Availability, Persistence, and Flexibility.
4. **Quality Metric Development**: To assess the ease of reproducibility of each study, we developed a quality metric for original study of each method, as outlined in [14]. This metric evaluates five characteristics: limitations, manual inspection, reproducibility package, method and data description, and improved version.

By aligning our methodology with Hevner's Design Science, we ensure a rigorous methodology to assessing the reproducibility of cybersecurity methods for firmware analysis. This methodology comprises two main sections. Firstly, in Sect. 4, through the implementation of algorithms proposed by each method, we identify any implementation challenges and determine the feasibility of reproducing the method despite these challenges. Secondly, in Sect. 5, by evaluating reproducibility attributes and employing a quality metric, we conduct a theoretical reproducibility assessment of the original studies related to the three selected methods.

4   Implementation and Challenges

In this section, we present the empirical experiments and evaluations conducted to investigate the reproducibility of various firmware analysis methods. We selected a set of studies to implement and evaluate, focusing on their methodology, implementation challenges, and the results obtained. This section is structured to align closely with the methodology outlined in Sect. 3.4, addressing Implementation and Challenges Identification.

We began by compiling a substantial list of potential papers, encompassing 21 studies relevant to firmware analysis methods. These papers represented a diverse range of methodologies within the field. After careful consideration, three papers were selected for implementation in our study, based on their clear implementation steps, pseudocode, or algorithm descriptions, balancing the effort required for implementation against our timeline constraints.

As seen in Fig. 1, the selected methods can be categorized into two distinct categories: TPL-detection based methods, aimed at identifying third-party libraries and software components within software, and Image Base Determination techniques, focused on locating the image base of binary executables. Within the TPL-detection category, we have one study, while the Image Base Determination category comprises two studies, each employing different methodologies: Function Entry Table (FET) and Matching Literal Pools (MLP). To implement these methods, we carefully extracted variables, data types, and functions outlined in each algorithm of the method by thoroughly studying each study multiple times. This section provides a concise overview of the method description, implementation steps undertaken, and the challenges faced during the process.

4.1 TPL Detection

An effective strategy for enhancing software security involves employing SCA, a methodology designed to evaluate the third-party or open-source software components employed in a product. SCA aims to identify potential issues such as outdated versions, vulnerabilities, or license non-compliance within these components [2]. Methods for detecting TPLs represent a subset of SCA methodologies.

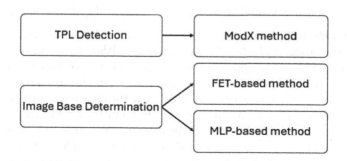

Fig. 1. The category of the selected methods

4.1.1 ModX Method

Yang et al. [15] propose the *ModX* method aimed at decomposing programs into finely-grained modules. Their method involves detecting partially imported TPL instances through both a binary-level program modularization algorithm and a semantic matching algorithm. The process unfolds in two main phases. In the first phase, the binary program modularization, consisting of two key components: Designing Module Quality Assessment and Modularization Algorithm. The former involves evaluating the quality score of grouping functions into clusters using a community detection algorithm. The latter component aims to optimize the quality score by combining functions and decomposing the binary into modules based on a quality metric. Additionally, the second phase of *ModX* framework concentrates on TPL detection, which entails implementing a Module Similarity Measurement algorithm based on semantics. This includes assessing Syntactic Similarity, Graph Similarity, and item Function Similarity.

Implementation. This section provides a comprehensive discussion on implementing reproducibility for the ModX method. The method comprises two distinct phases: Binary Modularization and TPL Detection, designed to forecast TPLs from a binary program. However, as the main input is the binary file, which must first be converted to the graph, an essential preliminary phase of graph creation is required. Therefore, we redefine the method to include three phases accordingly.

Phase 0 (Graph Creation): *Step 1) Generating and visualizing call graph.* Initially, the process involves creating a graph from the firmware file (binary source file). Subsequently, we visualize this graph to verify the correctness of the graph generation process. However, the study applies a function call graph, necessitating the compilation of a list detailing functions and their connections. Hence, the task involves determining the methodology to extract functions from firmware files. Radare2, a framework designed for reverse-engineering and analyzing binaries, is employed in this context to access and analyze the binary file, extracting the list of functions. When it comes to visualization, two alternatives are available: NetworkX and Graphviz. NetworkX visualization primarily serves ELF files, often encountering only nodes with minimal edge representation. Consequently, employing Graphviz proves to be a more effective solution.

Phase 1 (Binary Modularization): Subsequently, as the initial phase of their method, Yang et al. [15] clusters functions within the program to produce modules based on their Quality scores. This process involves breaking down firmware binary source files into modules. To discern the specific methodology employed, further investigation was conducted through references (i.e., 48, 49, 17, 46, 30). It is also necessary to examine the Community Algorithm to understand its function and the inputs and outputs it entails. *Step 2) Girvan-Newman Algorithm.* ModX employs the Girvan-Newman algorithm for detecting communities within the graph. However, the original Girvan-Newman algorithm lacks support for directed graphs, necessitating the creation of an undirected graph as input for this algorithm. *Step 3) calculating Quality Score.* After generating the function call graph and identifying communities using the Girvan-Newman Algorithm, the quality score of these discovered communities can be computed. *step 4) Function Volume Adjustment.* This step encompasses three functions: computing the volume value (number of statements), identifying end-nodes, and executing Backward Propagation. *Step 5, Step 6,* and *Step 7* correspond to the Modified Quality Metric, Modularization Algorithm, and Modularity Similarity Measurement, respectively.

Phase 2 (TPL Detection): Finally, at the second step, ModX performs TPL detection by matching program modules with TPL modules.

Challenges Identification. We faced the following challenges during the implementation and cross-testing of the *ModX* method:

- Data processing steps for generating graphs from raw data (i.e., software program) is not explained. Software, library, or package employed to generate graph is not introduced. Data is also not publicly available.
- There is no information regarding the implementation details such as programming language and libraries in the study.
- Furthermore, there is a dearth of information on the dataset utilized for evaluation, as well as details regarding the data, including input, output, and ground truth.
- The authors mention in the study that the entire program or library can be regarded as a graph with the functions representing the nodes. They also show on the overflow of ModX that the program file (e.g., EXE file) is converted to a function call graph but they don't mention how they do the conversion and which data structure they use to represent the graph (adjacency matrix, adjacency list or adjacency set).
- It is still unclear how binary files can be designated as distinct nodes and how their connections can be defined.
- Due to numerous uncertainties encountered during the implementation process, finishing the implementation became impossible.

4.2   Image Base Determination of Binary Executables

In the realm of reverse engineering, when disassembling an executable file, the disassembler must be aware of the processor type of its runtime environment and the image base of the executable file. While obtaining the processor type for a given embedded system firmware is relatively straightforward, determining the image base of the firmware poses a challenge. Properly configuring the image base in the disassembler during the initial import significantly improves the analysis of the firmware [17]. Various tools can be employed to determine the image base, including matching literal pool (MLP) [17], function entry table (FET) [16], matching function address [19], LDR instructions [18], and searching jump tables [20]. This section primarily examines FET-based [16] and MLP-based approaches [17].

4.2.1 FET-Based Method
In their study, Zhu et al. [16] propose two algorithms. The first algorithm, FIND-FET, is designed to identify Function Entry Table (FET) entries through a methodical approach involving sliding window analysis and FET gap assessment. FET entries are classified into discrete and continuous types, based on the adjacency of function pointers. Key definitions integral to this algorithm include the FET gap, denoting the number of words between adjacent function pointers within the same FET, and the sliding window, representing a continuous memory unit. Additionally, the size of the sliding window (wnd) is determined by the number of function entry addresses it encompasses. The algorithm adheres

to rules governing distance, uniqueness, and ARM/Thumb entry address criteria. The second algorithm, FIND-BASE, serves the purpose of determining the image base.

Implementation. To implement the FET-based method, we adhere to the following steps. Firstly, we load and read the binary file. Secondly, we locate the first function entry using the following steps: determine if the current position corresponds to a Thumb instruction, implement logic to verify if the instruction at the given position is a Thumb instruction, check if the instruction matches the Thumb-2 signature, and verify if the address is within the specified window size. Thirdly, we define three rules to filter the function entry addresses: Rule 1 checks the distance between each pair of function entry addresses in the window, ensuring it is not more than 64KB, Rule 2 ensures that function entry addresses within the sliding window are not the same, and Rule 3 checks ARM/Thumb entry address rules. Finally, we determine the image base by deduplicating and sorting function entry addresses and then calculating the image base. In this experiment, the parameter T is set to 40, as specified in the study.

Challenges Identification. We faced the following challenges during the implementation and cross-testing of the FET-based method:

- The study lacks precise details about the firmware file, firmware version, URL, or SHA256 of the analyzed input, making it challenging for future researchers to reproduce the results.
- It remains ambiguous what function MoveWindow serves in the FIND-FET algorithm. Based on our assumption, it appears to relocate a single window.
- The study lacks references for binary files and does not specify the exact firmware version, making it impossible to compare the model using the same binary file.
- The implemented method fails to identify any image base. The final condition in FIND-BASE is never met, as the ratio consistently remains below the threshold. Consequently, Thumb and ARM functions are inadequately represented in the current window.
- In the provided pseudocode, the output from Algorithm 1 (head, gap, table Size) does not directly match the input requirements for Algorithm 2 (binary file, function entry table, T). Consequently, in order to replicate the proposed method, researchers must independently determine the appropriate input for Algorithm 2 based on the output of Algorithm 1.

4.2.2 MLP-Based Method

Zhu et al. [17] introduce a two-step method for determining the image base of firmwares on ARM-based devices. Firstly, they propose the FIND-LP algorithm, which exploits the storage characteristics of strings in firmware files and the encoding features of literal pools containing string addresses to identify all possible literal pools. Secondly, they introduce the Determining image Base by Matching Literal Pools (DBMLP) algorithm to determine the image base.

DBMLP establishes the relationship between absolute addresses of strings and their corresponding offsets in the firmware file, generating a candidate list for the image base value. By analyzing the number of matched literal pools corresponding to each candidate image base, the correct image base is identified.

Implementation. In this section, we we delve into the detailed discussion of implementing reproducibility for the MLP-based method. Firstly, we begin by loading and reading the binary file. Secondly, we iterate through the binary data to extract string values, string addresses, string length vectors, and offset vectors. Thirdly, we employ three rules to identify literal pools. Rule 1 verifies if the distance between string addresses is no more than 64 KB. Rule 2 confirms if the string addresses in the same sliding window are unique. Rule 3 checks if the difference value between adjacent string addresses after sorting is less than 100. Subsequently, using the identified literal pool, we determine the image base by calculating the Euclidean distance between each vector and its sub-vectors. If the distance is 0, we consider it a successful match, and accordingly, the candidate image base can be calculated. Additionally, we assess whether the strings in each literal pool are stored in word-aligned format based on the features of addresses. If every string address in a literal pool is an exact multiple of 4, we conclude that these strings are stored in word-aligned format; otherwise, they are stored in unaligned format. Consequently, we discuss each case separately in the study.

Challenges Identification. The MLP-based method have been fully implemented, but there are several concerns regarding the precision of the implementation:

- The authors fail to identify or provide precise details about the firmware file, firmware version, URL, or SHA256 of the analyzed input, making it challenging for other researchers to replicate the proposed method. The download links for firmwares in their test set are presented in a table, but the majority of them are non-functional or not direct links to downloadable firmware files. Some may also require authorization to access the file. Moreover, their online storage system for firmwares is also not publicly available.
- The starting point for analyzing the binary file is unclear. One approach could involve initially checking the firmware header and then searching for strings following it. However, in our implementation, we opted to use 0x0 as the starting position.
- The study describes strings being separated by a string terminator (0 or 0x00). We've implemented the same logic to locate strings, yet we encounter a significantly higher number of strings and literal pools (LP) compared to the values provided in *"Table 1 – The experimental results (wndsize = 3)"* [17]. For example, in the "tintin_fw.bin" file, We've found 20887 strings and 259 LP, whereas the study reports 1580 strings and 175 LP.
- Defining or calculating the offsets of strings accurately is unclear. In our implementation, we define it as the count of blocks, regardless of whether they contain strings, from the beginning of the firmware file to the current string.

- There's ambiguity surrounding the MoveWindow() function in the FIND-LP algorithm. While we believe it involves shifting the current position by one sliding window, we are unsure if the authors employed the same function. Clarification on this matter is necessary to ensure consistency with the study's methodology.
- In our implementation, the DBMLP algorithm detects numerous image bases, but none of them are repeated. Consequently, no candidate image base can be selected, resulting in a failure.

5   Reproducibility Theoretical Evaluation

Building upon the implementation challenges outlined in Sect. 4, we now have a thorough understanding of the reproducibility of selected methods from experimental viewpoint. To further address all facets of reproducibility, we extend our evaluation to include a theoretical perspective. In this approach, we shift our focus from method to encompass the entirety of the original study, allowing us to assess the reproducibility of each study in this section. To theoretically evaluate the reproducibility level of these studies, we can leverage previous research in the field of reproducibility. Accordingly, inspired by papers [4] and [14], this section assesses reproducibility of selected methods from two perspectives: I) Reproducibility evaluation through an analysis of elements and their associated attributes that influence reproducibility (Sect. 5.1); II) Quality assessment conducted by addressing five questions aimed at measuring reproducibility (Sect. 5.2).

5.1   Reproducibility Assessment

According to [4], eight elements might influence reproducibility and are potentially reusable in future studies.

1. Data Source: This is where the real-world data is located.
2. Retrieval methodology: This involves the process of retrieving data using software tools.
3. Raw data: This refers to the unprocessed data obtained directly from the data source.
4. Extraction methodology: This is the process of extracting, cleaning, and storing data from the raw dataset.
5. Study parameters: These parameters control which part of the data is analyzed if not all data is available.
6. Processed dataset: This is the output of the extraction methodology and serves as the input to the analysis methodology.
7. Analysis methodology: This is where the processed dataset is analyzed to obtain the results dataset.
8. Result dataset: This dataset forms the basis for the research results and outcomes.

Furthermore, the extent of detail in which all identified elements are depicted in a study, along with their accessibility and characteristics, can significantly influence reproducibility. To measure this influence, it is essential to identify several attributes of these elements that impact reproducibility. These attributes encompass the *Identification* of the element's origin, *Description* of published information about the element, *Availability* of the element for researchers, *Persistence* of future availability of the item, and *Flexibility* of the element to adapt to new environments. We have identified the elements influencing reproducibility, along with their attributes for each study, resulting in the assessment outlined in Table 1, Table 2, and Table 3. By utilizing these assessment tables, it becomes feasible to determine whether a particular type of reproduction study is easy, difficult, or impossible, taking into account the rows in the table corresponding to the relevant elements.

The evaluation of the ModX study is detailed in Table 1. While their data sources, raw dataset, and study parameters are partially identifiable, there are notable limitations. The study describes their data collection process, which involved manual extraction from various publications and the use of package manager tools to gather binary files. However, they do not provide any links to the collected data. Moreover, there is no mention of the persistence and adaptability of their method. Although the study discusses the data collection process and retrieval methodology, reproducing the proposed methods seems impossible due to the inclusion of numerous sophisticated functions with unknown input and output parameters. Consequently, this study falls into the category of methods that are impossible to reproduce.

According to the reproducibility assessment in Table 2, the FET-based study falls into the category of methods that are impossible to reproduce from a data perspective. This is primarily due to the absence of direct downloadable links for all mentioned datasets, as well as the lack of version information. Additionally, there is no availability of raw or processed datasets online.

Table 3 also displays the reproducibility assessment for the MLP-based study, presenting these findings. All data sources could have been clearly identified and appropriately cited; mentioning the link to the firmware manufacturer is insufficient. The raw dataset, while published, was not easily accessible for reproduction and could have been provided in a more convenient format on a publicly-accessible platform. In summary, the MLP-based study faces significant obstacles in terms of data reproducibility.

Reviewing these table enables the identification of actions that would improve the reproducibility of the study. Although all three studies offer comprehensive details on their methods, whether through pseudocode or step-by-step formulas, they remain challenging to reproduce due to issues with presenting certain details about the data across different lifecycle phases and input and output parameters. For the ModX study, providing additional details on study parameters and offering a link to its datasets, or ideally, creating a reproducibility package, would be beneficial. Similarly, image base determination studies, FET-based and MLP-based, would benefit from similar enhancements. Additionally, MLP-based study should provide a direct link to its data source and consider selecting a more accessible online library for their data to ensure public accessibility.

Table 1. Reproducibility assessment for ModX study [15]

	Identification	Description	Availability	Persistence	Flexibility	Assessment
Data source	Partial	Partial	No	N/A	No	D
Retrieval meth.	Partial	Partial	No	N/A	No	D
Raw dataset	Partial	No	No	N/A	No	D
Extraction meth.	Partial	No	No	N/A	No	D
Parameters	No	No	No	N/A	N/A	N
Processed dataset	No	No	No	N/A	N/A	N
Analysis meth.	No	No	No	N/A	N/A	N
Results dataset	No	No	No	N/A	N/A	N

Tags for *Assessment*: U = Usable; N = Not usable; D = Usable with some difficulty; "*" = Flexible; "+" = Likely available in future; "–" = Irrelevant or nonexistent

Table 2. Reproducibility assessment for FET-based study [16]

	Identification	Description	Availability	Persistence	Flexibility	Assessment
Data source	Partial	Partial	No	N/A	Complete	D*
Retrieval meth.	–	No	–	N/A	–	N
Raw dataset	No	No	No	N/A	No	N
Extraction meth.	–	No	–	N/A	–	N
Parameters	No	No	No	N/A	No	N
Processed dataset	No	No	No	N/A	No	N
Analysis meth.	No	No	No	N/A	No	N
Results dataset	No	No	No	N/A	No	N

Tags for *Assessment*: U = Usable; N = Not usable; D = Usable with some difficulty; "*" = Flexible; "+" = Likely available in future; "–" = Irrelevant or nonexistent

Table 3. Reproducibility assessment for MLP-based study [17]

	Identification	Description	Availability	Persistence	Flexibility	Assessment
Data source	Complete	Detailed	Private	N/A	Complete	D
Retrieval meth.	–	No	–	N/A	–	N
Raw dataset	Partial	Detailed	Private	N/A	Complete	D
Extraction meth.	–	No	–	N/A	–	N
Parameters	No	No	No	N/A	No	N
Processed dataset	No	No	No	N/A	No	N
Analysis meth.	No	No	No	N/A	No	N
Results dataset	No	No	No	N/A	No	N

Tags for *Assessment*: U = Usable; N = Not usable; D = Usable with some difficulty; "*" = Flexible; "+" = Likely available in future; "–" = Irrelevant or nonexistent

5.2   Ease of Reproducibility Assessment

Rodriguez et al. [14] examines reproducibility and credibility in ESE through a case study, exploring how these aspects have been addressed in studies employing SZZ algorithm. Likewise, we can investigate reproducibility in firmware analysis through three case studies, examining how these aspects have been handled in studies employing TPL-detection or Image base determination approaches.

Based on the implementation obstacles highlighted in the preceding section, this section introduces the quality assessment for each study by addressing the five questions outlined by Rodriguez et al. [14], as follows:

Q1. Does the study report limitations of using firmware analysis method (whether TPL detection or image base determination)?

Q2. Do the authors carry out a manual inspection of their results?

Q3. Does the study point to a reproducibility package?

Q4. Does the study provide detailed description of the methods and data used?

Q5. Does the study use an improved version of firmware analysis method (whether TPL detection, or FET/MLP image-base determination)?

A positive score is assigned if the criteria are met, while a score of 0 is assigned if they are not. Aspects with a greater influence on the reproducibility of the studies are awarded 2 points. The individual scores are then aggregated to determine an overall score. Table 4 displays both the overall score and individual scores for each question across each method. In terms of reproducibility ranking, the overall score ranges are then labelled as follows: 0–1 ranks as *Poor*; 2–4 ranks as *Fair*; 5–6 ranks as *Good*; and 7 ranks as *Excellent*. According to the Table 4, all three studies fall within the third category, indicating a *Fair* level of ease of reproducibility. However, this level of reproducibility may not be sufficient for the reproducibility of firmware binary analysis.

In this paper, the primary reproducibility challenges of selected studies revovle around the second and fourth questions. While these studies explain operational procedures, they fall short in sharing exact data and detailing their initial setup. Specifically, studies employing Image base determination methodologies share their source code but omit data repositories. The ModX study explains procedures with equations, yet lacks comprehensive data sharing.

Table 4. Quality measure [14] of each study we attempted to reproduce

	ModX method [15]	FET method [16]	MLP method [17]
Score for Q1	2	0	1
Score for Q2	1	1	1
Score for Q3	0	0	0
Score for Q4	1	1	1
Score for Q5	0	0	0
Overal Score (Rank)	4 (Fair)	2 (Fair)	3 (Fair)

6   Discussion

Reproducibility enhances the influence of research [7] and ensuring reproducibility is fundamental for establishing credibility in firmware analysis studies. Furthermore, research endeavors that prioritize reproducibility are more prone to replication. Authors who furnish a replication package (or offer comprehensive

insights into the analysis, environment, and data used) facilitate others in replicating or reproducing their experiments, thereby enhancing the credibility of
their findings [7].

Depending on the type of artifacts manipulated in the experiment, various
challenges may arise during publication. Initially, source code is often the most
readily shared artifact alongside the study, enhancing transparency by detailing
the exact operations performed. However, relying solely on source code may
not suffice for achieving experiment reproducibility. Another challenge lies in
determining whether and how to disclose the data utilized during the experiment.
Additionally, the experiment's environment significantly influences its outcomes,
and with virtualization technologies, sharing the precise software environment
is typically straightforward. Moreover, the experiment setup plays a pivotal role
in determining the measured results, as an incorrect configuration can yield
divergent outcomes from the original study, thereby impacting fair methodology
comparisons [10].

The results and findings obtained from our experiments provide valuable
insights into the reproducibility of the selected firmware analysis methods. We
found that while some aspects of the implemented studies were reproducible
according to the predefined metrics, others posed challenges or inconsistency. For
instance, metrics introduced by [4] and [14] were used to assess the reproducibility of our implemented studies, revealing areas where improvements or clarifica-
tions were needed to ensure replicability. In discussing these results, it becomes
evident that reproducibility in firmware analysis is multifaceted, influenced by
factors such as the availability of data, the transparency of methodology descriptions, and the consistency of experimental setups. Our study highlights the need
for standardized practices and increased transparency in research methodologies
to enhance reproducibility in the field.

Our approach stands out from recent studies in that we implement firmware
analysis methods to assess reproducibility levels, whereas others may only examine it theoretically [5]. In our evaluation, we primarily focus on the availability of
data throughout various lifecycle phases, the methods used for data conversion
between steps, and whether the study addresses limitations and enhancements.
In contrast, other studies [5] may concentrate on aspects such as firmware acquisition and unpacking, heterogeneity, scalability, and establishing ground truth.

7   Conclusion

In this paper, we have independently reproduce and evaluate three selected
methods – ModX for third-party library determination, and FET and MLP for
firmware binaries base image determination – proposed in the field of firmware
security and firmware analysis. Unfortunately, despite all the efforts, we were not
able to fully reproduce either the methods or the results claimed in the respective studies. We have highlighted and motivated the main research and engineering challenges that prevented an independent reproduction and evaluation
of those studies. Also, we have used two different generic methodologies that are

used to assess the reproducibility of works that deal with algorithm implementation and software engineering. Our qualitative and quantitative evaluations show that the evaluated research studies somewhere between Medium and Low ranks of reproducibility scale. This suggests that independent evaluation and validation is highly unlikely without further details, data, and improvements from the respective authors.

The firmware analysis and firmware security community should give greater attention to reproducibility of the results, techniques, and other associated factors that guarantee a high-quality scientific and reproducible process. This will bolster the credibility of the associated research and engineering results, hence driving IoT and firmware security towards a more trustworthy path.

7.1   Future Work

Despite work in this direction starts to emerge [5], reproducibility is still a fairly unexplored concept within the realm of firmware security and firmware analysis, and many analysis methods and datasets have yet to be inspected from this perspective. Therefore, as immediate future work we aim to implement additional firmware analysis methods to evaluate the reproducibility standards within this expanding field relevant to both researchers and practitioners. Additionally, we will delve into other aspects of reproducibility such as firmware unpacking, heterogeneity, scalability, and ground truth. This comprehensive approach aims to provide a more thorough and robust solution for achieving reproducibility in firmware analysis.

Acknowledgment. Narges Yousefnezhad acknowledges the support of Jenny and the Antti Wihuri Foundation through the PoDoCo program (www.podoco.fi), grant number 141222. (Part of) This work was supported by the European Commission under the Horizon Europe Programme, as part of the project LAZARUS (https://lazarus-he.eu/) (Grant Agreement no. 101070303). The content of this article does not reflect the official opinion of the European Union. Responsibility for the information and views expressed therein lies entirely with the authors. (Part of this work was) Funded by the European Union (Grant Agreement Nr. 101120962, RESCALE Project). Views and opinions expressed are however those of the author(s) only and do not necessarily reflect those of the European Union or the Health and Digital Executive Agency. Neither the European Union nor the granting authority can be held responsible for them.

References

1. Abt, S., Stampp, R., Baier, H.: Towards reproducible cyber-security research through complex node automation. In: Badra, M., Boukerche, A., Urien, P. (eds.) 7th International Conference on New Technologies, Mobility and Security, NTMS 2015, Paris, France, 27–29 July 2015, pp. 1–5. IEEE (2015). https://doi.org/10.1109/NTMS.2015.7266527

2. Akiyama, M., Shiraishi, S., Fukumoto, A., Yoshimoto, R., Shioji, E., Yamauchi, T.: Seeing is not always believing: insights on iot manufacturing from firmware composition analysis and vendor survey. Comput. Secur. **133**, 103389 (2023). https://doi.org/10.1016/J.COSE.2023.103389

3. Cheng, Y., Chen, W., Fan, W., Huang, W., Yu, G., Liu, W.: Iotfuzzbench: a pragmatic benchmarking framework for evaluating iot black-box protocol fuzzers. Electronics **12**(14), 3010 (2023)

4. González-Barahona, J.M., Robles, G.: On the reproducibility of empirical software engineering studies based on data retrieved from development repositories. Empir. Softw. Eng. **17**(1–2), 75–89 (2012). https://doi.org/10.1007/S10664-011-9181-9

5. Helmke, R., Padilla, E., Aschenbruck, N.: Corpus christi: establishing replicability when sharing the bread is not allowed. arXiv preprint arXiv:2404.11977 (2024)

6. Hernandez, G., et al.: Firmwire: transparent dynamic analysis for cellular baseband firmware. In: 29th Annual Network and Distributed System Security Symposium, NDSS 2022, San Diego, California, USA, 24–28 April 2022. The Internet Society (2022). https://www.ndss-symposium.org/ndss-paper/auto-draft-200/

7. Juristo, N., Vegas, S.: Using differences among replications of software engineering experiments to gain knowledge. In: 2009 3Rd International Symposium on Empirical Software Engineering and Measurement, pp. 356–366. IEEE (2009)

8. Muench, M.: Dynamic binary firmware analysis: challenges & solutions. (Analyse dynamique de micrologiciels binaires: défis et solutions). Ph.D. thesis, Sorbonne University, France (2019). https://tel.archives-ouvertes.fr/tel-03143960

9. Neto, F.G.D.O., Torkar, R., Machado, P.D.: An initiative to improve reproducibility and empirical evaluation of software testing techniques. In: 2015 IEEE/ACM 37th IEEE International Conference on Software Engineering, vol. 2, pp. 575–578. IEEE (2015)

10. Olivier, P., Ngo, X., Francillon, A.: BEERR: bench of embedded system experiments for reproducible research. In: IEEE European Symposium on Security and Privacy, EuroS&P 2022 - Workshops, Genoa, Italy, 6–10 June 2022, pp. 332–339. IEEE (2022). https://doi.org/10.1109/EUROSPW55150.2022.00040

11. Peffers, K., et al.: The design science research process: a model for producing and presenting information systems research. In: 1st International Conference, pp. 83–106 (2006)

12. Raghupathi, W., Raghupathi, V., Ren, J.: Reproducibility in computing research: an empirical study. IEEE Access **10**, 29207–29223 (2022)

13. Rahman, M.M., Khomh, F., Castelluccio, M.: Works for me! cannot reproduce-a large scale empirical study of non-reproducible bugs. Empir. Softw. Eng. **27**(5), 111 (2022)

14. Rodríguez-Pérez, G., Robles, G., González-Barahona, J.M.: Reproducibility and credibility in empirical software engineering: a case study based on a systematic literature review of the use of the SZZ algorithm. Inf. Softw. Technol. **99**, 164–176 (2018)

15. Yang, C., Xu, Z., Chen, H., Liu, Y., Gong, X., Liu, B.: Modx: Binary level partially imported third-party library detection via program modularization and semantic matching. In: 44th IEEE/ACM 44th International Conference on Software Engineering, ICSE 2022, Pittsburgh, PA, USA, 25–27 May 2022, pp. 1393–1405. ACM (2022). https://doi.org/10.1145/3510003.3510627
16. Zhu, R., Tan, Y., Zhang, Q., Wu, F., Zheng, J., Xue, Y.: Determining image base of firmware files for ARM devices. IEICE Trans. Inf. Syst. **99-D**(2), 351–359 (2016). https://doi.org/10.1587/TRANSINF.2015EDP7217
17. Zhu, R., Tan, Y.A., Zhang, Q., Li, Y., Zheng, J.: Determining image base of firmware for arm devices by matching literal pools. Digital Invest. **16**, 19–28 (2016)
18. Zhu, R., Zhang, B., Mao, J., Zhang, Q., Tan, Y.A.: A methodology for determining the image base of arm-based industrial control system firmware. Int. J. Crit. Infrastruct. Prot. **16**, 26–35 (2017)
19. Zhu, R., Zhang, B., Tan, Y.A., Wan, Y., Wang, J.: Determining the image base of arm firmware by matching function addresses. Wirel. Commun. Mobile Comput. **2021**, 1–10 (2021)
20. Zhu, R., Zhang, B., Tan, Y.A., Wang, J., Wan, Y.: Determining the image base of smart device firmware for security analysis. Wirel. Commun. Mobile Comput. **2020**, 1–12 (2020)

Short Paper

Roles of Natural Language Generation for Requirements Engineering

Bert de Brock$^{(\boxtimes)}$ (iD)

Faculty of Economics and Business, University of Groningen, PO Box 800,
9700 AV Groningen, The Netherlands
E.O.de.Brock@rug.nl

Abstract. *Context*: In Requirements Engineering, communication problems are ubiquitous. Many users and user organizations cannot fully understand the artefacts which developers produce (such as domain models, (conceptual) schemas, data models, class diagrams, (system) sequence diagrams, other UML diagrams, etc.). We try to solve challenges that customers and practitioners face when dealing with requirements that are <u>not</u> expressed in Natural Language (NL).

Research questions: How could such artefacts be explained to and validated by the user organization in a systematic and user-understandable way?

Main idea: Well, users are of course supposed to understand their own native natural language. So, you might try to translate those artefacts to their own natural language in a systematic way. But under which conditions and what are the general mechanisms behind this, both for *static* and for *dynamic* aspects? With a clear and complete set of construction rules or even a grammar for your artefacts, you can (try to) construct practical translations to the target NL by systematically following those construction rules. This is independent of a particular development lifecycle within which the artefacts were produced.

Contribution: In the paper, we make these general mechanisms behind such NL generation explicit and mention the conditions under which these ideas can be applied. We illustrate the applicability and feasibility of the general theory for Conceptual Data Models (statics-based), using construction rules, and for System Sequence Descriptions (dynamics-based), using syntax-directed translations. We also establish the (easy) readability of the results.

Keywords: Requirements Engineering · Natural Language Generation · Generation Mechanisms · Statics · Dynamics · Conceptual Data Model · Use Cases · Validation · Explanation · Documentation

1 Introduction

In this paper we sketch and generalize the many roles that Natural Language Generation can play in Requirements Engineering (RE). In earlier papers (e.g., [1]) we worked it out for its role in explanation to and validation by the customer for the *statics* (e.g., for explaining a conceptual data model) as well as for the *dynamics* of a system to be built (e.g., for validating stylized forms of system sequence diagrams). In this paper we generalize this. We explain the general mechanism behind it and mention the conditions under which it can be applied. All in all, this paper generalizes [1].

© The Author(s), under exclusive license to Springer Nature Switzerland AG 2024
B. Shishkov (Ed.): BMSD 2024, LNBIP 523, pp. 229–239, 2024.
https://doi.org/10.1007/978-3-031-64073-5_14

We note that we are concentrating on NL generation from _conceptual_ artefacts, not from _software_ artefacts. So, the natural language generation can be used in an early development stage, for _explanation_ as well as for _validation_ purposes. We treat both the specification of the _statics_ and the specification of the _dynamics_ of a (future) system.

There is much literature on NL _Processing_ and there is also literature on NL _Generation_ from _software_ artefacts. However, we did not find literature presenting a unified theory of NL generation from various conceptual artefacts for both the _static_ and the _dynamic_ aspects of a system.

The rest of the paper is organized as follows: Sect. 2 gives some more background. If you have a clear and complete set of construction rules, Sect. 3 shows for Conceptual Data Models (regards _statics_) how to construct practical translations to English by systematically following their _construction_ rules. Section 4 shows for textual System Sequence Descriptions (regards _dynamics_) how to construct practical translations to structured use cases in English by systematically following their _grammar_ rules. Section 5 presents a generalization in case the artefacts are specified by means of a _context-free grammar_. Section 6 contains some conclusions and sketches our roadmap for future research in this area.

2   Background

NL _processing_ is typically applied to create artefacts from Natural Language expressions; see Fig. 1A. NL _generation_, on the other hand, can be used to come from artefacts to Natural Language: Once you obtained an artefact, independent of a particular development approach, NL Generation might be used in RE for _validation_ by the user organization (e.g., to check - and solve - RE communication problems), for _explanation_, and (later) for _documentation_ purposes; see Fig. 1B. As generally known, detecting defects in created artefacts in an early stage is very valuable and cost-effective, because the later defects are detected, the more expensive it is to repair them. NL Generation will contribute to validation though it might not be enough for _full_ validation.

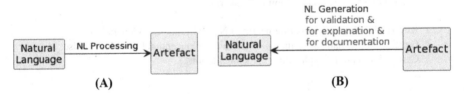

Fig. 1. A. NL Processing. **B.** NL Generation

As a result of NL Generation, the RE artefacts are expressed in Natural Language. Some examples of artefacts are _conceptual data models_, _class diagrams_, and _system sequence descriptions_ (SSDs). Unbounded use of natural language (i.e. English) is inherently prone to ambiguity, but our output concerns a bounded, unambiguous part of English.

Translations to different natural languages (English, Dutch, German, etc.) might then also be possible and useful, e.g., when the user organization uses a different native language or when different people in the user organization have different native languages (Fig. 2).

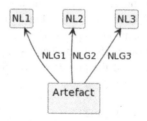

Fig. 2. Translating an artefact to different natural languages

Such translations can be used for explanation to and validation by the user organization (as well as for later documentation). In those cases, such translations can be preceded by the following text:

Target language	For *validation*	For *explanation* (and *documentation*)
English	*Is the following correct?*	*The situation is as follows:*
Dutch	*Klopt het volgende?*	*De situatie is als volgt:*
German	...	...
...	...	...

3 Simple Conceptual Data Models

A *Conceptual Data Model* (CDM) typically consists of a set of concepts each with a set of properties. A value for a property P might be optional, which we indicate by '[P]'. A property can be a Yes/No-property (a 'Boolean'), in which case the property has the form 'P?'. A property P can refer to another instance of a concept, which we indicate by '^P' (where P is usually the name of the referenced concept).

Moreover, a property or combination of properties of a concept might be uniquely identifying within that concept (a.k.a. a 'key'). This can be indicated by a '!' in front of the properties involved. If there is another uniqueness constraint within the same concept, that uniqueness constraint can be indicated by a '%' in front of the properties involved; e.g., see *Student* in Example 1.

So, in principle, a property expression can have the form [!^<txt >?] but the combination ^<txt>? does not make sense. The 12 remaining combinations can expressed by a small grammar:

N1 ::= <txt> | ^<txt> | <txt>?
N2 ::= N1 | ! N1
N3 ::= N2 | [N2]

Example 1: A Conceptual Data Model

We give an illustrative example of a CDM. It has some Yes/No-properties, some optional properties, and some combinations thereof. There are two references (^*Student* and ^*Course* in *Course Enrolment*). Furthermore, there are two uniqueness conditions within the same concept (*Student number* and *SSN* in *Student*), and two uniqueness conditions with two properties (e.g., *Faculty, Course code* in *Course*). If present, the value of the property *SSN* (Social Security Number) is unique.

Student:	Course:	Course Enrolment:
! Student number	! Faculty	! ^Student
[% SSN]	! Course code	! ^Course
Name	Name	Accepted?
[Phone number]	[Master course?]	
[Freshman?]	Description	
Birth date		

3.1 Explaining a Conceptual Data Model in English

For several reasons, it might be useful to express a Conceptual Data Model in Natural Language as well: The NL version might be used for *explanation to* and *validation by* the user organization (e.g., to check - and solve - communication problems) and for *documentation* purposes in a later stage.

If a Conceptual Data Model consists of concept C_1 with properties $P_{1,1}, ..., P_{1,n1}$, concept C_2 with properties $P_{2,1}, ..., P_{2,n2}, ...,$ until concept C_m with properties $P_{m,1}, ..., P_{m,nm}$, then our 'explanation' could run as below. We added the word 'relevant' because not each individual concept might be relevant for the organization or application.

The System Needs to Contain:

- **For each relevant C_1: $P_{1,1}, ...,$ and $P_{1,n1}$.**
- **For each relevant C_2: $P_{2,1}, ...,$ and $P_{2,n2}$.**
  $\vdots$
- **For each relevant C_m: $P_{m,1}, ...,$ and $P_{m,nm}$.**

Since a property expression can have a composite form, as just explained, we apply the following transformations to such a composite property expression, following the given grammar rules. We use that result instead of the property $P_{i,j}$ sec.

$F([n2]) \stackrel{\text{def}}{=}$ **optionally** $F(n2)$
$F(! \ n1) \stackrel{\text{def}}{=} F(n1)$ /* Uniqueness indications are ignored in this stage (see below)
$F(^\wedge\alpha) \stackrel{\text{def}}{=}$ **a reference to** $F(\alpha)$
$F(\alpha?) \stackrel{\text{def}}{=}$ **whether it is** $G(\alpha)$ /* 'he/she' instead of 'it'
                                   if the underlying concept C represents a human being
$F(\alpha) \stackrel{\text{def}}{=}$ **its** α /* 'his/her' (or 'their') instead of 'its'
                                   if the underlying concept C represents a human being

where $G(\alpha)$ is α, **a** α, or **an** α, according to the following grammar rules:

$G(\alpha) = \alpha$ if α is a *verb* (*phrase*) or a *mass noun* (*phrase*).

$G(\alpha) = $ **a** α if α is a *count noun* (*phrase*) and its first letter makes a consonant-type sound.

$G(\alpha) = $ **an** α if α is a *count noun* (*phrase*) and its first letter makes a vowel-type sound.

Examples of applying those rules in combination (if the underlying concept C does not represent a human being):

$F([!\alpha])$ = **optionally** $F(!\alpha)$ = **optionally** $F(\alpha)$ = **optionally its** α

$F([!^{\wedge}\alpha])$ = **optionally** $F(!^{\wedge}\alpha)$ = **optionally** $F(^{\wedge}\alpha)$ = **optionally a reference to** $F(\alpha)$ = **optionally a reference to its** α

$F([!\alpha?])$ = **optionally** $F(!\alpha?)$ = **optionally** $F(\alpha?)$ = **optionally whether it is** $G(\alpha)$ = **optionally whether it is (a(n))** α

For each property (combination) $P_1, \ldots, P_k$ of a concept C_i which is uniquely identifying within concept C_i, we can add the sentence.

'**The same [combination for]** $P_1, \ldots,$ **and** P_k **should not occur twice.**'

immediately after the complete sentence '**For each relevant** C_i**: ....**' for that concept.

The text '**combination for**' can be left out if $k = 1$, so if one property in itself is uniquely identifying. This constitutes an improved (i.e., more readable) version of [1].

Example 2: A Conceptual Data Model Explained

The CDM in Example 1 has one human being concept (*Student*) and two non-human being concepts (*Course* and *Course Enrolment*). Applying our 'explanation rules' to this CDM would result in:

  The system needs to contain:
- **For each relevant** Student: **their** Student number, **optionally their** SSN, **their** Name, **optionally their** Phone number, **optionally whether he/she is a** Freshman, **and their** Birth date.
- **The same** Student number **should not occur twice.**
- **The same** SSN **should not occur twice.**
- **For each relevant** Course: **its** Faculty, **its** Course code, **its** Name, **optionally whether it is a** Master course, **and its** Description.
- **The same combination for** Faculty **and** Course code **should not occur twice.**
- **For each relevant** Course Enrolment: **a reference to its** Student, **a reference to its** Course, **and whether it is** Accepted.
- **The same combination for** Student **and** Course **should not occur twice.**

  Without taking the reading aids such as newlines, bullets, empty lines, and bold text into account, the Readability Consensus of this sample text is Grade Level 10 (Reader's age: 14–15 yrs. old), with a standard/average Reading Level, according to [2]. The Readability Consensus is based on 7 readability formulas. See [3] and [4] for more background on *Readability*.

We refer to [1] for a further translation extension, i.e., with data types. There we mention the data type per property as well, e.g., by adding texts such as (**being a date and time**) or (**being a string of exactly** n **characters**) or for instance (**being** v1, v2, v3, v4, **or** v5) for an enumeration type. Other integrity constraints might follow similarly.

We tried this in a practical situation (a CDM with > 40 concepts and > 230 properties). Some presentation adjustments came forward, e.g., (a) Per concept, start with the *required* properties, followed by the *optional* properties, (b) Present each property on a new line, (c) Make the word '**optionally**'red. These readability adjustments were easily made.

4   Textual System Sequence Descriptions

System Sequence Descriptions (SSDs) are schematic representations of the interactions between the primary actor (user), the system (as a black box), and other participants (if any), including the messages between them. We present a grammar for *textual* SSDs (tSSDs) which is an extension of [5].

The grammar is given in BNF (Backus–Naur form). The terminals are written in **bold**. Non-terminals have the form <X >. The non-terminal <A> stands for 'atomic instruction' (or 'step'), <P> for 'participant' (or 'actor'), <M> for 'message'/'material', <T> for 'task', <S> for 'instruction' (or textual SSD), <C> for 'condition', <N> for 'instruction name', and <D> for 'definition':

<A> ::= <P> ➡ <P>: <M> | <P> **:** <T>
<P> ::= **System** | **User** | ...

<S> ::= <A> | <S> **;** <S> | **begin** <S> **end** | **if** <C> **then** <S> [**else** <S>] **end**
    | **while** <C> **do** <S> **end** | **repeat** <S> **until** <C> | **perform** <N>
    | <S> **,** <S> | **maybe** <S> **end** | **either** <S> **or** <S> **end** /* *These three constructs*
                                                                   introduce non-determinism
<D> ::= **define** <N> **as** <S> **end**

System represents the system under consideration. **User** represents the primary actor. Other actors are application-dependent. The actor often is a human user but it could as well be another system.

Informally, atomic instruction 'x → y: m' means 'x *sends m to y*'. Here, m can be intangible (e.g., a message, information, a request/command, etc.) or tangible (e.g., material such as ordered items, delivered goods, etc.). The atomic instruction 'x**:**t' means 'x *does t*' where x is an actor and t is a task. So, the step indicates the task that actor x has to do. (In that case, the actor is often **System**.)

Furthermore, the construct 's1; s2' indicates 'do s1 first; then do s2', while 's1, s2' indicates that the order is irrelevant ('do s1 and s2 in any order'). We use the binding rule that ',' binds stronger than ';' to avoid ambiguity.

The expression '**perform** ...' represents an *Include* or *Call*, '**maybe** s **end**' means 'do s or do nothing', and '**either** s1 **or** s2 **end**' means 'choose between doing s1 and doing s2'. The final '**end**' in some of the grammar rules is needed to avoid ambiguity.

The values for non-terminals <P >, <M >, <T >, <C >, and <N> are application-dependent, or 'domain specific' (except **System** and **User** for <P >). Those values will appear during the development of the specific application.

Example 3: A textual System Sequence Description

We give an illustrative example of a textual SSD. It is a variant of Larman's well-known real-world use case *Process Sale* [6]. The primary actor is the cashier. **InvSys** stands for the Inventory System. The blue underlined expressions are task names defined elsewhere and included/called here.

> **DEFINE** ProcessSale **as**
>   Cashier → System: start a new sale;
>   System ⦂ create a sale;
>   **repeat perform** <u>EnterItem</u>;
>   System ⦂ record sale line item ,
>   System → Cashier: description, price, and running total
>   **until** cashier sees it is done;
>   Cashier → System: end the sale;
>   System → Cashier: total with taxes;
>   Cashier → Customer: request for payment;
>   **maybe perform** <u>HandleCoupons</u> **end**;
>   **either perform** <u>HandleCashPayment</u>
>   **or perform** <u>HandleCreditPayment</u>
>   **end**;
>   System → InvSys: sale and payment info;
>   **if** system detects that printer is out of paper
>   **then perform** <u>HandlePaperShortage</u> **end**;
>   System → Cashier: receipt
> **END**

4.1 Turning a Textual SSD into a Structured Use Case

We recall and extend the mapping from textual SSDs to natural language (English in that case) as given in [7]. Function F below inductively maps textual SSDs to English, assigning to each textual SSD an expression in English in terms of the direct constituents of that tSSD, according to the *compositionality principle*: The meaning of a complex expression is determined by its structure and the meanings of its constituents [8]. Most mappings to English are straightforward, i.e., leave the language constructs as they are. We write out only two such straightforward examples: Rules 5 and 6. Some translation rules are not straightforward and are all given below. The final '**end**' in some of the grammar rules for tSSDs is retained in the translations in order to avoid ambiguity in the target language.

The type of parameters used in the translation rules are as follows: Participants x and y (often **User** and/or **System**), message/material z, task t, condition c, instruction name n, and textual SSDs s, s1, and s2.

1a. $F(x \rightarrow y: z)$ $\stackrel{\text{def}}{=}$ **The** $F(x)$ **sends** $F(z)$ **to the** $F(y)$ /* if z is a *noun phrase* (maybe + an *(in)definite article*)

1b. $F(x \rightarrow y: z)$ $\stackrel{\text{def}}{=}$ **The** $F(x)$ **asks the** $F(y)$ **to** $F(z)$ /* if z is an *affirmative imperative* (e.g., a command)

2. $F(x : t)$ $\stackrel{\text{def}}{=}$ **The** $F(x)$ **does** $F(t)$ /* t is an *affirmative imperative* expressing a task

3. $F(s1; s2)$ $\stackrel{\text{def}}{=}$ $F(s1)$. *<newline>* $F(s2)$ /* Sequential order will be indicated by a dot

4. $F(s1, s2)$ $\stackrel{\text{def}}{=}$ $F(s1)$ **and** *<newline>* $F(s2)$ /* Arbitrary order will be indicated by '**and**'

5. $F(\textbf{if } c \textbf{ then } s \textbf{ end})$ $\stackrel{\text{def}}{=}$ **if** $F(c)$ **then** $F(s)$ **end**

6. $F(\textbf{either } s1 \textbf{ or } s2 \textbf{ end})$ $\stackrel{\text{def}}{=}$ **either** $F(s1)$ **or** $F(s2)$ **end**

7. $F(\textbf{define } n \textbf{ as } s \textbf{ end})$ $\stackrel{\text{def}}{=}$ $F(n)$ **means:** $F(s)$ **end**

Essentially, the mapping boils down to replacing the basic steps by some standard sentence constructions (1a, 1b, 2), replacing ';' by '.', replacing ',' by '**and**', and replacing '**define** n **as**' by '$F(n)$ **means:**'. The final **end** in rules 5–7 is needed to avoid ambiguity. Implementing this algorithm is a typical nice exercise for a CS student.

A translation to, e.g., Dutch or German would lead to different translation rules. For Rule 6, for instance:

6D: $F(\textbf{either } s1 \textbf{ or } s2 \textbf{ end})$ $\stackrel{\text{def}}{=}$ **hetzij** $F(s1)$ **hetzij** $F(s2)$ **einde**

6G: $F(\textbf{either } s1 \textbf{ or } s2 \textbf{ end})$ $\stackrel{\text{def}}{=}$ **entweder** $F(s1)$ **oder** $F(s2)$ **ende**

The final **einde** in Rule 6D and the final **ende** in Rule 6G are needed to avoid ambiguity. The translations generate 'structured use cases', as illustrated by Example 4. A large example can be found in [9].

Example 4: The textual SSD translated
Applying our translation rules to the real-world tSSD in Example 3 would result in:

ProcessSale **means:**
   The Cashier asks the System to start a new sale.
   The System does create a sale.
   repeat perform EnterItem.
        The System does record sale line item **and**
        The System sends description, price, and running total **to the Cashier**
   until cashier sees it is done.
   The Cashier asks the System to end the sale.
   The System sends total with taxes **to the Cashier.**
   The Cashier sends request for payment **to the Customer.**
   maybe perform HandleCoupons **end.**
   either perform HandleCashPayment
      or perform HandleCreditPayment
   end.
   The System sends sale and payment info **to the InvSys.**
   if system detects that printer is out of paper
      then perform HandlePaperShortage **end.**
   The System sends receipt **to the Cashier**
end

According to [2], the Readability Consensus of this sample text is Grade Level 7–8 (Reader's age: 11–14 yrs. old) with a standard/average Reading Level.

5 Generalization

If you have clear and complete set of construction rules for your artefacts, then you can (try to) construct translations to the target natural language by following the construction rules. If you even have a 'grammar' for your artefacts, then you can (try to) construct *syntax-directed* translations to the target natural language, i.e., a translation rule for each grammar rule. In this section, we generalize the situation in Sect. 4, where the artefacts are specified by means of a *context-free grammar*.

In a context-free grammar, each rewriting rule R has one non-terminal on its left hand side and an expression E_R with zero or more non-terminals on its right hand side. The non-terminal on the left can also occur on the right.

The general form of such a grammar rule R is as follows (where $<N_1>, ..., <N_n>$, and $<N>$ indicate non-terminals and $n \geq 0$):

$$<N> ::= E_R(<N_1>, ..., <N_n>)$$

Some examples from Sect. 4:

(a) $<S> ::= $ **if** $<C>$ **then** $<S>$ **end**
(b) $<D> ::= $ **define** $<N>$ **as** $<S>$ **end**

A translation function F is defined inductively by assigning to an expression E_R according to a grammar rule R an expression TE_R in the target language, expressed in terms of the direct constituents of that source expression. For example, translation rule 7 in Sect. 4:

$$F(\textbf{define } n \textbf{ as } s \textbf{ end}) \stackrel{\text{def}}{=} F(n) \textbf{ means: } F(s) \textbf{ end}$$

The general form of such a syntax-driven translation rule for the grammar rule $<N> :: = E_R(<N_1>, ..., <N_n>)$ is:

$$F(E_R(e_1, ..., e_n)) \stackrel{\text{def}}{=} TE_R(F(e_1), ..., F(e_n))$$

where e_k is an $<N_k>$ -expression (i.e., an expression derived from the non-terminal $<N_k>$). In words: F assigns to the source expression $E_R(e_1, ..., e_n)$ an expression TE_R in the target language in terms of the translation results $F(e_1), ..., F(e_n)$. See [8] for more background.

Often, the target expression TE_R is the same expression

$$E_R: \quad F(E_R(e_1, ..., e_n)) \stackrel{\text{def}}{=} E_R(F(e_1), ..., F(e_n))$$

Translation rules 5 and 6 in Sect. 4 are examples:

$$F(\textbf{if } c \textbf{ then } s \textbf{ end}) \quad \stackrel{\text{def}}{=} \textbf{ if } F(c) \textbf{ then } F(s) \textbf{ end}$$
$$F(\textbf{either } s1 \textbf{ or } s2 \textbf{ end}) \stackrel{\text{def}}{=} \textbf{ either } F(s1) \textbf{ or } F(s2) \textbf{ end}$$

As another concrete application of this very general principle, [9] even contains rules to translate *textual* SSDs to *graphical* SSDs (i.e., UML sequence diagrams): Some people understand and (in)validate diagrams better.

6 Conclusions and Future Work

Natural Language Generation plays an essential role in several areas of software engineering, and requirements engineering in particular should be no exception. As outlined and illustrated in this paper, if you have a clear and complete set of construction rules for your conceptual artefacts, then you can try to construct translations to the target natural language of the customer by following the construction rules. If you even have a context-free grammar for your artefacts, then you can construct syntax-directed translations to the target natural language, as we worked out for the general case (Sect. 5). Then, a generator could even *generate* the translations.

All those translation results can be used for explanation to and validation by the user organization (and later for documentation). Therefore, we also paid attention the readability of the results. Based on the Readability Consensus [3, 4], we can conclude that the results are easily readable.

As we illustrated, it might also be possible to translate those artefacts to different target natural languages (English, Dutch, German, etc.), e.g., when the user organization uses a different native language or when different people in the user organization have different native languages.

Our aim is to solve challenges that customers and practitioners face when dealing with requirements that are _not_ expressed in NL. In particular, we treated Conceptual Data Models (statics-based), where we used construction rules, and textual System Sequence Descriptions (dynamics-based), where we used syntax-directed translations.

Our further road map is as follows: Currently, we are developing grammars (!) for a class of graphical Sequence Diagrams, Activity Diagrams, and fragments of BPMN. Once we have grammars for those graphical artefacts, we want to apply NL Generation in a similar way as sketched in this paper. This might help for validation and explanation of those artefacts towards the customer as well.

Acknowledgment. I want to thank Coen Suurmond for our many discussions.

References

1. de Brock, E.O., Suurmond, C.: NLG4RE: How NL Generation Can Support Validation in RE. NLP4RE (2022)
2. https://readabilityformulas.com/free-readability-formula-tests.php. Accessed 5 May 2024
3. DuBay, W.H.: The Principles of Readability (2004). https://eric.ed.gov/?id=ed490073. Accessed 5 May 2024
4. Scott, B.: What Are Readability Formulas? https://readabilityformulas.com/articles/what-are-readability-formulas.php. Accessed 5 May 2024
5. de Brock, E.O.: On system sequence descriptions. In: Sabetzadeh, M., et al. (eds.) Joint Proceedings of REFSQ-2020 Workshops, Doctoral Symposium, and Tracks. Pisa (2020)
6. Larman, C.: Applying UML and Patterns. Pearson Education (2005)
7. de Brock, E.O.: An NL-based Foundation for Increased Traceability, Transparency, and Speed in Continuous Development of Information Systems. NLP4RE (2019)
8. Stanford Encyclopedia of Philosophy (in particular Compositionality). Stanford, https://plato.stanford.edu/about.html, https://plato.stanford.edu/entries/compositionality/
9. de Brock, E.O.: Developing Information Systems Accurately - A Wholistic Approach. Springer (2023)

Developing Functional Specifications of an Information System a Personal Overview

Bert de Brock[(✉)] [ID]

Faculty of Economics and Business, University of Groningen, PO Box 800,
9700 AV Groningen, The Netherlands
E.O.de.Brock@rug.nl

Abstract. How to develop the functional specifications of an information system in a straightforward way, given some problem space?

Both *data* (the *statics*) and *processes* (the *dynamics*) must be developed, in an integrated way. The statics and dynamics of a system are closely related: Actually, they are the two sides of the same coin. We will sketch a concrete and complete development path for functional requirements, from initial (vague) user wishes via functional specifications until software specifications.

Importantly, the development steps are mutually aligned. Our aligned development pipeline supports *traceability* which, in turn, supports *adaptability*. The development pipeline includes concrete validation and explanation steps.

An intermediate *Conceptual Model* (CM) has a central role in this development. The CM is a functional 'blue print' and is implementation-independent. From the CM we can deduce the software specifications for the target platform in a straightforward way ('model-driven'). The original question now concentrates on the question how to *specify* the functional requirements for a given problem space. This actually splits *Developing* into *Specifying* and *Realizing*.

The Conceptual Model of a system should model the *statics* as well as the *dynamics* of the system. The *statics* can be specified by a Conceptual *Data* Model (CDM) and the *dynamics* by a Conceptual *Process* Model (CPM). So, in short: CM = CDM ⊕ CPM. A CDM consists of one data model, while a CPM typically consists of several (usually *many*) 'interaction descriptions', e.g., in the form of System Sequence Descriptions (SSDs). Important to note is that the constructions in our SSD-language have a formal semantics.

Keywords: Information System · Functional Requirements · Statics ·
Dynamics · Data · Processes · Mutual Alignment · Conceptual Model · Complete
Development Path · Traceability · Semantics · Model-Driven

1 Introduction

How to develop the functional requirements (FRs) of an information system, given some problem space? That is, for problems that might be solved by means of an information system. Figure 1 illustrates this question. To answer it, we start at a global high level and then zoom in step by step. We will concentrate on the *functional* requirements of

© The Author(s), under exclusive license to Springer Nature Switzerland AG 2024
B. Shishkov (Ed.): BMSD 2024, LNBIP 523, pp. 240–250, 2024.
https://doi.org/10.1007/978-3-031-64073-5_15

the system. Although quality requirements (a.k.a. 'non-functional' requirements) are important too, they are outside the scope of this paper. This position paper presents the overall picture of our approach, mainly based on our earlier publications.

It is very useful to specify a *Conceptual Model* (CM) of the system, which specifies the functionality of the system (i.e., its *functional requirements*). The Conceptual Model is a kind of (implementation-independent) 'blue print' of the system and should model (the relevant part of) the problem space. The CM forms the basis for a realization of the system: From the CM we can deduce the software specifications for the target platform in a straightforward, 'model-driven' way, as indicated by the exclamation marks in Fig. 2. Figure 2 essentially expresses to split *Developing* into *Specifying* and *Realizing*.

In short: **Develop => Specify + Realize**

The two steps are quite different in nature: The specification step needs much discussion and feedback (requirements engineering), while the realization step is more straightforward (software engineering); see Fig. 3. The original question now concentrates on the question how to *specify* the functional requirements for a given problem space.

In this paper, the green boxes are on conceptual level.

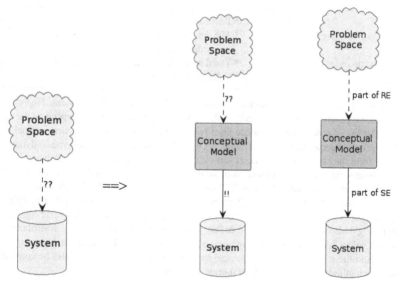

Fig. 1. How to develop the FRs of an information system, given some problem space?

Fig. 2. A Conceptual Model will help enormously

Fig. 3. Nature of the steps to develop the FRs

A *Conceptual Model* of a system should model the *statics* as well as the *dynamics* of the system, and in an <u>integrated</u> way. The *statics* can be specified by a Conceptual *Data* Model and the *dynamics* by a Conceptual *Process* Model. A Conceptual Data Model consists of <u>one</u> data model, while a Conceptual Process Model typically consists of several (usually *many*) 'interaction descriptions'. Such an interaction description is often given in the form of a *Use Case*, an *Activity Diagram*, or a *System Sequence Description* (SSD), to mention a few possibilities. The *statics* and *dynamics* of a system are closely related and must be mutually aligned. They are the two sides of the same coin, so to say. Figure 4 summarizes the foregoing and Example 1 shows some mutual alignment issues.

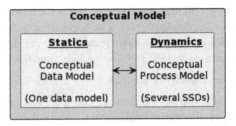

Fig. 4. The ingredients of a Conceptual Model: CM = CDM ⊕ CPM

Example 1: Alignment between static and dynamic aspects
Let's consider the following process fragment (a *dynamic* aspect), with explanation:

⋮	/* Previous actions
Choose order type	/* The data model or current state contains the order types to choose from
Create order (of that type)	/* The data model contains the attributes of an order
⋮	/* Subsequent actions

This is okay as a first approximation: It says that there are essentially two steps: First choose the order type and then create an order of that type. The attribute set might depend on the type.

The list of order types to choose from (e.g., customer order, supply order, internal production order) comes from the data model or current state (if the list of order types is dynamic), hence from the *static* part. A modest example of alignment between statics and dynamics.

The attributes of an order come from the data model, so also from the *static* part. But who fills in the values for those attributes? The user, you might say/think. That might hold for many of the attributes but maybe not for all attributes. E.g., what about the Order ID? To be filled in by the user? Or maybe to be generated by the system? But, then, based on what? Moreover, there might also be attributes that get default values upon order creation. Which attributes get default values? And which default value does each of them get? This all has to be specified as well. And these specifications (*dynamics*) and data model (*statics*) should also be consistent with each other! Another example of mutual alignment.

In one of our applications, a user creating an order does not always fill in the same list of order attributes: If the order type is 'recipe-based production order', then the user has to fill in one 'multiplication factor', to be applied to the units in the standard recipe (*statics*), after which several order attributes are filled in by the system itself, not by the user. Alignment again.

All in all, this little, simple example already illustrates the interaction between the statics and dynamics, which should be carefully aligned!

As a generic example of a frequent alignment issue: The creation of an instance of a concept must specify the value of *each* property of that concept mentioned the data model. On the other hand, if the creation of an instance of a concept introduces another property of that concept, then that property should be added to the data model. And, of course, for *each* concept in the data model, it should be possible to create instances.

Although all this might sound waterfall-like, this approach can be applied in an incremental way, i.e., specifying and realizing a Conceptual Model 'piece-by-piece' [1].

The rest of this paper is organized as follows. Section 2 works out the static part, while Sect. 3 works out the dynamic part. Section 4 presents an example of a complete development path for an individual functional requirement. Section 5 gives some further background and Sect. 6 contains some conclusions.

2 Statics

Figure 5 sketches the possible ingredients for the *static* part (see [1] and [2]):

- Via elicitation and other means (company visit etc.), you might sketch a *domain model*, typically consisting of the relevant **concepts**, their mutual **associations**, and maybe already some of their **properties**
- But a domain model is far from complete and insufficiently precise. It usually lacks:

  - the *association details*, e.g., the **references**
  - how instances of a concept can be **uniquely identified**
  - per property, its **possible values** and whether a value is **required** or **optional**
  - remaining **constraints** (a.k.a. *integrity rules*)

- So, more requirements engineering (RE) is needed before you have a Conceptual Data Model (CDM)
- From a *textual* CDM, we can generate a *graphical* CDM and/or a description in a natural language, useful for validation, explanation, and documentation purposes

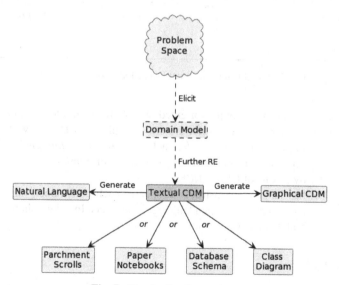

Fig. 5. Developing the *static* part

- The CDM is platform-independent but forms the basis for a realization of the static part of the system. The realization might be by means of parchment scrolls (a few centuries ago), paper notebooks (a century ago), a relational database, or an OO-system, to mention a few possibilities

---

Example 2: Developing a Fragment of a Conceptual Data Model

From the problem space we might elicit an association *Student follows Course*, between the relevant concepts *Student* and *Course*. The association is 'many-to-many' because a student can follow several courses and a course can be followed by several students. Represented in a domain model (where each '*'indicates a 'many'-aspect):

$$\text{Student} \;\frac{\blacktriangleright \text{follows}}{*\qquad\quad *}\; \text{Course}$$

As argued in [1], a 'many-to-many' association should be split into two 'many-to-one' associations, around a newly introduced (and formerly hidden) concept. In this case, the concept will be something like 'Participation' (of a Student in a Course):

$$\text{Student} \;\frac{\blacktriangleleft \text{of}}{1\quad *}\; \text{Participation} \;\frac{\blacktriangleright \text{in}}{*\quad 1}\; \text{Course}$$

Further requirements engineering (RE) might reveal that a student can follow the same course several times, in different course years.

The system also needs a few 'digital number dispensers', e.g., for new student numbers and for new course numbers. They can be collected in the concept *Dispenser*.

Further RE should reveal the relevant properties, references, uniqueness constraints, and the optionality of property values. The resulting graphical Conceptual Data Model for this small example is shown in Figure 6. The symbol '^' indicates a reference, '[' and ']' indicate the optionality of a property value, and per concept, the uniqueness constraint is indicated by a '!' in front of all the properties involved. In other words, within each concept the value of the property (combination) preceded by '!' is unique.

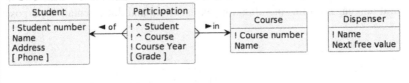

Fig. 6. Graphical Conceptual Data Model for our example

If the target system is an object-oriented system for example, then each concept is implemented as a *class*. If the target system is a relational DBMS with SQL, then each concept is implemented as a *table*, each reference as a *foreign key* constraint, each uniqueness constraint as a *primary key* constraint or a *unique key* constraint, and (non)optionality by means of (NOT) NULL.

Where SQL has language constructs to specify such constraints, imperative programming languages usually lack such language constructs. In [2] we show how to take care of such constraints in a systematic way.

3   Dynamics

Figure 7 sketches the possible ingredients for the *dynamic* part (see [1] and also [2]):

- Via elicitation (and other means), *user wishes* will appear (e.g., *Register an Order*)
- Augmenting a user wish with a role and optionally its benefit(s), we get what is known as a *user story*, e.g., in the form of the popular Connextra template [3]:

  As a <role>, **I want to** <user wish> [**so that** <benefit(s)>]

- A user story is not enough. We also need to know the interaction with the system, i.e., which steps? That could be expressed in a *Use Case*, i.e., a text in natural language that describes a sequence of actions in one session with the system
- We stylize the use case in the form of a *textual* System Sequence Description (tSSD). A tSSD is a kind of stylised Use Case which schematically depicts the tasks of and interactions between the user, the system (as a black box), and other actors (if any), including the messages between them
- If desired, from a *textual* SSD we can generate a *graphical* SSD and/or a description in a natural language. This is useful for validation and for explanation purposes
- Applying the well-known general MVC design pattern (Model-View-Controller), we can turn our *black box* view of the system into a *grey box* view, where the system consists of an Interface and a Kernel, which communicate with each other [2]:

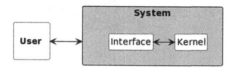

The MVC design pattern is an important basic software design pattern that allows to separate internal representations of information from the ways information is presented to, and accepted from, the user [4]. E.g., the kernel could send error codes, while the interface can convert those error codes into human-understandable text. That text might even depend on the native language of the user at hand

- Since the grey box result is a textual SSD, we can generate a *graphical* SSD of the grey box as well
- A grey box may contain several interactions with the Kernel. Each interaction must be worked out in detail, leading to a detailed *white box*. Since a white box is a textual SSD too, we can generate a *graphical* SSD of a white box as well

In Summary

User Story	≡ User Wish + role [+ benefit(s)].
Use Case	≡ User Wish + steps (in natural language).
tSSD	≡ schematic Use Case.
gSSD	≡ tSSD in graphical form.
grey box	≡ System as Interface & Kernel.
white box	≡ details of an interaction with the Kernel.

In this way, the specification of the dynamics of the system can grow incrementally, 'User Wish by User Wish' (or even 'Scenario by Scenario' within a User Wish).

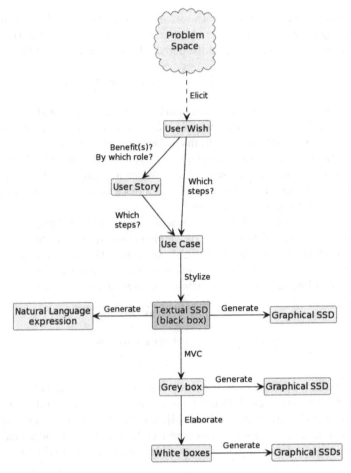

Fig. 7. Overview of developing a single user wish (as part of the *dynamics*)

4 Developing a User Wish: An Example

This section presents a complete development path for the user wish *Register a student*, say, originating from the Central Student Administration (CSA) of a university. Following Fig. 7, the path consists of a User Wish, a User Story, a Use Case, a textual SSD, a Grey box, and a White box. Note the traceability of the development path. In between, we generate graphical SSDs from the textual SSD and from the Grey box.

User Wish *Register a student*

User Story *As a CSA-administrator,*
I want to *Register a student with a given name, address, and maybe phone number*
so that *that student can follow a study here and we have another (paying) student*

The first benefit is actually a benefit for the student, the second one is the actual benefit for the university…

The user wish sounds 'stupidly simple', but still there are some subtleties (as usual in practice). Requirements Engineering revealed that upon registration, a new student must get a system-generated student number and that a student number is a natural number divisible by 11 (meant for simple checks). Moreover, the system must manage the ('consecutive') student numbers. This is taken into account in the subsequent Use Case:

Use Case

1. The CSA-administrator (user) asks the system to

   Register a student with a given name, address, and maybe phone number

2. The system uses the *next free student number* as the new student number
3. The system registers that student number, name, address, and (maybe) phone number
4. The system returns the assigned student number to the user
5. The system increases the *next free student number* by 11

Textual SSD

1. User-> System: RegisterStudent(<name >, < address > [, < phone number >]);
2. System -> System: take the *next free student number* as the new student number;
3. System -> System: CreateStudent(<student nr >, < name >, < address > [, <phone nr >]);
4. System -> User: "Assigned student number is" < student nr >;
5. System -> System: increase the *next free student number* by 11

Graphical SSD

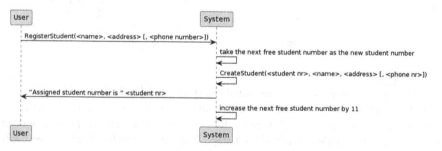

So, as informally described in the Use Case and schematically depicted in the SSDs: once the system receives the RegisterStudent-request, then

- the system uses the *next free student number* as the new student number,
- registers that student number, name, address, and (maybe) phone number,
- returns the assigned student number to the user, and
- increases the *next free student number* by 11.

Grey Box

In the *grey box* view, where the system consists of an Interface and a Kernel, the Interface receives the user-request (maybe submitted as a filled-in form taken from a menu) and sends the corresponding command to the Kernel. The Kernel executes that command and sends the assigned student number to the Interface. The Interface sends the assigned student number provided with a proper text to the user and the Kernel increases the *next free student number* by 11. In the MVC design below, the correspondence with the SSD step numbers is indicated:

U -> I : RegisterStudent(<name>, <address> [, <phone nr>]);	(1)
I -> K : EXECUTE CreateStudent(@n = <name>, @a = <address>, @p = <phone nr>);	(1)
K -> K: execute CreateStudent with the *next free student number* as new student number;	(2,3)
K -> I : <student nr>;	(4)
I -> U : "Assigned student number is " <student nr>;	(4)
K -> K: increase the *next free student number* by 11	(5)

Graphical SSD of the Grey Box

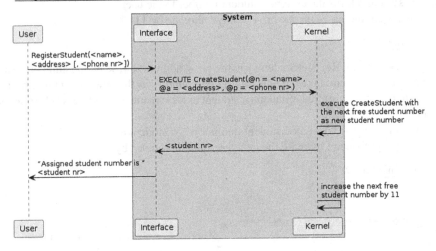

White Box

If the target system is, e.g., a relational DBMS, then the *white box* can be a so-called stored procedure, say `CreateStudent`, with a *name*, *address*, and *phone number* as input variables and an `OUTPUT` variable for the student number. The procedure determines the next free student number (SSD-step 2), adds a tuple to the table `Student` with the proper values (an `INSERT`, corresponding to step 3), and increases the Dispenser called *Next Free Student Number* by 11 (an `UPDATE`, corresponding to step 5).

The procedure must be an 'all-or-nothing' transaction, a.k.a. an *atomic* transaction, implying that the body of the procedure starts with `BEGIN TRANSACTION` and ends with `COMMIT TRANSACTION`. All in all, this leads to the following stored procedure (where the correspondence with the SSD-steps are marked yellow):

```
CREATE PROCEDURE CreateStudent @n varchar, @a varchar, @p varchar,
                               @NUSN integer OUTPUT
AS BEGIN
    BEGIN TRANSACTION
(2)   SELECT @NUSN = Current_value FROM Dispenser
      WHERE Name = 'Next Free Student Number'
(3)   INSERT INTO Student(Student_number, Name, Address, Phone)
          VALUES(@NUSN, @n, @a, @p)
(5)   UPDATE Dispenser
      SET   Current_value = Current_value + 11
      WHERE Name = 'Next Free Student Number'
    COMMIT TRANSACTION
    END
```

Similarly, if the target system is an object oriented system, then the *white box* can be implemented as a *method* CreateStudent.

5 Further Background Ingredients of Our Approach

We worked out most parts of our vision in much more detail in several other papers.

References [1] and [5] present a general grammar for tSSDs, while [6] gives a formal semantics to the tSSD-constructs. Moreover, [1] contains rules to map tSSDs to *natural language* (English in this case) and rules to map them to *sequence diagrams*. We also constructed rules to map tSSDs to *activity diagrams* and rules to map tSSDs to *BPMN diagrams* [7]. See Fig. 8. The natural language equivalent and/or diagram equivalent can be useful for explanation and validation, and in a later stage also for documentation.

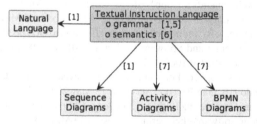

Fig. 8. Validation opportunities (with background publications)

A Conceptual Model must be implementation-independent and should subsequently be implementable on various platforms. For instance, [1] explains in depth how to come from a *conceptual model* (data as well as processes) to an implementation in a *relational DBMS* using SQL, while [2] explains how to come from a *conceptual model* to an *OO-implementation*. The implementation of the conceptual model could be on another (old, current, or new) technology instead. As an illustration, [1] sketches:

(a) an implementation with parchment scrolls ('write once' storage), quill pens ('write-heads' for scrolls), slates ('rewritable memory'), slate pencils, and a sponge
(b) an implementation using (paper) notebooks

See also Fig. 9.

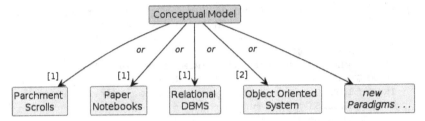

Fig. 9. A Conceptual Model must be implementation-independent

6   In Conclusion

We gave a concrete sketch of a *complete* development path for the *statics* (the data) and the *dynamics* (the processes) of a system: all the way from initial (vague) user wishes via functional specifications to software specifications, with mutually aligned development steps, plus concrete validation and explanation steps. Static and dynamic aspects are taken into account in an <u>integrated</u> way. They are the two sides of the same coin.

New in this paper is the overall composition ('picture') of our approach to develop functional requirements. It is based on our earlier separate publications. Our approach 'automatically' provides a good traceability (as the examples illustrate). It therefore improves adaptability as well.

References

1. de Brock, E.O.: Developing Information Systems Accurately - A Wholistic Approach. Springer, Cham (2023).https://doi.org/10.1007/978-3-031-16862-8. Accessed May 13 2024
2. de Brock, E.O., Smedinga, R.: From conceptual specification to OO specification. In: Shishkov, B. (ed.) Business Modeling and Software Design. LNBIP, vol. 483, pp. 180–199. Springer, Cham (2023). https://doi.org/10.1007/978-3-031-36757-1_11
3. Cohn, M.: User Stories Applied: For Agile Software Development. Addison Wesley (2004). https://dl.acm.org/doi/10.5555/984017. Accessed 13 May 2024
4. SWEBOK (Software Engineering Body of Knowledge). https://www.computer.org/education/bodies-of-knowledge/software-engineering. Accessed 13 May 2024
5. de Brock, E.O.: From business modeling to software design. In: Shishkov, B. (ed.) Business Modeling and Software Design, LNBIP 391, pp. 103–122. Springer, Cham (2020). https://doi.org/10.1007/978-3-030-52306-0_7. Accessed 13 May 2024
6. de Brock, E.O.: Declarative semantics of actions and instructions. In: Shishkov, B. (ed.) Business Modeling and Software Design, LNBIP 391, pp. 297–308. Springer, Cham (2020). https://doi.org/10.1007/978-3-030-52306-0_20. Accessed 13 May 2024
7. de Brock, E.O.: Assigning Declarative Semantics to some UML Activity Diagrams and BPMN Diagrams. BMSD 2024 (2024)

Context Awareness and External Factors

Boris Shishkov[1,2,3]([envelope])

[1] Institute of Mathematics and Informatics, Bulgarian Academy of Sciences, Sofia, Bulgaria
[2] Faculty of Information Sciences, University of Library Studies and Information Technologies, Sofia, Bulgaria
[3] Institute IICREST, Sofia, Bulgaria
b.b.shishkov@iicrest.org

Abstract. The adequate functioning of most current software systems assumes the capability to adapt with regard to numerous circumstances; we call a (software) system "context-aware" if it can deliver "behavior" that is relevant to a particular context situation, as opposed to rigid systems that cannot easily adapt to the changing environment. Most context-aware (software) systems are sensitive to changes in the situation of the user while others are sensitive to changes concerning their own operation. Nevertheless, sensitivity to changes that concern external factors (such as public values, regulations, and norms) is insufficiently covered by most current context-aware software systems. This paper touches upon context awareness and external factors, justifying the need for a more thorough consideration of public values, regulations, and norms in the specification of context-aware software systems. Our analytical contribution is not backed by proof-of-principle / proof-of-concept because we report research in progress and plan to do this in the future.

Keywords: Context awareness · Public values · Regulations · Norms

1 Introduction

Twenty years ago today the Information and Communication Technology (ICT) marked a significant progress and for the first time we could count on powerful portable devices supported not only by global telecommunications and networking but also by rich digital multimedia and wireless sensors. Hence, it was possible to determine the user situation while delivering ICT services – an example of this is the AWARENESS platform [1]. It was about health tele-monitoring and the services delivered to the monitored person, would depend on his/her situation: when all is "normal", vital signs are captured and archived while in case of established "urgent needs", transportation to a care center would be arranged. We label such kind of servicing drive "**maximization of the user-perceived effectiveness**". After some years, situation sensitivity was "extended" to also cover changes in the operation of the ICT system itself. For instance, while a drone is performing a mission in the sky (for example: monitoring), for the benefit of a user, if system-internal issues would pop up (for example: fuel/battery is low), then

B. Shishkov (Ed.): BMSD 2024, LNBIP 523, pp. 251–257, 2024.
https://doi.org/10.1007/978-3-031-64073-5_16

the service delivery would change: the drone may stop monitoring and head towards the base station. We label such kind of servicing drive "**system-internal optimization**". The *maximization of the user-perceived effectiveness* and the *system-internal optimization* were considered as *"categories of context-aware systems"* in [2] where also a third "category" was considered, namely the adaptation of service delivery to relevant *public values*, such as safety, accountability, traceability, and so on [3]. In this regard, we have provided useful conceptualizations leaning towards top-down designs guaranteeing that the social world is governing the systems world, and not vice versa [4, 5].

As "**HARD**" concerns in such designs we consider the abovementioned drives towards maximization of the user-perceived effectiveness and system internal optimization, in the sense that any (technical) system is to be expected to fulfill some user needs and to also take care of its own "health".

On the other hand, as "**SOFT**" concerns we consider the drives towards keeping the (ICT) servicing in concert with societal *values*, *norms*, and *regulations*, in the sense that unlike the *hard concerns* (that are obviously essential in realizing a technical design), such societal issues come "in addition" even though they are not to be considered less important. Hence, in this we are broadening the view of context from public values (which have been considered in previous work [2]) to also cover regulations and norms. Further, we propose designating the *soft concerns* as "***external factors***". Finally, we argue that *external factors* (*public values* included) are receiving less attention to date, compared to the abovementioned *hard concerns* with regard to the development of context-aware software systems.

Thus, considering *external factors* is three-fold: (i) Relating service delivery to relevant **public values** (see above), for example: when realizing monitoring, the service delivery system is to be *privacy-sensitive*; (ii) Aligning service delivery to underlying **regulations**, for example: an autonomous vehicle is to stick to the *traffic regulations*; (iii) Adapting service delivery to imposed **norms**, for example: if several autonomous vehicles are traveling in synch, then a rule (norm) may be imposed such that a vehicle should stop and wait if the other ones are delaying, such that in the end they arrive together at the destination point.

The contribution of this paper is two-fold: (a) We make a justified appeal to software designers to take not only *hard concerns* (effectiveness and optimization) into account, but also the *external factors*; (b) We consider the *external factors* perspective in more detail to cover not only *public values* (as in [2]) but also *regulations* and *norms*.

Our analytical contribution is not backed by proof-of-principle / proof-of-concept because we report research in progress and plan to do this in the future.

The remainder of this paper is structured as follows: Background information featuring *context awareness*, *public values*, *regulations*, and *norms* is provided in Sect. 2. We present our proposed analysis in Sect. 3. Finally, we conclude the paper in Sect. 4.

2 Background

The visionary views of Mark Weiser have inspired the computer world since the early 1990s, featuring "ubiquitous" environments where many connected devices work together for the benefit of the user, adapting their behavior, both to the user and to the environment [6]. Nevertheless, it took many years until this was possible to implement in practice. In our view, this was partially due to the needed but unavailable enabling technologies such as affordable connectivity, portable devices, and sensing technology [7–14]. Unfortunately, we still mainly see technology-driven solutions, as opposed to user-centric solutions (user-centric designs would really "force" the technology system to adapt to the situation of the user and/or the environment) [4]. We claim that among the reasons for this is the software rigidity, where typically one standard process and several possible variants are identified. In such a way, it is often possible to achieve adaptation to the user's situation and/or to system-internal changes but if *external factors* are to be also considered, then the "standard process + variants" approach would often fail, in our view. That is because *public values*, *regulations*, and *norms* concern the system environment which in turn is hard to predict at design time: such *external factors* are outside our primary design scope and we certainly have limited knowledge and information about them. Such a limitation seems obvious for technology-driven servicing where the "World" is supposed to adapt to what a platform is offering. In contrast, we stand for top-down designs that are user-centric, Society-driven, and so on. They would hence allow developers to carefully look into the USER NEEDS, to adequately consider SYSTEM NEEDS, and to also address SOCIETAL CONCERNS. That is how developers would be able to weave both *HARD concerns* and *SOFT concerns* in a robust design. Said otherwise, in achieving context awareness with regard to *external factors*, we would lean towards top-down solutions. Further in the current section, we will briefly consider *public values*, *regulations*, and *norms*.

With regard to **PUBLIC VALUES**, such as *safety*, *privacy*, *accountability*, and *trust* [3] – they may be put at risk with all abovementioned technical and technological developments, as studied in [15] As it concerns SAFETY, can we always guarantee that localization would not put at risk a stakeholder, for example: a border security officer who may become a target for trespassers / smugglers? As it concerns PRIVACY, can we guarantee that upon gathering situation-specific data concerning the service user, *privacy-sensitive* details would not "leak out"? As it concerns ACCOUNTABILITY, can we guarantee accountability in cases where multiple stakeholders and technical systems are contributing to the service delivery, for example when services are delivered by drones that are often driven by several technical systems (the drone hardware/software, the ground hardware/software, and so on) and several stakeholders (the mission "owner", the controlling institutions, and so on)? As it concerns TRUST, can we guarantee adequate cooperation of users and stakeholders, that in turn requires *minimal levels of trust* in the system and/or in the relevant institutions? We observe that to date those issues are not covered exhaustively. This is considered a concern firstly with the growing pervasion of hardware/software into our lives, secondly with the broad global availability of large data volumes, and thirdly with the increased complexity of human-machine interaction [16–18]; we then have a problem when multiple stakeholders interact, using data provided by multiple sources [19], with no powerful mechanisms to "control" the data and its usage. Most technical systems have been designed with an essential focus on *service effectiveness* and with insufficient attention on *public values*, as mentioned above. From other perspectives, however, "controlling" data and its usage may be dangerous by itself. And in the end, there may be *tensions* among different *public values*, requiring harmonization and synchronization. This implies that the way current ICT systems are implemented should be improved, by accommodating VALUE-SENSITIVE DESIGN [3, 20].

With regard to **REGULATIONS**, they are about the *legal obligations* an organization faces as part of its operation; hence, regulations are a legal form of *governance* that is predicated on legislation and oversight, typically from a governmental or adjacent regulatory body [21]. It is to be noted that *regulations* may concern the service delivering system (for example: an autonomous vehicle that is to stick to traffic regulations), the user (for example: a person who is in the vehicle and who has the obligation to carry a valid IT document), and so on. Hence, even though *regulations* are an *external factor*, they still may concern the user and/or the system, and this "duality" is important.

With regard to **NORMS**, they govern the entities' *behavior*, representing the *rules and patterns of behavior*, either formal or informal, explicit or implicit, existing within a society, an enterprise, or even a small group of people working together to achieve a common goal [22]. *Norms* are determined by Society or collective groups and serve as a *standard for the members to coordinate their actions*. An individual member uses the knowledge of *norms* to guide his or her actions. If the *norms* can be identified, the *behaviors* of the individuals, hence their collective *behaviors*, are mostly predictable. From this perspective, to specify an organization can be done by specifying the *norms* [23] and this holds also for enterprises. Taking the perspective of *Organizational Semiotics*, in business processes and software operations, most *rules* fall into the category of *behavioral norms* prescribing what people *must*, *may*, and *must not* do, which are equivalent to three *deontic operators*: "is obliged", "is permitted", "is prohibited" [24].

It is essential to recognize that *norms* are not as rigid as logical conditions. If a person does not drink water for a certain duration of time (s)he cannot survive. But an individual who breaks the working pattern of a group does not have to be punished in any way. For those actions that are permitted, whether the agent will take an action or not is seldom deterministic. This elasticity characterizes business processes, therefore is of particular value to understand the corresponding enterprise(s).

3   Analysis

As a starting point in our analysis, we emphasize on the three key *Context Awareness* (*CA*) viewpoints (perspectives), discussed already: (i) *maximizing the user-perceived effectiveness*; (ii) *optimizing internal processes*; (iii) *sticking to external factors*.

This is partially in tune with [2], with the key difference that the third viewpoint (perspective) covers not only *public values* but also *regulations* and *norms* (rules), as discussed already. In this nevertheless we do not claim exhaustiveness – we just argue that *public values*, *regulations*, and *norms* are three essential things to be considered as *external factors* with regard to context-aware (software systems).

All above mentioned is illustrated in Fig. 1 and as the underlined text above suggests, our particular focus is on *external factors*. Hence, we consider the following as important, with regard to our analysis:

- Sometimes *external factors* may concern issues that belong to another viewpoint (perspective) – imagine that service delivery is to be adapted to *regulations* but those

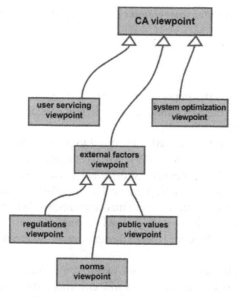

Fig. 1. Context awareness viewpoints

regulations concern the user or imagine that some *norms* that are to be considered that in turn concern system-internal processes. Then it would not be straightforward establishing whether service delivery adaptation is user-driven/system-driven or driven by external factors.

- There may be *tensions* among different *external factors* – imagine that some service-delivery *norms* assume disclosing user data but this goes against *privacy* standards. We argue that to resolve such issues, it would be necessary applying some *prioritization hierarchies*. This would be nevertheless challenging because of the very characteristic of *norms* being highly *heterogeneous*. Hence, constructing useful *hierarchies of norms* would not be straightforward and would require additional analyses. Anyway, adequate *norm hierarchies* would allow for usefully enforcing *prioritizations* that in turn would help resolve *tensions*.

- It is possible that one *external factor* is "mixed up" with another one – in the above example, user data may be not only about *norms/regulations* but also about *public values*. Hence, *prioritization* is needed here as well.

- We argue that *Quality-of-Service* considerations are not straightforward because *quality* from a *user perspective* is one thing, *quality* from a *system optimization perspective* is another thing and *quality* from the perspective of fulfilling *external factors* is yet another thing; in our view, current *value-driven* Society would often put *external factors* above all (because sticking to *public values* and observing the Law is a "must") but sometimes serving the user may be life-critical – hence, balancing in such situations should be a matter of *"trade-offs"*.

- Since servicing the user is related to requirements and system optimizations concern the operation of a technical artefact, those are more location-invariant; in contrast, *external factors may differ from country to country*, depending on the relevant *public values* and *laws*.

4   Conclusions

This paper has analyzed the importance of context-aware (software) systems, in general, and in particular: the adaptation perspective that concerns relevant *public values*, *regulations* and *norms*.

This is considered a step forward with regard to previous work [2] and the claimed analytical contribution drive is two-fold: (i) We have made a justified appeal to software designers to take not only *hard concerns* (effectiveness and optimization) into account, but also the *external factors*, namely: *public values*, *regulations*, and *norms*, and we have analyzed accordingly each of these contextual elements; (ii) With regard to the *external factors* themselves, we have not only focused on *public values* (as in previous work) but we have "coined" the broader label *"external factors"* to cover also *regulations* and *norms*.

Finally, the limitations of our work are two-fold: (a) We have not justified exhaustiveness with regard to the *external factors* with covering *public values*, *regulations*, and *norms*; (b) We have not provided validation with regard to our analytical claims, leaving this for future work.

Acknowledgement. I express sincere gratitude to my Dutch Friends and Colleagues, *Alexander Verbraeck*, *Marten van Sinderen*, and *Coen Suurmond*, for inspiring discussions touching upon context awareness, which discussions have helped me in my progress in the area.

References

1. Wegdam, M.: AWARENESS: a project on context AWARE Mobile NEtworks and ServiceS. In: Proceedings of the 14th Mobile & Wireless Communications Summit. EURASIP
2. Shishkov, B., Larsen, J.B., Warnier, M., Janssen, M.: Three categories of context-aware systems. In: Shishkov, B. (ed.) BMSD 2018. LNBIP, vol. 319, pp. 185–202. Springer, Cham (2018). https://doi.org/10.1007/978-3-319-94214-8_12
3. Veluwenkamp, H., van den Hoven, J.: Design for values and conceptual engineering. Ethics Inf. Technol. **25**, 2 (2023). https://doi.org/10.1007/s10676-022-09675-6
4. Shishkov, B., van Sinderen, M.: Towards well-founded and richer context-awareness conceptual models. In: Shishkov, B. (ed.) BMSD 2021. LNBIP, vol. 422, pp. 118–132. Springer, Cham (2021). https://doi.org/10.1007/978-3-030-79976-2_7
5. Shishkov, B., van Sinderen, M.: On the context-aware servicing of user needs: extracting and managing context information supported by rules and predictions. In: Shishkov, B. (eds.) Business Modeling and Software Design. BMSD 2022. LNBIP, vol. 453. Springer, Cham (2022). https://doi.org/10.1007/978-3-031-11510-3_15
6. Weiser, M.: The Computer for the 21st Century. SIGMOBILE Mob. Comput. Commun. Rev. 3, 3 (July 1999), 3–11. ACM, New York (1999)
7. Shishkov, B., van Sinderen, M.: From user context states to context-aware applications. In: Filipe, J., Cordeiro, J., Cardoso, J. (eds.) ICEIS 2007. LNBIP, vol. 12, pp. 225–239. Springer, Heidelberg (2008). https://doi.org/10.1007/978-3-540-88710-2_18

8. Dey, A., Abowd, G., Salber, D.: A conceptual framework and a toolkit for supporting the rapid prototyping of context-aware applications. Hum.-Comput. Interact. **16**, 2 (2001)

9. Dey, A.K., Newberger, A.: Support for context-aware intelligibility and control. In: Proceedings of the SIGCHI Conference on Human Factors in Computing Systems. ACM, USA (2009)

10. Bosems, S., van Sinderen, M.: Models in the design of context-aware well-being applications. In: Meersman, R., et al. (eds.) OTM 2014. LNCS, vol. 8842, pp. 37–42. Springer, Heidelberg (2014). https://doi.org/10.1007/978-3-662-45550-0_6

11. Alegre, U., Augusto, J.C., Clark, T.: Engineering context-aware systems and applications. J. Syst. Softw. **117**, C (July) (2016)

12. Alférez, G.H., Pelechano, V.: Context-aware autonomous web services in software product lines. In: Proceedings 15th International SPLC Conference, CA, USA. IEEE (2011)

13. Abeywickrama, D.B., Ramakrishnan, S.: Context-aware services engineering: models, transformations, and verification. ACM Trans. Internet Technol. J. **11**(3), Article 10. ACM (2012)

14. Shishkov, B.: Designing Enterprise Information Systems, Merging Enterprise Modeling and Software Specification. Springer, Cham (2020). https://doi.org/10.1007/978-3-030-22441-7

15. Shishkov, B., Garvanova, M.: Telecommunications and remote sensing: a public values perspective. In: Shishkov, B., Lazarov, A. (eds.) Telecommunications and Remote Sensing. ICTRS 2023. Communications in Computer and Information Science, vol 1990. Springer, Cham (2023)

16. Bartneck, C., Lütge, C., Wagner, A., Welsh, S.: Autonomous vehicles. In: An Introduction to Ethics in Robotics and AI. SpringerBriefs in Ethics. Springer, Cham (2021). https://doi.org/10.1007/978-3-030-51110-4_10

17. Fotohi, R., Abdan, M., Ghasemi, S.: A self-adaptive intrusion detection system for securing UAV-to-UAV communications based on the human immune system in UAV networks. J. Grid Comput. **20**, 22 (2022). https://doi.org/10.1007/s10723-022-09614-1

18. Hernigou, P., Lustig, S., Caton, J.: Artificial intelligence and robots like us (surgeons) for people like you (patients): toward a new human–robot-surgery shared experience. What is the moral and legal status of robots and surgeons in the operating room?. Int. Orthop. (SICOT) **47**, 289–294 (2023). https://doi.org/10.1007/s00264-023-05690-4

19. Han, J., Kamber, M., Pei, J.: Data Mining: Concepts and Techniques, 3rd edn. Morgan Kaufmann Publ. Inc., San Francisco, CA, USA (2011)

20. Friedman, B.: Value-sensitive design. ACM Interact. Mag. **3**(6), 16–23 (1996)

21. Ghanavati, S., Humphreys, L., Boella, G., Di Caro, L., Robaldo, L., van der Torre, L.: Compliance with multiple regulations. In: Yu, E., Dobbie, G., Jarke, M., Purao, S. (eds.) ER 2014. LNCS, vol. 8824, pp. 415–422. Springer, Cham (2014). https://doi.org/10.1007/978-3-319-12206-9_35

22. Stamper, R., Liu, K., Hafkamp, M., Ades, Y.: Signs plus norms – one paradigm for organizational semiotics. In: The Proceedings of the 1st International Workshop on Computational Semiotics, May 26–27, 1997, Paris, France (1997)

23. Stamper, R.: Language and computer in organized behavior. In: Riet, R.P.V.D., Meersman, R.A. (eds.) Linguistic Instruments in Knowledge Engineering. Elsevier Science, Amsterdam (1992)

24. Liu, K.: Semiotics in Information Systems Engineering. Cambridge University Press, Cambridge (2000)

Managing Multi-site Artificial Neural Networks' Activation Rates and Activation Cycles
Experiments on Cross-Enterprise, Multi-site Deep Learning Systems

Marcus Grum$^{(\boxtimes)}$ ⓘ

J.-Chair of Business Information Systems, esp. AI-based Appl. Sys.,
University of Potsdam, Potsdam 14482, Germany
marcus.grum@uni-potsdam.de

Abstract. Traditionally, business models and software designs used to model the usage of artificial intelligence (AI) at a very specific point in the process or rather fix implemented application. Since applications can be based on AI, such as networked artificial neural networks (ANN) on top of which applications are installed, these on-top applications can be instructed directly from their underlying ANN compartments [1]. However, with the integration of several AI-based systems, their coordination is a highly relevant target factor for the operation and improvement of networked processes, such as they can be found in cross-organizational production contexts spanning multiple distributed locations. This work aims to extend prior research on managing artificial knowledge transfers among interlinked AIs as coordination instrument by examining effects of different activation types (respective activation rates and cycles) on by ANN-instructed production machines. In a design-science-oriented way, this paper conceptualizes rhythmic state descriptions for dynamic systems and associated 14 experiment designs. Two experiments have been realized, analyzed and evaluated thereafter in regard with their activities and processes induced. Findings show that the simulator [2] used and experiments designed and realized, here, (I) enable research on ANN activation types, (II) illustrate ANN-based production networks disrupted by activation types and clarify the need for harmonizing them. Further, (III) management interventions are derived for harmonizing interlinked ANNs. This study establishes the importance of site-specific coordination mechanisms and novel forms of management interventions as drivers of efficient artificial knowledge transfer.

Keywords: AI-based Software Specification · Artificial Neural Networks · Experiments · Simulation

1 Introduction

Traditionally, business models and software designs are implemented as more or less static tools being programmed with software and hardware routines, which

B. Shishkov (Ed.): BMSD 2024, LNBIP 523, pp. 258–269, 2024.
https://doi.org/10.1007/978-3-031-64073-5_17

are used to realize value-adding production steps [3]. Principally, if artificial intelligence (AI) has been used to enhance the tool's capabilities, the AI usage has been modeled at a very specific point in the process implemented or customized beforehand [1]. In contrast to this, AI systems can be combined and represent a foundation for applications, such as networked artificial neural networks (ANN) on top of which applications are installed. So, these on-top applications can be instructed directly by their underlying ANN compartments. Here, the AI induces application-specific process behaviors and static software and hardware routines are made more flexible: if the AI base works efficiently, it automatically reorganizes resource allocation and improves ongoing processes [1]. However, common AI usage has not yet been standardized in application systems. Hence, knowledge flows among AI-based systems are rather inefficient [4].

These missing standards are particularly problematic if AI is introduced to networks of applications, such as in organization-wide networks of production machines (cyber-physical systems, short: CPS) or cross-organization-wide interacting networks of cyber-physical production systems (short: CPPS) [5]. The controlling of multi-site production facilities via Artificial Neural Networks (ANN) - each machine and site can be represented as individual *cognitive production network* [1] - is challenging because of different characteristics: Activation patterns might vary at machine-, site- and vendor-specific levels for instance as well as follow organization-specific routines and processes. So, AI-based knowledge flows in overarching, interwoven cognitive production networks might become destructive [6] and inefficient [7] in the entire network's context. As this research shows, reasons can be found at different activation rates and activation cycles. In a worse case, correctly working outcomes of the activated ANNs either are overwritten or lost in disharmonious ANN structures. If it was possible to bring isolated, machine-specific or site-specific ANN networks in harmony, one can expect joint multi-site ANN-based systems to have (a) more efficient knowledge transfers as individual machines and facilities can adapt to the specific knowledge conversion, (b) destructive activations of sub-systems can be reduced, so that for instance waste, energy and time consumption can be reduced in cross-organization production chains, and (c) ANN-based networks become controllable in a way that management interventions can be applied to improve artificial knowledge transfers in advance.

While Grum designs a prototype of *Open Source simulation systems for ANN-based CPPS* that implements the multi-site ANN simulation system construction [2], this article contributes with experiments about multi-site ANN-based application systems and applies the prototype of *Open Source simulation systems for ANN-based CPPS* [2] for realizing them. It so clarifies inefficient and destructive ANN-based knowledge flows and demonstrates the prototype worked out. Further, the experiments clarify the leverage points for a mechanism of action: the improvement of these kinds of knowledge transfers by management intervention. It is so considered a separate contribution. Thus, the following research will address the improvement of ANN knowledge transfers and focuses on the following research question: *"How can different activation types of rate and cycle combinations in multi-site ANN be researched and improved?"*

The research does not intend to provide a sophisticated empirical proof of improved and coordinated ANN knowledge transfers because of managed multi-site ANNs. It rather intends to clarify the basis of such an instrument in production contexts. This article further contributes with a new versatile kind of state descriptions (in the sense of system analysis) as an auxiliary instrument for structuring management interventions presented.

The research approach is intended to be design-oriented in accordance with the Design-Science-Research Methodology (DSRM) [8]. Thus, building on (1) the background of multi-site ANN simulation system construction being presented by Grum [2] as well as (2) the concrete requirements for the global, neuronally instructed production network having multiple production facilities and (3) the artifact of Open Source simulation systems for ANN-based Cyber-Physical Production Systems (CPPS) designed, the remainder presents the artifact demonstration in form of experiments. The article is thus structured as follows: The experiments will be designed in section two. These issue how to examine the effects of ANN activation rates and cycles on AI-based production routines and clarify how to intervene by management. In section three, it will be evaluated inhowfar the artifact design is suitable to enhance multi-site ANN-based CPPS. Finally, the findings are concluded.

2   Experiment Design

For researching multi-site ANN activation rate and activation cycle combinations (here referred to as activation type), the design-science-oriented research proceeding by [2] has been carried out: the here-provided Open Source simulation system for ANN-based CPPS has been used to realize the following experiment task:

– General experiment task: *An AI-based production chain with at least two neuronally instructed production facilities is to be operated, whereby the activation types of the production facilities are varied with regard to the activation cycle and the activation rates and the ANN-based knowledge bases used are retained and confronted with different experiment variants in such a way that any faults that may occur due to different activation rates and cycles in production operations can be investigated.*

As experiments differentiate the production facility's activation cycles in the two variants "coupled" (also referred to as "synchronous") and "uncoupled" (also called "unsynchronized") as well as their activation rates in the two variants "equal" and "different", in principle, a 2×2 matrix with four experiment variants is constructed. Each variant or task serves to test one of the four initial hypotheses:

– Hypothesis 1: The synchronization of activation cycles with the same activation rates of distributed production sites promotes the trouble-free operation of production chains.

- Hypothesis 2: Decoupled activation cycles with equal activation rates of distributed production sites lead to disruptions in production chains.
- Hypothesis 3: Different activation rates in synchronized cycles of neural systems of distributed production sites lead to disruptions in production chains.
- Hypothesis 4: Different activation rates in asynchronized cycles - in the opposite sense of a standard of distributed production sites - prevent the operation of neuronally instructed production chains.

However, the four initial hypotheses are differentiated in 14 greater levels of detail, because they show the realistic and possible permutations of activation rates and cycles. These arise if a) activations are carried out early or late, b) activation rates are at regular intervals or multiples of each other, c) activation rates are at irregular intervals of each other or d) activation rates are completely variable in relation to each other. The corresponding mapping of initial hypotheses and more versatile cycle and rate operations can be seen in the comparison of the rows 'hypothesis', 'cycles' and 'rates' in Fig. 1.

The concrete operationalization of the activation rates and cycles at the two production facilities *CPS1* and *CPS2* with which the 14 Experiemnts have been started, can be seen at the row 'parameters' in Fig. 1. The by the ANN induced production behavior of the two production facilities and their machines is visualized below at the row 'visualization'. Using a global simulation system clock, in this row, the individual production facility's activities becomes apparent (visualized in black and blue arrows in Fig. 1). Thus, a system analysis allows for the identification of stable or unstable production states being in a production equilibrium or not.

The **system analysis** has shown that IDs 1–6 and 9–12 result in a periodic dynamic system state and IDs 7–8 and 13–14 result in a chaotic dynamic system state (see 'system state' in Fig. 1). It should be noted that the system state identified here (periodic or chaotic) says nothing about the disruptions or inefficiencies that arise in the production chain simulated here. This occurs due to ANN activation and is measured in the operational production space. However, since the analyses of neuronally induced behavior (presented in detail in the demonstration section) showed that the two system states of dynamic systems (periodic and chaotic) do not allow sufficient differentiation for neuronal activation rates and cycles in the sense of common system analysis, the 14 previously mentioned, more detailed, novel state descriptions were derived in the sense of a *musical rhythm analysis*. These are displayed at the row 'system state' in Fig. 1. Using these novel **rhythmic state descriptions of dynamic systems**, the experimental tasks can now be clearly divided into distinguishable categories based on the type of activation cycle-activation rate combination. Further, using these, the present multi-site activation type can be described unambiguously, which simplifies communication about stacking ANN systems and addressing their interactions. Going beyond, these are particularly helpful if category-specific disruption patterns are identified for these. So, these can be used to derive corrective management interventions, which will be described in

ID	1	2	3	4	5	6	7
Hypothesis	H1	H2	H3$_a$	H3$_b$	H3$_c$	H3$_d$	H3$_e$
Cycles	coupled /synchronous	decoupled /asynchronous	coupled /synchronous	coupled /synchronous	coupled /synchronous	coupled /synchronous	coupled /synchronous
Rates	same	same	different (divisible)	different (duplicable)	different (indivisible)	different (unduplicable)	different (single irregular)
Parameters (examples)	Start CPS1 at 0:00 Start CPS2 at 0:00 Rate CPS1 = 1 cycle Rate CPS2 = 1 cycle	Start CPS1 at 0:00 Start CPS2 at 0:15 Rate CPS1 = 1 cycle Rate CPS2 = 1 cycle	Start CPS1 at 0:00 Start CPS2 at 0:00 Rate CPS1 = 1 cycle Rate CPS2 = 1/3 cyc.	Start CPS1 at 0:00 Start CPS2 at 0:00 Rate CPS1 = 1 cycle Rate CPS2 = 3 cycles	Start CPS1 at 0:00 Start CPS2 at 0:00 Rate CPS1 = 1 cycle Rate CPS2 = 1/Pi cyc.	Start CPS1 at 0:00 Start CPS2 at 0:00 Rate CPS1 = 1 cycle Rate CPS2 = 1*Pi cyc.	Start CPS1 at 0:00 Start CPS2 at 0:00 Rate CPS1 = 1 cycle Rate CPS2 = variable
Visualization	0:00: 0:00-1:00 / 0:00-1:00; 1:00: 1:00-2:00 / 1:00-2:00; 2:00: 2:00-3:00 / 2:00-3:00; 3:00:	0:00: 0:00-1:00 / 0:15-1:15; 1:00: 1:00-2:00 / 1:15-2:15; 2:00: 2:00-3:00 / 2:15-3:15; 3:00:	0:00: 0:00-1:00 / 0:00-0:20 / 0:20-0:40 / 0:40-1:00; 1:00: 1:00-2:00 / 1:00-1:20 / 1:20-1:40 / 1:40-2:00; 2:00: 2:00-3:00 / 2:00-2:20 / 2:20-2:40 / 2:40-3:00; 3:00:	0:00: 0:00-1:00 / 1:00-2:00 / 2:00-3:00; 3:00: 3:00-6:00 / 3:00-4:00 / 4:00-5:00 / 5:00-6:00; 6:00: 6:00-9:00 / 6:00-7:00 / 7:00-8:00 / 8:00-9:00; 9:00:	0:00: 0:00-3:00 / 0:00-0:19 / 0:19-0:38 / 0:38-0:57; 1:00: 1:00-2:00 / 0:57-1:16 / 1:16-1:35 / 1:35-1:54; 2:00: 2:00-3:00 / 1:54-2:13 / 2:13-2:32 / 2:32-2:51; 3:00:	0:00: 0:00-3:08 / 0:00-1:00 / 1:00-2:00 / 2:00-3:00; 3:08: 3:08-6:16 / 3:00-4:00 / 4:00-5:00 / 5:00-6:00; 6:16: 6:16-9:25 / 6:00-7:00 / 7:00-8:00 / 8:00-9:00; 9:25:	0:00: 0:00-1:00 / 0:00-0:19 / 0:19-0:28 / 0:28-0:54; 1:00: 1:00-2:00 / 0:54-1:12 / 1:12-1:36 / 1:36-1:45; 2:00: 2:00-3:00 / 1:45-3:13; 3:00:
System state (rhytmic interpretation)	periodically (on the beat)	periodically (on the offbeat)	periodically (on the interval-beat)	periodically (on the manifold-beat)	periodically (off the interval-beat)	periodically (off the manifold-beat)	chaotic (off the beat)

ID	8	9	10	11	12	13	14
Hypothesis	H3$_f$	H4$_a$	H4$_b$	H4$_c$	H4$_d$	H4$_e$	H4$_f$
Cycles	coupled /synchronous	decoupled /asynchronous	decoupled /asynchronous	decoupled /asynchronous	decoupled /asynchronous	decoupled /asynchronous	decoupled /asynchronous
Rates	different (double irregular)	different (divisible)	different (duplicable)	different (indivisible)	different (unduplicable)	different (single irregular)	different (double irregular)
Parameters (examples)	Start CPS1 at 0:00 Start CPS2 at 0:00 Rate CPS1 = variable Rate CPS2 = variable	Start CPS1 at 0:00 Start CPS2 at 0:15 Rate CPS1 = 1 cycle Rate CPS2 = 1/3 cyc.	Start CPS1 at 0:15 Start CPS2 at 0:00 Rate CPS1 = 1 cycle Rate CPS2 = 3 cycles	Start CPS1 at 0:00 Start CPS2 at 0:02 Rate CPS1 = 1 cycle Rate CPS2 = 1/Pi cyc.	Start CPS1 at 0:02 Start CPS2 at 0:00 Rate CPS1 = 1 cycle Rate CPS2 = 1*Pi cyc.	Start CPS1 at 0:00 Start CPS2 at 0:02 Rate CPS1 = 1 cycle Rate CPS2 = variable	Start CPS1 at 0:00 Start CPS2 at 0:02 Rate CPS1 = variable Rate CPS2 = variable
Visualization (examples)	0:00: 0:00-0:48 / 0:00-0:19 / 0:19-0:28 / 0:28-0:54; 1:00: 0:48-1:46 / 0:54-1:12 / 1:12-1:36 / 1:36-1:42; 2:00: 1:46-2:36 / 1:42-3:15; 3:00:	0:00: 0:00-1:00 / 0:15-0:35 / 0:35-0:55 / 0:55-1:15; 1:00: 1:00-2:00 / 1:15-1:35 / 1:35-1:55 / 1:55-2:15; 2:00: 2:00-3:00 / 2:15-2:35 / 2:35-2:55 / 2:55-3:15; 3:00:	0:00: 0:00-3:00 / 0:15-1:15 / 1:15-2:15 / 2:15-3:15; 3:00: 3:00-6:00 / 3:15-4:15 / 4:15-5:15 / 5:15-6:15; 6:00: 6:00-9:00 / 6:15-7:15 / 7:15-8:15 / 8:15-9:15; 9:00:	0:00: 0:00-1:00 / 0:02-0:21 / 0:21-0:40 / 0:40-0:59; 1:00: 1:00-2:00 / 0:59-1:18 / 1:18-1:37 / 1:37-1:56; 2:00: 2:00-3:00 / 1:56-2:15 / 2:15-2:34 / 2:34-2:53; 3:00:	0:00: 0:00-3:08 / 0:02-1:02 / 1:02-2:02 / 2:02-3:02; 3:08: 3:08-6:16 / 3:02-4:02 / 4:02-5:02 / 5:02-6:02; 6:16: 6:16-9:25 / 6:02-7:02 / 7:02-8:02 / 8:02-9:02; 9:25:	0:00: 0:00-1:00 / 0:02-0:21 / 0:21-0:30 / 0:30-0:56; 1:00: 1:00-2:00 / 0:56-1:14 / 1:14-1:38 / 1:38-1:47; 2:00: 2:00-3:00 / 1:47-3:15; 3:00:	0:00: 0:00-0:48 / 0:02-0:21 / 0:21-0:30 / 0:30-0:56; 1:00: 0:48-1:46 / 0:56-1:14 / 1:14-1:38 / 1:38-1:47; 2:00: 1:46-2:36 / 1:47-3:15; 3:00:
System state (rhytmic interpretation)	chaotic (no beat)	periodically (on shifted interval-beat)	periodically (on shifted manifold-beat)	periodically (off shifted inverval-beat)	periodically (off shifted manifold-beat)	chaotic (off the shifted beat)	chaotic (shifted no beat)

Legend:
- • - Start of AI usage of *Machine1*   ▶ - End of AI usage of *Machine1*   •→ - Period of AI Usage of *Machine1*   abc - Time state of global system clock
- • - Start of AI usage of *Machine2*   ▶ - End of AI usage of *Machine2*   •→ - Period of AI Usage of *Machine2*

Fig. 1. The DoE on activation rates and activation cycles of multi-site ANN

detail at the corresponding evaluation section. In particular, the following IDs are relevant for an initial investigation, as explained below:

-ID1: The activation of CPS1 and CPS2 is realized as it was originally planned and intended when the neural production chain was built, trained and installed. It is thus considered as the *reference scenario*.

-ID14: Probably the most realistic task setting because organizations probably do not synchronize production processes - CPS1 and CPS2 are activated as required by the subjective circumstances of a production site or as desired by production managers. This means, for example, the arbitrary activation of any CPS without having a view of efficient global production chains.

These IDs will be examined in more detail as part of the examination presented here, whereby further IDs are to be systematically investigated thereafter in on-building research. So, management interventions can be identified for relevant IDs and collected systematically. These management interventions are conceptualized to eliminate disruptions in global, neuronally instructed production chains. Furthermore, the management interventions identified in this research are to be tested immediately to be applied for, so that a catalog of interventions for the trouble-free operation of neuronally instructed global production chains for application-oriented research and practice is created.

3   Demonstration

In accordance with design-oriented research [8], the application of designed artifacts demonstrates their use, so that one is able to evaluate if the original research problem can be overcome. In this research context, the experiments designed in Sect. 2 are carried out. Each can be considered as artificial knowledge transfer scenario. Since all these research artifacts are brought together by one new type of device simulating global production chains being instructed by ANNs, the experiments draw attention to the interplay of different types of ANN activation rates and cycles in multi-site CPPS.

3.1   Experiment 1 - ID1

During the execution of the simulated production scenario with the ID1, the behavior described below was observed (behavior description). The activity analysis of the associated neuronal structures provides possible behavioral analyses and explanations:

1st cycle: The machine called M1, that is associated with CPS1, recognizes the 1st fruit delivery of good quality and the short conveyor belt transports this fruit delivery to its right side. Meanwhile, the machine M2, which is associated with CPS2, recognizes a "no fruit" picture (cf. "no-fruit pic" in Figs. 5–7 in [2]), as the position detected by a camera does not show a fruit delivery or is empty. M2 therefore remains idle or M2 is paused.

2nd cycle: M1 must pause because the fruit delivery has not yet been taken over by CPS2 or its conveyor belt system and is still on the short conveyor belt system of CPS1. As the position for image analysis is unoccupied, M1 recognizes the image "no fruit" at the time of activation. At the same time, M2 recognizes the image "no fruit", as its position for image analysis is still not occupied and transports the fruit from the left side to the image analysis at M2 using the long conveyor belt system.

3rd cycle: M1 recognizes the second fruit of good quality, which has now been fed in by the letter carrier. The short conveyor belt thus transports the fruit delivery from the image analysis position to the right-hand side of the short conveyor belt system (transfer position to the long conveyor belt system). Meanwhile, M2 identifies the good quality fruit and the long conveyor belt transports the fruit delivery to the right to the transfer position to the connected Lego model system or the fischertechnik model system.

The performance analysis showed that the following key performance indicators (KPIs) could be collected in the simulated production scenario and in the experimental task with ID1:
- Fruit deliveries sent by the automated letter carrier at CPS1: 2
- Successful productions detected at CPS2: 1
- Production defects detected in the product: 0
- Completion of production compared to planning: on time

To achieve this performance, the individual system analysis of the experimental task with ID1 shows the following neuron-induced activities:
- 3 fruit analyses performed, of which
  - fruit analyses performed for M1: 2
  - Fruit analyses performed for M2: 1
- 3 "no-fruit" analyses performed, of which
  - "No-fruit" analyses performed at M1: 1
  - "No-fruit" analyses performed for M2: 2
- 2 pause instructions carried out, of which
  - pause instructions carried out for the short conveyor system: 1
  - pause instructions carried out on the long conveyor system: 1
- 4 transportation instructions carried out, of which
  - transport instructions carried out on the short conveyor system: 2
  - Transport instructions carried out on the long conveyor system: 2

3.2   Experiment 2 - ID14

When running the simulated production scenario with the ID14, the observed behavior could be analyzed and explained as described below (behavior analysis and explanation approaches):

1st cycle: M1 recognizes the 1st fruit delivery of good quality and the short conveyor belt starts transporting the fruit delivery to its right side. Meanwhile, M2 recognizes a "no fruit" image for three iterations (cf. "no-fruit pic" in Fig. 5-7 in [2]), as the position detected with a camera does not show a fruit delivery or is empty. M2 therefore remains idle for three iterations or M2 pauses.

2nd cycle: M1 recognizes "no fruit" image, as the fruit delivery is still on its way to the right side of the short conveyor belt system (transfer position to CPS2) and the image analysis position at M1 is empty. A pause is therefore instructed. The underlying ANN has not learned to continue the transport for intermediate iterations. This means, for example, that the workpiece is lost between the sensory perceptions of the CPS1. As the idle command overwrites the ongoing transport process of CPS1, the workpiece has to be sorted out manually (unnecessarily). Meanwhile, M2 recognizes the image "no fruit" in three iterations and instructs idle or pause of the long conveyor belt system, as the transport of the workpiece to the right side of CPS1 has not yet been completed.

3rd cycle: M1 recognizes the second fruit of good quality, which has now been fed in by the letter carrier. CPS1 therefore starts transporting the fruit delivery using the short conveyor belt from the image analysis position at M1 to the right-hand side of the short conveyor belt system (transfer position to the long conveyor belt system). Meanwhile, M2 identifies the "no fruit" image and starts the pause of the long conveyor belt system.

The performance analysis showed that the following key performance indicators (KPIs) could be collected in the simulated production scenario and in the experimental task with ID14:
- Fruit deliveries sent by the automated letter carrier at CPS1: 2
- Successful productions detected at CPS2: 0
- Production defects detected in the product: 1
- Completion of production compared to plan: no completion, late

To achieve this performance, the individual system analysis of the experimental task with ID14 shows the following neuron-induced activities:
- 2 fruit analyses performed, of which
  - fruit analyses performed for M1: 2
  - Fruit analyses performed for M2: 0
- 9 "no-fruit" analyses performed, of which
  - "No-fruit" analyses performed for M1: 2
  - "No-fruit" analyses performed for M2: 7
- 9 pause instructions carried out, of which
  - pause instructions carried out for the short conveyor system: 2
  - pause instructions carried out on the long conveyor system: 7
- 2 transport instructions carried out, of which
  - transport instructions carried out on the short conveyor system: 2
  - Transport instructions carried out on the long conveyor system: 0

4   Evaluation

In order to satisfy design-science-oriented research approaches [8], it has been evaluated inhowfar knowledge transfers have been improved in the knowledge transfers scenarios demonstrated.

4.1   Experiment 1 - ID1

Since the production behavior shown here produces no waste and has no inefficiencies - all activities are required to successfully complete the production process - the **efficiency analysis** of the entire simulated production chain results in the following:
- 0 inefficient image analyses performed
- 0 inefficient breaks performed

As an **interpretation** of the neuron-instructed production behavior, the performance achieved and the individual system activities, the following can be concluded: There are no disruptions in the simulated production chain, as every neuronal output of CPS1 can be used efficiently by CPS2. There are no irrelevant pauses and image analyses.

As production in the scenario of the experimental task with ID1 runs efficiently and smoothly, corrective intervention by management is not necessary. There is therefore no need to derive **management interventions**, as the scenario is classified as "on the beat" (see system status in Fig. 1). Optionally, the management could act proactively and (1) install a global scheduling mechanism that flexibly waits for the completion of each element of the production chain (the state of ID1 is thus guaranteed), or (2) the management could guarantee the ability of all ANNs to deal with the different variants of activation rate-activation cycle combinations of ID 1–14. In addition, (3) the outputs can be cached and a system-specific data provisioning mechanism can be installed that stores activation inputs and activation outputs in a time-dependent manner (thus guaranteeing that no values are accidentally overwritten) and injects corresponding time-relevant activations into the respective ANNs. The mechanism therefore provides the data provision logic as well as the rate and coupling management including a necessary time reset of recurrent ANNs.

In the **hypothesis conclusion**, it can be stated that the initial hypothesis H1 ("The synchronization of activation cycles with the same activation rates of distributed production sites promotes the trouble-free operation of production chains.") can thus be confirmed on the basis of the analyses carried out here.

4.2   Experiment 2 - ID14

Since the production behavior shown here produces a reject and not a successful production product as well as various inefficiencies - not all activities are required to successfully carry out the production process - the **efficiency analysis** of the entire simulated production chain results in the following:
   - 5 inefficient image analyses performed
   - 7 inefficient pauses performed

The **interpretation** of the neuron-instructed production behavior, the performance achieved and the individual system activities can be concluded as follows: Disruptions occur in the simulated production chain because neural processing in the neural fabric is unable to handle (1) interval activations, (2) multiple activations, and (3) postponed (delayed/early) activations. Neural outputs from CPS1 cannot be used because CPS1 self-destructs correctly initiated production activities due to unknown training tasks (tasks different from ID1). Even if a usable output from CPS1 is transferred to CPS2, it cannot be used here because CPS2 itself destroys correctly initiated production activities due to the unknown training task (compared to ID1). Irregularities in terms of (a) activation cycles, (b) activation rates in (c) all types of systems thus show the most complex analyses, the most non-transparent behavior and the most possibilities for errors as well as the most possibilities for inefficiencies.

Since production in the scenario of the experimental task with ID14 is inefficient and not running smoothly, corrective intervention by management is necessary. A derivation of **management interventions** could be realized as follows: Since the scenario is classified as "shifted no beat" (cf. system state in Fig 1), management could first bring the neuronal production chain to the shifted interval-beat, so that the state "on the shifted interval-beat" of the rhythmic state descriptions of dynamic systems is achieved. The management interventions of ID9 can then be applied. Namely, this refers to the following:

- Management could first bring the neural production chain to the interval-beat so that the state "on the interval-beat" of the rhythmic state descriptions of dynamic systems is achieved. The management interventions of ID3 could then be applied.

- Having achieved ID 3, management should eliminate irrelevant interval activations so that the state "on the beat" of the rhythmic state descriptions of dynamic systems is achieved.

Alternatively, additional sensors can be installed and the ANNs of CPS1 and CPS2 can be retrained to efficiently handle (1) interval and multiple activations, (2) irregular activation rates, (3) regularly delayed and premature activation shifts, and (4) irregular delays and premature activations. Alternatively, the output values can also be temporarily stored and a system-specific data provision mechanism can be installed that stores activation inputs and activation outputs on a time-dependent basis (and thus guarantees that no values are accidentally overwritten) and injects the corresponding time-relevant activations into the respective ANNs. The mechanism therefore provides the data provision logic as well as the rate and coupling management including a necessary time reset of recurrent ANNs.

As a **hypothesis conclusion**, it can be stated that the initial hypothesis H4 ("Different activation rates in asynchronized cycles - in the opposite sense of a standard of distributed production sites - prevent the operation of neuronally instructed production chains.") can also be confirmed in the experimental task with the ID14 based on the analyses carried out here.

5   Conclusion

In accordance with the DSRM [8], design-science oriented research demands for being communicated. Thus, the following concludes the paper by outlining insights achieved and justifying its contribution to the state-of-the-art.

Summary. This paper has used the artifact design of [2] and presented demonstration for cross-organization-wide, interacting ANN-based production system following different activation rates and activation cycles. These metaphorically are equivalent to multiple interwoven artificial brains being more or less in synchronization. It so extends the state-of-the-art of production system building and provides a new example for AI-based CPPS. The demonstration has clarified the usefulness of the prototype in the marmalade glass production scenario in multiple experiment settings examining different types of activation rate and cycle combinations. It so contributes with further examples of destructive and inefficient artificial knowledge transfers and novel coordination mechanisms for ANN-based decision support systems or rather distributed cognitive production networks. Further, the demonstration has confirmed that requirements of multi-site CPPS that are based on ANN instructions (or rather global, neuronally instructed production chains having multiple production facilities), that were specified in advance [2], have been satisfied, which is demanded by the design-oriented artifact creation [8].

Critical Appraisal and Contributions. The research question (*"How can different activation types of rate and cycle combinations in multi-site ANN be researched and improved?"*) can be answered with regard to the design of ANN-based production chains: The simulation system prototype constructed [2] enables the simulation of global AI-based production networks containing multiple production facilities being instructed by ANN. Embedding this new simulated production chain infrastructure implemented in the experiment design worked out, the research of ANN activation rates and cycles is enabled. Facing experiments and analyses realized, new kinds of management interventions are derived with which inefficiencies and failures can be reduced because of harmonized ANN activation types. Thus, the knowledge base of Enterprise Architecture Management is extended. However, AI organization and collaboration standards are extended, because the harmonization of ANN activation types opportunities can be controlled and used for improving multi-site ANN with the aid of *rhythmic state descriptions for dynamic systems* easily.

Limitations and Outlook. The results and insights presented here need to be limited in regard with the validation level. The technical functionality has been proven by a demonstrator, and the effects of different activation rates and cycles have been clarified by selected simulation scenarios. Validated knowledge transfer models have been applied for this. Future research will therefore examine the empirical examination of ANN-instructions and respective management interventions identified and stress the artifacts created by real-world conditions. This will be realized the aid of experiments offering the artifacts presented at this contribution.

References

1. Grum, M.: Construction of a Concept of Neuronal Modeling. Springer (2022). https://doi.org/10.1007/978-3-658-35999-7
2. Grum, M.: Researching multi-site artificial neural networks' activation rates and activation cycles - the provision of an open source simulation system for examining ANN-based, multi-site cyber-physical production systems. In: Business Modeling and Software Design: 14th International Symposium, BMSD, pp.1–18. Springer (will be published soon), Luxembourg (2024)
3. Bergweiler, S.: Smart factory systems–fostering cloud-based manufacturing based on self-monitoring cyber-physical systems. Development **2**, 3 (2016)
4. Grum, M., Thim, C., Gronau, N.: Aiming for Knowledge-Transfer-Optimizing Intelligent Cyber-Physical Systems. In: Andersen, A.L., Andersen, R., Brunoe, T.D., Larsen, M.S.S., Nielsen, K., Napoleone, A., Kjeldgaard, S. (eds.) CARV/MCPC - 2021. LNME, pp. 149–157. Springer, Cham (2022). https://doi.org/10.1007/978-3-030-90700-6_16

5. Bender, B., Grum, M., Gronau, N., Alfa, A. and Maharaj, B.T.: Design of a world-wide simulation system for distributed cyber-physical production networks. In: 2019 IEEE International Conference on Engineering, Technology and Innovation (ICE/ITMC), pp. 1–7. IEEE (2019)
6. Deng, J., Chen, C., Xue, S., Su, D., Poon, W.S., Hou, H., Wang, J.: Microglia-mediated inflammatory destruction of neuro-cardiovascular dysfunction after stroke. Front. Cell. Neurosci. **17**, 1117218 (2023)
7. Grum, M.: Managing human and artificial knowledge bearers: the creation of a symbiotic knowledge management approach. In: Business Modeling and Software Design: 10th International Symposium, BMSD 2020, Berlin, Germany, pp. 182–201. Springer (2020)
8. Peffers, K., Tuunanen, T., Gengler, C.E., Rossi, M., Hui, W., Virtanen, V., Bragge, J.: The design science research process: a model for producing and presenting information systems reseach. In: 1st International Conference on Design Science in Information Systems and Technology (DESRIST), vol. 24, pp. 83–106. (2006)

Software Architecture for Object Detection in Images Based on Color Features with Integrated Artificial Intelligence

Georgi Tsonkov[1], Gabriela Garvanova[2,3], Ivan Garvanov[2(✉)],
and Magdalena Garvanova[2]

[1] Elektro Mechanik Sonnenschein GmbH, Bischofswiesen, Germany
`gtsonkov@tsoftcomputers.de`
[2] University of Library Studies and Information Technologies, Sofia, Bulgaria
`gabigarvanova@abv.bg, {i.garvanov,m.garvanova}@unibit.bg`
[3] Institute of Information and Communication Technologies, Bulgarian Academy of Sciences,
Sofia, Bulgaria

Abstract. This article proposes a software architecture for object detection in video materials, integrating advanced object recognition through the utilization of artificial intelligence (AI) and the capabilities of an object detection algorithm employing color characteristics. The proposed algorithm significantly enhances the accuracy and efficiency of detection, enabling better adaptation to varying lighting conditions and a diversity of objects. The article highlights how the integration of artificial intelligence and machine learning can enrich the analysis of video data, offering new possibilities for application in various domains.

Keywords: Software architecture · object-oriented programming · artificial intelligence

1 Introduction

In today's rapidly evolving technological landscape, the realms of video processing and analysis are assuming ever greater importance across a multitude of sectors. Responding to this growing demand, a plethora of software products have emerged, offering diverse capabilities for analyzing various types of video data [1–3]. Of particular significance in the contemporary context is the analysis of video content within the realm of security and safety. Advanced software solutions now boast an extensive repertoire of algorithms and functionalities that significantly streamline the video analysis process [4–6]. These algorithms facilitate tasks such as object detection, facial recognition, motion analysis, and more. They empower users to extract valuable insights from video content, serving a wide range of purposes, including incident prevention, criminal investigation, business process optimization, and improved user experience. Consequently, the advancement of modern software solutions for video content analysis not only streamlines and enhances the work of video data processors but also holds considerable potential to redefine our interactions with video materials and leverage the information they contain.

© The Author(s), under exclusive license to Springer Nature Switzerland AG 2024
B. Shishkov (Ed.): BMSD 2024, LNBIP 523, pp. 270–282, 2024.
https://doi.org/10.1007/978-3-031-64073-5_18

Amidst the array of video analysis methodologies, including object recognition [7], image focusing [8, 9], motion detection, and facial recognition [10, 11], there exists the opportunity for object detection based on their color characteristics. While object and facial recognition represent crucial components of video analysis, circumstances may arise where these tasks pose significant challenges or are rendered unattainable due to factors such as poor lighting, image blurring, limited viewing angles, and privacy regulations prohibiting the storage and/or use of training data for algorithms without explicit consent from relevant parties. In such scenarios, leveraging color attributes for object and facial detection emerges as a viable strategy, presenting considerable potential for effectiveness, particularly in the absence of alternative information about the target entities.

In paper [12], we proposed an algorithm for object detection in video materials using color characteristics. The proposed algorithm demonstrates significant potential across various applications, from security to automation. In this context, the present article introduces the next step in our research - the integration of artificial intelligence for object recognition, as a strategy for significantly enhancing the accuracy and efficiency of our object detection systems.

This article will delve into the technical aspects of integrating artificial intelligence into existing software for object detection based on color characteristics. This leads to a significant improvement in the accuracy and efficiency of the object detection system and represents a strategy for increasing the system's capacity to recognize and identify objects in video materials.

In addition to the technical implementation, potential applications of this integration in various domains will also be explored, along with its impact on future developments in the field of video analysis and image processing.

The remaining part of this article is organized as follows: Sect. 2 focuses on the functionalities and usage of the YOLO [13] models for object detection and recognition in video surveillance. Section 3 describes the process of integrating object recognition technologies within the .NET environment, with a focus on the use of pre-trained YOLO models and the optimization of this process through the use of ONNX Runtime and Microsoft.ML. The aim is to present a detailed architecture of a module that can be integrated into an already created application within the .NET environment, while also being designed with the flexibility to be used for the integration of YOLO into other applications utilizing this platform. This is achieved thanks to the structure of the module, which is developed to be universal and easily reusable. In Sect. 4, a real-life example of the result from the operation of the YOLO integration module is provided, which is successfully applied with a color filter described in [9], allowing for the isolation of objects within a specific color range set by the user. This demonstrates our proposed innovative approach that enables the detection of objects by external characteristics and the filtering of them by color features. Finally, we conclude our study in Sect. 5 by drawing conclusions, making recommendations, and outlining plans for our future research.

2 Principles and Application of YOLO

YOLO (You Only Look Once) represents an object detection algorithm that made its debut in the scientific paper authored by Joseph Redmon, Santosh Divvala, Ross Girshick, and Ali Farhadi titled "You Only Look Once: Unified, Real-Time Object Detection" [13] in 2015. Ever since its inception, this algorithm has been a game-changer in real-time object detection, surpassing its predecessor - the Region-based Convolutional Neural Network (R-CNN). When we, as humans, analyze objects within an image, we typically glance at the image just once and immediately comprehend the objects depicted and their respective locations. This innate ability enables us to effortlessly undertake relatively complex tasks like driving, searching, and identifying objects in our surroundings. YOLO accomplishes this task similarly, employing a single convolutional network that predicts multiple bounding boxes and the associated probabilities of classes for these boxes. YOLO is trained using entire images and directly optimizes detection performance, a departure from other object detection methods that utilize classifiers to detect objects by evaluating them at various locations and scales within the image [13, 14].

Since YOLO treats detection as a regression problem, there is no need for a complex system of components. A neural network is simply launched on the image. This gives YOLO a significant advantage, making it fast and efficient for real-time object recognition [13]. YOLO adopts a global approach to image reasoning when making predictions. Unlike sliding window techniques and region-based predictions, YOLO sees the entire image during both training and testing, thus implicitly encoding contextual information about classes and their appearances. This significantly reduces the likelihood of errors, making YOLO highly accurate in its predictions [13].

Over time, YOLO has undergone continuous improvement and optimization. As of the present day, the latest iteration is YOLO8. This version employs a single forward pass of CNN (convolutional neural network), which partitions the image into regions and concurrently predicts bounding boxes and probabilities for each region. Such refinement enhances both the precision and expediency of detection while concurrently diminishing the requisite computational resources. YOLO8 concentrates on refining network architecture, streamlining for swiftness and accuracy, as well as enhancing the capability to discern small and intricate objects. Generally, YOLO8 integrates cutting-edge machine learning and artificial intelligence techniques to elevate its performance compared to antecedent versions [15, 16].

In the recent versions of YOLO, it has become an anchor-free model, meaning that the model directly predicts the center of the object instead of offsetting from a given anchor box. Anchor boxes were problematic in earlier YOLO models, as they may represent the distribution of bounding boxes in the target test set but not in a customized dataset. Detection without anchor boxes reduces the number of predictions for bounding boxes, thus accelerating Non-Maximum Suppression (NMS), a complex step in the subsequent processing of detected objects, which sifts through the detection candidates after extracting information. This innovation leads to a significant increase in performance and reduces the likelihood of erroneous predictions [16].

Another advantage of this version is the C2f module at the core of the model, as opposed to the previous version where the C3 module was utilized. The distinction between the two lies in how the C2f model concatenates the outputs of all bottleneck modules, whereas the C3 model employs the output of the final bottleneck module. The bottleneck module comprises residual bottleneck blocks, which enhance performance in deep learning networks. This accelerates the training process and improves the flow of gradients through the neural network [14, 16].

In summary, the architecture of YOLO can be presented as follows [14]:

- Backbone Network: The foundation of the architecture, which utilizes convolutional neural networks to extract features from the input image.
- Neck: A component module situated between the backbone and the head of the network, serving to merge and aggregate features from different levels of the backbone network.
- Head: The final segment of the network, which utilizes processed features from pre-ceding parts of the network to make precise predictions about the location and iden-tification of objects in the input image. This segment of the network is critical for the effectiveness of the detection model, as the accuracy of predicted boundary boxes, confidence scores, and class probabilities directly influence the quality of detection.
- Non-Maximum Suppression (NMS) In conclusion, post-processing is performed to eliminate overlapping predictions of boundary boxes, ensuring that each object is detected precisely once without redundancy.

The workflow is also indicated by the architecture presented in Fig. 1. Initially, the input image is loaded and processed through the backbone network, where it is partitioned.

Once the necessary features are extracted, they pass through the neck component of the network, where they are merged and aggregated to effectively synthesize infor-mation across different scales. Subsequently, the actual detection takes place, utilizing the extracted features to determine the boundary boxes, confidence scores, and classes for each detected object. Finally, as previously mentioned, post-processing with NMS is performed to define the detected objects and remove overlaps. This ensures with high certainty that each object is detected precisely once [14, 16].

This is where it should be noted that YOLO is used not only for object detection but also for instance segmentation and image classification. This makes it one of the most efficient and widely used tools in these fields. The effectiveness, productivity, and continuous development and improvement of YOLO make it increasingly desired and successful. These are the main reasons for choosing it as the preferred model for further development of the product described in the article. For the purposes of this software, we will currently focus solely on using YOLO for object detection.

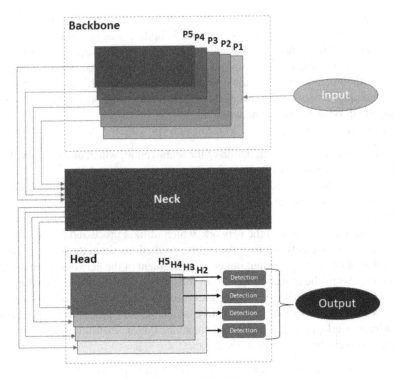

Fig. 1. YOLOv8 Architecture

3   Architecture of the YOLO Integration Module in a .Net Environment

Within the current project scope, integration of artificial intelligence technologies for object detection developed on the .NET platform is envisaged. This integration encompasses the capability to apply pretrained YOLO models within the specified environment, facilitated by the development of a specific interface to streamline interaction with these models. The architecture of the module we propose, which facilitates this integration, is designed to be reusable in other applications operating within the .NET environment. This module is exceptionally useful due to the widespread use of .NET as one of the most popular platforms for software development. This compatibility provides convenience and flexibility, allowing developers to use YOLO models in conjunction with existing .NET applications or to integrate them very easily with other software components within the .NET ecosystem. This offers opportunities for rapid expansion of the functionality of software applications and enhances the flexibility of development. The implementation of ONNX Runtime through Microsoft.ML represents a key component in this process, ensuring the necessary compatibility and efficiency in executing machine learning models. The interface is utilized to ensure seamless integration and interaction between .NET applications and complex AI models, enabling their effective utilization within the project.

Microsoft.ML is a machine learning library from Microsoft designed for .NET developers, aimed at facilitating the integration of machine learning into software applications. It offers a wide range of pre-defined algorithms for various machine learning tasks, including classification, regression, clustering, and anomaly detection. With Microsoft.ML, developers can process and analyze data, train models, and evaluate their effectiveness within the context of .NET applications using convenient APIs. This library also supports integration with ONNX, enabling the use of models trained outside the .NET ecosystem, thus enriching the development capabilities for intelligent applications [17].

ONNX (Open Neural Network Exchange) represents an innovative open standard for machine learning models, simplifying their sharing and deployment across various frameworks and platforms without the need for conversion or reconfiguration. It's developed to standardize the representation of AI models, thus facilitating their portability and optimization. ONNX supports a wide range of deep learning and traditional machine learning models, making it a universal tool for developers. ONNX Runtime, on the other hand, is a high-performance execution environment that accelerates the execution of models defined in the ONNX format. This environment is optimized for fast and efficient operation across various operating systems, including cloud environments. ONNX Runtime ensures compatibility between different machine learning frameworks and provides APIs for multiple programming languages, thus facilitating the integration and utilization of AI models in various applications and platforms [18].

The architecture of the module we propose, which facilitates the integration of the YOLO model into the .NET environment, is implemented as shown in Fig. 2.

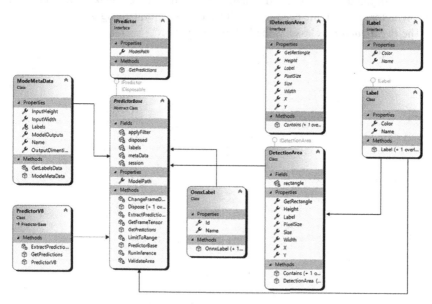

Fig. 2. Class Diagram of Module Interface for YOLO Integration

The *IPredictor* interface defines the core methods and properties that any class implementing it must have in order to integrate into the system and perform the expected functionalities. This interface has the following general structure:

```
public interface IPredictor
{
    public string? ModelPath { get; }

    public IEnumerable<DetectionArea>
        ExtractPredictions(DenseTensor<float> output,
                                            Image frame);
}
```

The abstract class PredictorBase serves as the foundation for all predictors (classes that will be in this role) in the architecture, providing a common implementation of the logic needed to execute machine learning models (for this case YOLO) in the .NET environment through ONNX Runtime. It includes methods for loading models, preparing input data, and processing predictions from the neural network. Using the abstract class PredictorBase as a base allows the specialization of this functionality for specific models like YOLO while preserving the possibility for further use of the common logic. This is a good practice as it enables easy and seamless expansion of the architecture. Inheriting from IPredictor in PredictorBase is crucial for ensuring consistency and coherence in the behavior of all predictors in the system. It guarantees that every class implementing IPredictor shares a common set of methods and properties, facilitating the integration and usage of various machine learning models within a unified framework. This provides flexibility in the development and maintenance of the system, making it easier to add new predictors without the need for significant architectural changes.

The *PredictorBase* class has the following structure:

```
public abstract class PredictorBase : IPredictor, IDisposable
{
    private readonly InferenceSession session;
    private readonly ModeMetaData metaData;
    private List<OnnxLabel> labels;
    private bool applyFilter;
    private bool disposed;
        //Constructor
    public PredictorBase(string path, string[]? objects, bool applyFilter =
false)…

    public abstract IEnumerable<DetectionArea> GetPredictions(Image frame);

    public string? ModelPath { get; private set; }

    public void Dispose()…

    protected virtual void Dispose(bool disposing)…
    protected virtual IEnumerable<DetectionArea> ExtractPredictions
    (List<Tensor<float>> output, Image frame)…
    protected virtual IEnumerable<DetectionArea> ExtractPredictions
    (Image frame, Tensor<float> output, bool useFilter, object[]? filters)…
    protected List<Tensor<float>> RunInference(Image frame)…

    private Tensor<float> GetFrameTensor(Image frame)…
    private Image ChangeFrameDimension(Image frame)…
    private float LimitToRange(float min, float max, float x)…
    private DetectionArea ValidateArea(DetectionArea currentArea)…
}
```

Since **PredictorBase** is an abstract class, it cannot be directly instantiated. Instead, the current architecture is designed to work with YOLO v8 models, for which the **PredictorV8** class is created. This class is specifically designed to interact with the respective version of the model. As a class that inherits from **PredictorBase**, **PredictorV8** inherits all the basic functionalities provided in the base class, allowing for their utilization. Additionally, by inheriting the interfaces, **PredictorV8** ensures that all methods and behaviors expected from the interface will be implemented, ensuring compatibility and stability in the program code. This allows for greater flexibility, a higher level of abstraction, and code reusability, facilitating easy maintenance and extensibility of the system in the future.

The class **PredictorV8** is instantiated within the engine of the core logic for working with objects. As seen from the provided excerpt of the structural architecture (Fig. 2), the constructor of this class requires parameters for the path (the directory where the YOLO model to be used is stored), a boolean argument indicating whether object filtering based on their visual characteristics will be applied (by default, this boolean value is false), and a list (in this case, an array) of object names to be filtered (if this option is chosen). After creating an instance of the class and successfully loading the model, the actual object detection can commence. For this purpose, the **PredictorV8** class implements the abstract method **GetPredictions(Image frame)**, which is responsible for initiating object detection on the provided image (photo, frame, etc.) in the respective format, as determined by the Image class (in this case, Bitmap). Once the frame is provided, it will be processed, and all detected objects will receive coordinates and labels, crucial for their representation in the user interface. These data are stored in instances of the **DetectionArea** object, as seen in Fig. 2. The described architecture outlines the module responsible for establishing the connection between the neural network, the extracted data, and their provision within the .NET environment. Adhering to the fundamental SOLID principles [19] and encapsulating the logic enables easy integration of this model into other applications operating in this environment. Another significant benefit is the ease of expansion and optimization of the model. Due to the clear separation of responsibilities among the various components of the software architecture, each part can be modified or enhanced without disrupting the functionality of the others.

After executing the logic for detection and filtering of objects based on their visual characteristics, the program proceeds to the next stage. This stage involves applying an additional filter that examines each detected region of the frame to determine if it matches the user-defined color characteristics. The user can specify the desired color range for the objects of interest by defining the lower and upper bounds of the color range. This is necessary because it can be difficult to determine the exact color of an object and how it will be registered by the video processor of individual video capture devices. The operation of this algorithm is detailed and presented in [12]. This functionality is particularly useful in scenarios where the objects that the user is searching for have specific colors or characteristics that distinguish them from the surrounding environment.

Each of these filters can operate autonomously, meaning that the user has complete freedom to decide whether to use only the color filter, only the object detection, or a combination of both. This is crucial when searching for different types of objects. In some situations, AI may fail to recognize the desired objects, but nonetheless, when the color filter is applied to the entire frame, these objects can be detected based on their color characteristics. These options empower the user to personalize the object recognition process according to their specific needs and requirements. Such an app-roach enhances the reliability of the system and provides a broader range of capabilities for image processing. Ultimately, the combination of physical and color recognition improves the efficiency of the object recognition program and increases the accuracy of the results, making the application highly valuable across various domains such as video surveillance, robotics, medical imaging, and others.

4 Results

The architecture presented above is currently undergoing integration into the application [12] and will be provided for testing to some agencies in Germany in the field of security and rescue operations. Its aim is to support and facilitate their work.

To demonstrate the capabilities of the application, a video was captured using a drone. The goal of the current experiment is to detect cars of a specific color captured in an active urban environment. Due to the movement of both the cars themselves and the drone, it will be challenging for the operator to visually cover and analyze all objects in the video. Additionally, a shooting mode with relatively low resolution was chosen to showcase the algorithm's maximum capabilities at the moment. To preserve confidentiality and ensure privacy, frames without faces and identifiable signs were selected.

In the test scenario, cars are being sought using a pre-trained model for this purpose. The application incorporates the use of a color filter, which is applied to the regions detected by the neural network. For this purpose, the following settings for the color filter, shown in Fig. 3, have been defined. The program offers the option to select two separate color ranges to be applied individually for each detected object.

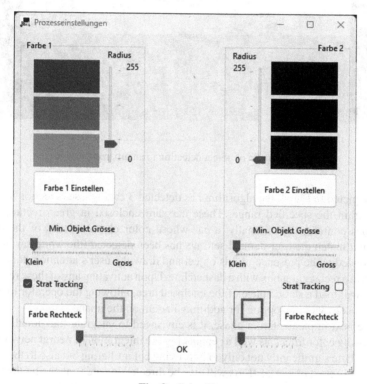

Fig. 3. Color filter

This is a particularly useful feature in many cases where objects with a combination of colors need to be searched for. For demonstration purposes, a filter based on only one color range set in the "Farbe 1" area will be used. By checking the "Start Tracking" box, upon activating the video, the algorithm will start processing frame by frame, searching for objects that match the description "car", and at the next step, the algorithm will apply the color filter to each found object of this type. As shown in Fig. 4, the algorithm has detected 3 cars whose detection areas have colors within the specified range. These cars are enclosed in green rectangles with continuous contours. Additionally, a car whose color characteristics of the detected area do not match the user-defined settings has been detected (the white car in Fig. 4).

Fig. 4. Example of object detection in an urban environment

As depicted in Fig. 4, the algorithm has detected 3 cars whose detection areas have colors within the specified range. These cars are enclosed in green rectangles with continuous contours. Additionally, a car whose color characteristics of the detected area do not match the user-defined settings has been detected (the white car in Fig. 4). To acknowledge the presence of this object and draw the user's attention, this object is enclosed in a rectangular box with a dashed line. Upon activating any of these rectangular boxes, it will load a static image of the enclosed area, allowing the operator to examine it more closely, with the option for additional zoom on the image.

In the next implementation phase, it is envisaged to integrate functionalities based on improving color filters, as well as enhancing the integration of neural networks. This will contribute significantly not only to improving color filtering but also to the ability to recognize different objects. Efforts will also be directed towards enhancing the software architecture and optimizing the algorithms to improve the scalability and efficiency of the application.

5   Conclusions

The presented architecture is well-structured and provides an efficient and flexible way to detect objects based on both visual and color characteristics. Utilizing concepts of clean code and applying SOLID principles [20] enables easy and seamless extension of the architecture to accommodate the use of newer versions of YOLO in the future. Additionally, optimization of color filters, such as integrating new color masks, can be achieved without necessitating changes to the functionality and architecture of the application.

By combining various methods of object recognition and filtering, the program provides the capability for precise and reliable object detection based on their unique attributes. On the other hand, the color characteristics of objects also play a crucial role in the detection process. Through color filtering, the program allows for the detection of objects that match specific colors or combinations of colors. This aspect enhances the ability to recognize objects in various scenarios where their colors are important for identification.

The ability to choose the method of applying color filters and detecting objects based on their visual characteristics provides the product with additional flexibility, making it applicable in various fields such as security, defense, surveillance, etc.

Combining physical and color characteristics in the object detection process provides greater reliability in object recognition across different conditions and environments. This approach offers a high degree of flexibility and adaptability to the program, making it suitable for various applications in the field of computer vision and object recognition.

Acknowledgement. This work is supported by the Bulgarian National Science Fund, Project title "Innovative Methods and Algorithms for Detection and Recognition of Moving Objects by Integration of Heterogeneous Data", KP-06-N 72/4/05.12.2023.

References

1. Garvanov, I., Garvanova, M., Ivanov, V., Lazarov, A., Borissova, D., Kostadinov, T.: Detection of unmanned aerial vehicles based on image processing. In: Proceedings of the Eleventh International Conference on Telecommunications and Remote Sensing – ICTRS'22, 21–22 November 2022, Sofia, Bulgaria. Springer, Book series Communications in Computer and Information Science (CCIS, volume 1730) (2022). ISBN: 978-3-031-23225-1. https://doi.org/10.1007/978-3-031-23226-8_3
2. Kinovea (2023). https://www.kinovea.org/
3. Darfish (2023). https://sourceforge.net/software/product/Dartfish
4. Yuan, H.: Image target detection algorithm based on computer vision technology. In: 2022 International Conference on 3D Immersion, Interaction and Multi-sensory Experiences (ICDIIME), Madrid, Spain, 2022, pp. 10–13 (2022). https://doi.org/10.1109/ICDIIME56946.2022.00010
5. Li, Z., Jiang, D., Wang, H., Li, D.: Video image moving target recognition method based on generated countermeasure network. Comput. Intell. Neurosci. **2022**, Article ID 7972845, 8 pages (2022). https://doi.org/10.1155/2022/7972845
6. Shishkov, B., Garvanova, M.: The societal impacts of drones: a public values perspective. In: Proceedings of the Eleventh International Conference on Telecommunications and Remote Sensing – ICTRS'22, 21–22 November 2022, Sofia, Bulgaria. Communications in Computer and Information Science, vol. 1730, pp. 61–71. Springer, Cham (2022). ISBN 978-3-031-23225-1, Electronic ISBN 978-3-031-23226-8, Print ISSN 1865-0929, Electronic ISSN 1865-0937. https://doi.org/10.1007/978-3-031-23226-8_5
7. Dange, V., Pophale, S., Raut, N., Shadrach, F., Chowdhury, S., Ramya, G., Dutta, P.: Image processing and pattern recognition-based car classification for intelligent transportation system. In: 6th Smart Cities Symposium (SCS 2022), Hybrid Conference, Bahrain, 2022, pp. 271–275 (2022). https://doi.org/10.1049/icp.2023.0520

8. Garvanova, M., Ivanov, V.: Quality assessment of defocused image recovery algorithms. In: 3rd International Conference on Sensors, Signal and Image Processing – SSIP 2020, October 9–11, 2020, Prague, Czech Republic. ACM International Conference Proceeding Series, pp. 25–30. New York, NY, USA: Association for Computing Machinery (2020). ISBN 978-1-4503-8828-3, ISSN 2153-1633. https://doi.org/10.1145/3441233.3441242

9. Garvanova, M., Ivanov, V.: Quality assessment of image deburring algorithms. In: IOP Conference Series: Materials Science and Engineering, vol. 1031 (1), pp. 1–5, Print ISSN 1757–8981 (2021). Online ISSN 1757-899X, doi: https://doi.org/10.1088/1757-899X/1031/1/012051

10. Maria Dominic Savio, M., Deepa, T., Bonasu, A., Anurag, T.S.: Image processing for face recognition using HAAR, HOG, and SVM algorithms. Journal of Physics: Conference Series, Volume 1964, Advances in Computational Electronics and Communication Engineering (2021). DOI: https://doi.org/10.1088/1742-6596/1964/6/062023

11. Shishkov, B., Garvanova, M.: Telecommunications and remote sensing: a public values perspective. In: Proceedings of the Twelfth International Conference on Telecommunications and Remote Sensing – ICTRS'23, 18–19 September 2023, Rhodes, Greece. Communications in Computer and Information Science, vol. 1990, pp. 77–89. Springer, Cham (2023). ISBN 978-3-031-49262-4, Electronic ISBN 978-3-031-49263-1, Print ISSN 1865-0929, Electronic ISSN 1865-0937. https://doi.org/10.1007/978-3-031-49263-1_6

12. Tsonkov, G., Garvanova, M.: Objects detection in an image by color features. In: Telecommunications and Remote Sensing. ICTRS 2023. Communications in Computer and Information Science, vol. 1990. Springer, Cham (2023). https://doi.org/10.1007/978-3-031-49263-1_5

13. Redmon, J., Divvala, S., Girshick, R., Farhadi, A.: You only look once: unified, real-time object detection. In: 2016 IEEE Conference on Computer Vision and Pattern Recognition (CVPR), Las Vegas, NV, USA, 2016, pp. 779–788 (2015). https://doi.org/10.1109/CVPR.2016.91

14. Dive into YOLOv8: How does this state-of-the-art model work? (2023). OpenMMLab. https://openmmlab.medium.com/dive-into-yolov8-how-does-this-state-of-the-art-model-work-10f18f74bab1

15. Jacob Solawetz, F.: What is YOLOv8? The Ultimate Guide. [2024]. Roboflow Blog, 11 January 2023. https://blog.roboflow.com/whats-new-in-yolov8/

16. Garvanova, M., Shishkov, B.: Capturing human authority and responsibility by considering composite public values. Business Modeling and Software Design. BMSD 2019. Lecture Notes in Business Information Processing, vol. 356, pp. 290–298. Springer, Cham (2019). ISBN (Print) 978-3-030-24853-6, ISBN 978-3-030-24854-3 (eBook), ISSN 1865-1348, ISSN 1865-1356 (electronic) (2019). https://doi.org/10.1007/978-3-030-24854-3_22

17. Microsoft ML.NET Documentation (2024). https://learn.microsoft.com/en-us/dotnet/machine-learning/

18. Garvanova, M., Shishkov, B., Janssen, M.: Composite public values and software specifications. In: Business Modeling and Software Design. BMSD 2018. Lecture Notes in Business Information Processing, vol. 319, pp. 412–420. Springer, Cham (2018). ISBN (Print) 978-3-319-94213-1, ISBN (eBook) 978-3-319-94214-8, ISSN 1865-1348, ISSN 1865-1356 (electronic). https://doi.org/10.1007/978-3-319-94214-8_32

19. Microsoft.ML.OnnxRuntime (2024). https://onnxruntime.ai/docs/api/csharp/api/Microsoft.ML.OnnxRuntime.html

20. Cabral, R., Kalinowski, M., Baldassarre, M., Villamizar, H., Escovedo, T., Lopes, H.: Investigating the impact of SOLID design principles on machine learning code understanding. In: CAIN 2024 (2024). Doi:https://doi.org/10.1145/3644815.3644957

Challenges in Geolocation for Logistics Delivery: A Case Study on the Accuracy in Bulgaria of Google Maps Directions API

Iliyan Iliev[1]([✉]) [iD], Katia Rasheva-Yordanova[1] [iD], and Daniela Borissova[2] [iD]

[1] University of Library Studies and Information Technologies, Sofia, Bulgaria
{i.iliev,k.rasheva}@unibit.bg
[2] Institute of Information and Communication Technologies, Bulgarian Academy of Sciences, Sofia, Bulgaria
daniela.borissova@iict.bas.bg

Abstract. The article deals with the problem of geolocation concerning the logistics that have changed the way in which deliveries are made. The core idea is to reveal the current challenges in the field of delivery logistics. The present study is focused on the analysis of the accuracy of the Google Maps Directions API in Bulgaria and the challenges faced by logistics operators due to the insufficient accuracy of geolocation data. As the logistics infrastructure plays a key role in the day-to-day operations of companies, the accuracy of geolocation data plays a crucial role in the efficient functioning of deliveries. By analyzing real cases and data, system performance is investigated and challenges arising in real delivery scenarios are identified. The results of the study highlight the importance of geolocation data accuracy to improve operational efficiency and optimize logistics processes in Bulgaria. To cope with such challenges, a generalized approach to improve the accuracy and efficiency of geolocation delivery systems is proposed. This approach is composed of 4 modules where the machine learning module is used to improve the accuracy. The proposed approach is preliminarily tested and the results demonstrate the applicability of the proposed approach.

Keywords: Geolocation · Logistics Delivery · Accuracy of Data

1 Introduction

In the modern world, where e-commerce and online services are at their peak, logistics in deliveries play a crucial role in meeting the needs of customers [1]. The e-commerce market is fiercely competitive, and achieving just-in-time delivery to customers is a key issue in many studies [2–4]. In this context, geolocation accuracy is essential for the successful execution of deliveries. While unstructured addresses are easy for people to understand and locate, they are difficult for computers to work with. To allow the use of unstructured address information by these applications, one of the prerequisites is the automatic assignment of correct geographic locations to the addresses. This process is usually called address geolocation [5].

© The Author(s), under exclusive license to Springer Nature Switzerland AG 2024
B. Shishkov (Ed.): BMSD 2024, LNBIP 523, pp. 283–292, 2024.
https://doi.org/10.1007/978-3-031-64073-5_19

Generally speaking, geolocation refers to the process of determining location, while positional accuracy measures the degree of precision of this information or the distance by which the geocoded position differs from the geographic latitude/longitude of the reference location [6]. In recent years, achieving accurate geolocation of geographical objects has become increasingly important, with significant applications in various fields including military reconnaissance, disaster monitoring, geodesy, and cartography [7–9]. In the context of delivery logistics, high positional accuracy is essential to ensure accurate and timely deliveries, reducing the risk of losses, delays, and customer dissatisfaction.

Effective management of delivery positional accuracy can lead to significant cost savings and increased customer satisfaction [10]. The lack of accurately defined spatial information in delivery logistics can lead to several problems, as described in Table 1.

Table 1. Link between the problem and its consequences in the execution of deliveries due to spatial data inaccuracy [1, 10–12]

Problem	Consequence
Delivery delays	Vehicles may become lost or travel on detours
Inefficiency	Delivery providers waste time searching for addresses or correcting their course, reducing their overall efficiency and increasing delivery costs
Poor customer service	If customers expect timely deliveries and their shipments are delayed due to inaccuracies in positioning, this can lead to customer dissatisfaction and potential loss for the business [1, 10, 12]
Increased costs	Vehicles deviating from their course or wasting time due to inaccurate positions may consume more fuel, leading to increased operational costs [10, 11]
Poor planning	Inaccurate location data can lead to poor route planning, over-loading resources and reducing productivity
Compliance with regulatory requirements	In some industries, accurate positioning is necessary to comply with regulations, such as in healthcare or transportation of hazardous materials

The accuracy of geocoding from postal codes may vary [6]. For this reason, geocoding based on the Google Maps Directions API tool is often resorted to, which usage frequently poses challenges for delivery providers. We observe specific issues related to geolocation in Bulgaria, primarily involving deviations from correct addresses, incorrect locations, and other discrepancies between the actual delivery location and the information provided by the geolocation system. These issues can lead to significant delays in parcel delivery, wasting time and resources for both couriers and clients.

This article is structured into three relatively independent sections. The first presents an analysis of the complexities arising when working with the Google geolocation tool in urban environments in Bulgaria. The second section examines the importance of calculating distances between points and demonstrates the presence of a problem using the Haversine formula and the Google Maps Directions API. The third section offers suggestions for overcoming existing challenges by introducing structured addresses and validating input data and proposes a machine-learning model for correcting deviations.

2 Analysis of the Accuracy of the Google Geolocation Tool for Logistics Purposes

The current section aims to clarify whether the most widely used geolocation tool, Google Maps Directions API, provides sufficiently reliable results for location accuracy in Bulgaria. Our hypothesis is that the positional accuracy of this tool is not at a level that ensures efficient parcel delivery without additional difficulties for couriers and recipients.

For the purposes of this study, data provided by a delivery provider operating on the territory of Bulgaria is used. The data includes records of 1,023 successful deliveries to addresses made by a single courier in his area over a period of time and contains the following attributes as shown in Table 2:

Table 2. Description of used data

Attributes	Description
City	The city specified by the sender
Address	The address specified by the sender
Postal Code	The postal code provided by the sender
Geographic latitude and longitude of the specified address	The point corresponding to the recipient's address when entered into Google Maps
Geographic latitude and longitude of the parcel delivery	The point where the courier actually delivered the parcel to the recipient, obtained from the device the courier uses to scan the parcel on-site
Date and Time	The date and time when the courier delivered the parcel

The data clearly indicates that the widely used Google Maps Directions API does not provide a sufficiently reliable location accuracy in Bulgaria with a precision that is acceptable for pedestrian distances, without delaying the courier or the receipt of the parcel by the client. Factors such as changes in city infrastructure, construction of new buildings, removal of old ones, and other events that could lead to changes in addresses

Table 3. Challenges and opportunities when using the Haversine formula to calculate the distance between two points

Limitation	Possibilities
Applicability in real-world scenarios	Accuracy of calculations
Need for precise geographic coordinates	Integration with technologies like Google Maps Directions API

seem to render the Google Maps Directions API outdated. When submitting an address entered by the client from the logistics provider's system to the GMD API, often the addresses do not match. There are several types of problems as described below:

2.1 Small Deviation from the Correct Point with Significant Importance

This type of problem can be observed in deliveries made on streets with one-way traffic, especially on major boulevards. An example of such a problem is observed on Tsarigradsko Shosse Boulevard in Sofia, Bulgaria. The starting delivery point appears to have a minor deviation, but upon closer inspection, it becomes clear that it is located on one side of the boulevard, while the actual delivery location is on the other side of the boulevard.

The client provides the following address: "metro station "IEC Tsarigradsko Shose", room No. 12". The coordinates determined by Google Maps for this location are latitude 42.649587 and longitude 23.393634. The courier delivered the parcel at a location less than 5 m away from the specified coordinates. Analysis shows that the points are on different sides of the boulevard. This complicates pedestrian access and requires additional time for car movement. The delay in the current delivery affects the overall delivery time realized by the same provider within the day.

The initial location of the courier ("IETS Tsarigradsko Shose" metro station, room #12" according to Google Maps Directions API: lat. 42.649587 long. 23.393634), as well as the address to which the courier actually delivered the parcel (lat. 42.649183 long. 23.393555) are shown in Fig. 1.

Fig. 1. Demo of discrepancies between a physical address in the application and in the real world: a) lat. 42.649587 long. 23.393634; b) lat. 42.649183 long. 23.393555

Inaccuracies in calculating the object's position in the above-described scenario lead to the following consequences:

- Time expenditure – the seemingly insignificant distance requires technical time for correction of at least 4 min;
- Excessive fuel consumption – correcting the route necessitates covering an additional 3.1 km.
- Additional difficulties – these delays do not account for the time that will be allocated for communication between the courier and the client, as well as any traffic complications during delivery. Such delays affect not only one but all subsequent shipments.

2.2 Wrong Location with a Significant Deviation from the Correct Point

Another potential problem arises when the address provided to the provider is completely inaccurate. From the available database, we encounter another case where the client provides the address "AVI BUSINESS CENTRE". The problem is more complex. Firstly, the client does not provide a real address but rather a location name. Secondly, this location is missing from the Google Maps database. When entering the input data provided by the client into the system, we obtain the following coordinates: latitude 42.697708, longitude 23.321868. Despite the presence of a populated place and postal code, the system manages to orient to the city level, but when the address cannot be localized successfully, we simply receive coordinates in the center of the city (see Fig. 2).

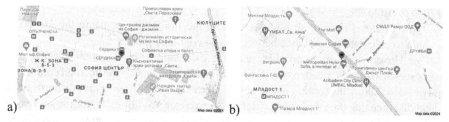

Fig. 2. Demonstration of errors when an address is provided incorrectly: a) lat. 42.697708, long. 23.321868; b) lat. 42.657780, long. 23.382591

The actual delivery location this time is significantly further from the initially provided point – with latitude 42.657780 and longitude 23.382591. The straight line between the point from Fig. 2 and the new point measures 6.6 km.

To determine the actual distance between two points, taking into account that a car cannot travel in a straight line in the real world, we again use Google Maps to see the distance and duration of travel between them. The experiment showed the shortest distance of 6.6 km between the two points.

This time it's clear that it's not just a matter of a few meters' difference, but actually several kilometers (7.5 km), and the travel time is about 13 min, which was not previously planned in the delivery schedule.

The consequences of inaccurate delivery address and coordinates can be significant: loss of time and resources, unnecessary fuel expenses, negative impact on delivery schedules, and inability to achieve accuracy in planning, which also affects customer satisfaction.

3   Determination of the Distance Using the Haversine Formula and the Google Maps Directions API to Demonstrate the Problem of Geolocation in Logistics Delivery

The Haversine formula is a powerful tool for calculating the distance between two points on a sphere, using the geographic coordinates of those points. This method provides fairly accurate results over large distances, which is useful for determining the shortest path between two locations using the following dependencies:

$$a = sin^2\left(\frac{\Delta lat}{2}\right) + cos\,cos(lat_1).cos\,cos(lat_2).sin^2(\frac{\Delta long}{2}) \qquad (1)$$

$$c = 2.atan2(\sqrt{a}, \sqrt{1-a}) \qquad (2)$$

$$d = R.c \qquad (3)$$

where Δlat is the difference in geographic latitude between the two points; $\Delta long$ is the difference in geographic longitude between the two points; lat_1 and lat_2 are the geographic latitudes of the two points; R is the radius of the Earth (average radius = 6371 km); a is the square of half the length of the chord between the points; c is the angular distance in radians; and d is the distance between the two points on the surface of the sphere.

Table 2 shows the possibilities as well as the limitations of using the Haversine formula to calculate the distance between two geographic points.

The Haversine formula provides accurate calculations, but its application in real-world scenarios can be challenging due to various factors such as traffic, road conditions, and obstacles along the route. This means that the calculated distance may differ from the actual distance that the courier or carrier needs to cover. Additionally, for the successful application of the Haversine formula, it is crucial to have precise geographic coordinates for the starting and ending points of the route. Inaccuracies or lack of coordinates can lead to incorrectly determined routes and loss of time and resources. At the same time, the Haversine formula ensures high accuracy in calculating distances between points on a sphere. This enables carriers and providers to determine the exact distance between the starting and ending points of the route, which is essential for planning and optimizing deliveries.

Since the Haversine formula provides us with the length of a straight line (in this case, an arc on a sphere) between two points or the so-called "as the crow flies" distance, we need to find the shortest path that a vehicle can travel from point A to point B. To find the most optimal distance and the average time required to cover this distance, we use the Google Maps Directions API. This facilitates the process of calculation and optimization of routes through the Haversine formula and provides opportunities for automated and optimized route planning, leading to more efficient deliveries and reduced operational costs.

To make a valid API data call, it is needed to know following 4 parameters: *ORIGIN_LATITUDE*; *ORIGIN_LONGITUDE*; *DESTINATION_LATITUDE*; and *DESTINATION_LONGITUDE*. Origin latitude and long are the coordinates of the starting point, while destination latitude and longitude are the coordinates of the final point. This information can be used to make an API call to the following address:

```
https://maps.googleapis.com/maps/api/directions/json?origin=
ORIGIN_LATITUDE,ORIGIN_LONGITUDE&destination=DESTINATION_ LAT-
ITUDE,DESTINATION_LONGITUDE&key=API_KEY
```

If the provided parameters meet the conditions, we get a response that retrieves the most optimal distance between the two points and the average travel time between them. After processing all addresses, the following findings were found:

- 2 records to find the address but no successful route finding.
- 141 correct addresses, assuming addresses with a difference of 500 m or less are correct.
- 339 incorrect addresses, assuming addresses with a difference of 501 m or more are wrong.
- 541 times the Google Maps API failed to find the position of the address.
- 36.36 km the average deviation from the address specified by the customer to the delivery address (driving distance).
- 1288 min (21 h 28 min) the average time deviation.
- There are three addresses that Google Maps defines as outside Bulgaria, which distorts the statistics. After removing these results, the average time deviation changes significantly to 166 min.
- There are also three addresses that Google Maps identifies as outside the courier's area, and these records have been filtered to provide clear urban statistics. The end result that is obtained is a 5 min average deviation for delivery.

All this proves once again the need to improve geolocation accuracy for logistics.

4   An Approach to Improve Geolocation for Logistics Delivery

Often web forms for entering addresses consist of a single field where the user enters their complete address – Including street, block, entrance, floor, apartment, and other details. This allows the user to enter their address in a format they deem most convenient. As a result, the database of addresses may have different formatting for each entry.

Creating a more detailed form with a field for each individual attribute of the address allows for easy formatting of the address in the desired format by the user. This ensures integrity and improved readability of address data. As a result, all addresses follow a common format.

Therefore, when using a specific algorithm, it can be more precisely tuned, taking into account the details of each part of the address. In this regard, an approach is proposed to improve delivery logistics by combining several modules as shown in Fig. 3.

The proposed approach is composed of the following modules: UI; accuracy improvement by machine learning module; optimization module; and module for validation.

The input data includes addresses provided by customers and their corresponding actual coordinates obtained by the courier during delivery are entered by proper UI.

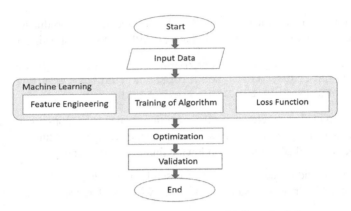

Fig. 3. An approach for improvement of delivery logistics

Our contribution is focused on a machine learning module that aims to improve accuracy through 3 separate steps namely: feature engineering; algorithm training and loos function. Feature engineering as a pre-processing step of machine learning is used to transform raw data into features. That means feature engineering can add, delete, combine, and mutate data sets to improve machine learning model training, thus getting better performance and greater accuracy. So, to prepare data for training, feature engineering is needed, which includes extracting features from the address components such as street names, cities, postal codes, and others. That is why in the proposed module such an element is involved. Algorithms for supervised learning, such as regression models or neural networks could be used to train the model. The second step is the training of the selected algorithm based on feature engineering. This is a core where different algorithms can be used to analyze data patterns, learn from discrepancies, and adjust predictions accordingly. Ultimately, over time these algorithms become more accurate and efficient as they process more data thus improving the accuracy of geolocation data for logistics delivery. This step aims to correct deviations between the addresses provided by customers and their actual locations on Google Maps. The aim of the used loss functions like Mean Squared Error or Mean Absolute Error is to evaluate the difference between predicted and actual coordinates during training. In fact, this is the third step of the proposed module. It helps the model to correct and improve its predictions, thus enhancing the overall accuracy of the system.

The optimization module is intended to find the shortest path to the endpoint of the delivery address. This could be realized by using different shortest-path algorithm techniques [13, 14]. The shortest path problem can be defined for graphs whether undirected, directed, or mixed.

The validation module serves to verify the integrity of the data inputs, filtering out errors and ensuring the reliability of the information used for training and prediction, thus enhancing the precision of the system. It is extremely important as it allows filtering out fake addresses, and user input errors when entering addresses. It could be used to cope with other potential problems that can arise during input. Errors in entering any of the attributes, such as town, city/village, and postal code, are extremely easy to verify and prevent the entry of invalid data. Removing a field where free text is entered and replacing it with a list or autocomplete function eliminates the likelihood of entering invalid data. For the remaining attributes, this approach may not be as effective, and other methods should be considered.

Once the model is successfully trained and validated, it can be deployed as a service or integrated into the system for real-time or batch processing of address deviation correction.

5   Conclusion

The article discusses problems related to supply logistics. For this purpose, a sample of delivery records for 1023 addresses was analyzed. From the analysis, it was found that there are discrepancies between the addresses provided by the customers and their actual locations determined by Google Maps. 339 incorrect addresses with a difference of 501 m and more have been identified. To address this problem, an accuracy improvement approach in supply logistics is proposed, composed of a module for input data, an accuracy improvement module, an optimization module, and a validation module. The authors propose to use an accuracy improvement module in which the feature extraction processes used in a suitable machine learning model are sequentially implemented, and finally, the loss function is applied. In this way, it is possible to correct deviations using the coordinates provided by the courier when scanning the package at the place of delivery.

Accurate geolocation is crucial for the efficient functioning of logistics processes and deliveries, as this is associated not only with the loss of more time but also with fuel costs. Technologies such as the Google Maps Directions API play an important role in this area, but there are challenges regarding the accuracy of geolocation data. Using the proposed approach could be seen as an important step towards improving logistics processes and improving the accuracy of geo-location data for deliveries. This will contribute not only to reducing deviations in addresses but also to improving customer satisfaction as a result of the observed delivery time. As future research, the use of different algorithms for machine learning and analysis of the obtained results are planned to identify the appropriate algorithms leading to better results.

Acknowledgment. This work is supported by the Bulgarian National Science Fund by the project "Mathematical models, methods and algorithms for solving hard optimization problems to achieve high security in communications and better economic sustainability", KP-06-H52/7/19-11-2021.

References

1. Tadić, S., Krstić, M., Stević, Ž., Veljović, M.: Locating collection and delivery points using the p-Median location problem. Logistics **7**, 10 (2023). https://doi.org/10.3390/logistics7010010

2. Long, L.: Accurate delivery analysis of distributed e-commerce based on Word2vector. In: 2019 International Conference on Machine Learning, Big Data and Business Intelligence (MLBDBI), Taiyuan, China, 2019, pp. 64–66. https://doi.org/10.1109/MLBDBI48998.2019.00020

3. Arnold, F., Cardenas, I., Sörensen, K., Dewulf, W.: Simulation of B2C e-commerce distribution in Antwerp using cargo bikes and delivery points. Europ. Transport Res. Rev. **10**(2) (2018). https://doi.org/10.1007/s12544-017-0272-6

4. Kandula, S., Krishnamoorthy, S., Roy, D.: A prescriptive analytics framework for efficient E-commerce order delivery. Decis. Support Syst. **147**, 113584 (2021). https://doi.org/10.1016/j.dss.2021.113584

5. Qian, C., Yi, C., Cheng, C., Pu, G., Liu, J.: A: coarse-to-fine model for geolocating Chinese addresses. ISPRS Int. J. Geo Inf. **9**(12), 698 (2020). https://doi.org/10.3390/ijgi9120698

6. Khan, S, Pinault, L., Tjepkema, M., Wilkins, R.: Positional accuracy of geocoding from residential postal codes versus full street addresses. Health reports/Statistics Canada, Canadian Centre for Health Information = Rapports sur la santé/Statistique Canada, Centre canadien d'information sur la santé (2018)

7. Li, Y., Zhang, W., Li, P., Ning, Y., Suo, C.: A method for autonomous navigation and positioning of UAV based on electric field array detection. Sensors **21**, 1146 (2021)

8. Qiao, C., Ding, Y., Xu, Y., Xiu, J.: Ground target geolocation based on digital elevation model for airborne wide-area reconnaissance system. J. Appl. Remote. Sens. **12**, 016004 (2018)

9. Wang, X., Liu, J., Zhou, Q.: Real-time multi-target localization from unmanned aerial vehicles. Sensors **17**, 33 (2017)

10. Kandula, S., Krishnamoorthy, S., Roy, D.: A prescriptive analytics framework for efficient E-commerce order delivery. Decision Support Syst. **147**, 113584 (2021). ISSN 0167-9236 (2021). https://doi.org/10.1016/j.dss.2021.113584

11. Gevaers, R., Van de Voorde, E., Vanelslander, T.: Characteristics and typology of last- mile logistics from an innovation perspective in an urban context. In: Macharis, C., Melo, S. (eds.) City Distribution and Urban Freight Transport; pp. 56–71. Edward Elgar Publishing, Cheltenham (2011)

12. Rao, S., Rabinovich, E., Raju, D.: The role of physical distribution services as determinants of product returns in Internet retailing. J. Oper. Manag. **32**, 295–312 (2014)

13. Dimitrova, Z., Dimitrov, V., Borissova, D., Garvanov, I., Garvanova, M.: Two-stage search-based approach for determining and sorting of mountain hiking routes using directed weighted multigraph. Cybernetics Inf. Technol. **20**(6), 28–39 https://doi.org/10.2478/cait-2020-0058

14. Borissova, D., Mustakerov, I.: E-learning tool for visualization of shortest paths algorithms. Trends J. Sci. Res. **2**(3), 84–89 (2015)

Understanding SBOMs in Real-World Systems – A Practical DevOps/SecOps Perspective

Narges Yousefnezhad[1]([✉])([iD]) and Andrei Costin[2]([iD])

[1] Binare Oy, Jyväskylä, Finland
narges.yousefnezhad@binare.io
[2] University of Jyväskylä, Jyväskylä, Finland
ancostin@jyu.fi
https://binare.io/ , https://jyu.fi/it/

Abstract. Vulnerabilities in third-party and open-source components pose significant risks to numerous systems, as evidenced by recent incidents like the XZ backdoor. Software Bill of Materials (SBOM) serves as a vital tool for identifying and isolating such vulnerabilities, and in some cases, it is a legally-mandated requirement to enhance supply-chain security within the digital ecosystem (e.g., Executive Order 14028). Despite its significant benefits, there are limitations in generating, using, and interpreting SBOMs effectively. In this paper, we aim to take an objective look on the state-of-the-art cybersecurity tools, particularly examining their contributions to or challenges from the practical SBOM perspective. The insights we present help improve existing tools and their usage in DevSecOps and compliance scenarios to maximize the effectiveness of SBOM standardization and requirements.

Keywords: SBOM · software bill of materials · DevOps · DevSecOps · software supply-chain · supply-chain security

1 Introduction

In recent years, software development and cybersecurity have undergone significant evolution, highlighting the importance of Software Bill of Materials (SBOMs). These documents are crucial for detailing software component composition, enhancing transparency, resilience, and security in digital ecosystems. The issuance of Executive Order 14028, "Improving the Nation's Cybersecurity," by President Biden emphasizes the pivotal role of SBOMs in national cybersecurity infrastructure [3]. The mandate to provide SBOMs to purchasers, either directly or through public dissemination, underscores the urgent need to integrate SBOM practices into DevOps and SecOps methodologies. This directive reflects the government's commitment to promoting uniformity and compatibility in SBOM implementation, facilitating adoption across various sectors.

B. Shishkov (Ed.): BMSD 2024, LNBIP 523, pp. 293–304, 2024.
https://doi.org/10.1007/978-3-031-64073-5_20

However, despite the growing recognition of SBOMs' importance, there are significant challenges in their practical implementation. The complexity of modern software systems, coupled with the dynamic nature of the software supply chain, often leads to difficulties in reliably generating, utilizing, and interpreting SBOMs. In particular, existing SBOM tools may fall short in effectively addressing the subtle requirements of DevOps and SecOps workflows, leaving organizations vulnerable to supply chain attacks and compliance gaps.

This paper attempts to address these challenges and provides valuable insights into the practical implications of SBOM adoption within real-world systems. It offers a novel perspective on SBOM tools, contrasting them with conventional categorizations to highlight their weaknesses and strengths. By exploring the intersection of SBOMs with DevOps and SecOps methodologies, we identify areas for enhancement to improve the security of the supply chain. Our contribution lies in bridging the gap between SBOM theory and practice, offering actionable recommendations for researchers, practitioners, and policymakers to enhance the resilience of digital ecosystems.

The paper is structured as follows: Sect. 2 offers background information on SBOMs and their formats. Section 3 reviews related work in the field. Section 4 discusses the practical challenges of SBOM adoption in DevOps and SecOps, highlighting current limitations and improvement opportunities. Section 5 provides an analysis of SBOM tools, discussing their practical strengths and weaknesses. Finally, Sect. 6 wraps up the paper.

2 Background

SBOM serves as a comprehensive inventory of software components, recognizing and enumerating each element while also describing the relevant information about them and illustrating the relationships within the supply chain [11]. SBOMs come in various formats, customized to fulfill distinct objectives. Additionally, this section explains the connections between SBOMs and three software development and security paradigms: DevOps, SecOps, and DevSecOps.

2.1 SBOM Formats

Three common SBOM formats include Software Package Data Exchange (SPDX), CycloneDX (CDX), and Software Identification (SWID). SPDX [13] and CDX [6], both open-source and machine-readable, are products of Linux Foundation and Open Web Application Security Project (OWASP). SPDX focuses on ensuring compliance and transparency in managing open-source and proprietary code for development teams and corporations. CDX is a lightweight SBOM format designed for easy adoption and automation of SBOM generation throughout the software development pipeline. SWID tags [4], functioning more as a software identifier than an SBOM format, provide a straightforward way to transparently track software inventory by storing specific release information.

2.2   DevOps, SecOps, and DevSecOps

DevOps, SecOps, and DevSecOps are all closely related to SBOM in various ways. DevOps, a trending technology, enhances software development operations by unifying the development and operations teams in a single process, leading to greater flexibility in meeting customer requirements [10]. SBOM fits into DevOps practices by providing transparency into the software components used throughout the development lifecycle. Security is a notable challenge limiting DevOps adoption. Terms like SecOps and DevSecOps have emerged to address this. SecOps integrates security into DevOps by encouraging collaboration between security and operation teams. SBOMs play a crucial role in SecOps by providing security teams with visibility into the software components and dependencies used in applications. This visibility allows security teams to assess the security posture of software components, identify vulnerabilities, and enforce security policies throughout the development and deployment lifecycle. DevSecOps, combining DevOps and SecOps, emphasizes embedding security in applications during development through collaboration among development, operations, and security teams [17]. SBOMs are an essential tool in DevSecOps as they provide the foundation for implementing security practices such as vulnerability management, risk assessment, and compliance monitoring.

3   Related Work

This section showcases various research efforts aiming to address vulnerabilities and challenges associated with SBOM adoption. However, despite these attempts, significant gaps remain, including the need for clearer benefits, improved generation quality, and standardized adoption methods. These gaps emphasise the ongoing relevance and necessity of the paper's contributions, which aim to address the identified shortcomings and advance the state-of-the-art in SBOM adoption and security enhancement.

The emergence of SBOM signifies a crucial advancement in software supply chain management and risk mitigation. However, security remains a critical concern due to potential vulnerabilities during active SBOM usage. Camp and Andalibi [5] outlines these vulnerabilities and corresponding recommendations, such as ensuring consistent contributor entities to prevent takeover or hijack risks. This measure safeguards against unauthorized updates, preserving code integrity. Moreover, SBOM adoption hinges on accessible tools for generation and management. Arora et al. [1] classify SBOM tools into "produce," "consume," and "transform" categories, covering various aspects like interface type, repository, and Application Programming Interface (API) support. FOSSology is a flexible SBOM tool, supporting all three functionalities but limited to generating SPDX format.

To analyze the SBOM adoption, empirical studies can be employed involving interviews and surveys. Xia et al. [20] conducted empirical studies, gathering data from 17 interviewees and 65 survey respondents across 15 countries on five continents, utilizing both qualitative and quantitative methods. Their findings emphasize the need for further investigation to expedite SBOM adoption by enhancing generation quality, clarifying benefits and use cases for consumption, and reducing sharing barriers. Sehgal et al. [16] examined various SBOM types, identifying vulnerability identification and tracking components as key security challenges that SBOM can address. Similarly, Chaora et al. [6] explored socio-technical factors and challenges surrounding SBOM through ethnographic studies, highlighting the necessity for clarification on SBOM formats, sharing mechanisms, IT infrastructure, and usability factors.

SBOM has the potential to enhance security across diverse domains. Hyeon et al. [9] propose a blockchain-based model for IoT firmware updates that incorporates SBOM, enhancing reliability and integrity through private blockchain networks. This model addresses limitations like resource and network overhead, thereby improving firmware update availability. Similarly, Wu et al. [19] introduce an intelligent security detection and warning scheme based on SBOM, employing a System Component Dependency Tree (CDT) and Bloom filter for vulnerability assessment. Their method demonstrates applicability on diverse open-source software terminal systems, including IoT devices.

4 SBOM Realities and Challenges

The National Telecommunications and Information Administration (NTIA) advises generating an SBOM for each new release of a component, covering various phases of the lifecycle [14]. Thus, an SBOM can be created from the source code, during build-time, at runtime, from the binary, or from a container image, be declarative in nature (self-declaration), or a combination of all the previous based on full or partial information available to the toolset and the analyst. Cybersecurity & Infrastructure Security Agenecy (CISA) has categorized SBOM into six distinct types (Design, Source, Build, Analyzed, Deployed, and Runtime), with each dedicated to one or several phases of the software development lifecycle [7]. Our present paper classifies SBOM into four primary types: source-code/ built-time, binary and post-build, runtime-host perspective (filesystem level and process level), and runtime-network perspective. Herein, the source-code or build-time SBOMs corresponds to the design, source, and build SBOMs as categorized by CISA. Similarly, the binary and post-build SBOM aligns with the Analyzed and Deployed SBOM categories. Finally, the runtime-host perspective and runtime-network perspective correspond to the Runtime category as defined by CISA.

Each technique possesses its own set of strengths and weaknesses, and an optimal solution would involve combining all approaches. However, managing all of these dependencies can be challenging. Effective software composition analysis (SCA) tooling can assist in this regard. The most comprehensive SCA tools are capable of identifying dependencies in various aspects such as applications, source code, files, build artifacts, container images, libraries, firmware, and beyond. Moreover, SBOM creation should be viewed as a process rather than merely producing a document. While an individual SBOM outlines application ingredients, treating SBOM creation as a methodology allows for dynamic supply chain visibility and upstream risk management [18].

4.1   Source-Code/Build-Time SBOMs

This category typically encompasses SBOMs accessible to developers and DevOps tools at various stages, including code design, source code analysis, and build phases. Engineering workflows such as git for version control and CI/CD pipelines automate SBOM generation during pipeline builds ("build-time" SBOMs). These automated processes eliminate manual errors and ensure precise component identities. Moreover, automated SBOM creation enables automated signing, thereby enhancing auditability. SBOMs are generated using tools integrated with build systems, package managers, and CI servers, providing both technical and business advantages. The resulting SBOM, delivered as an additional artifact specific to the software version built, can be further refined and enhanced throughout the pipeline [12].

Source code SBOMs may encounter certain issues: Firstly, while they generally offer the most comprehensive perspective, they can sometimes present an unrealistic view due to factors like complex build systems. Secondly, not all third-party dependencies referenced in the code are necessarily linked in the final deployed binary, leading to a significant amount of white noise and inherent/false positives compared to the actual running system in the real world.

JBOM produces Runtime SBOMs for Java applications, aligning with source code and build-time stages. Tools like *Microsoft.Sbom.Tool* and *Cyclonedx-npm*, *Cyclonedx-gomod*, and *Cyclonedx-python* are specialized for particular programming languages, facilitating SBOM generation. Other tools include *Build-info-go*, *Covenant, Meterian BOSS scanner*, and *SecureStack*.

4.2   Binary and Post-Build SBOMs

This category covers SBOMs resulting from various analyses like binary reverse engineering and Software Composition Analysis (SCA), as well as deployment. Older systems developed without modern version control or continuous integration methods may not be included in build-time SBOM generation. For these cases, acquiring data for a "post-build" SBOM should prioritize obtaining component information early in the engineering process. This post-build SBOM may aggregate data from multiple sources, including suppliers, processes, and tools. Binary scanning, often conducted with code analysis tools, can help populate SBOM information for components obtained from upstream suppliers, particularly for commercial components. Ensuring the integrity and authorship of the post-build SBOM is crucial, often involving timestamping, versioning, and digital signatures. Additionally, binary analysis involves directly examining application binaries to identify third-party SDKs, providing software consumers with insights into their dependencies. It allows for determining transitive dependencies recursively. However, dynamic code inclusion and on-the-fly app compilation by platforms like Apple and Google may lead to inaccuracies in pre-compiled SBOM assessment.

Addressing vulnerabilities within SBOMs presents a significant challenge, particularly when these vulnerabilities arise during the operation of SBOM tools post-build or post-packaging. SBOM generators rely on files generated by compilers or package programs, including Rust's cargo.lock, NPM's package-lock.json, or an apt-cache. The gap between the build and SBOM creation introduces a potential security loophole, allowing malicious manipulation of the SBOM report, leading to the creation of inaccurate SBOMs.

The *CycloneDX Maven plugin* generates a comprehensive SBOM containing both direct and transitive dependencies of a project. *Trivy*, a user-friendly vulnerability scanner for containers, identifies vulnerabilities in both operating system packages and application dependencies. It also offers Trivy-SBOM feature for generating SBOMs in CycloneDX format, which can be integrated with Dependency-Track for centralized management. *Cyclonedx Gradle Plugin* analyzes dependencies in Gradle-based projects, while *CycloneDX CocoaPods Plugin*, *CycloneDX module for .NET*, and *CycloneDX PHP Composer Plugin* generate SBOMs for CocoaPods projects, .NET NuGet projects, and PHP's Composer, respectively. *Jake* scans Python environments and applications, producing CycloneDX SBOMs and reporting vulnerabilities. Other tools include *Rebar3-sbom* for Erlang Rebar3 projects, *Distro2sbom* for package or system SBOMs, and *DaggerBoard* for vulnerability scanning and assessment of software dependencies. Additional tools for binary and post-build SBOM include *CodeSentry, Cybellum SBOM, Fortress File Integrity Assurance, NetRise Turbine, NowSecure Platform, ONEKEY firmware analysis platform, OpenRewrite*, and *CAST Highlight*.

4.3   Runtime SBOMs: Host Perspective

Runtime dependencies, referring to external elements utilized by a software object but not inherently included within it, are not encompassed within the current interpretation of the SBOM [2]. Examining only source files or build manifests has certain limitations. These methods fail to account for the runtime environment in which the software operates, as well as the system dependencies utilized, which may not be explicitly stated in the source files or manifests. Consequently, the analysis is confined to the inventory of software components alone. The runtime SBOM is often produced by instrumenting the system and executing the software to capture components within the system, as well as external call-outs or dynamically loaded components. In certain contexts, this may also be termed as an "Instrumented" or "Dynamic" SBOM. This type of SBOM is typically generated using tools that interact with a system to document the artifacts present in a running environment and/or those that have been executed [7].

Generating SBOMs at runtime provides several benefits [15]: Capturing both invoked and uninvoked dependencies; Documenting system dependencies inherent to the underlying platform or operating system; Recording details and settings pertaining to the runtime environment; Documenting the utilization and dependence on external services, including those accessed via HTTP and MQTT. Examples of tools for runtime SBOM encompass *Oligo Runtime SBOM, Rezilion Dynamic SBOM, Contrast Security, Vuls*

Two approaches exists for generating SBOMs during runtime: Host and network perspectives. The former can be managed at the filesystem or running process level.

Filesystem-Level SBOMs. This type of SBOM primarily targets filesystems and operating systems, and various tools serve this purpose. For example, to generate CycloneDX SBOMs for Linux distributions, it is feasible to utilize the *cyclonedx-linux-generator* tool. Additionally, *Syft* is capable of generating SBOMs for container images, filesystems, archives, and other formats to identify packages and libraries. *Grype*, a vulnerability scanner, is compatible with Syft, a robust SBOM tool used for analyzing container images and filesystems. *Clair* also provides the capability to audit SBOMs. It is an open-source project designed for the static analysis of vulnerabilities in application containers, which currently support OCI and Docker formats. Users can leverage the Clair API to index their container images and compare them against known vulnerabilities. *KubeClarity* serves as a solution for detecting and managing SBOM and vulnerabilities within container images and filesystems. It conducts scans across both runtime Kubernetes clusters and CI/CD pipelines to bolster software supply chain security. On the other hand, *meta-dependencytrack* generates CycloneDX SBOM from root filesystems.

Process-Level SBOMs. This is derived from the active processes, similar to the functionality of the 'ps' command in Linux operating systems. *Snyk*, a developer security platform, seamlessly integrates into development workflows and automation pipelines, allowing teams to effortlessly detect, prioritize, and resolve security vulnerabilities within code. While Snyk Open Source constructs a comprehensive dependency graph for vulnerability detection, it collaborates with various tools to compile and enrich SBOMs. This integration addresses critical supply chain security concerns, aiding in inventory management, integrity assurance, and provenance verification.

4.4   Runtime SBOMs: Network Perspective

Not every software component running on a host system engages in network communication or exposes network ports. In other words, only a subset of the installed software participates in network-related tasks, like transmitting or receiving data over the network or monitoring specific network ports for incoming connections. This subset of software components that interact with network services and ports may possess certain characteristics: a) They can be detected by black-box scanning tools such as Nmap; b) They are accurately identified and associated with the correct version. However, limitations in tools like Nmap, AMAP, and Ettercap [8], as well as protective measures like firewalls and IDS, might result in some components being incorrectly identified or failing to expose network interfaces. This leads to what we refer to as inherent or implicit "false negatives".

CycloneDX Generator (cdxgen) is a versatile toolset comprising a Command Line Interface (CLI) tool, library, REPL, and server. It enables the creation of compliant CycloneDX SBOM by aggregating all project dependencies. When utilized alongside plugins, CDXGen extends its capabilities to generate SBOMs for Linux Docker images and virtual machines (VMs) running on Linux or Windows operating systems. Additionally, CDXGen incorporates an "evinse" tool for generating component evidence. CDXGen stands out as a user-friendly, precise, and comprehensive universal SBOM generator and it doesn't align with any specific types of SBOM. *Nmap* can be employed for real-time SBOM generation. It assists in identifying active services and applications along with their specific attributes such as application name, version, and port number. Additionally, Nmap can aid in vulnerability identification. On the other hand, *JDisc Discovery* is a network discovery tool that identifies CycloneDX SBOMs and imports component inventory into the platform.

5   Discussion

In our investigation, we undertook a comprehensive categorization of existing SBOM tools, utilizing both CISA's established classification and our own devised framework tailored to the DevOps/SecOps context. Our analysis revealed that these tools support a range of SBOM formats, such as SPDX and CycloneDX. While CISA primarily identifies tools like "Nmap" and "KubeClarity" as real-time SBOM generators, emphasizing their role in bolstering software supply chain security, our categorization unveils a broader spectrum of tools facilitating SBOM runtime across various dimensions, including both host and network perspectives. Furthermore, our framework delves into the granularity of SBOM generation, discerning between file-system level and process-level perspectives, offering a deeper insight into their deployment within runtime environments. For instance, "Syft" falls within the "runtime:host perspective (file-system level)" category, contrasting with "Jdisk discovery," which is situated under the "runtime: network perspective." While both are classified as runtime tools by CISA, our approach illuminates their distinct perspectives and granularity levels.

Table 1 provides a comprehensive comparison of the SBOM tools discussed in this document, along with the supported formats for each tool. For some tools, where the information on supported formats is not explicitly stated, we denote it as N/A. Rezilion Dynamic SBOM claims to support all formats, which we denote as All. Additionally, some tools support not only CDX and SPDX formats but also Syft's format. It's worth noting that the number of SBOM tools supporting CDX is significantly higher than those supporting SPDX. Generally, if a tool supports SPDX, it implies support for CDX as well, but the reverse is not necessarily true.

The table categorizes each tool into two groups: one based on CISA classification and the other based on the categorization proposed within this paper.

Table 1. Comparison of selected SBOM tools

SBOM Tool	Support format	CISA's category	Proposed category	Application
JBOM	CDX	Build	Source-code/Build-time	Java
Microsoft.Sbom.Tool	SPDX	Source	Source-code/Build-time	Many App
Cyclonedx-npm	CDX	Build	Source-code/Build-time	NPM
Build-info-go	CDX	Build	Source-code/Build-time	CLI
Covenant	SPDX & CDX	Source & build	Source-code/Build-time	.Net, NPM
Meterian BOSS scanner	CDX	Source	Source-code/Build-time	Many App
SecureStack	CDX	Source	Source-code/Build-time	Cloud
Cyclonedx-python	CDX	Build	Source-code/Build-time	Python
cyclonedx-gomod	CDX	Build	Source-code/Build-time	Go modules
Cyclonedx-Rust-Cargo	CDX	Build	Source-code/Build-time	Rust cargo
Cargo-Sbom	SPDX & CDX	Build	Source-code/Build-time	Cargo/Rust
Rebar3-sbom	CDX	Build	Source-code/Build-time	Rebar3
OpenRewrite	CDX	Deployed	Binary and Post-Build	Java
CycloneDX Maven plugin	CDX	Analyzed	Binary and Post-Build	Maven
Cyclonedx Gradle Plugin	CDX	Analyzed	Binary and Post-Build	Gradle
CycloneDX CocoaPods Plugin	CDX	Analyzed	Binary and Post-Build	iOS, SWIFT
CycloneDX module for .NET	CDX	Analyzed	Binary and Post-Build	.NET
CycloneDX PHP Composer Plugin	CDX	Analyzed	Binary and Post-Build	PHP
Jake	CDX	Build & Analyzed	Binary and Post-Build	Python
Distro2sbom	SPDX & CDX	Deployed	Binary and Post-Build	RPM distro
Trivy	CDX	Analyzed	Binary and Post-Build	Scanner
DaggerBoard	SPDX & CDX	Analyzed	Binary and Post-Build	Scanner
CodeSentry	CDX	Analyzed	Binary and Post-Build	SCA
Cybellum SBOM	N/A	Analyzed	Binary and Post-Build	Scanner
Fortress File Integrity Assurance	N/A	Analyzed	Binary and Post-Build	API
NetRise Turbine	N/A	Deployed	Binary and Post-Build	Risk analysis
NowSecure Platform	CDX	Analyzed	Binary and Post-Build	Mobile
ONEKEY	N/A	Analyzed	Binary and Post-Build	Vuln. report
CAST Highlight	N/A	Source & Analyzed	Binary and Post-Build	Many App
Oligo Runtime SBOM	CDX	Runtime	Runtime: Host pers.	VEX
Rezilion Dynamic SBOM	All	Runtime	Runtime: Host pers.	SCA
Contrast Security	CDX	Runtime	Runtime: Host pers.	IAST & RASP
Vuls	CDX	Runtime	Runtime: Host pers.	Linux/FreeBSD
Syft	SPDX & CDX & Syft's format	Runtime	Runtime: Host pers. (FS)	CLI
Grype	SPDX & CDX	Runtime	Runtime: Host pers. (FS)	Many App
Clair	N/A	Runtime	Runtime: Host pers. (FS)	Container
KubeClarity	SPDX & CDX & Syft's format	Runtime	Runtime: Host pers. (FS)	K8s clusters & CI/CD
Meta-dependencytrack	CDX	Runtime	Runtime: Host pers. (FS)	Meta-layer
Snyk	SPDX & CDX	Runtime	Runtime: Host pers. (Pr)	JSON, XML
Nmap	SPDX & CDX	Runtime	Runtime: Network pers.	ICS
CycloneDX Generator	CDX	Runtime	Runtime: Network pers.	Many App
JDisc Discovery	SPDX	Runtime	Runtime: Network pers	Many App

Abbreviations: FS (FileSystem), Pr (Process), NPM (Node Package Manager), VEX (Vulnerability Exploitability eXchange), CI/CD (Continuous Integration/Continuous Delivery), XML (eXtensible Markup Language), ICS (Industrial Control System)

Notably, "source" and "build" from CISA's classification correspond to the "source-code/build-time" category in our classification, while "deployed" and "analyzed" in CISA are equivalent to the "build and post-build" category. The "runtime" category in CISA aligns with either the Runtime: Host perspective (whether Filesystem or Process level) or network perspective in our classification. Some tools, like Covenant, fall into two categories according to CISA classification, making it challenging to determine the exact type of SBOM they represent. Furthermore, the table indicates the application for which each SBOM tool can be used. Most SBOM tools cover only one application, although a few of them span across multiple applications.

Despite the availability of these tools, there are still gaps in the SBOM ecosystem. Many essential features or tools are missing, hindering efforts to streamline SBOM adoption and compliance. To illustrate, while existing tools offer capabilities for generating SBOMs, there's a lack of comprehensive solutions for managing and integrating SBOMs seamlessly into DevOps and SecOps workflows. Just as the "ps" command in Linux provides a powerful tool for viewing process information, there's a need for similarly robust and comprehensive tools in the SBOM landscape to make the process of SBOM generation and utilization easier and more compliant for organizations.

6   Conclusion

In this paper, we conducted a comprehensive review of the primary types of SBOMs, along with their major formats, and explored cybersecurity tools suitable for generating various types and formats as demanded by DevSecOps and compliance processes. Additionally, we highlighted the primary limitations inherent in different SBOM types and tools, particularly in their ability to address key DevSecOps and compliance scenarios. The insights presented herein aim to contribute to the enhancement of existing tools and their effective utilization within the realms of DevSecOps and compliance. Future work could focus on increasing the interoperability between different SBOM formats to ensure seamless integration across various tools and platforms. Additionally, expanding the coverage of SBOMs to include more detailed information about software dependencies and vulnerabilities could further enhance their utility in cybersecurity and compliance.

Acknowledgments. Narges Yousefnezhad acknowledges the support of the Jenny and Antti Wihuri Foundation through the PoDoCo program (www.podoco.fi), grant number 141222. (Part of) This work was supported by the European Commission under the Horizon Europe Programme, as part of the project LAZARUS (https://lazarus-he. eu/) (Grant Agreement no. 101070303). The content of this article does not reflect the official opinion of the European Union. Responsibility for the information and views expressed therein lies entirely with the authors. (Part of this work was) Funded by the European Union (Grant Agreement Nr. 101120962, RESCALE Project). Views and opinions expressed are however those of the author(s) only and do not necessarily reflect those of the European Union or the Health and Digital Executive Agency. Neither the European Union nor the granting authority can be held responsible for them.

References

1. Arora, A., Wright, V.L., Garman, C.: SoK: a framework for and analysis of software bill of materials tools. Tech. rep, Idaho National Laboratory (INL) (2022)
2. Bendix, L., Göransson, A.: A Comprehensive View of Software Bill of Materials (2023)
3. Biden, J.R.: Executive Order on Improving the Nation's Cybersecurity . https://www.whitehouse.gov/briefing-room/presidential-actions/2021/05/12/executive-order-on-improving-the-nations-cybersecurity/ (2021)
4. Birkholz, H., Fitzgerald-McKay, J., Schmidt, C., Waltermire, D.: RFC 9393 Concise Software Identification Tags (2023)
5. Camp, L.J., Andalibi, V.: SboM vulnerability assessment & corresponding requirements. NTIA Res. Not. Req. Comments Softw. Bill Mater. Elem. Consid. (2021)
6. Chaora, A., Ensmenger, N.L., Camp, L.J.: Discourse, challenges, and prospects around the adoption and dissemination of software bills of materials (SBOMs). In: IEEE International Symposium on Technology and Society, ISTAS 2023, Swansea, United Kingdom, September 13-15, 2023, pp. 1–4. IEEE (2023). https://doi.org/10.1109/ISTAS57930.2023.10305922, https://doi.org/10.1109/ISTAS57930.2023.10305922
7. CISA: Types of Software Bill of Material (SBOM) Documents. https://www.cisa.gov/sites/default/files/2023-04/sbom-types-document-508c.pdf (2023)
8. Ghanem, W.A.H., Belaton, B.: Improving accuracy of applications fingerprinting on local networks using NMAP-AMAP-ETTERCAP as a hybrid framework. In: 2013 IEEE International Conference on Control System, Computing and Engineering, pp. 403–407. IEEE (2013)
9. Hyeon, D.E., Park, J.H., Youm, H.Y.: A secure firmware and software update model based on blockchains for internet of things devices using SBOM. In: 18th Asia Joint Conference on Information Security, AsiaJCIS 2023, Koganei, Japan, August 15-16, 2023, pp. 53–58. IEEE (2023). https://doi.org/10.1109/ASIAJCIS60284.2023.00019
10. Mohan, V., Othmane, L.B.: SecDevOps: is it a marketing buzzword?-mapping research on security in DevOps. In: 2016 11th International Conference on Availability, Reliability and Security (ARES), pp. 542–547. IEEE (2016)
11. Muirí, É.Ó.: Framing software component transparency: establishing a common software bill of material (SBOM). NTIA, Nov 12 (2019)
12. NTIA: Software Suppliers Playbook: SBOM Production and Provision. https://www.ntia.gov/sites/default/files/publications/software_suppliers_sbom_production_and_provision_-_final_0.pdf (2021)
13. NTIA: Survey of Existing SBOM Formats and Standards. https://www.ntia.gov/files/ntia/publications/ntia_sbom_formats_and_standards_whitepaper_-_version_20191025.pdf (2021)
14. NTIA: The Minimum Elements For a Software Bill of Materials. https://www.ntia.doc.gov/files/ntia/publications/sbom_minimum_elements_report.pdf (2021)
15. OWASP: Authoritative Guide to SBOM- Implement and Optimize use of Software Bill of Materials. https://cyclonedx.org/guides/sbom/generation/ (2024)
16. Sehgal, V.V., Ambili, P.: A taxonomy and survey of software bill of materials (SBOM) generation approaches. In: Analytics Global Conference, pp. 40–51. Springer (2023)
17. Shiff, L.: SecOps vs DevSecOps: What's The Difference? https://www.bmc.com/blogs/secops-vs-devsecops/ (2020)

18. Synopsys: Which of CISA's Six Types of SBOMs Are Right for You? https://www.synopsys.com/software-integrity/resources/ebooks/cisa-sboms-guide.html+ (2024)
19. Wu, W., Wang, P., Zhao, L., Jiang, W.: An intelligent security detection and response scheme based on SBOM for securing IoT terminal devices. In: 11th International Conference on Information, Communication and Networks (ICICN), pp. 391–398. IEEE (2023)
20. Xia, B., Bi, T., Xing, Z., Lu, Q., Zhu, L.: An empirical study on software bill of materials: where we stand and the road ahead. In: 45th IEEE/ACM International Conference on Software Engineering, ICSE 2023, Melbourne, Australia, May 14-20, 2023, pp. 2630–2642. IEEE (2023). https://doi.org/10.1109/ICSE48619.2023.00219, https://doi.org/10.1109/ICSE48619.2023.00219

Correction to: Business Modeling and Software Design

Boris Shishkov

Correction to:
**B. Shishkov (Ed.): *Business Modeling and Software Design,*
LNBIP 523, https://doi.org/10.1007/978-3-031-64073-5**

In the originally published version of Bookfrontmatter, there was a missing Abstract before TOC. This has been corrected.

The updated version of this book can be found at
https://doi.org/10.1007/978-3-031-64073-5

Author Index

B. Shishkov (Ed.): BMSD 2024, LNBIP 523, p. 305, 2024.
https://doi.org/10.1007/978-3-031-64073-5